How Language Speaks to Music

Linguistische Arbeiten

Edited by
Klaus von Heusinger, Agnes Jäger,
Gereon Müller, Ingo Plag,
Elisabeth Stark and Richard Wiese

Volume 583

How Language Speaks to Music

Prosody from a Cross-domain Perspective

Edited by
Mathias Scharinger and Richard Wiese

DE GRUYTER

ISBN 978-3-11-153213-4
e-ISBN (PDF) 978-3-11-077018-6
e-ISBN (EPUB) 978-3-11-077025-4
ISSN 0344-6727

Library of Congress Control Number: 2022934837

Bibliographic information published by the Deutsche Nationalbibliothek
The Deutsche Nationalbibliothek lists this publication in the Deutsche Nationalbibliografie;
detailed bibliographic data are available on the Internet at http://dnb.dnb.de.

© 2024 Walter de Gruyter GmbH, Berlin/Boston Typesetting: Integra Software Services Pvt.

This volume is text- and page-identical with the hardback published in 2022.

www.degruyter.com

Contents

Mathias Scharinger & Richard Wiese
Introduction: How to conceptualize similarities between language and music —— 1

Pauline Larrouy-Maestri, David Poeppel & Peter Q. Pfordresher
Pitch units in music and speech prosody —— 17

Mathias Scharinger
Melody in speech and music —— 43

Dicky Gilbers & Teja Rebernik
A constraint-based approach to structuring language and music: Towards a roadmap for comparing language and music cross-culturally —— 71

Jasmin Pfeifer, Silke Hamann
Word stress perception by congenital amusics —— 105

Richard Wiese
Rhythmic structure – parallels between language and music —— 135

Heini Arjava & Gerrit Kentner
Alignment of prosodic weight and musical length in Finnish vocal music textsetting —— 161

Elena Girardi & Ingo Plag
Metrical mapping in text-setting: Empirical analysis and grammatical implementation —— 191

Christina Domene Moreno & Barış Kabak
Prominence alignment in English and Turkish songs: Implications for word prosodic typology —— 223

Sonja A. Kotz
Bridging speech and music – A neural common ground perspective on prosody —— 259

Index —— 267

Mathias Scharinger & Richard Wiese
Introduction: How to conceptualize similarities between language and music

> Music is the universal language of mankind, – poetry their universal pastime and delight.
> Henry Wadsworth Longfellow (1835) [Longfellow, 1835]

Abstract: In this introduction, we first address the question of how to find the appropriate level for the comparison between language and music. Secondly, we argue that the appropriate level for this comparison is the one of prosody, subsuming supra-segmental properties such as rhythm, meter and melody. We then provide a bibliometric analysis of recent contributions on the topics most central to this comparison. Finally, we introduce the contributions to the present volume.

Keywords: language, music, prosody, bibliometric analysis

The famous quote by 19th century novelist Henry Wadsworth Longfellow and many of its similar reformulations underscore the insight that music and language are essential human cognitive abilities. In his influential book, Aniruddh Patel goes as far as expressing these as identifying human features: "Language and music define us as human." (Patel, 2010, p. 3). Indeed, all modern humans use language (e.g., Pagel, 2017 and references therein), and there is no culture without music (Mehr et al., 2019). Longfellow's quote has received direct support by Mehr et al. (2019) who were able to demonstrate that there are indeed universal properties of music, e.g., its omnipresence, and most likely, its tonality. Other properties, by contrast, vary, albeit in structured ways, e.g., along arousal or religiosity. The ongoing quest for language universals, by comparison, has apparently been less successful, or, put more positively, has revealed variability along a vaster set of dimensions (e.g., Greenberg, 1978).

It is obvious, then, that music and language are related to each other in several ways, displaying commonalities while also maintaining specific differentiations. As briefly mentioned above, musicologists and linguists alike attempt to

---

Mathias Scharinger, Philipps-Universität Marburg, Pilgrimstein 16, D-35032, Marburg, e-mail: mathias.scharinger@uni-marburg.de
Richard Wiese, Philipps-Universität Marburg, Pilgrimstein 16, D-35032, Marburg, e-mail: wiese@uni-marburg.de

https://doi.org/10.1515/9783110770186-001

define universals in either domain. One such overarching universal feature seems to be the expression of emotions and/or affect. In this respect, music has been ascribed a direct link (Koelsch, 2011; Scherer, 1995; Timmers & Loui, 2019), while language shows rather variable and more or less direct links to emotions and/or affects. In language, emotions can be communicated by semantic features or pragmatic conventions, or they can be expressed (more directly) by prosody (e.g., Liebenthal et al., 2016; Nygaard & Queen, 2008; Paulmann et al., 2012).

1 Prosody in language and music

In general, prosody as a system of suprasegmental linguistic information such as stress, prominence, meter, rhythm, tone and intonation (e.g., Fox, 2002; Nespor & Vogel, 1986; Selkirk, 1995) is a prime candidate for looking at the relation between language and music in a principled way. This claim is based on several aspects, as elucidated in the following paragraphs.

First, prosody is concerned with the perceptual correlates "length", "pitch" and "perceived intensity" of the acoustic bases of language and music that are directly comparable with each other by their physical properties duration, frequency and intensity. Syllables in language, for instance, have a temporal extent and their vocalic nucleus is characterized by fundamental frequency contours as well as specific intensities. Tones in music also have a temporal extent and bear specific tone heights. They may also differ in their intensities. Syllables and tones are emitted as sound pressure waves in the air and perceived through the same peripheral auditory system. When focusing on human singing, syllables and tones are merged objects produced by the same tripartite human language production system: respiratory source, phonatory larynx and filtering vocal tract.

Second, prosodic accounts, most prominently, Nespor & Vogel (1986), suggest a hierarchical organization of prosodic units, the so-called "prosodic hierarchy", that not only resembles a syntactic hierarchy, but is viewed as (part of) an interface to syntax (Bennett & Elfner, 2019). Hierarchical structures in music, akin to syntactic (or prosodic) structures in language, have been proposed and formalized by Lerdahl and Jackendoff (Lerdahl & Jackendoff, 1977; 1983). Importantly, the model relates prosodic phrases from language to phrases from music. The hierarchical phrase structure contains heads and complements and accounts for the multi-tiered aspects of prominences on more local (individual tones or syllables) or more global levels (groups of individual tones or syllables, cadences or "feet").

Third, prosody provides a very promising ground for evolutionary accounts of language and music. Scientific approaches to the evolution of language and music have sparked interest for decades in many different fields. The probably most influential evolutionary theory of the last millennium also includes important hypotheses about the role of music. To this end, Darwin suggested a song-like communication system that pre-dates human language (Darwin, 1981 [1871]). This view has been expressed in many subsequent accounts in which a common pre-cursor for both language and music is assumed (e.g., Masataka, 2007; 2009). A similar pre-cursor is discussed in a more language-oriented framework (Bickerton, 1990). Accounts hence differ as to whether this pre-cursor rather resembled music or language. Further, there are ongoing discussions about the evidence for a co-evolution of language and music. In this respect, there are different opinions on how to account for the apparent differences in adaptive benefits between language and music. On an extreme side, music is ascribed no such direct benefit or evolutionary advantage at all, expressed in the "auditory cheesecake hypothesis" (Pinker, 1997). According to Pinker, music is a recent, rather "ornamental" development in human evolution with strong emphasis on aspects of pleasure and aesthetics. Others maintain the hypothesis that even though no direct evolutionary advantages of music may be identified, clearly some aspects co-evolved, e.g., with conspecific calls and vocalizations, with social bonding or with credibility signaling (Mehr et al., 2020; Savage et al., 2020). Fitch presents a comparative account that also discusses aspects of co-evolution (Fitch, 2005; 2006). For instance, he critically assesses the "spandrel" hypothesis, according to which music evolved as a byproduct during the selection for features and mechanisms enabling human language. An interesting argument is made regarding articulatory control. According to this argument, singing requires finer respiratory control than speech. This supports the hypothesis that singing may have evolved earlier or simultaneously with speaking (Fitch, 2006). A similar stance is taken by Wray (2002), suggesting that complex signals (e.g., spoken or sung sounds) evolve first, and only later, (compositional) meaning is added (for discussion, see also Fitch, 2005). Importantly, arguments in favor of co-evolution or shared proto-stages for both language and music crucially involve prosodic aspects, based on a definition of prosody that may be applied to both language and music. Some approaches, following the "musi-language" hypothesis (Mithen, 2005), therefore assume joint prosodic sources for music and language (Brown, 2000; 2017). Similar views are expressed by Heffner & Slevc (2015) and Fenk-Oczlon & Fenk (2009), although the latter two accounts are not primarily of evolutionary nature, but rather describe structural parallels between language and music that are most prominently seen on the level of prosody. Fenk-Oczlon & Fenk (2009) speculate about all three possibilities of the sequential evolution of music language, considering a "music before language", "language before music" and a precursor/simultaneous scenario, while arguing that either the "music before language" or the "musical precursor" scenario is the most likely one. They attribute a special role to singing and consider vowels as essential units of a music-language precursor that was essentially of prosodic nature (Fenk-Oczlon, 2017). Besides approaches with a focus on frequency/pitch properties, such as provided by the aforementioned authors, there are also very intriguing accounts with an emphasis on rhythm. In their review on the evolution of rhythm processing, Kotz et al. (2018) argue that, in essence, rhythm serves the social synchronization across domains and species. Rhythm thus seems to fulfill a similar social bonding role than music as a whole (Savage et al., 2020). The role and importance of synchronization by means of a (common) rhythm is also expressed in Filippi et al. (2019). The authors argue that temporal modulations aid the expression of emotions. For instance, slower articulation rates are associated with sadness, while faster articulation rates are associated with joy. Temporal modulations are also assumed to support the delineation of basic units in either language or music. The latter aspect is very prominently expressed in oscillatory approaches to language and music (e.g., Ding et al., 2017; Ghitza & Greenberg, 2009). Basically, these approaches assume that the processing of basic (prosodic) units in music and language is based on a successful parsing ("chunking") of the continuous acoustic signal by means of the brain's oscillatory mechanisms. More precisely, it is suggested that cortical rhythms, such as the oscillation in the theta-range (between 4 and 8 Hz), are beneficial in tracking and thereby processing syllabic or tonal information by "quantizing" the acoustic information into packages that correspond to the respective units, i.e., syllables or tones. The exact role of cortical rhythms for segmenting and recognizing the respective acoustic input is currently still discussed.

The fourth reason of why prosody is particularly well-suited for approaching the relation of language and music concerns the shared neural substrates of linguistic and musical prosody. Many studies have shown that music and language share cortical and subcortical resources (e.g., Koelsch et al., 2002; Patel, 2003; Peretz & Zatorre, 2003), while others have identified specific biases for language- versus music-processing, and thus suggested rather separate and specialized processing resources (Bever & Chiarello, 1974). The latter authors established (and confirmed) the special role of the left cerebral hemisphere for language processing (cf. Broca, 1863), and the special role of the right cerebral hemisphere for music processing. Later studies have provided evidence for a more general hemispheric bias that depends on the level of processing of musical and linguistic input. In sum, it is assumed that initial processing of acoustic input (both musical and linguistic), after the stages of the peripheral auditory system, occurs bilateral, up to primary auditory cortex around Heschl's Gyrus in the temporal cortices. Later processing stages differentiate between rapid and rather temporal event processing (in the left) and slower, rather spectral event processing (in the right) hemisphere (e.g., Albouy et al., 2020; Poeppel, 2003; Zatorre & Belin, 2001). Importantly, though, right-temporal areas have been identified to support the processing of both linguistic and musical prosody, especially when focusing on frequency/pitch and intonation (e.g., Sammler et al., 2015). The processing of rhythm or meter, on the other hand, may be biased towards the left hemisphere, at least for trained musicians (Vuust et al., 2005). Higher processing levels of language and music also seem to share neural resources. Here, the emphasis is on structural and syntactic processing that is supported by left inferior frontal structures (e.g., Kunert et al., 2015; Sammler et al., 2011), ascribing them rather domain-independent roles in sequencing, coordinating or combining information from smaller constituent units (syllables, words or tones). The involvement of these structures in both language and music also supports the aforementioned generative model of musical structure by Lerdahl and Jackendoff (Lerdahl & Jackendoff, 1977; 1983).

The fifth (but certainly not last) reason to focus on prosody when illustrating the relation between language and music relates to transfer effects between the two domains. This transfer can go in either direction and is best illustrated on the level of prosody. The language-to-music transfer can be exemplified by absolute pitch, the rare skill to assign arbitrary tone heights the correct (musical) label (Levitin & Rogers, 2005). Deutsch and colleagues have shown that speakers of a tone language are more likely to show absolute pitch than speakers of a non-tone language (Deutsch et al., 2006). This suggests that language experience in assigning labels to fundamental frequency/pitch in speech sounds transfers to music. A recent study (Maggu et al., 2021) provides further evidence for a common mechanism underlying fundamental frequency/pitch encoding in music and speech. The music-to-language transfer, on the other hand, seems to have received far more attention. Again, the level of prosody is prominently focused at when investigating these transfer effects. For instance, trained musicians have been found to show greater sensitivity to fundamental frequency in the native language (Schön et al., 2004) as well as in foreign languages (Marques et al., 2007). Musicians also show greater sensitivity to metric structure in language (Marie et al., 2011). Positive influences of musical training on general phonological skills have been attested by numerous researchers (Anvari et al., 2002; Jones et al., 2009; Moreno et al., 2009), for more discussion see Besson et al. (2011). Thompson et al. (2004) provide evidence that musically trained persons are better in decoding emotional speech prosody than untrained persons. This exemplary and by no means exhaustive list of studies shows that music and language do not only show overlap in neural structures (Peretz et al., 2015) but apparently use partially identical mechanisms such that the training of these mechanisms in one domain has direct effects for the respective other domain.

The discussion above emphasizes that it is a fruitful endeavor to use prosody for a principled comparison of language and music, an endeavor that we attempt to pursue in this book. Prosody, in very broad terms, refers to the sound structure of communicative systems and may be considered a "meta"-language that formalizes the way of "how music speaks to language and vice versa". Prosody is firmly established within linguistic theory, particularly, phonology, but is also applied in the musical domain (e.g., Glaser, 2000; Palmer & Hutchins, 2006; Palmer et al., 2001; Palmer & Kelly, 1992). Therefore, prosody is not just a field of inquiry that shares elements or features between music and language (e.g., sound/tone durations and frequency/tone height), but may provide a common conceptual ground.

A final argument that prosody is a very fruitful approach to study the relations between language and music stems from a bibliometric analysis introducing and framing the specific approaches to the prosodic link between the two domains made by the authors in this volume.

2 A bibliometric analysis on prosody in music and language

Bibliometric analyses are an emerging statistical and visual technique to describe and quantify a scientific landscape around a certain topic as well as its impact on science as a whole (Cobo et al., 2011; Pritchard, 1969). A topic-search in "Web of Science" (WoS, https://apps.webofknowledge.com, retrieved on March 11th, 2021) with the three keywords "language", "music", and "prosod*" (the star being a place holder for either the noun or adjective ending), combined with logical "and" yielded a total of 268 documents (among them 234 journal articles) published between 1993 and 2021. The output of the search is essentially a bibliographic list in which each document is fully referenced, including title, author, co-authors, affiliations, keywords and cited references. The search was analyzed by the bibliometric package "bibliometrix" (Aria & Cuccurullo, 2017). The results showed documents of a total of 664 authors, 57 of which produced single-authored documents and 607 of which participated in multi-authored documents. A total of 11 618 references were cited in all retrieved documents matching the search terms.

A closer look at the development of the scientific landscape between 1993 and 2021 revealed a number of citations peak in 2017 (Figure 1 A), mainly driven

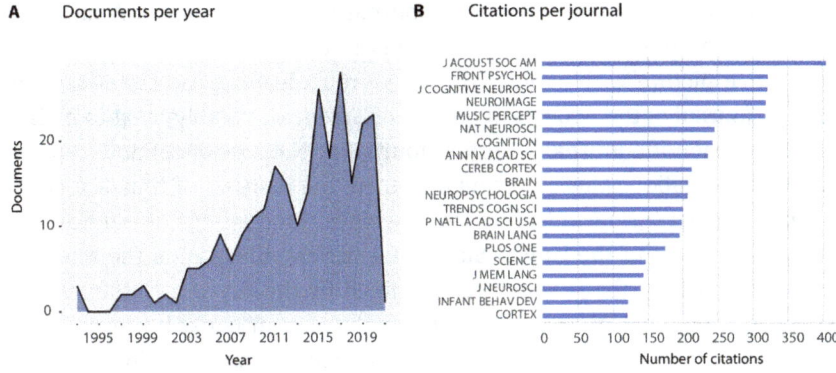

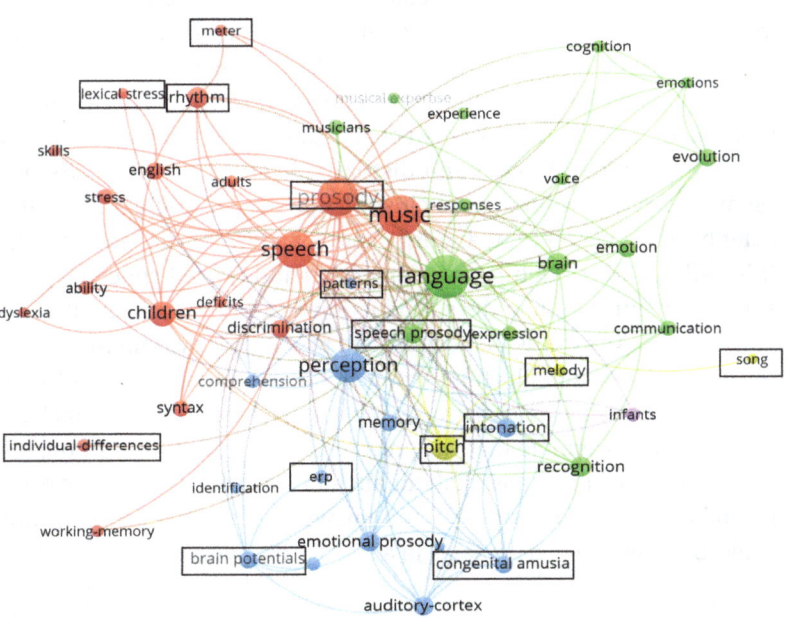

Figure 1: Illustration of the bibliometric analysis on the search terms "language", "music" and "prosod*". A: Number of articles containing the search terms as a function of the years of their appearance. B: The twenty most-cited journals in the documents found by the WoS search. C: Co-occurence network of the key words (total: 788) found in the 268 documents of the WoS search. Absolute number of occurrences are coded in font size, with higher numbers corresponding to larger font sizes, co-occurrences are indexed by the number of connecting lines. Clustering was done in VosViewer and is based on co-citation measures described in more detail in van Eck & Waltman (2010). Depicted are the 50 most frequent keywords with at least 7 occurrences.

by publications on language and in the journal family "frontiers". A more detailed analysis on the journals that were cited in the 234 articles shows a quite representative picture with acoustic-based journals leading the citation count (Figure 1 B, Journal of the Acoustical Society of America). Notably, next to highly-ranked neuroscientific journals (Cortex, Journal of Neuroscience) and journals within music cognition (Music Perception), there are journals of broadest scope and highest impact (Science, Nature Neuroscience, Proceedings of the National Academy of Sciences of the United States of America), illustrating the scientific interest and impact of the research field defined by the key words "language", "music" and "prosody". Most importantly for the current book, however, is the visualization of keyword co-occurrences in the network depicted in Figure 1 C (created with VosViewer, van Eck & Waltman, 2010). Not surprisingly, the three search items have a prominent position, with their font size positively correlated with their number of occurrence in the search results. The keyword are organized into color-coded clusters (see van Eck & Waltman, 2010 for details on the clustering technique), based on citation co-occurrences. A prominent red cluster is dominated by key words on language and speech prosody, including terms such as lexical stress, meter and rhythm. A green cluster subsumes terms on language, emotion(s) and evolution. A small and distributed yellow cluster is based on song, melody and pitch, while a blue cluster shows a neuroscientific character, with emphasis on perception, auditory cortex and event-related potentials (ERPs). It is perhaps worth noting that perception and related concepts play a much more prominent role than does production as another fundamental perspective in cognition. Key words that correspond to key topics within this volume are marked by rectangles and illustrate how well the present book covers the scientific landscape defined by the three search terms "language", "music" and "prosody". It is also discernible that the green cluster is not covered in this volume. This very plausibly illustrates that our attempt was not to provide an evolutionary prosodic account for language and music, but rather to reveal fruitful prosodic links between the two domains in a synchronic perspective.

3 Contributions to the present volume

The current volume thus takes prosody (in its wider sense) as an overarching framework for investigating how each domain may profit from insights from the other domain. Since most contributions stem from authors with a linguistic background, it is natural that the focus is on the language side. There are, however, also outlooks on how both directions of the transfer between language and music may be explored in a fruitful way.

The **first part** of the book is concerned with underlying prosodic units based on fundamental frequency/pitch. What is the appropriate granularity of these units, and how can they be quantified, particularly with respect to the recurrence structure in melodic contours?

The first aspect defines the core of the chapter by **Pauline Larrouy-Maestri, David Poeppel and Peter Q. Pfordresher**. They start out by describing units which occur in both language and music and acknowledge that even though these units may differ in the respective domains, the operations applied to them may be similar. The focus is then on so-called pitch "scoops", i.e., deviations in frequency, or small-scale frequency sweeps, which are introduced as a musical phenomenon. Based on the observation that pitch deviations are tolerated to certain degrees in music, scoops illustrate that the alleged discreteness of tone height does not hold across the board. The magnitude of scoops rather depends on context and musical skills of the performers. Therefore, pitch scoops provide counter-evidence to the widely assumed difference between frequency/pitch in language (more variable, less discrete) and frequency/pitch in music (less variable, discrete, cf. Zatorre & Baum, 2012). Importantly, the authors elaborate on the evaluation of musical scoops and distinguish between aesthetic and auditory evaluations. However, their empirical data from experiments reported in this chapter suggest that auditory correctness ratings ("in-tune") correspond to (aesthetic) preferences.

Mathias Scharinger, on the other hand, argues that syllable-pitch in speech is interpreted in a more discrete way than the aforementioned pitch differences between speech and music might suggest (Zatorre & Baum, 2012). Starting out from the assumption that fundamental frequency in syllables can be quantized in a discrete way, he defines speech melody as consisting of structured sequences of syllable pitches, possibly dependent on the intrinsic pitch of the syllables' nuclei. Melodic contours are then proposed to be statistically describable by autocorrelations of mean fundamental frequency (equated with pitch), the degree of which seems to correlate with aesthetic judgments. The autocorrelation structure of speech melody can also be seen in relation to a 1/f power law that is reminiscent of one of the universal features of music discussed in Mehr et al. (2019). In fact, when using a derived measure based on pitch autocorrelation, melodic structure in language and music seems to follow a gradient, with poetry occupying a particular middle-ground between the two domains, as has been assumed since antiquity (Winn, 1984).

The **second part** of the book is concerned with rhythm and stress and pursues the question of how they compare across the domains. This part also discusses data from electrophysiological experiments that highlight the role of shared mechanisms (rather than shared units) between language and music with respect to rhythm and stress.

First, **Dicky Gilbers and Teja Rebernik** pursue the general approach of assuming that language experience structures the way the corresponding musical system is structured. They therefore emphasize the role of transfer effects, specifically transfer from language to music, and argue that phonological and prosodic properties take on a key role in this transfer. The structural similarities between language and music are modelled within an Optimality Theory framework, in which surface patterns are derived through the interaction of different constraints and their respective relative ranking to each other (Prince & Smolensky, 2004). They capitalize on the alleged universal status of these constraints and their language-specific rankings, that in turn are thought to structure music. With their exemplary analyses on different levels of description, including segments, syllables, tones, chords and rhythmic structure, they attempt to arrive at a comparative typology. Their innovative approach subsumes aspects of universals in language and music (Greenberg, 1978; Mehr et al., 2019) and generative structure building in both domains (Lerdahl & Jackendoff, 1977; 1983).

Jasmin Pfeifer and Silke Hamann are also interested in shared mechanisms accounting for observations in music and language. They focus on a transfer from music to language. Their general approach is to study relationships between the two domains by looking at impairments in one domain (music) and the respective consequences for the other domain (language). To this end, they look at amusia as a specific musical disability that essentially describes the lack of musicality with many different consequences (Ayotte et al., 2002). More recent research, as illustrated in the chapter, supports the view that amusia is accompanied by a disruption of more domain-general mechanisms pertaining not only to pitch processing in music, but also to rhythm and stress processing in language. The hypothesis that persons with amusia are worse in processing linguistic stress is tested with a behavioral study, while an electrophysiological study provides complementary data on subconscious processing of linguistic stress patterns. Their most intriguing finding is that persons with amusia seem to rely more on duration cues than on pitch cues, illustrating not only transfer effects from music to language, but also effects of between-domain compensation.

Richard Wiese provides an overview of rhythmic similarities between language and music. His claim is that the two domains are more similar on the background of rhythm and stress than previously assumed. He sets out to illustrate similarities in the structural notations of prominence in music and language while acknowledging that complete regular rhythm in language is impeded by higher-order, syntactic and morphological constraints. Only when these constraints are lifted – as, for instance, in poetry – can rhythmic regularity prevail. Wiese argues that the functions of rhythm may be similar in the two domains and be best described by referring to predictive mechanisms as currently discussed in Predictive Coding frameworks applied to both language and music (Lewis & Bastiaansen, 2015; Vuust et al., 2009). Five studies from a neurolinguistic and a corpus-linguistic paradigm support the claim that regularity and predictiveness, while less strong in language than in music, are still essential principles in organizing events in time.

The **third part** of this volume is concerned with a topic at the true middle ground between language and music: text-setting. Text-setting, either understood as setting words to music or composing music to words illustrates the intricacy of the spoken and the sung utterance. It has previously been established that linguistic and musical prosodic properties (e.g., meter) align in text-setting (Temperley & Temperley, 2013), but principled accounts with an emphasis on prosody are relatively rare.

Heini Arjava and Gerrit Kentner are the first in this book to fill the aforementioned gap. They focus on text-setting in Finnish, a quantity-based language. The overall topic is the alignment of prosodic information between music and language. In music, prosodic properties are thought to subsume note duration, while in speech, the equivalence is assumed to be prosodic weight. The study they present highlights possible ways in which composers may be affected by the prosodic system of the language that they attempt to set to music. Based on a Finnish song collection, the prosodic relationship between language and music is analyzed in symmetric and asymmetric music duration contexts. Detailed analyses reveal that the correspondence of long notes and prosodic prominence is driven by the syllabic nucleus, not the coda. Their analyses further suggest that text-setting is also based on relative durations, i.e., durations in context, rather than absolute prosodic unit characteristics.

Elena Girardi and Ingo Plag also examine text-setting from a prosodic perspective but put more emphasis on the musical structure, namely, musical meter, note value and note height, relating this to poetic meter and syllabic prominence on the linguistic side. They model text-setting within an Optimality-Theory framework (Prince & Smolensky, 2004) and thereby attribute grammatical aspects to the process of text-setting. They attempt to answer the question of whether the mapping from text to music is direct or mediated through metrical structure. The example of classical English songs composed by Joseph Haydn reveals a systematic mapping of text meter to musical meter, with prominence positions in the songs almost categorically aligning with the text. The authors further show that the strongest metrical positions co-occur with longer notes (replicating the findings of Heini Arjava and Gerrit Kentner for Finnish). Pitch, on the other hand, seems to play only a minor role for the mapping between text and music, i.e., metrically prominent positions do not consistently align with pitch prominences in music. The authors thus observe a general and intriguing trend according to which it is mainly higher-order prosodic features which are matched between language and music in text-settings! This view is complemented by the modeling results from their Optimality Theory approach.

Christina Domene Moreno and Barış Kabak, finally, extend and complement the chapter by Elena Girardi and Ingo Plag in at least two ways. First, they focus on the psychological reality of the prosodic linguistic properties under investigation, and second, they compare languages and musical genres, enabling to draw conclusions about universal, language- and culture-specific mapping principles. They attempt a classification of languages according to the degree to with which they incorporate pitch into the marking of prominence, thereby distinguishing tone, stress, and pitch accent languages. The empirical basis for their claims is a corpus of 42 children's songs in Turkish, about half of which composed in the Makam tradition and the other half composed in the Western music tradition. The Turkish songs are furthermore compared to 18 English children's songs. Their main findings show that word stress corresponds to metrical prominence in Turkish, replicating findings from English in the chapter by Elena Girardi and Ingo Plag. This was not true for Makam music. A further finding is that linguistic stress is also aligned with melodic prominence (i.e., pitch-based prominence) in Turkish, but not in English, again replicating the findings by Elena Girardi and Ingo Plag. The authors conclude that the alignment of prosodic structure in text-setting is based on the most informative cue for stress in the respective language. This provides another important example for the fruitful transfer effects between language and music.

Finally, the book concludes with a perspective paper by **Sonia Kotz**. The author argues that "an integrative cognitive and neural perspective" on prosody in language and music is crucial for further progress in elucidating the human ability of processing acoustic events of all types. Particular emphasis is put on the role of different cortical and subcortical components for handling increasingly complex aspects of the structure of sounds.

References

Albouy, Philippe, Lucas Benjamin, Benjamin Morillon & Robert J. Zatorre. 2020. Distinct sensitivity to spectrotemporal modulation supports brain asymmetry for speech and melody. *Science* 367(6481). 1043–1047.

Anvari, Sima H., Laurel J. Trainor, Jennifer Woodside & Betty Ann Levy. 2002. Relations among musical skills, phonological processing, and early reading ability in preschool children. *Journal of Experimental Child Psychology* 83(2). 111–130.

Aria, Massimo & Corrado Cuccurullo. 2017. Bibliometrix: An R-tool for comprehensive science mapping analysis. *Journal of Informetrics* 11(4). 959–975.

Ayotte, Julie, Isabelle Peretz & Krista Hyde. 2002. Congenital amusia: A group study of adults afflicted with a music-specific disorder. *Brain* 125(2). 238–251.

Bennett, Ryan & Emily Elfner. 2019. The syntax-prosody interface. *Annual Review of Linguistics* 5. 151–171.

Besson, Mireille, Julie Chobert & Céline Marie. 2011. Transfer of training between music and speech: Common processing, attention, and memory. *Frontiers in Psychology* 2. 94.

Bever, Thomas G. & Robert J. Chiarello. 1974. Cerebral dominance in musicians and nonmusicians. *Science* 185(4150). 537–539.

Bickerton, Derek. 1990. *Language and species*. Chicago, IL: The University of Chiacgo Press.

Broca, Paul. 1863. Localisations des fonctions cérébrales. Siège de la faculté du langage articulé. *Bulletin de la Société D'anthropologie* 4. 200–208.

Brown, Steven. 2000. The "musilanguage" model of music evolution. In: Nils L. Wallin, Bjorn Merker, Steven Brown, editors. *The origins of music*, 271–300. Cambridge, Mass.: MIT Press Ltd.

Brown, Steven. 2017. A joint prosodic origin of language and music. *Frontiers in Psychology* 8. 1894.

Cobo, M. J., A. G. López-Herrera, E. Herrera-Viedma & F. Herrera. 2011. Science mapping software tools: Review, analysis, and cooperative study among tools. *Journal of the American Society for Information Science and Technology* 62(7). 1382–1402.

Darwin, Charles. 1981 [1871]. *The descent of man and selection in relation to sex [originally published in 1871]*. Princeton: Princeton University Press.

Deutsch, Diana, Trevor Henthorn, Elizabeth Marvin & HongShuai Xu. 2006. Absolute pitch among American and Chinese conservatory students: Prevalence differences, and evidence for a speech-related critical period. *The Journal of the Acoustical Society of America* 119(2). 719–722.

Ding, Nai, Aniruddh D. Patel, Lin Chen, Henry Butler, Cheng Luo & David Poeppel. 2017. Temporal modulations in speech and music. *Neuroscience and Biobehavioral Reviews* 81(Pt B). 181–187.

Fenk-Oczlon, Gertraud. 2017. What vowels can tell us about the evolution of music. *Frontiers in Psychology* 8. 1581.

Fenk-Oczlon, Gertraud & August Fenk. 2009. Some parallels between language and music from a cognitive and evolutionary perspective. *Musicae Scientiae* 13(2). 201–226.

Filippi, Piera, Marisa Hoeschele, Michelle Spierings & Daniel L. Bowling. 2019. Temporal modulation in speech, music, and animal vocal communication: Evidence of conserved function. *Annals of the New York Academy of Sciences* 1453(1). 99–113.

Fitch, W. Tecumseh. 2005. The evolution of language: A comparative review. *Biology & Philosophy* 2–3(20). 193–203.

Fitch, W. Tecumseh. 2006. The biology and evolution of music: A comparative perspective. *Cognition* 100(1). 173–215.
Fox, Anthony. 2002. *Prosodic features and prosodic structure: The phonology of suprasegmentals*. Oxford: Oxford University Press.
Ghitza, Oded & Steven Greenberg. 2009. On the possible role of brain rhythms in speech perception: Intelligibility of time-compressed speech with periodic and aperiodic insertions of silence. *Phonetica* 66(1–2). 113–126.
Glaser, Susan. 2000. The missing link: Connections between musical and linguistic prosody. *Contemporary Music Review* 19(3). 129–154.
Greenberg, Joseph H. 1978. *Universals of human language*. Stanford, CA: Stanford University Press.
Heffner, Christopher C. & L. Robert Slevc. 2015. Prosodic structure as a parallel to musical structure. *Frontiers in Psychology* 6. 1962.
Jones, Jennifer L., Jay Lucker, Christopher Zalewski, Carmen Brewer & Dennis Drayna. 2009. Phonological processing in adults with deficits in musical pitch recognition. *Journal of Communication Disorders* 42(3). 226–234.
Koelsch, Stefan. 2011. Toward a neural basis of music perception – a review and updated model. *Frontiers in Psychology* 2. 110.
Koelsch, Stefan, Thomas C. Gunter, D. Yves v Cramon, Stefan Zysset, Gabriele Lohmann & Angela D. Friederici. 2002. Bach speaks: a cortical "language-network" serves the processing of music. *NeuroImage* 17(2). 956–966.
Kotz, Sonja A., Andrea Ravignani & W. Tecumseh Fitch. 2018. The evolution of rhythm processing. *Trends in Cognitive Sciences* 22(10). 896–910.
Kunert, Richard, Roel M. Willems, Daniel Casasanto, Aniruddh D. Patel & Peter Hagoort. 2015. Music and language syntax interact in Broca's Area: An fMRI study. *Plos One* 10 (11). e0141069.
Lerdahl, Fred & Ray Jackendoff. 1977. Toward a formal theory of tonal music. *Journal of Music Theory* 21. 111–171.
Lerdahl, Fred & Ray Jackendoff. 1983. *A generative theory of tonal music*. Cambridge, MA: The MIT Press.
Levitin, Daniel J. & Susan E. Rogers. 2005. Absolute pitch: Perception, coding, and controversies. *Trends in Cognitive Sciences* 9(1). 26–33.
Lewis, Ashley Glen & M. C. Bastiaansen. 2015. A predictive coding framework for rapid neural dynamics during sentence-level language comprehension. *Cortex* 68. 155–168.
Liebenthal, Einat, David A. Silbersweig & Emily Stern. 2016. The language, tone and prosody of emotions: Neural substrates and dynamics of spoken-word emotion perception. *Frontiers in Neuroscience* 10(506).
Longfellow, Henry Wadsworth. 1835. *Outre-Mer: A pilgrimage beyond the sea*. New York: Harper & Brothers.
Maggu, Akshay R., Joseph C. Y. Lau, Mary M. Y. Waye & Patrick C. M. Wong. 2021. Combination of absolute pitch and tone language experience enhances lexical tone perception. *Scientific Reports* 11(1). 1485.
Marie, Céline, Cyrille Magne & Mireille Besson. 2011. Musicians and the metric structure of words. *Journal of Cognitive Neuroscience* 23(2). 294–305.
Marques, Carlos, Sylvain Moreno, São Luis Castro & Mireille Besson. 2007. Musicians detect pitch violation in a foreign language better than nonmusicians: Behavioral and electrophysiological evidence. *Journal of Cognitive Neuroscience* 19(9). 1453–1463.

Masataka, Nobuo. 2007. Music, evolution and language. *Developmental Science* 10(1). 35–39.
Masataka, Nobuo. 2009. The origins of language and the evolution of music: A comparative perspective. *Physics of Life Reviews* 6(1). 11–22.
Mehr, Samuel A., Max M. Krasnow, Gregory A. Bryant & Edward H. Hagen. 2020. Origins of music in credible signaling. *Behavioral and Brain Sciences* 44. e60.
Mehr, Samuel A., Manvir Singh, Dean Knox, Daniel M. Ketter, Daniel Pickens-Jones, S. Atwood, Christopher Lucas, Nori Jacoby, Alena A. Egner, Erin J. Hopkins, Rhea M. Howard, Joshua K. Hartshorne, Mariela V. Jennings, Jan Simson, Constance M. Bainbridge, Steven Pinker, Timothy J. O'Donnell, Max M. Krasnow & Luke Glowacki. 2019. Universality and diversity in human song. *Science* 366(6468). 1–17.
Mithen, Steven. 2005. *The singing Neanderthals: The origins of music, language, mind and body*. London: Weidenfeld and Nicolson.
Moreno, Sylvain, Carlos Marques, Andreia Santos, Manuela Santos, São Luis Castro & Mireille Besson. 2009. Musical training influences linguistic abilities in 8-year-old children: More evidence for brain plasticity. *Cerebral Cortex* 19(3). 712–723.
Nespor, Marina & Irene Vogel. 1986. *Prosodic phonology*. Dordrecht: Foris Publications.
Nygaard, Lynne C. & Jennifer S. Queen. 2008. Communicating emotion: Linking affective prosody and word meaning. *Journal of Experimental Psychology: Human Perception and Performance* 34(4). 1017–1030.
Pagel, Mark. 2017. What is human language, when did it evolve and why should we care? *BMC Biology* 15(64). 1–6.
Palmer, Caroline & Sean Hutchins. 2006. What is musical prosody? *Psychology of Learning and Motivation* 46. 245–278.
Palmer, Caroline, Melissa K. Jungers & Peter W. Jusczyk. 2001. Episodic memory for musical prosody. *Journal of Memory and Language* 45(4). 526–545.
Palmer, Caroline & Michael H. Kelly. 1992. Linguistic prosody and musical meter in song. *Journal of Memory and Language* 31(4). 525–542.
Patel, Aniruddh D. 2003. Language, music, syntax and the brain. *Nature Neuroscience* 6. 674–681.
Patel, Aniruddh D. 2010. *Music, language, and the brain*. New York: Oxford University Press.
Paulmann, Silke, Debra Titone & Marc D. Pell. 2012. How emotional prosody guides your way: Evidence from eye movements. *Speech Communication* 54(1). 92–107.
Peretz, I., D. Vuvan, M. E. Lagrois & J. L. Armony. 2015. Neural overlap in processing music and speech. *Philosophical Transactions of the Royal Society B-Biological Sciences* 370(1664). 68–75.
Peretz, Isabelle & Robert J. Zatorre. 2003. *The cognitive neuroscience of music*. Oxford: Oxford University Press.
Pinker, Steven. 1997. Words and rules in the human brain. *Nature* 378. 547–548.
Poeppel, David. 2003. The analysis of speech in different temporal integration windows: Cerebral lateralization as 'asymmetric sampling in time'. *Speech Communication* 41. 245–255.
Prince, Alan & Paul Smolensky. 2004. *Optimality Theory – Constraint interaction in Generative Grammar*. Malden, MA: Blackwell Publishing.
Pritchard, Alan. 1969. Statistical bibliography or bibliometrics. *Journal of Documentation* 25. 348–349.

Sammler, Daniela, Marie-Hélène Grosbras, Alfred Anwander, Patricia E. G. Bestelmeyer & Pascal Belin. 2015. Dorsal and ventral pathways for prosody. *Current Biology* 25(23). 3079–3085.

Sammler, Daniela, Stefan Koelsch & Angela D. Friederici. 2011. Are left fronto-temporal brain areas a prerequisite for normal music-syntactic processing? *Cortex* 47(6). 659–673.

Savage, Patrick E., Psyche Loui, Bronwyn Tarr, Adena Schachner, Luke Glowacki, Steven Mithen & W. Tecumseh Fitch. 2020. Music as a coevolved system for social bonding. *Behavioral and Brain Sciences* 44. e59.

Scherer, Klaus R. 1995. Expression of emotion in voice and music. *Journal of Voice* 9(3). 235–248.

Schön, Daniele, Cyrille Magne & Mireille Besson. 2004. The music of speech: Music training facilitates pitch processing in both music and language. *Psychophysiology* 41(3). 341–349.

Selkirk, Elizabeth. 1995. Sentence prosody: Intonation, stress, and phrasing. In: John Goldsmith, editor. *The handbook of phonological theory*, 550–569. Cambridge, MA: Blackwell Publishers.

Temperley, Nicholas & David Temperley. 2013. Stress-meter alignment in French vocal music. *The Journal of the Acoustical Society of America* 134(1). 520–527.

Thompson, William Forde, E. Glenn Schellenberg & Gabriela Husain. 2004. Decoding speech prosody: Do music lessons help? *Emotion* 4(1). 46–64.

Timmers, R. & P. Loui. 2019. Music and Emotion. *Foundations in music psychology: Theory and research*, 783–825.

van Eck, Nees Jan & Ludo Waltman. 2010. Software survey: Vosviewer, a computer program for bibliometric mapping. *Scientometrics* 84(2). 523–538.

Vuust, Peter, Leif Ostergaard, Karen J. Pallesen, Christopher Bailey & Andreas Roepstorff. 2009. Predictive coding of music – brain responses to rhythmic incongruity. *Cortex* 45(1). 80–92.

Vuust, Peter, Karen Johanne Pallesen, Christopher Bailey, Titia L. van Zuijen, Albert Gjedde, Andreas Roepstorff & Leif Østergaard. 2005. To musicians, the message is in the meter: Pre-attentive neuronal responses to incongruent rhythm are left-lateralized in musicians. *NeuroImage* 24(2). 560–564.

Winn, James Anderson. 1984. *Unsuspected eloquence: History of the relations between poetry and music*. New Haven, CT: Yale University Press.

Wray, Alison. 2002. *Formulaic language and the lexicon*. Cambridge: Cambridge University Press.

Zatorre, Robert J. & Shari R. Baum. 2012. Musical melody and speech intonation: Singing a different tune. *PLoS Biology* 10(7). e1001372.

Zatorre, Robert J. & Pascal Belin. 2001. Spectral and temporal processing in human auditory cortex. *Cerebral Cortex* 11(10). 946–953.

Pauline Larrouy-Maestri, David Poeppel & Peter Q. Pfordresher
Pitch units in music and speech prosody

Abstract: Music and language processing have been repeatedly compared but similarities and differences between domains are challenging to quantify. This chapter takes a step back and focuses specifically on the role of fine-grained changes in pitch, which play a role in both domains but are not widely studied. In addition to describing the units, we provide empirical evidence for the specific role of small units in music: scoops, which are small dynamic pitch change at the start or end of sung notes within a melody. We report results from a new experiment that builds on a recent study that addressed two distinct processes for the evaluation of pitch accuracy (Larrouy-Maestri & Pfordresher, 2018). The present study compared accuracy ratings to a more ecologically valid listening task: preference judgments. By replicating and extending previous findings, we describe the processing of small units in music perception and propose research directions to further investigate such units in speech perception, and ultimately gain the necessary insight to make meaningful cross-domain comparisons.

Keywords: Fundamental frequency, Note, Scoop, Preference, Perception

1 General introduction

Researchers have long been intrigued by the degree to which language and music share acoustic properties, and whether our brain processes input from each domain using similar or distinct resources (Jackendoff, 2009; Patel, 2008).

Acknowledgments: We are grateful to Pol van Rijn for his help with Figure 1, to Shi En Gloria Huan for helping with the data collection of preference judgments, and to Madita Hörster and Carmel Raz for edits. This research was supported in part by NSF Grant BCS-1848930 awarded to Peter Q. Pfordresher and by the Max Planck Society.

Pauline Larrouy-Maestri, Neuroscience Department, Max-Planck-Institute for Empirical Aesthetics, Germany; Max-Planck-NYU Center for Language, Music, and Emotion, New York, USA
David Poeppel, Neuroscience Department, Max-Planck-Institute for Empirical Aesthetics, Germany; Max-Planck-NYU Center for Language, Music, and Emotion, New York, USA; Psychology Department, New York University, USA; Ernst Strüngmann Institute for Neuroscience, Frankfurt-am-Main, Germany
Peter Q. Pfordresher, Department of Psychology, University at Buffalo, State University of New York, USA

https://doi.org/10.1515/9783110770186-002

However, the comparison of these two domains is challenging, as has been discussed by Fritz and collaborators (2013). One key point of that chapter, focused on the neurobiology of language, speech, and music, is that while the 'units' or 'primitives' that define perceptually separable events in each domain (phonemes, syllables versus notes, melody, etc.) might be different in kind, many cognitive or computational operations (e.g. segmentation, concatenation, hierarchy formation, categorization, etc.) might be similar.

A first key step towards such cross-domain investigation and comparison consists, on this perspective, in identifying the relevant units and processes to be compared in each domain. In this chapter, we focus on one feature: fundamental frequency (f_0) dynamics, associated with melodies in music and intonation or prosody in speech. f_0 is important both in human communication and in conveying musical melodies. A next step consists of testing different hypotheses regarding the integration of f_0 units of different timescales. Theoretically, one hypothesis is that auditory processing is *statistical* in nature: listeners' perception is based on a summary statistic (say mean f_0) across a larger unit, taking into account the dynamic pitch information contained in the smaller one(s). A different hypothesis is that auditory processing is *teleological*. On this view, listeners perceive small units based on their relationship to larger units, assuming that the larger unit constitutes the endgoal point for a (motor) plan. This form of listening focuses on the sound sequence trajectory formed by larger-scale units as opposed to summary statistics within a unit. Note that these two hypotheses are not necessarily exclusive, but could be combined or varied, depending on the function of the process.

This chapter lays the ground for a meaningful comparison between the music and language domains. We first propose an overview of the role of pitch in both speech prosody and music, with a focus on small f_0 units. Then, we provide empirical data that allow to further examine the perception of pitch in the context of singing performances. In addition to shedding light on the processes involved in the perception of pitch when listening to music, such findings offer a reference for cross-domain comparison of underlying mechanisms to process relevant pitch units, and thus pave the way for a better understanding of auditory sequence processing in general.

2 Role of pitch in speech prosody and music

Listeners' sensitivity to pitch variation is usually examined with pitch discrimination tasks (see, e.g., the tasks in the toolbox of Soranzo & Grassi, 2014). Thresholds are generally far lower than necessary to process pitch changes in music.

This is particularly true for listeners with formal musical training, and they vary slightly from one individual to the other (e.g., Micheyl et al., 2006; Moore, 1973). For larger contexts (i.e., non isolated sounds), the literature on dynamic changes highlights the perception of glides between pure tones (Lyzenga et al., 2004) and glides at the end of pure tones (Wang et al., 2013), confirming the perceptual relevance of quick pitch movements. Such dynamic changes influence the perception of tone sequences (Kerivan & Carey, 1976). However, it should be emphasized that not every pitch change is perceived. For instance, listeners don't identifying the sweep direction in frequency-modulated signals if the stimulus is less than twenty milliseconds long (Gordon & Poeppel, 2002; Luo et al., 2007). Also, the rate of frequency rise (or fall) should be more than $0.16/T^2$, where T is the duration of the glide (Hart et al., 1990) to be perceived.

Besides the discrimination abilities of listeners and the f_0 characteristics of a stimulus, the perceptual relevance of pitch obviously depends on the context. For instance, Warrier & Zatorre (2002) observed that small pitch manipulations are better perceived in melodic contexts compared to isolated intervals. In fact, the perceptual relevance of pitch (and its role) is highly sensitive to the domain under consideration.

2.1 Pitch in speech prosody

In the speech prosody literature, pitch is described in terms of single values such as mean pitch, that do not take into account the temporal aspect of speech prosody, or in a more dynamic way, in terms of intonation, or pitch direction (e.g., utterances interpreted as statements or questions, Bolinger, 1986; Ladd, 1996), or pitch accent (e.g., Ladd et al., 1999), or prosodic patterns (e.g., Dilley & McAuley, 2008; Kraljic & Brennan, 2005). Whatever the descriptors used to characterize speech prosody, it is now well established that speech conveys both linguistic and paralinguistic information in part through pitch.

When focusing on the paralinguistic information, there is evidence that the acoustic properties of speech provides hints about speaker sex (e.g., Hillenbrand & Clark, 2009; Latinus & Belin, 2011; Latinus et al., 2013), age (see Gamba, 2014, for a review; Shigeno, 2016), size (e.g., Rendall et al., 2007), and personality (e.g., McAleer et al., 2014). More generally, speech prosody has a social function. For instance, Zoghaib (2019) observed that speakers with high-pitched voices were perceived as the most competent, whereas Pavela Banai and collaborators (2016) report that political "winners" (according to presidential election outcomes) had lower-pitched voices, and Ponsot and collaborators (2018) observed pitch contours associated with the perception of speakers' dominance. Cheng and collaborators (2016) observed that people spontaneously modulate their vocal pitch, which influenced listeners' perception of their 'rank', supporting that pitch has a key role in human interactions.

Importantly, pitch gives information about the emotional state of the speaker, which is a crucial ingredient of human communication, since affective communication has an adaptive value and influences the behavior of the communication partner (Bandstra et al., 2011; Fischer & Manstead, 2008; Keltner & Haidt, 1999; Shariff & Tracy, 2011; Sinaceur et al., 2015; Wubben et al., 2011). Numerous studies using filtered, foreign, or pseudo-language material have confirmed that emotions can be identified well above chance level on the basis of acoustic cues alone (e.g., Bänziger & Scherer, 2005; Bryant & Barrett, 2008; Dromey et al., 2005; Pell et al., 2009; Pell & Skorup, 2008; Scherer et al., 2001; Wildgruber et al., 2005). Relevant features are not limited to pitch-related ones (e.g., Banse & Scherer, 1996; Juslin & Laukka, 2003) but pitch has been repeatedly reported as crucial (already by Fairbanks & Pronovost, 1938).

In line with the general statement that speech prosody conveys speakers' intention (Grice, 1957) that shapes communication (see the speech act theory; Austin, 1962; Searle, 1969), the non-exhaustive list of examples provided above illustrates the role of acoustic cues, including pitch, on the identification of the speakers' identity, social status or emotional state, and thus on human communication. Whereas the exact nature of pitch features remains to be clarified, their perceptual relevance in the context of speech communication is well documented.

2.2 Pitch in music

The organization of pitch in time provides information that allows listeners to recognize, evaluate, and enjoy a musical performance. In different musical styles, tones are associated with various symbols that have been developed since the late middle ages (Cohen, 2002). Tones are usually defined as the smallest discrete unit in Western music and their organization along the melody defines its tonality that plays an important role in the expectations of the listeners of a specific culture. There exist different musical systems, each with its scales, rules, and grammars (Cross, 2001; Krumhansl, 1979; Lerdahl & Jackendoff, 1983; Ringer, 2002; Thompson, 2016).

Western musical culture is generally based on the equal temperament system, arguably the most common tuning system for the past few hundred years (Parncutt & Hair, 2018). The smallest theoretical distance in tempered systems between the tones of a scale is called a semitone (assumed to be equal), and musical intervals can be described in terms of number of semitones. Studies exploring the perception of intervals confirmed the relevance of semitones as discrete categories (Burns & Ward, 1978; Zarate et al., 2012), which is a much larger difference than the pitch discrimination thresholds observed in a general population. In other words, pitch perception in music is linked to the musical system and cannot be explained only by pitch discrimination abilities. In principle, the identity of a musical piece should remain invariant when other acoustic dimensions such as timbre or tempo are altered, as long as the tones fall within the right semitone category. For instance, "Jingle Bells" played on a keyboard, a trombone, or sung by a young child, at a slow or fast tempo remains "Jingle Bells" as long as the relationship between tones that compose this melody is preserved. Note that a melody transposed is still recognized (Stalinski & Schellenberg, 2010), which supports the notion that the general pitch height is not relevant as long as the size of the intervals between consecutive notes is preserved.

In addition to the relevance of pitch in melody recognition, pitch manipulations affect the correctness of a musical performance. By growing up in a specific culture, listeners develop an internal representation of what is 'correct' in terms of pitch accuracy (Larrouy-Maestri et al., 2013; Larrouy-Maestri et al., 2015). Larrouy-Maestri (2018) reported a series of experiments designed to clarify the amount of pitch deviation that causes listeners to evaluate a musical sequence as correct or incorrect. Listeners' tolerance with regard to mistuning (i.e., the range of pitch variability heard as correct) was examined by presenting parametrically manipulated melodies to a large group of listeners with different musical expertise and asking them to identify each version as in-tune or out-of-tune. In four experiments, listeners' tolerance with regard to mistuning was compared across melodies to examine the effect of interval (i.e., size, direction, and position), and familiarity. Taken together, the results support the existence of a 'tolerance zone' when evaluating the correctness of a melody and show that listeners accept pitch deviations that are both larger than the typical pitch discrimination thresholds and smaller than a semitone.

Listeners' perception of correctness in naturalistic music of different genres can now be quantified with the newly developed Mistuning Perception Test (MPT, Larrouy-Maestri et al., 2019). Interestingly, previous exposure plays a role in the shaping of a correctness category. Indeed, the notion of correctness is slightly different when the melody to evaluate has been mostly previously heard as slightly 'deviant,' such as the song, "Happy Birthday to You", which is rarely performed accurately (Larrouy-Maestri, 2018). Even if a direct comparison of correctness judgment and preferences/liking would be necessary to confirm the relevance of pitch in non-technical judgments, it seems reasonable to assume that difficult-to-recognize or totally out-of-tune performances would rarely be the most appreciated.

3 Definition of pitch units

3.1 Units in speech prosody

Banse & Scherer (1996) foundational study underscores that the average of f_0 over sentences is a parameter that contributes to the perception of different emotions such as hot anger, panic fear, anxiety, desperation, elation, boredom, and contempt. The pitch height of entire sentences conveys information about an intended (and perceived as such) emotional state. In other words, listeners might process pitch information at the sentence level. Of course, mean f_0 information along sentences is not only relevant in the case of emotional prosody but has a key role in other aspects of human communication (Pavela Banai et al., 2016; Zoghaib, 2019).

Besides the relevance of large units such as sentences, the multi-time resolution hypothesis suggests that dynamic changes in small time windows are relevant to listeners for speech comprehension (Poeppel, 2003; Teng et al., 2016). Linguistic elements of different sizes, such as vowel, segments, syllables, words, phrases, and sentences, are concurrently tracked and temporally integrated (Ding et al., 2017; Ding et al., 2016; Keitel et al., 2018). With regard to emotional prosody, it seems reasonable to hypothesize that units of different size exist and are integrated over time (Jiang et al., 2015; Pell & Kotz, 2011; Waaramaa et al., 2010). Whereas the most obvious carrier of emotional prosody is the intonation contour over entire phrases or sentences, words carry prosodic information (e.g., Ponsot et al., 2018). Likewise, syllables and even single phonological segments might carry prosodic information as well, which support the need of studies investigating units of very different levels of organization and abstraction.

Several arguments suggest the existence of smaller units for emotional prosody comprehension. For instance, the modulation of f_0 along sentences seems to play a role, as shown by the significant contribution of the standard deviation of the f_0 in the recognition of hot anger, anxiety, desperation, and contempt (Banse & Scherer, 1996). Also, previous research has focused on other units such as segments (e.g., Shami & Kamel, 2005), syllables (e.g., Agrima et al., 2019), phonemes (e.g., Bitouk et al., 2010), or selected vowels (e.g., Goudbeek et al., 2009). The fact that emotional states can be described or recognized from these temporally shorter units indicates that the information is not equally distributed over the full sentence. Pell & Kotz (2011) as well as Nordström & Laukka (2019) reached the same conclusion with a different approach. They used a gating paradigm and showed that the size of units in speech affected the identification of specific emotions. Recognition improved over time and thus depended on the amount of information accumulated (i.e., gate duration), which suggests that emotional prosody might be a dynamic signal constituted of small units (i.e., smaller than the full sentence) containing critical acoustic information, including f_0, potentially integrated over time.

The role of the acoustic content in small units (e.g., formant transitions, Stevens & Klatt, 1974) is not questioned anymore. In the case of pitch, the hypothesis of the relevance of small windows in prosody has also been supported by recent studies using the reverse correlation method which permits access to mental representations without presenting the actual/stereotypical target. For instance, Ponsot and collaborators (2018) presented pairs of randomly manipulated pitch contours of single words to listeners and observed specific contours associated with attitudes such as 'dominance,' as well as great individual differences. Using morphing methods, other studies confirmed the role of intonation (see Belin et al., 2017, about the perception of trustworthiness; Sammler et al., 2015, about the perception of questions/statements). Altogether, these studies provide evidence for the perceptual and social relevance of pitch contours. The exact nature of pitch movements over time is under study. For example, van Rijn and collaborators (under review) developed new features describing slopes, general shapes, and pitch changes of spoken sentences. The addition of these features to an existing standard feature set (eGemaps of Eyben et al., 2016) significantly improves the classification of emotions. The preliminary results offer promising perspectives with regard to the identification of small units in speech prosody.

3.2 Units in music

3.2.1 Documented units

Several models (e.g., Pearce, 2005; Temperley, 2013) have been proposed to describe the organization of tones within the more general structure of musical phrases, thereby quantifying listeners' expectations grounded both in Gestalt-like principles and in statistical learning (Morgan et al., 2019). Whereas the exact cause of listeners' expectations remains to be clarified, it appears that lay listeners use tone units and implicitly develop knowledge about the music system of their culture (Bigand & Poulin-Charronnat, 2006; Hannon & Trainor, 2007; Larrouy-Maestri, 2018; Marmel et al., 2008; McDermott et al., 2016). It has also been repeatedly shown that irregularities with regard to the music system are detected in the brain responses of listeners (e.g., Koelsch & Friederici, 2003). In addition to behavioral arguments about melodic recognition and evaluation, these findings again support the organization of tones in larger structures following specific rules. Taken together, studies on music perception have repeatedly confirmed the perceptual relevance of two units of different size: tones and melodies.

Whereas tones are commonly described as the smallest discrete units that allow for the construction of structured melodies in the tonal system of Western culture, one might wonder whether smaller units, such as pitch fluctuations within the tones themselves, have relevance in music. It has been shown that pitch alterations such as vibrato rate and extent are important features in pitch perception (e.g., van Besouw & Howard, 2009) and in music evaluation (e.g., Larrouy-Maestri et al., 2017). Considered as a vocal quality developed through training (Mürbe et al., 2007), vibrato is appreciated in highly trained voices (Garnier et al., 2007). Even if vibrato is not limited to operatic voices, it remains something special, and is rarely associated with the singing of occasional/untrained singers. As illustrated in Figure 1A, a series of sung tones can be described as a series of flat lines (f_0) in a spectrogram, but zooming in (see Figure 1B) reveals the presence of unsteady parts. In order to examine widely present pitch fluctuations, we focus here on pitch movements happening at the start and end of tones: 'scoops.'

3.2.2 Definition of scoops

Singing requires fine control of the vocal instrument (e.g., Sundberg, 2013; Titze, 2000), leading to unavoidable motor adjustments (Hutchins et al., 2014). Even highly trained singers produce pitch transitions toward or away from a target pitch (Hutchins & Campbell, 2009; Mori et al., 2004; Saitou et al., 2005; Stevens & Miles, 1928). Besides the physiological constraints of singing, these pitch movements may be used expressively. In fact, scoops do not only reflect mere noise in the motor system. Note that in the psychophysical literature, pitch movements in small time windows are often referred to as "glides" or "sweeps." In line with the terminology proposed by Larrouy-Maestri & Pfordresher (2018), we use the term "scoop" to refer to dynamic changes at the start or end of sung tones, whether produced voluntarily or not.

Scoops have been investigated by examining the singing productions of occasional singers varying greatly in terms of singing accuracy (Larrouy-Maestri & Pfordresher, 2018). Appendix A of that study described the characteristics of

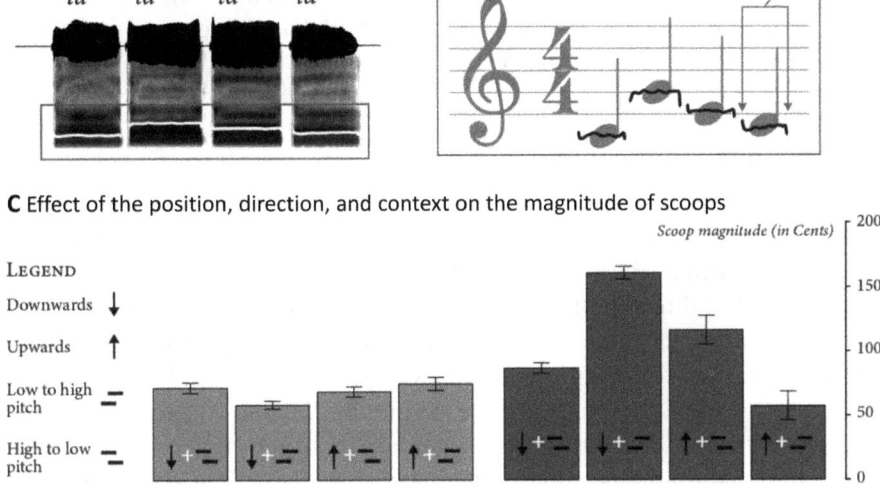

Figure 1: Description of scoops. A. Illustration of a 4-tone sequence produced with the syllable /ta/ by an occasional singer. The wave form of each syllable as well as their spectrum are represented, the white lines (in the frame) show the position of the relatively stable fundamental frequency (f_0). B. Superposition of the f_0 and the musical notation illustrating that the f_0 of each tone is not perfectly straight. C. Mean magnitude of scoops (in Cents) of 1461 tones analyzed (i.e., not aggregated per singer), according to the position (starting or ending), the direction (up-/downwards), and the pitch height of the tone adjacent to the scoop (higher or lower than the target) in the melody. Plus signs (+) represent the combination of variables 'direction' and 'context'. Bars represent standard error of the mean. This panel is based on the re-analysis of the material recorded by Pfordresher & Mantell (2014).

scoops at the start and end of musical sung tones that were used to synthesize realistic material for the listening task of the main experiment. The focus was on the amplitude and rate of scoops before and after the stable middle part of the tone (i.e., the asymptote). To do so, the f_0 values of a total of 1,874 single tones of about 1 s length were selected from existing recordings (Pfordresher & Mantell, 2014). The analysis adapted the model of Large et al. (2002), originally designed to quantify variations in temporal perturbation, in order to predict how f_0 changes at the beginning and ending of a sung tone (see Equation A2 and Figure A1, of Larrouy-Maestri & Pfordresher, 2018). From a total of 1,461 tones (78% of the available tones), information about the amplitude of the scoop, that is, the difference between the median of the stable part of the tone and the pitch at the start or end, was extracted. Other features were estimated, such as the rate of the scoop (time to reach the stable part or to end the tone), and the oscillation around the stable part (periodic fluctuations in f_0 before or after this part). As visible in Figure 1C, there was a large variability in terms of scoop magnitude, with means ranging from 50 to 150 cents.

3.2.3 Variability of scoops

Besides estimating the scoop magnitude of occasional singers, the sung material used in Larrouy-Maestri & Pfordresher (2018) offered the possibility of testing the effect of direction (upward vs. downward), position (start vs. end), and context (adjacent tone higher or lower than the target tone) on scoop characteristics. As illustrated in Figure 1C and extensively described in Larrouy-Maestri & Pfordresher (2018, Appendix A), the magnitude of scoops varied considerably depending on the direction (larger magnitude for downward scoops, $p = .006$, $\eta_p^2 = .249$) and on the position (larger magnitude for ending scoops, $p = 001$, $\eta_p^2 = .440$). There was also a significant three-way interaction among position, direction, and context ($p = .001$, $\eta_p^2 = .564$). In other words, the magnitude of the scoop varied systematically depending on the position, direction, and surrounding musical context. By contrast, no significant effects of these variables were found for the rate of scoops or oscillation features.

In addition to this information about scoop variability, we revisited this dataset to examine the variability according to singer quality. Indeed, participants (recorded by Pfordresher & Mantell, 2014) were categorized as accurate (if the mean pitch deviation between the sung tones and the target pitches was less than 50 cents), or inaccurate (if the mean deviation was greater than 50 cents) by the authors (see Dalla Bella, 2015, or Pfordresher & Larrouy-Maestri, 2015, for discussion about cutoff criteria). As a consequence, we were able to compare the scoops of two contrasting groups: accurate singers (n = 12) and poor-pitch singers (n = 19). As illustrated in Figure 2A, poor-pitch singers performed with a greater scoop magnitude ($M = 121$ cents) than accurate singers ($M = 89$ cents), $t(15.78) = 2.54, p = .022$.

Because the magnitude of scoops varied greatly even within groups, we also examined the relationship between the magnitude of the scoops and the amplitude of the global deviation of the asymptote of the tones analyzed (Figure 2B). The Spearman coefficient correlation did not reach significance level ($r(28) = .218$, $p = .254$). Note that the same profile was observed for accurate (black circles) and inaccurate singers (grey circles) when the analysis was performed separately ($p > .05$), supporting the lack of direct relationship between mistuning of the stable part and magnitude of scoops even if inaccurate singers show generally more deviation in both compared to accurate singers. Altogether, the additional analyses performed on the dataset described in Larrouy-Maestri and Pfordresher (2018, Appendix A) support the claim that scoops greatly depend on both the musical material and the singing abilities of the performer.

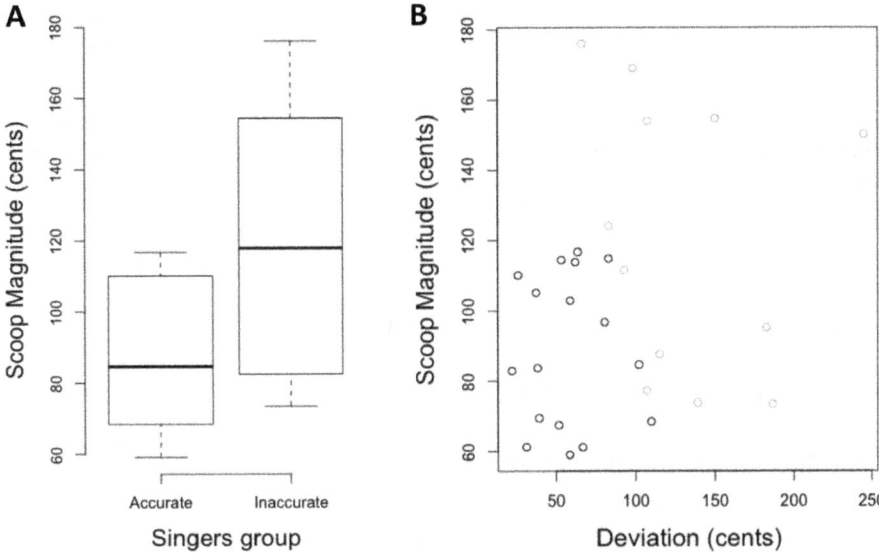

Figure 2: Summary of the distribution of magnitude of scoops (in cents) for accurate and inaccurate singers (re-analysis of the material recorded by Pfordresher & Mantell, 2014). The bottom and top of the boxes represent the 25th and 75th percentiles (lower and upper quartiles), with a line at the median. Error bars: lowest and highest scores within a 1.5 interquartile range (IQR). B. Relationship between the global pitch deviation of the stable middle part from the target and the absolute value of the scoops magnitude. Black circles represent the accurate singers and grey circles represent the inaccurate singers.

3.2.4 Perceptual relevance of scoops

The scoop magnitudes and rates discussed above (cf. Figure 1) were above the perceptual thresholds proposed so far. Therefore it was assumed that scoops would be heard when listening to music. In Larrouy-Maestri & Pfordresher (2018), 110 participants were asked to evaluate the intonation of 4-tone melodies in which the third tone's tuning could vary within the stable part of tones, or by virtue of scoops at the beginning and/or end of the tone. Note that the material consisted in synthesized vocal sounds in order to precisely manipulate scoops. As expected, it was observed that listeners' ratings of pitch accuracy were affected by the presence of scoops: lower ratings were given to melodies in which dynamic changes occured at the end of tones (Experiments 1, 2, and 3 of Larrouy-Maestri & Pfordresher, 2018), or when they were present at both the start and the end of tones (Experiment 2 of the same study). Note that units of small size are not limited to pitch dynamics at the start and/or end of tones but can also take place in the form of frequency modulations (Gockel et al., 2001) or vibrato (Larrouy-Maestri et al., 2017; van Besouw & Howard, 2009) and should be specifically examined. Nevertheless, the findings of Larrouy-Maestri & Pfordresher (2018) confirmed that scoops are treated as informative when listening to music, supporting the claim that the auditory system processes units that are considerable smaller than tones. Below we report a follow-up study that replicates and expands on the results of this previous research.

4 Processing small units: The case of scoops in music perception

4.1 Background and hypotheses

Since a strong advance has been made regarding the identification of small units in music perception (i.e., scoops) – whereas the ongoing research is still in progress in the speech prosody domain – this section focuses on the musical domain. As discussed, Larrouy-Maestri and Pfordresher's (2018) study confirmed the perceptual relevance of scoops. In addition, they tested two hypotheses about the process behind the perception of scoops in correctness judgments by examining listeners' perception of melodies containing manipulated tones (Figure 3):
- The *statistical* hypothesis assumes that listeners' perception is based on the average f_0 across a sung tone. As a consequence, listeners would perceive melodic performances as more in tune when the addition of a scoop would lead to a smaller pitch deviation of the entire tone. For instance, if the middle stable part of a tone is too sharp and the starting scoop goes upward and/or the ending scoop goes downward, the average f_0 of the sung tone will be less sharp than if the scoops go in the other direction (making the average f_0 of the tone even sharper), and thus will be perceived as less out-of-tune. In other words, scoops compensating for the deviation of the sung tone would be perceived as leading to a more correct pitch than scoops that failed to compensate.
- The *teleological* hypothesis assumes that listener's perception of scoops depends on the general trajectory of the melody, the singers' goals corresponding to the middle stable part of the sung tone. This hypothesis treats

scoops as distinct from the way in which a scoop influences the average f_0 across the entire tone, but interprets them in relation to the surrounding context of the sung tone manipulated. Concretely, of scoops can either enhance *continuity* across successive discrete tones, or *anticontinuity* between adjacent tones. Continuity between pitches has been associated with speech whereas sung performances have been described in terms of fixed tones of steady pitch (Sievers, 1912). However, recent findings highlight that pitch glides (i.e., continuity) leads to the impression of singing and does not enhance the impression of speaking (Merrill & Larrouy-Maestri, 2017). In any case, the teleological hypothesis supports that small units are interpreted in a more general context, in a continuous or discontinuous manner.

To summarize, Larrouy-Maestri & Pfordresher (2018) highlighted the coexistence of two mechanisms behind the perception of scoops: statistical and teleological. Listener perception of scoops is based both on the relationship of the scoop to the tuning of the associated tone (higher scores for stimuli in which the scoops compensated the pitch deviation of the tone) as well as on the relationship of the scoop to the broader melodic context (higher scores for stimuli in which the scoops were not continuous between the two adjacent tones). These findings clarify an important point in the perception of correctness. However, they might not be generalizable to more typical auditory tasks. Indeed, as listeners commonly attend to musical performances for pleasure and appreciation, rather than to judge their technical correctness, the sensitivity to dynamic change in small time windows might vary depending on the question under study. For instance, the relevance of scoops might be lessened or enhanced when the judgment refers to melodic recognition or aesthetic/beauty judgments rather than to pitch accuracy (as tested in Larrouy-Maestri & Pfordresher, 2018). Also, if scoops are relevant, their role might differ depending on the question. For instance, we could observe a preference for continuity for aesthetic judgments and the opposite for pitch accuracy judgments (which is the case in Larrouy-Maestri & Pfordresher, 2018). Such pattern would not be surprising since performances in which the transition between notes is perceived as rather continuous seem to be liked better (Merrill & Larrouy-Maestri, 2017). Note however that the material used in this latter study is not typically sung but standing between speech and sung performances (speechsong or Sprechgesang in German; Stadlen, 1981). Finally, the processes themselves (statistical or teleological) might differ according to the question. As a consequence, it seems challenging to generalize the present findings when focusing only on a specific type of judgment.

The direct comparison of different types of judgments, examined with similar methods was proposed to address the effect of the task on the perception of scoops. Concretely, the study reported here aimed at 1) replicating the findings of Larrouy-Maestri & Pfordresher (2018) with a new sample of participants, and 2) extending the examination of scoops to a more natural listening condition: preference judgment.

4.2 Methods

4.2.1 Participants

Fifty-two students at the State University of New York at Buffalo (29 self-reported as females, 23 self-reported as males), ranging from 18 to 23 years old (M = 19.02, SD = 1.33), participated in the experiment in exchange for course credit. Participants reported normal hearing abilities, and a few of them reported a limited amount of formal music training (up to 8 years, M = 0.94, SD = 1.85). The general musical sophistication scores estimated with the Gold-MSI self-report questionnaire (Müllensiefen et al., 2014) ranged from 48 to 91, with a mean of 72.04, which stand within the range of the scores examined by Müllensiefen et al. (2014), meaning that they were comparable to the scores of a general population.

4.2.2 Material

The stimuli were identical to the set used in Larrouy-Maestri and Pfordresher (2018, Experiment 1). Four tones were synthesized using a male timbre (Vocaloid, Zero-G Limited, Okehampton, England) and arranged in two melodies: C3 (131 Hz) – E3 – D3 – G3 and G3 – D3 – E3 – C3, using equal temperament. Each tone was 900 milliseconds long and articulated with the syllable /da/. The characteristics of the third tone of each melody were manipulated at two different levels: the central portion of the tone (correct, flattened, or sharpened by 50 cents from ideal equal tempered tuning, 100 cents = 1 semitone), and/or the scoop at the start or end of the tone. The scoop magnitude was chosen according to the analyses of pitch fluctuations (Figure 1C) in order to propose realistic stimuli to the listeners. The direction of scoops was defined relative to the middle part: an upward scoop at the start of the tone starts lower than the middle part whereas an upward scoop at the end of the tone ends higher than the middle part. Contrasting tones manipulation were proposed to test the role of continuity (Figure 3A) and compensation (Figure 3B) of scoops on melodic perception.

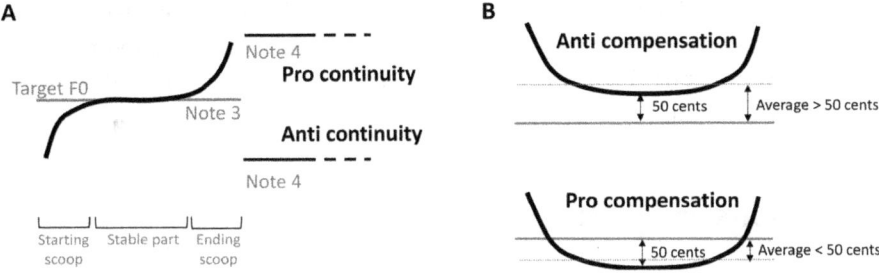

Figure 3: Illustration of the conditions. A. Example of an ending scoop up leading to melodic continuity (when the following note is higher) of discontinuity (when the following note is lower). B. Example of tuning compensation for a note with starting and ending scoops up and positive (up) or negative (down) asymptotic mistuning.

4.2.3 Procedure

The task was similar to the one described in Larrouy-Maestri & Pfordresher (2018), except that, in addition to a block in which participants made correctness judgments, the material was also presented in a block in which participants made preference judgments. Within a block, each participant was exposed to two sets of 15 variants of a melody (n = 105 pairs per melody) and was asked to select one performance of each pair according to the question "Which performance is more in tune?" or "Which performance do you prefer?". Participants could choose between the first one, the second one, but had also the option to say that performances were equally in tune or preferred (depending on the block). We manipulated the order of the questions / melodies between participants, with half of the participants listening to variations of Melody 1 first (followed by Melody 2), the other half listening to variations of Melody 2 first (followed by Melody 1). For each group defined by which melody was heard first, half started with the block dedicated to the "correctness" question and the other half with the block dedicated to the "preference" question. All possible stimulus pairs were presented once in each block, in a random order, and were thus evaluated for each combination of melody and question.

Aggregated ratings of preference and correctness were computed for a participant in the following way: For each stimulus and each condition (correctness versus preference judgment), the initial score was set to zero and was increased by one if that condition was selected as more correct/preferred relative to the other stimulus of the trial (a score of 0.5 was recorded if neither stimulus was selected). The final score for each condition was computed by accumulating points over trials, ranging from 0 (i.e., stimulus never selected) to 14 (i.e., stimulus always selected). This rating procedure enables the ranking of the manipulated melodies from the most out-of-tune to the most in-tune or from the least to the most preferred, depending on the block. The highest scores were thus associated to correct or preferred stimuli.

4.3 Results and discussion

First, we focused on the correctness judgments of the current study and observed the replication of the findings reported in Larrouy-Maestri & Pfordresher (2018). The ANOVA performed on the new data confirmed the main effect of scoops ($p < .001$, $\eta_p^2 = .28$). As illustrated in Figure 4, stimuli without scoops were rated significantly higher (i.e., more correct) than stimuli with scoops at

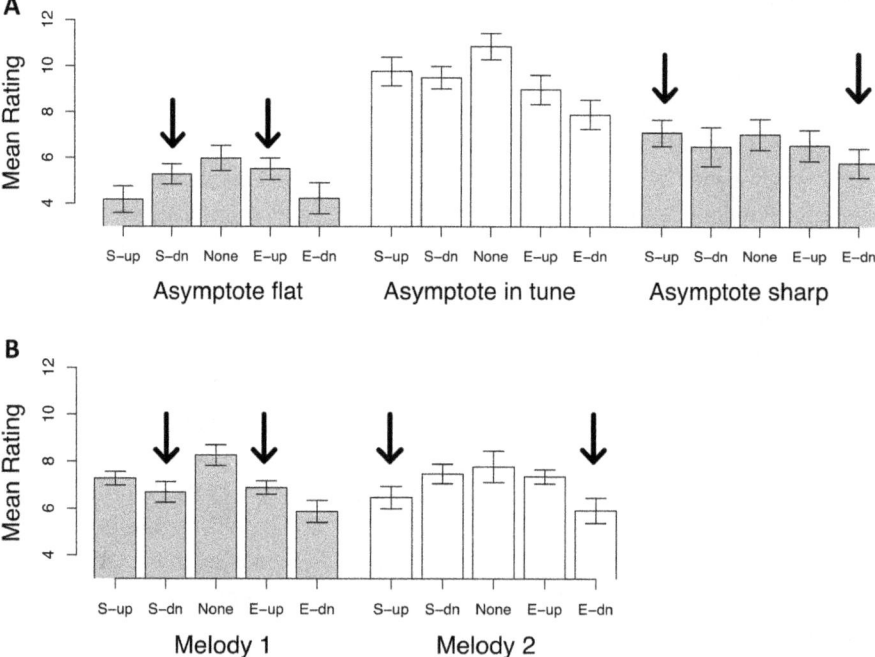

Figure 4: Mean ratings (95% CI) of the stimuli when evaluating correctness. A. illustrates the interaction observed between scoops and deviation of the asymptote. Arrows highlight conditions for which the scoop compensates for asymptotic mistuning. B. illustrates the interaction observed between scoops and melody. Arrows highlight conditions for which the scoop promotes continuity in the transition from one note to the next. S=start, E=end, dn=down.

the start or end of the tone. We also observed an interaction between scoops and deviation of the asymptote ($p = .004$, $\eta_p^2 = .05$, Figure 4A) as well as with the melody ($p < .001$, $\eta_p^2 = .07$, Figure 4B).

Figure 5A illustrates the high reliability between the ratings provided by two independent groups of participants (reference study and new data), each dot representing a stimulus (n = 30, 3 asymptotic tunings x 5 scoop types x 2 melodies). These results confirm the salience of small-timescale vocal scoops on judgements of "correct" intonation. Then, we directly compared the ratings provided in the correctness and preference blocks. Figure 5B illustrates the strong relationship between the two types of ratings. The high degree of similarity between the two types of ratings supports the claim that in-tune stimuli are preferred. Because it is possible that a carry-over effect increased these associations, we also analyzed the correlation between correctness and preference ratings within the first half of the experiment (i.e., before participants transitioned to the other task). This association was still highly significant though smaller in magnitude, $r^2 = .71$.

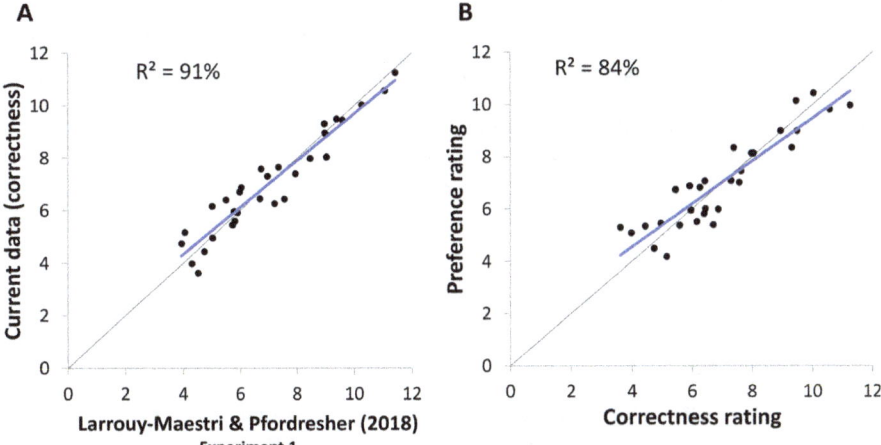

Figure 5: Judgements for vocal scoops. A. Relation between correctness judgements obtained from the participants of Larrouy-Maestri and Pfordresher (2018, Experiment 1) and correctness judgements from the participants of the current study. Each dot corresponds to a stimulus (n = 30) B. Relation between correctness and preference judgements from the current study. Thick lines represent least-squares linear regression, plotted in comparison to the unity line. Both $p < .001$.

This new dataset replicated the findings reported in Larrouy-Maestri & Pfordresher (2018), confirming the perceptual relevance of scoops when judging the correctness of sung performances, while also providing a way to compare different types of judgments: technical evaluation versus listeners' preferences. As shown in Figure 6, we observed the same pattern of results whatever the type of judgment, with the higher scores for the anti-continuity condition (Figure 6, left panel) and for the compensation condition (Figure 6, right panel). This means that listeners prefer scoops when they enhance the *discreteness* or *discontinuity* of tones and listeners also integrate scoops as *part of the tone*, whatever the question asked (correctness judgment in white and preference judgment in grey). In other words, our findings support both the statistical or teleological hypotheses when listening to melodies.

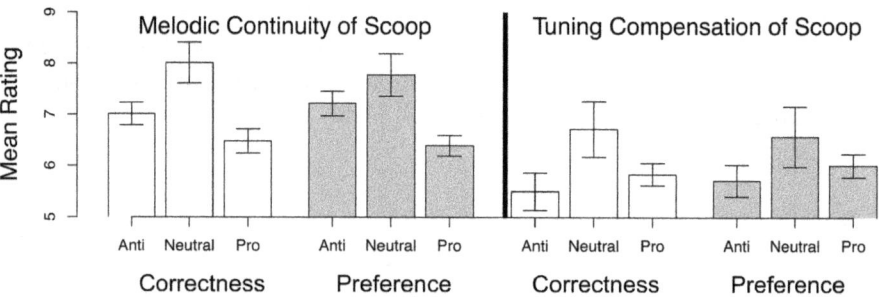

Figure 6: Parallel between correctness and preference ratings. Mean ratings (95% CI) given to stimuli for which scoops favor or not melodic continuity and tuning compensation, in the two tasks (white bars for correctness and grey bars for preference judgments).

5 Conclusion – outlook

Examining similarities and differences across domains requires insights about the nature of respective units (Fritz et al., 2013). In music, it is now clear that pitch is an important feature for judging the technical (i.e., correctness) and aesthetic quality of a performance and that units of different timescales are used in combination. More specifically, both the data reported in Larrouy-Maestri & Pfordresher (2018) and the data reported in this chapter highlight the unique contribution of *scoops*, whatever the type of judgment, and support the coexistence of two distinct mechanisms: averaging pitch across the duration of the tone and processing fluctuations in relation to the surrounding context. Research in speech prosody is advancing considerably, both regarding the identification of relevant units and the exploration of underlying mechanisms to process pitch information. As an example, van Rijn and collaborators (under review) quantified the role of pitch movements in speech production. Also, we currently investigate further the specific role of such pitch movements within words by observing mental representations of contrasting communicative intentions with the reverse correlation method described by Ponsot and collaborators (2018). This promising line of research not only provides a deeper understanding of the role of pitch in speech prosody but also allows to identify the nature of the units to be manipulated to extent the methods presented here to speech material. Ultimately, we will be able to confront the effect of our manipulations with the findings replicated and generalized in music (i.e., coexistence of statistical and teleological hypothesis). We believe that the direct comparison of pitch perception and processes in both domains promises to shed light on the long-standing and nevertheless still open debate about similarities and differences between music and speech.

References

Agrima, Abdellah, Abdelmajid Farchi, Laila Elmazouzi, Ilham Mounir & Badia Mounir. Emotion recognition from Maroccan dialect speech and energy band distribution. Proceedings of International Conference On Wireless Technologies, Embedded And Intelligent Systems (Wits); 2019; Fez, Morocco. p 1–6.

Austin, John L. 1962. *How to do things with words*. Oxford: Oxford University Press.

Bandstra, Nancy F., Christine T. Chambers, Patrick J. McGrath & Chris Moore. 2011. The behavioural expression of empathy to others' pain versus others' sadness in young children. *Pain* 152(5). 1074–1082.

Banse, Rainer & Klaus R. Scherer. 1996. Acoustic profiles in vocal emotion expression. *Journal of Personality and Social Psychology* 70(3). 614–636.

Bänziger, Tanja & Klaus R. Scherer. 2005. The role of intonation in emotional expressions. *Speech Communication* 46(3–4). 252–267.

Belin, Pascal, Bibi Boehme & Phil McAleer. 2017. The sound of trustworthiness: Acoustic-based modulation of perceived voice personality. *Plos One* 12(10). e0185651.

Bigand, Emmanuel & Bénédicte Poulin-Charronnat. 2006. Are we "experienced listeners"? A review of the musical capacities that do not depend on formal musical training. *Cognition* 100(1). 100–130.

Bitouk, Dmitri, Ani Nenkova & Ragini Verma. 2010. Class-level spectral features for emotion recognition. *Speech Communication* 52. 613–625.

Bolinger, Dwight L. M. 1986. *Intonation and its parts: Melody in spoken English*. Stanford, CA: Stanford University Press.

Bryant, Gregory A. & H. Clark Barrett. 2008. Vocal emotion recognition across disparate cultures. *Journal of Cognition and Culture* 8(1–2). 135–148.

Burns, Edward M. & W. Dixon Ward. 1978. Categorical perception – phenomenon or epiphenomenon: Evidence from experiments in the perception of melodic musical intervals. *The Journal of the Acoustical Society of America* 63(2). 456–468.

Cheng, Joey T., Jessica L. Tracy, Simon Ho & Joseph Henrich. 2016. Listen, follow me: Dynamic vocal signals of dominance predict emergent social rank in humans. *Journal of Experimental Psychology: General* 145(5). 536–547.

Cohen, David. 2002. *Notes, scales, and modes in the Earlier Middle Ages*. Cambridge: Cambridge University Press.

Cross, Ian. 2001. Music, cognition, culture, and evolution. *Annals of the New York Academy of Sciences* 930. 28–42.

Dalla Bella, Simone. 2015. Defining poor-pitch singing: A problem of measurement and sensitivity. *Music Perception* 32(3). 272–282.

Dilley, Laura C. & J. Devin McAuley. 2008. Distal prosodic context affects word segmentation and lexical processing. *Journal of Memory and Language* 59(3). 294–311.

Ding, Nai, Lucia Melloni, Aotian Yang, Yu Wang, Wen Zhang & David Poeppel. 2017. Characterizing neural entrainment to hierarchical linguistic units using electroencephalography (EEG). *Frontiers in Human Neuroscience* 11. 481.

Ding, Nai, Lucia Melloni, Hang Zhang, Xing Tian & David Poeppel. 2016. Cortical tracking of hierarchical linguistic structures in connected speech. *Nature Neuroscience* 19(1). 158–164.

Dromey, Christopher, Jose Silveira & Paul Sandor. 2005. Recognition of affective prosody by speakers of English as a first or foreign language. *Speech Communication* 47(3). 351–359.

Eyben, Florian, Klaus R. Scherer, Björn W. Schuller, Johan Sundberg, Elisabeth André, Carlos Busso, Laurence Y. Devillers, Julien Epps, Petri Laukka, Shrikanth S. Narayanan & Khiet P. Truong. 2016. The Geneva minimalistic acoustic parameter set (GeMAPS) for voice research and affective computing. *IEEE Transactions on Affective Computing* 7(2). 190–202.

Fairbanks, Grant & Wilbert Pronovost. 1938. Vocal pitch during simulated emotion. *Science* 88(2286). 382–383.

Fischer, Agneta H. & Anthony S. R. Manstead. 2008. Social functions of emotions. In: Michael Lewis, Jeannette Haviland-Jones, Lisa F. Barrett, editors. *Handbook of emotions*, 456–468. New York: The Guilford Press.

Fritz, Jonathan, David Poeppel, Laurel Trainor, Gottfried Schlaug, Aniruddh D. Patel, Isabelle Peretz & Lawrence M. Parsons. 2013. The neurobiology of language, speech, and music. In: Michael A. Arbib, editor. *Language, music, and the brain: A mysterious relationship* 417–459. Cambridge, MA: The MIT Press.

Gamba, Marco. 2014. Vocal tract-related cues across human and nonhuman signals. *Italian Journal of Cognitive Sciences* 1. 49–65.

Garnier, Maëva, Nathalie Henrich Bernardoni, Michèle Castellengo, David Sotiropoulos & Danièle Dubois. 2007. Characterisation of voice quality in western lyrical singing: From teachers' judgements to acoustic descriptions. *Journal of Interdisciplinary Music Studies* 1(2). 62–91.

Gockel, Hedwig, Brian C. J. Moore & Robert P. Carlyon. 2001. Influence of rate of change of frequency on the overall pitch of frequency-modulated tones. *The Journal of the Acoustical Society of America* 109(2). 701–712.

Gordon, Michael & David Poeppel. 2002. Inequality in identification of direction of frequency change (up vs. down) for rapid frequency modulated sweeps. *Acoustics Research Letters Online – Acoustical Society of America* 3. 29–34.

Goudbeek, Martijn B., Jean Philippe Goldman & Klaus R. Scherer. 2009. Emotion dimensions and formant position. *Tenth Annual Conference of the International Speech Communication Association*. Brighton, UK: ISCA.

Grice, H. Paul. 1957. Meaning. *The Philosophical Review* 66. 377–388.

Hannon, Erin E. & Laurel Trainor. 2007. Music acquisition: Effects of enculturation and formal training on development. *Trends in Cognitive Sciences* 11(11). 466–472.

Hart, Johan 't, René Collier & Antonie Cohen. 1990. *A Perceptual Study of Intonation: An Experimental-Phonetic Approach to Speech Melody*. Cambridge: Cambridge University Press.

Hillenbrand, James M. & Michael J. Clark. 2009. The role of f0 and formant frequencies in distinguishing the voices of men and women. *Attention, Perception, & Psychophysics* 71(5). 1150–1166.

Hutchins, Sean & David Campbell. 2009. Estimating the time to reach a target frequency in singing. *Annals of the New York Academy of Sciences* 1169(1). 116–120.

Hutchins, Sean, Pauline Larrouy-Maestri & Isabelle Peretz. 2014. Singing ability is rooted in vocal-motor control of pitch. *Attention, Perception, & Psychophysics* 76(8). 2522–2530.

Jackendoff, Ray. 2009. Parallels and nonparallels between language and music. *Music Perception* 26(3). 195–204.

Jiang, Xiaoming, Silke Paulmann, Jessica Robin & Marc D. Pell. 2015. More than accuracy: Nonverbal dialects modulate the time course of vocal emotion recognition across cultures. *Journal of Experimental Psychology. Human Perception and Performance* 41(3). 597–612.

Juslin, Patrik N. & Petri Laukka. 2003. Communication of emotions in vocal expression and music performance: Different channels, same code? *Psychological Bulletin* 129(5). 770–814.

Keitel, Anne, Joachim Gross & Christoph Kayser. 2018. Perceptually relevant speech tracking in auditory and motor cortex reflects distinct linguistic features. *Plos Biology* 16(3). e2004473.

Keltner, Dacher & Jonathan Haidt. 1999. Social functions of emotions at four levels of analysis. *Cognition and Emotion* 13(5). 505–521.

Kerivan, John E. & Bernhard J. Carey. 1976. Pattern identification of pure tones and frequency glides by untrained listeners. *Perception & Psychophysics* 20(6). 489–492.

Koelsch, Stefan & Angela D. Friederici. 2003. Toward the neural basis of processing structure in music. *Annals of the New York Academy of Sciences* 999. 15–28.

Kraljic, Tanya & Susan E. Brennan. 2005. Prosodic disambiguation of syntactic structure: For the speaker or for the addressee? *Cognitive Psychology* 50(2). 194–231.

Krumhansl, Carol L. 1979. The psychological representation of musical pitch in a tonal context. *Cognitive Psychology* 11(3). 346–374.

Ladd, D. Robert. 1996. *Intonational Phonology*. Cambridge: Cambridge University Press.

Ladd, D. Robert, Dan Faulkner, Hanneke Faulkner & Astrid Schepman. 1999. Constant "segmental anchoring" of f0 movements under changes in speech rate. *The Journal of the Acoustical Society of America* 106(3). 1543–1554.

Large, Edward W., Philip Fink & J. A. Scott Kelso. 2002. Tracking simple and complex sequences. *Psychological Research* 66. 3–17.

Larrouy-Maestri, Pauline. 2018. "I know it when I hear it": On listeners' perception of mistuning. *Music & Science* 1. 1–17.

Larrouy-Maestri, Pauline, Peter M. C. Harrison & Daniel Müllensiefen. 2019. The mistuning perception test: A new measurement instrument. *Behavioral Research Methods* 51(2). 663–675.

Larrouy-Maestri, Pauline, Yohana Lévêque, Daniele Schön, Giovanni Antoine & Dominique Morsomme. 2013. The evaluation of singing voice accuracy: A comparison between subjective and objective methods. *Journal of Voice* 27(2). 251–259.

Larrouy-Maestri, Pauline, David Magis, Matthias Grabenhorst & Dominique Morsomme. 2015. Layman versus professional musician: Who makes the better judge? *Plos One* 10(8). e0135394.

Larrouy-Maestri, Pauline, Dominique Morsomme, David Magis & David Poeppel. 2017. Lay listeners can evaluate the pitch accuracy of operatic voices. *Music Perception* 34(4). 489–495.

Larrouy-Maestri, Pauline & Peter Q. Pfordresher. 2018. Pitch perception in music: Do scoops matter? *Journal of Experimental Psychology: Human Perception and Performance* 44(10). 1523–1541.

Latinus, Marianne & Pascal Belin. 2011. Human voice perception. *Current Biology* 21(4). 143–145.

Latinus, Marianne, Phil McAleer, Patricia Bestelmeyer & Pascal Belin. 2013. Norm-based coding of voice identity in human auditory cortex. *Current Biology* 23(12). 1075–1080.

Lerdahl, Fred & Ray Jackendoff. 1983. An overview of hierarchical structure in music. *Music Perception* 1(2). 229–252.

Luo, Huan, Anthony Boemio, Michael Gordon & David Poeppel. 2007. The perception of FM sweeps by Chinese and English listeners. *Hearing Research* 224(1–2). 75–83.

Lyzenga, Johannes, Richard P. Carlyon & Brian C. J. Moore. 2004. The effects of real and illusory glides on pure-tone frequency discrimination. *The Journal of the Acoustical Society of America* 116(1). 491–501.

Marmel, Frédéric, Barbara Tillmann & Walter J. Dowling. 2008. Tonal expectations influence pitch perception. *Perception & Psychophysics* 70(5). 841–852.

McAleer, Phil, Alexander Todorov & Pascal Belin. 2014. How do you say "hello"? Personality impressions from brief novel voices. *Plos One* 9(3). e90779.

McDermott, Josh H., Alan F. Schultz, Eduardo A. Undurraga & Ricardo A. Godoy. 2016. Indifference to dissonance in native Amazonians reveals cultural variation in music perception. *Nature* 535. 547–550.

Merrill, Julia & Pauline Larrouy-Maestri. 2017. Vocal features of song and speech: Insights from Schoenberg's Pierrot Lunaire. *Frontiers in Psychology* 8. 1108.

Micheyl, Christophe, Karine Delhommeau, Xavier Perrot & Andrew J. Oxenham. 2006. Influence of musical and psychoacoustical training on pitch discrimination. *Hearing Research* 219(1–2). 36–47.

Moore, Brian C. J. 1973. Frequency difference limens for short-duration tones. *The Journal of the Acoustical Society of America* 54(3). 610–619.

Morgan, Emily, Allison Fogel, Anjali Nair & Aniruddh D. Patel. 2019. Statistical learning and gestalt-like principles predict melodic expectations. *Cognition* 189. 23–34.

Mori, Hiroki, Wakana Odagiri, Hideki Kasuya & Kiyoshi Honda. Transitional characteristics of fundamental frequency in singing. Proceedings of the 18th International Congress on Acoustics; 2004; Kyoto.

Müllensiefen, Daniel, Bruno Gingras, Jason Musil & Lauren Stewart. 2014. The musicality of non-musicians: An index for assessing musical sophistication in the general population. *Plos One* 9(2). e89642.

Mürbe, Dirk, Thomas Zahnert, Eberhard Kuhlisch & Johan Sundberg. 2007. Effects of professional singing education on vocal vibrato-a longitudinal study. *Journal of Voice* 21(6). 683–688.

Nordström, Henrik & Petri Laukka. 2019. The time course of emotion recognition in speech and music. *The Journal of the Acoustical Society of America* 145(5). 3058–3074.

Parncutt, Richard & Graham Hair. 2018. A psychocultural theory of musical interval: Bye bye Pythagoras. *Music Perception* 35(4). 475–501.

Patel, Aniruddh D. 2008. *Music, Language, and the Brain*. Oxford: Oxford University Press.

Pavela Banai, Irena, Benjamin Banai & Kosta Bovan. 2016. Vocal characteristics of presidential candidates can predict the outcome of actual elections. *Evolution and Human Behavior* 38(3). 309–314.

Pearce, Marcus T. 2005. The construction and evaluation of statistical models of melodic structure in music perception and composition [Doctoral Dissertation]. London: City University London.

Pell, Marc D. & Sonja A. Kotz. 2011. On the time course of vocal emotion recognition. *Plos One* 6(11). e27256.

Pell, Marc D., Laura Monetta, Silke Paulmann & Sonja A. Kotz. 2009. Recognizing emotions in a foreign language. *Journal of Nonverbal Behavior* 33(2). 107–120.

Pell, Marc D. & Vera Skorup. 2008. Implicit processing of emotional prosody in a foreign versus native language. *Speech Communication* 50(6). 519–530.

Pfordresher, P. Q. & Pauline Larrouy-Maestri. 2015. On drawing a line through the spectrogram: How do we understand deficits of vocal pitch imitation? *Frontiers in Human Neuroscience* 9. 271.

Pfordresher, Peter Q. & James T. Mantell. 2014. Singing with yourself: Evidence for an inverse modeling account of poor-pitch singing. *Cognitive Psychology* 70. 31–57.

Poeppel, David. 2003. The analysis of speech in different temporal integration windows: Cerebral lateralization as 'asymmetric sampling in time'. *Speech Communication* 41. 245–255.

Ponsot, Emmanuel, Juan José Burred, Pascal Belin & Jean-Julien Aucouturier. 2018. Cracking the social code of speech prosody using reverse correlation. *Proceedings of the National Academy of Sciences of the United States of America* 115(15). 3972–3977.

Rendall, Drew, John R. Vokey & Nemeth Christie. 2007. Lifting the curtain on the Wizard of Oz: Biased voice-based impressions of speaker size. *Journal of Experimental Psychology: Human Perception and Performance* 33(5). 1208–1219.

Ringer, Alexander L. 2002. Melody: Definition and origins. The New Grove Dictionary of Music Online.

Saitou, Takeshi, Masashi Unoki & Masato Akagi. 2005. Development of an f0 control model based on f0 dynamic characteristics for singing-voice synthesis. *Speech Communication* 46(3–4). 405–417.

Sammler, Daniela, Marie-Hélène Grosbras, Alfred Anwander, Patricia E. G. Bestelmeyer & Pascal Belin. 2015. Dorsal and ventral pathways for prosody. *Current Biology* 25(23). 3079–3085.

Scherer, Klaus R., Rainer Banse & Harald G. Wallbott. 2001. Emotion inferences from vocal expression correlate across languages and cultures. *Journal of Cross-Cultural Psychology* 32(1). 76–92.

Searle, John R. 1969. *Speech acts: An essay in the philosophy of language.* Cambridge: Cambridge University Press.

Shami, Mohammad T. & Mahamed S. Kamel. Segment-based approach to the recognition of emotions in speech. Proceedings of IEEE International Conference on Multimedia and Expo (LCME) 2005; Amsterdam. IEEE.

Shariff, Azim F. & Jessica L. Tracy. 2011. Emotion expressions: On signals, symbols, and spandrels – A response to Barrett (2011). *Current Directions in Psychological Science* 20 (6). 407–408.

Shigeno, Sumi. 2016. Speaking with a happy voice makes you sound younger. *International Journal of Psychological Studies* 8(4). 71–76.

Sievers, Eduard. 1912. *Rhythmisch-melodische Studien: Vorträge und Aufsätze (1893–1908).* Heidelberg: Carl Winter.

Sinaceur, Marwan, Shirli Kopelman, Dimitri Vasiljevic & Christophe Haag. 2015. Weep and get more: When and why sadness expression is effective in negotiations. *Journal of Applied Psychology* 100(6). 1847–1871.

Soranzo, Alessandro & Massimo Grassi. 2014. Psychoacoustics: A comprehensive Matlab toolbox for auditory testing. *Frontiers in Psychology* 5. 712.

Stadlen, Peter. 1981. Schoenberg's speech-song. *Music Letter* 62. 1–11.

Stalinski, Stephanie M. & E. Glenn Schellenberg. 2010. Shifting perceptions: Developmental changes in judgments of melodic similarity. *Developmental Psychology* 46(6). 1799–1803.

Stevens, Francis A. & Walter R. Miles. 1928. The first vocal vibrations in the attack in singing. *Psychological Monographs* 39(2). 200–220.

Stevens, Kenneth N. & Dennis H. Klatt. 1974. Role of formant transitions in the voiced-voiceless distinction for stops. *The Journal of the Acoustical Society of America* 55(3). 653–659.

Sundberg, Johan. 2013. Perception of singing. In: Diana Deutsch, editor. *The Psychology of Music,* 171–214. London: Elsevier.

Temperley, David. 2013. Computational models of music cognition. In: Diana Deutsch, editor. *The Psychology of Music,* 327–368. London: Elsevier.

Teng, Xiangbin, Xing Tian & David Poeppel. 2016. Testing multi-scale processing in the auditory system. *Scientific Reports* 6. 1–13.

Thompson, William F. 2016. Intervals and scales. In: Diana Deutsch, editor. *The Psychology of Music,* 107–140. London: Elsevier.

Titze, Ingo R. 2000. Principles of voice production (2nd edition). National Center For Voice And Speech, Iowa City, IA..

van Besouw, Rachel M. & David M. Howard. 2009. Effects of carrier and phase on the pitch of long-duration vibrato tone. *Musicae Scientiae* 13(1). 139–161.

Waaramaa, Teija, Anne-Maria Laukkanen, Matti Airas & Paavo Alku. 2010. Perception of emotional valences and activity levels from vowel segments of continuous speech. *Journal of Voice* 24(1). 30–38.

Wang, Wen-Jie, Chin-Tuan Tan & Brett A. Martin. 2013. Auditory evoked responses to a frequency glide following a static pure tone. *The Journal of the Acoustical Society of America* 133(5). 3429.

Warrier, Catherine M. & Robert J. Zatorre. 2002. Influence of tonal context and timbral variation on perception of pitch. *Perception & Psychophysics* 64(2). 198–207.

Wildgruber, Dirk, Axel Riecker, Ingo Hertrich, Michael Erb, Wolfgang Grodd, Thomas Ethofer & Hermann Ackermann. 2005. Identification of emotional intonation evaluated by fMRI. *Neuroimage* 24(4). 1233–1241.

Wubben, Maarten J. J., David de Cremer & Eric van Dijk. 2011. The communication of anger and disappointment helps to establish cooperation through indirect reciprocity. *Journal of Economic Psychology* 32(3). 489–501.

Zarate, Jean Mary, Caroline R. Ritson & David Poeppel. 2012. Pitch-interval discrimination and musical expertise: Is the semitone a perceptual boundary? *The Journal of the Acoustical Society of America* 132(2). 984–993.

Zoghaib, Alice. 2019. Persuasion of voices: The effects of a speaker's voice characteristics and gender on consumers' responses. *Recherche et Applications en Marketing (English Edition)* 34(3). 83–110.

Mathias Scharinger
Melody in speech and music

Abstract: Melody – in its basic sense – is an orderly sequence of pitches. As such, melody refers both to tone sequences in music, and pitch sequences (or intonation contours) in speech. There have been numerous attempts to account for melodies in speech and music in a similar way. However, the characteristics and constraints of melodies in the two domains also differ. Is it thus still possible that melodies in speech and music can be described within the same formal system? Is it feasible to consider melodies in speech and music to be based on a descriptive continuum, where clear instances of musical melodies and clear instances of speech melodies lay on opposite ends, and where pitch sequences that oscillate between speech and music will fall on middle regions of such a continuum?

In this chapter, I attempt to provide a unifying framework for the description of musical melodies and speech melodies. The underlying assumption is that melodies in speech and music share organizational principles by which they are perceived as "melodious".

Keywords: Melody, music, speech, pitch, autocorrelations

1 Introduction

Melody has been used to describe aspects of language and music alike. This is etymologically evident from its referents "song" and "ode" to be used synonymously in Greek (Bonds, 2003) and from the word stem "μέλ" that can be part of word for "singer", "song" and "songwriter", as well as "poet" and "bard" (Hüschen, 1961). Recent research has further highlighted that melody in speech plays a particular role in poetry recitals (Menninghaus et al., 2018) or silent reading of poetry (Menninghaus et al., 2017). Despite the etymological background and the relevance of melody for aesthetic speech such as poetry, the literature on music and language has not agreed on a succinct notion of "melody". Most definitions, however involve the statement that a melody describes the ordered succession of tones or pitches in time (e.g., Randel, 2003; Rousseau, 1768).

At the same time, the succession of tones in musical melodies – at least those following the tonal conventions of Western music – differs from the

---

Mathias Scharinger, Philipps-Universität Marburg, Institute of German Linguistics, Pilgrimstein 16, 35032 Marburg, Germany

https://doi.org/10.1515/9783110770186-003

succession of pitches in spoken language. Eduard Sievers exemplifies this observation in the following statement:

> Im Gesang gebrauchen wir die Singstimme, in der Rede die Sprechstimme, die an sich durch ein Mindermaß musikalischer Eigenschaften charakterisiert ist. Die Musik arbeitet hauptsächlich mit festen Tönen von gleichbleibender Tonhöhe, die Sprache bewegt sich vorwiegend in Gleittönen, die innerhalb einer und derselben Silbe von einer Tonhöhe zur anderen auf- oder absteigen. Insbesondere aber bindet sich die Sprache nicht an die fest bestimmten Tonhöhen und Intervalle der musikalischen Melodien: sie kennt nur ungefähr bestimmte Tonlagen, und ihre Tonschritte sind zwar meist der Richtung nach (ob Steigschritt oder Fallschritt) fest gegeben, aber nicht auch der Größe nach, vielmehr kann diese nach den verschiedensten Gesichtspunkten wechseln. (Sievers, 1912, p. 57)
>
> *During singing, we use the singing voice, during speaking, the speaking voice, characterized by a smaller degree of musical properties. Music mainly works with fixed tones of discrete height, speech distinguishes between frequency movements, that is, tone heights that change within single syllables by moving upwards or downwards. In particular, speech is not bound to fixed tone heights and intervals of a musical melody: there are only vague tonal centers; and tonal steps are determined by their direction (upwards vs. downwards), but not by their size, the latter being subject to change due to several different aspects. [own translation]*

This view is elaborated in Nadel & Baker (1930) and Patel (2010). Patel (2010) further argues that the main differences between speech and music is that speech uses pitch patterns which are usually not in the focus of attention, while music uses pitch patterns in and for themselves.

Despite these differences in the *nature* of melody between speech and music, the term is commonly used to describe the *perceived* aspect of melodicity of spoken and sung language as well as instrumental music. In this vein, Magdics (1963) speaks of a functional difference between melody in speech and melody in music, with its components differing in character and nature, while the "ground substance" is shared between the two domains. Palmer & Hutchins (2006) concede that this ground substance is to be looked for within the prosodies of speech and music. They state that song and speech share elements of pitch accent, tone and intonation. Tone is described as referring to pitch targets and glides, while intonation equals melodic contours.

1.1 Musical melody

Musical melodies in Western traditions are (usually) based on discrete tones. Tone can be defined as simple or complex sound that is characterized by the perceptual quality of tone height or pitch. In simple, sinusoidal tones, pitch directly correlates with its fundamental frequency, i.e., its sinusoidal frequency.

In more complex tones, pitch may correlate with its fundamental frequency (repetition rate), but may also be derived from its spectral properties, particular harmonic constituents in simple numerical relations to its fundamental frequency (Krumhansl, 1990; 2000; Oxenham, 2012; 2018; 2019). Besides (perceived) height, tones are characterized by their duration, giving rise to the perception of tone length, speed and rhythm. Furthermore, tones may differ in their intensity, relating to the physical loudness, and in their spectral shape, oftentimes referred to as "timbre" (McAdams & Siedenburg, 2019). Timbre relates to the intensities of a tone's spectral constituents (harmonic parts etc.) and can, for instance, be used to differentiate between musical instruments.

All four basic acoustic properties of tones (fundamental frequency, duration, physical loudness, spectral shape) have perceptual correlates that are directly relevant to melodies, namely tone height, length, intensity and timbre. Musical theory and praxis has provided examples for melodies being solely based on timbre ("klangfarbenmelodie"; McAdams & Siedenburg, 2019; Schönberg, 1911), however, in this chapter, the emphasis will be on tone height as dominant feature for constituting musical melodies. This can be inferred from the tradition of notating musical melodies, where "height" directly corresponds to the height of note placement. Melodic contours as movements or changes in tone height thus have a direct visual correlate. Melodic contours can be conceived of as holistic objects, "gestalts" in the sense of Wertheimer (Wertheimer, 1924), while changes in tone height are more locally and analytically describable as tone intervals. Both properties – melodic contour and tone intervals – play important roles for melody memory and melody recognition (e.g., Dowling, 1978; Zatorre & Baum, 2012).

Experimental work in music cognition has shown that in order for melodies to be processed and recognized, it is not sufficient that there are local interval relations between successive tones; it is additionally required that globally, melodies are being mapped onto contours (Lee & Noppeney, 2014). The gestalt-principle of melodic contours may be fundamental for the ability of recognizing melodies played by different instruments and in different transpositions (Lee et al., 2015; Narmour, 1990). Melodic intervals and motives can be recognized independent from instruments they are played on and independent from starting tones (tonal centers). Schellenberg & Habashi (2015) provided evidence that the recognition of melodies is independent of the speed (tempo) and the key in which they are presented. However, they also demonstrated that changes in timbre affected melody recognition in negative ways.

Despite the relative independence of melodic processing from tempo, temporal aspects within melodic sequences do play a crucial role during recognition. Narmour (1989) and Narmour (1990) showed that the relative and temporally even-spaced emphasis of tones within a sequences of tones, giving rise to the "beat", is essential for remembering and recognizing melodies. Melodies thus crucially involve distributional properties of tone length, intensity and emphasis (beat), that is, rhythmical properties.

Musical melodies have also to be considered within a tonal system. This system is crucial for perceiving and interpreting melodies because it defines the melody's tonal center (Krumhansl, 1990). Tonal systems in the Western tradition are based on octave equivalence, i.e., the perceptual similarity between a tone and its octave-transposed comparison tone (Dowling & Harwood, 1986). This similarity comes about by shared spectral properties (shared harmonics) of two tones in octave relation. The acoustic definition of an octave is the multiplication of a tone's fundamental frequency by the factor two (higher octave) or ½ (lower octave). A consequence of octave equivalence is that equivalent tonal targets within an octave receive the same labels (letters A, B, C etc.). Tones with the same label are said to have the same chroma (Bachem, 1950). The music of different cultures uses a limited amount of tones within an octave, commonly 5 to 7 (Gill & Purves, 2009; Patel, 2010). It is hypothesized that this limit is rooted in the constraints on working memory to maximally hold between 5 and 7 items (Miller, 1956). In well-tempered musical systems, octaves are split in 12 semi-tones.

Musical melodies as sequence of tonal pitches are further characterized by harmonic changes (Holleran et al., 1995), phrase boundaries (Deliege, 1987; Lerdahl & Jackendoff, 1977; 1983), rhythm and meter (Jones, 1987) as well as tone expectancies (Narmour, 1990). The latter property is thought to provide a specific level of musical meaning (Patel, 2010), also related to surprise. Recent research has shown that aesthetic pleasure in musical melodies in fact derives from an interplay of uncertainty and surprise (Cheung et al., 2019).

1.2 Melody in speech

The notion of melody in speech is generally related to prosodic aspects, in particular, intonation and durational properties such as rhythm and meter. Prosody subsumes all speech properties that go above and beyond single speech sounds or segments. Prosodic properties are thus suprasegmental properties of speech and comprise speaking rate, rhythm, accentuation, meter, tone and intonation (Cutler et al., 1997; Dahan, 2015; Nespor & Vogel, 1986). Speech prosody may also be interpreted emotionally (Cruttenden, 1997). Note that linguistic tone is defined as the use of pitch to express lexical and grammatical distinctions (Pulleyblank, 1986; Yip, 2002; Yip, 1980). Even in cases where a language is usually not considered a tone language (e.g., German), tones can be used for lexical distinctions in some dialects of that language (e.g., Schmidt, 1986) or show substantial modulations across larger units (e.g., Zimmermann, 1998). However, a detailed discussion of the relationship between linguistic tone and musical tone is beyond the scope of this chapter. Therefore, linguistic tone will not be considered any further.

Speech melody is mostly based on intonation, pitch targets and pitch movements. Pitch targets can be applied to all voice speech sounds, preferably to elements in syllable nuclei. While thereby, syllables can receive different tones, independent of the speech material, vowels are additionally characterized by intrinsic pitch (Lehiste & Peterson, 1961). Intrinsic pitch refers to the observation that high vowels (with high tongue position or close production) have higher fundamental frequencies than low vowels (with low tongue position or open production). This also refers to the common observation that low vowels indeed sound lower than high vowels. Intrinsic pitch has been observed not only in isolated vowel productions, but also in connected speech (Ladd & Silverman, 1984), and in several different languages (Whalen & Levitt, 1995). The underlying principle of intrinsic pitch is still discussed. One possibility is that intrinsic pitch emerges through articulatory coupling (Whalen et al., 1999). Other accounts discuss the possibility of voluntary control allowing for specific adjustments (Jacewicz & Fox, 2015) or for generally for enhancing vowel contrasts (Diehl, 1991; Kingston, 1992).

Speech melody can also express emotions and affects (Nygaard & Queen, 2008) and thus realize an additionally level of communicative function. Xu (2005) describe a general model for the communicative function of intonation in speech, focusing on melodic units on the syllable level.

Since speech melody is considered a prosodic aspect of language, speech melody analyses have primarily focused on functional prosodic aspects of tone and intonation. To this end, a prominent notational system has been developed (Beckman et al., 2004) that accounts for several effects emerging from the assumed hierarchical architecture of speech prosody (Nespor & Vogel, 1986; Selkirk, 1984). The so-called ToBI system (Tones and Break Indices) provides a set of conventions for annotating and transcribing speech prosody. Tonal elements in this system comprise pitch accents, phrase accents, and boundary tones. Derived from the F0 information over time (pitch track), pitch accents refer to either high (H) or low (L) tones, i.e., locally high F0 plateaus or locally low F0 plateaus. A combination of high and low tones can account for pitch movements (glides, i.e., falling or rising tones). The ToBI system therefore provides a notational, descriptive account of prosodic phrases in terms of their accompanying F0-information that may be interpreted as speech melody. It is a phonological, rather than a musical or melodic framework to describe the distributions of tones in spoken language.

Musical approaches to speech melody, by contrast, have focused on describing characteristic F0 modulations, sometimes with notational systems resembling those of Western music tradition. A prominent example of such an attempt is Joshua Steele (1700–1791) who tried to capture the speech melody of talented actors and orators (Alkon, 1959; Kassler, 2005; Steele, 1775). His notational system included a way of indicating the direction of pitch glides within syllables (illustrated in Kassler, 2005).

Applied musical approaches to speech melody stem from composers who were either inspired by F0 modulations of the human voice or used these modulations directly in their compositions. An example of the former sort is Leos Janácek (1854–1928). Janácek started transcribing intonation contours towards the end of the 19th century and continued this endeavor for almost 30 years. His focus (in contrast to Steele) was on ordinary speech. Intonation contours, according to his conviction, were indicative of speaker's emotional and psychological state and offered inspirations for his compositions, in particular for his vocal works (Christiansen, 2004; Pearl, 2006; Wingfield, 1992).

A different approach is taken by contemporary composers who use speech material (audio or video recordings) in order to assemble compositions from speech melodic raw material. One example is provided by Steve Reich in his composition "The Cave" (Prieto, 2002). Herein, Reich uses video recordings to assemble melodies in a "ready-made" manner. In a similar vein, Peter Ablinger integrates voices (from speech recordings) in his compositions. His approach is based on mutual relationships between speech and music since he tries to construe melody from speech and speech from musical instruments (here: the piano).

1.3 Comparing melodies in speech and melodies in music

As can be discerned from the aforementioned approaches to speech melody, there is a specific level on which melodic properties of speech and music resemble each other. However, there are specific properties in each domain that constitute essential differences. When focusing on Western music with a semi-tone system, one essential of such differences concerns the tonal targets. Musical melody is based on discrete tone levels (heights), while speech melody is rather continuous (Zatorre & Baum, 2012) and includes pitch movements (glides). Pitch movements can be realized within a single syllable and are usually not perceived as sequence of discrete tones, but rather as "ups" and "downs". However, some approaches to speech melody have provided evidence that most syllable-based tones are in fact of a nearly steady-state character and below a glide or glissando threshold (D'Alessandro et al., 1998; Hart, 1981) such that an approximation of melodic contours in speech can be achieved by extracting mean fundamental frequency per syllable (Patel et al., 2006). On the other hand, "gliding" aspects are not entirely absent in musical melodies. This is most obvious in glissandi, but also discernible in tremolo (i.e., varying tone levels) or vibrato (i.e., varying sung tone levels).

A further difference between melodies in speech and music relates to their tonal inventory and tonal system. In the music of several different cultures, tone heights are taken from limited sets of tones, commonly five or seven (Gill & Purves, 2009; Patel, 2010), arranged in octaves. Specific interval relations between tones in these systems constitute tonal systems or modes (major, minor, etc.). A direct equivalent of tonal systems in speech does not exist (Zatorre & Baum, 2012). However, recent research suggests that the cues to tonal modes such as major and minor scales as well as their affective and emotional interpretation is shared by speech and music (Bowling, 2013; Poon & Schutz, 2015). Bowling (2013) argues that musical modes may have a vocal basis. Poon & Schutz (2015) suggest the pitch-based cues for major and minor musical modes to be the same as those for distinguishing emotions derived from speech prosody (e.g., happy from sad voices).

A third aspect of differences concerns the concept of tonality and tonal relationships in music. Tones in music are ordered in a hierarchical manner and yield tonal family relations. The principle of tonality (Krumhansl, 1990) does not apply to speech.

Lastly, the range of different F0 levels differs noticeable from the range of different tones in a musical melody. Considering the speaking versus the singing voice, the range difference is about one octave. While the speaking voice roughly covers one octave (Fant, 1956), the singing voice usually covers two octaves (Fischer, 1993). The difference is even more pronounced if instrumental music is considered.

2 Quantifying melodic properties in speech and music

In order to go beyond the descriptive level of melodic properties in speech and language, empirical approaches attempt to quantify melodies or their physical bases. In general, one can distinguish between two foci. On the one hand, cognitive musicologist try to establish acoustic and statistic measures that characterize melodies (Dowling & Harwood, 1986; Krumhansl, 2000; Müllensiefen &

Frieler, 2007; Müllensiefen & Halpern, 2014). Basically, acoustic properties such as tone height or tone duration are examined by means of descriptive statistical analyses, e.g., in order to describe the mean tone height or standard deviation from a mean tone height that indexes the melodic range. Other measures involve automatic detection of tonality, the frequency of different intervals, but also more complex measures such as contour approximations by means of higher order polynomials. Müllensiefen (2009) proposes a set of more than 50 acoustic-statistical measures in order to describe melodies and to quantify melodic similarities.

The distribution of musical events in time, i.e., tone heights, durations and intensities, has also been described by frequency spectra of these discrete events (Colley & Dean, 2019; Hsü & Hsü, 1991; Levitin et al., 2012; Voss & Clarke, 1975; 1998; Wu et al., 2015). These frequency spectra indicate the strength of a particular frequency, i.e., of a repetition rate. Thereby, it is possible to quantify to what degree events repeat in time and at what temporal lags these repetitions occur (e.g., every second note). It has been observed that spectra of discrete musical events obey the 1/f power law according to which spectral power decreases with increasing frequencies. In log-log spectra, i.e., when both power and frequency are translated to their natural logarithm, the decrease can be approximated by a linear function whose slope is indicative of the spectral shape of the underlying musical piece and thus of its repetition structure. Previous research has suggested that the 1/f structure applies to intensities of musical events (Voss & Clarke, 1975; 1998), to durations (Levitin et al., 2012) and to tone intervals (Colley & Dean, 2019; Hsü & Hsü, 1991; Wu et al., 2015). Voss & Clarke (1975) additionally showed that loudness fluctuations in speech are describable by the 1/f power law. In essence, the 1/f structure indexes fractal properties of biological and physical signals. It is a means of visualizing and quantifying self-similarity and repetition- or recurrence structure and thus potentially capable of providing a mathematical means of describing melodies.

Musically inspired analyses of speech events (i.e., prosodic units) are relatively rare. The most natural equivalent to tones in music is the unit of the syllable (Patel, 2005; 2010; Patel & Daniele, 2003; Patel et al., 2006). Syllables provide the rhythmic structure of speech, particularly if their realizations are governed by meter and rhyme, i.e., prosodic and segmental regularities indicative of aesthetic speech as e.g., in poetry.

There exist some approaches of extracting syllable-based F0 information from speech that contain semi-automatic algorithms, combined with modelling F0 transitions and contours. These approaches attempt to extract prosodic information that is relevant for perception and that is the basis for prosodic annotations. Some approaches focus on prosodic models, while others center around specific algorithms of F0 extraction, modification and stylization. Among those emphasizing particular ways of prosodic modelling, Dilley and colleagues provide an account that is based on ToBI (Beckman et al., 2004), but extends it by several prosodic principles such as the Obligatory Contour Principle (OCP, Leben, 1973). The so-called Rhythm and Pitch system (RaP, Breen et al., 2012; Dilley & Brown, 2005) additionally includes a level of rhythm, allowing for the assignment of strong beats to metrically stressed syllable according to metrical phonology (Nespor & Vogel, 1986). Thereby, RaP approximates musical notation systems insofar as rhythmic structure is acknowledged. RaP differs from musical notation, however, because it treats the rhythmic tier separately from the intonation tier.

Systems focusing on algorithmic aspects include MOMEL (Hirst et al., 2000; Hirst & Espesser, 1993) and a tonal perception model based on Prosograms (Hart et al., 1990; Mertens, 2004), applied in the comparative studies of Patel (Patel, 2006; Patel et al., 2006). MOMEL is an algorithm that provides an automatic translation of raw F0 information into a phonetic representation (Hirst et al., 2000; Hirst & Espesser, 1993; Hirst, 2005). It is based on two components, a microscopic and a macroscopic component. The macroscopic component describes intonation contours by combining individual tones or tonal targets by quadratic spline functions. The microscopic component deals with deviations from the macroscopic curve, caused by individual tonal targets on different speech sounds (voiced, unvoiced) or in different contexts (end of phrases, before pauses etc.). The MOMEL algorithm is considered to provide both a model of intonation and a stylization of F0.

The aspect of F0 stylization is fundamental to the concept of Prosograms (Hart et al., 1990; Mertens, 2004). In essence, a Prosogram is a stylized version of raw F0 information. The specific aspect in this tonal perception model concerns the resolution of pitch glides or glissandos into a semi-tone notation. Psycho-acoustic research has established the so-called glissando threshold (D'Alessandro et al., 1998; Hart, 1981), an empirical measure that determines whether the perceived pitch is a static tone or a tone variation. The glissando threshold crucially varies as a function of pitch duration and in dependency of context, in particular, pause context. Prosograms are based on an initial segmentation into syllable nuclei based on intensity peaks and take into account the glissando threshold, its contextual dependency, as well as the differential glissando threshold, determined by a perceived change in the slope of the glissando (i.e., variations of the glissando speed). Prosograms provide an ideal basis for comparing melodic aspects between speech and music because they are based on a stylized transformation of F0, a semi-tone representation and a resolution of F0 movements on syllables or longer prosodic units. They can provide the basis for subsequent melodic analyses.

Chow & Brown (2018) take F0 stylization and the microscopic/macroscopic differentiation a step further and additionally incorporate rhythmic information in their notational system. The authors provide a musical annotation system, based on semi-tones, and map F0 information onto a musical system in which note symbols denote tone height and tone duration, akin of Joshua Steele's approach (Steele, 1775). The advantage of their approach is not only that intonation and rhythm is combined in a notational system, but also that they can represent the pitch of every syllable in spoken utterances. By averaging across speakers, they are able to examine relative pitch changes as a function of sentence types (declarative, question-types, etc.) or even text-type. While their syllabic approach neglects syllable-internal F0 movements by averaging F0 across the syllable and mapping raw F0 values onto semi-tones, thus ignoring glissando thresholds, this simplification appears acceptable because most syllable-based F0 movements are usually below the glissando threshold (Patel et al., 2006). The musical approach of Chow & Brown, 2018 is thus one of the few that provides the basis of directly comparing intonation patterns in speech with melodic properties in music. In the next section, I will provide a unifying account that combines a semi-automatic F0 stylization and quantization with a statistical method of quantifying melodic properties, most notably, recurrence structure.

3 A unified approach of quantifying melodic properties in speech and music

3.1 F0 extraction

We have recently proposed that speech melody is not only a metaphorical construct, but has actually explanatory power for aesthetic speech (i.e., poetry, Menninghaus et al. (2018)), and can be described and quantified by means beyond existing linguistic systems such as ToBI or RaP. Some of the basic assumptions are shared with accounts briefly reviewed in the above section.

For quantifying melodic properties of speech, we take the syllable to be the essential unit of processing and analysis. This is in accordance with several previous studies (e.g., Chow & Brown, 2018; Patel, 2006; Patel et al., 2006). The simplifying assumption we made is that in most syllables, pitch movements are actually below the glissando threshold. Therefore, our first approximation to melodic contours is achieved by using mean fundamental frequency values of voiced parts of each syllable from spoken language recordings. In the study by Menninghaus et al. (2018), the analyzed speech corpus consists of 40 poems primarily from between the 18th and 19th century, 20 of which have subsequently been put to music. The selection of these poems followed criteria discussed elsewhere (Menninghaus et al., 2017). For the purposes of our account, the recorded speech material was annotated by setting syllable boundaries. First, spoken poems and their orthographic transcriptions were subjected to the WEBMAUS Basic service (Kisler et al., 2017), a web application that automatically aligns syllable boundaries to recorded speech. The output of WEBMAUS is a so-called TextGrid annotation that can be read by the phonetic software application PRAAT (Boersma & Weenink, 2019). Within PRAAT, syllable boundaries were manually controlled by a phonetically trained, native speaker of German. Subsequently, all syllable boundaries were shifted to zero-crossings of the amplitude-over-time (oscillographic) speech information. Then, mean fundamental frequency values per syllable were calculated. This procedure involved the detection of voiced parts within the syllable. As first pass, F0 values in a larger possible pitch range (60–700 Hz) were considered. We then followed the approach suggested by Hirst (Hirst, 2011) and constrained the second-pass pitch extraction to F0 values comprising of the second and third quantiles of the first pass. We measured F0 from three positions within the syllable: the beginning, the middle, and the end. When none of the three positions yielded measurable F0 values, the syllable received the mean fundamental frequency value calculated from the preceding and the following syllable. We then compared whether the first two positions or the last two positions were closer in F0. If so, we took their respective mean values for representing the syllable's final F0. Otherwise, we took the mean F0 across all three measurement positions. For this chapter, I additionally implemented a syllable nucleus approach and calculated the mean fundamental frequency aligned to the intensity peak within each syllable. This is approximating the Prosogram approach by Mertens (2004). When comparing the mean F0 time series of our original approach with the intensity-adjusted approach, I obtain a median F0 difference of 3.6 Hz and a correlation of F0 with $r=0.93$. Thus, the basic F0 extraction procedure is comparable to those used in the Prosogram approach.

Following the rationale of Chow & Brown (2018), the mean F0 values per syllable were subsequently mapped onto a well-tempered system, consisting of semi-tones. Syllable durations were quantized to correspond to a minimum of a 1/32 note. In the temporal domain, the shortest syllable could be 31.25 ms, the longest 8 s. The lower limit was motivated by typical minimum durations of CV syllables consisting of a plosive consonant and a reduced vowel (Stevens, 1998). The quantized syllables thereby contained both F0 and duration information, overcoming limits of RaP (Breen et al., 2012; Dilley & Brown, 2005) as discussed in Chow & Brown (2018). As such, F0 and duration can easily be expressed by a notational system. This is illustrated in Figure 1A.

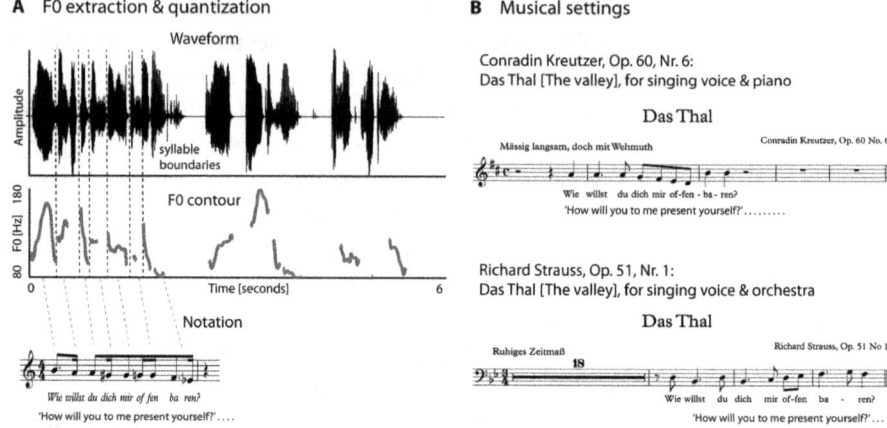

Figure 1: A. Illustration of F0 extraction and quantization. Digital recordings of spoken poems were first assigned syllable boundaries. The examples shows the first phrase of Johann Ludwig Uhlands "Das Thal" (The Valley) from 1824. After syllabic annotation, F0 contours were estimated using PRAAT. From three measurement positions within each syllables, a mean F0 value per syllable was calculated and mapped onto a well-tempered semitonal system. Syllable durations were quantized to musical length expressed between full-measure and 1/32 note lengths. Quantized F0 and durations were subjected to further analyses. B. Example of musical settings of Johann Ludwig Uhlands poem "Das Thal" by Conradin Kreutzer and Richard Strauss. Matching the speech recording, only the first phrase of the singing voice is depicted.

3.2 Describing the distribution of syllable F0 and duration in time

Quantized syllable F0 and durations allows for descriptive statistics regarding their distribution in time, exemplified with the poem "Das Thal", written by Johann Ludwig Uhland in 1811 (Figure 1B). Descriptive statistic values from the spoken version of the poem are compared to the notated singing voice of two musical settings of this poem, one by Conradin Kreutzer in 1824, and one by Richard Strauss in 1902. The spoken poem yields a F0 range of 13 semitones, thus a little more than an octave. The same range applies to Kreutzer's musical setting, thereby suggesting a certain affinity to the range of the speech melody. Indeed, when comparing the first phrase of the quantized speech melody with the first phrase of the musical setting, the overall gestalt is quite comparable.

Richard Strauss' composition, by contrast, differs remarkably and yields a range of 22 semitones, i.e., almost two octaves. Therefore, the musical setting of Kreutzer is closer to the range of the human speaking voice, while the musical setting of Strauss is closer to the range of the human singing voice (Fant, 1960; Sundberg, 1977).

Another measure of tonal distribution is the standard deviation from F0 mean. This measure yields the dynamics of the respective melody. In the speech example, the standard deviation is 2.8 semitones. Kreutzer's composition shows a deviation of 3.4 semitones, while Strauss' composition shows the largest deviation with 5 semitones. These deviations indicate that the speech melody prefers relatively small intervals while intervals in music tend to be larger. This might be one reason for Chow & Brown (2018) to argue that speech melody is rather atonal. If directly looking at mean interval sizes, the aforementioned interval preferences are substantiated: The mean interval size of the speech melody is 2.2 semitones, while it is 2.5 in Kreutzer's musical setting and 2.7 in Strauss' musical setting.

3.3 Autocorrelation analyses of syllable F0 and durations

Repetition structure of time-evolving signals can be visualized and quantified by so-called autocorrelation analyses. An autocorrelation is the correlation of a signal with itself at different time lags (Korotkov et al., 2003). In essence, autocorrelations can be calculated at n different shifts of the copy of a signal relative to the original signal with k datapoints (or length k). At shift $n=0$, the signal is perfectly correlated with itself. At shifts $0 < n < k$, the mean correlation across all data points reveals at which time lag the signal "repeats" itself. For this reason, autocorrelation analysis is a standard technique to derive the repetition rate of the human voice during speaking (Cheveigné & Kawahara, 2002; Meddis & O'Mard, 1997; Paliwal & Rao, 1981; Yost, 2009), but also to determine higher-order repetition structure such as meter in music and speech (Brown, 1993; Cocco & Bavaud, 2015; Eck, 2006; Liu et al., 2013; Toiviainen & Eerola, 2006; Vos et al., 1994). Note that the signal cannot be shifted more or equal than k lags; usually, the maximal shift is $0.95 * k$.

When applied to syllable-based F0 in speech or to tones in music, the autocorrelation structure reveals the repetition or recurrence structure of the signal (i.e., a spoken utterance or a musical piece). The most obvious repetition occurs when individual tones repeat in strophic music. An example is provided in Figure 2A. Here, the German strophic song "Der Mond ist aufgegangen [The moon has been appearing]" by Johann Abraham Peter Schultz with words by Matthias Claudius has been subjected to an autocorrelation analysis based on the notation of the singing voice Figure 2B.

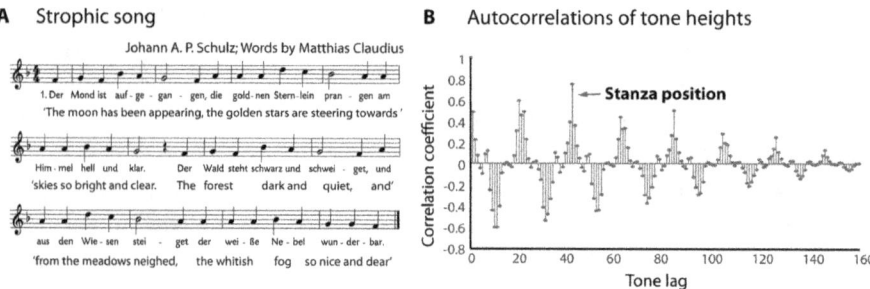

Figure 2: Illustration of applying an autocorrelation analysis to a strophic song, Johann Abraham Peter Schulz's tune to Matthias Claudius' "Der Mond ist aufgegangen" [The moon has been appearing]. A. The melodic line in standard musical notation with the translation of the first stanza. B. Autocorrelation representation of the F0 values obtained by conversion from the musical notation into semitones using the MIDI convention. The highest (positive) correlation coefficient occurs at a tone lag corresponding to the distance between stanzas (the stanza position). Note that the time series of semitones comprised three stanzas. This coefficient indicates that the notes are repeating in each stanza.

For this illustration, the musical notation has been translated into semitones according to the MIDI convention. In this system, each note receives a positive integer value, referenced to the anchor tone of 440 Hz. The series of tone height values (i.e., semitones) subsequently underwent a standard autocorrelation analysis carried out in MatLab (The Mathworks, Inc., Nattick, USA; Version 2018a). Positive and negative correlation coefficients are calculated for each tone lag, up to 95% of the entire length of the time series. It is apparent that the highest positive autocorrelation coefficient occurs at a tone lag that corresponds to the tone distance between stanzas. This is not surprising, given that the musically notated tones are completely repeated in each stanza. The fact that the value does not equal "1" has to with the algorithm that arrives at a mean correlation with regard to the entire time series length; however, since the number of lags must necessarily be smaller than the number of notes, only the correlation at lag 0 has an average correlation coefficient of 1.

It is now relatively straightforward to feed syllable-based F0 values from spoken recordings of poems into the autocorrelation algorithm. The emerging structure is then indicative of a potential repetition structure regarding F0 or syllable duration. If applied to the spoken rendition of the poem "Das Thal" by Johann Ludwig Uhland, the autocorrelation structure depicted in Figure 3A emerges.

The autocorrelation representation of the spoken rendition shows two prominent correlation coefficient peaks, one at the syllable lag corresponding to rhyme distances, and one at the syllable lag corresponding to stanza distances. The

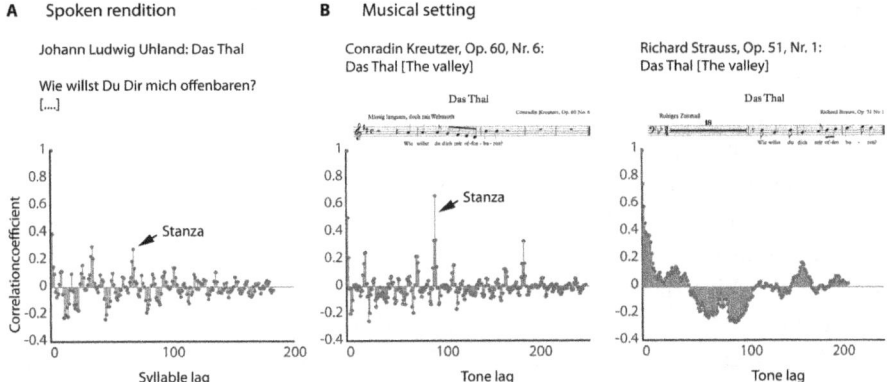

Figure 3: Ilustration of autocorrelation analyses applied to a spoken rendition of the poem "Das Thal" [The valley] by Johann Ludwig Uhland (A), and to two musical settings (B), one by Conradin Kreutzer (middle) and one by Richard Strauss (right). The spoken rendition shows prominent correlation coefficients at syllable lags corresponding to the distance between rhymes and stanzas. The musical setting by Kreutzer yields a particularly large autocorrelation coefficient at the stanza lag, which is the consequence of the strophic structure of the piece. By contrast, the piece by Straus has no strophic structure and therefore does not yield prominent (positive) autocorrelation coefficients, rather patterns that correspond to the tripartite musical structure.

musical setting of Kreutzer (Figure 3B) reveals a strong stanza-related peak, indicating the strophic structure of the song. The musical setting by Strauss, by contrast, shows no stanza effect, but rather a tripartite structure that can also be motivated on musical grounds.

It is discernible that the autocorrelation representation of the spoken rendition of the poem shows F0 recurrences across stanzas. While in music, stanzas with identical melody are common, it is not expected that the melodic structure in speech repeats across poem stanzas. The example above is indicative of a general pattern that has been reported in Menninghaus et al. (2018) and that seems independent of speakers. Strophic structure in poems corresponds to high autocorrelation coefficients at syllable lags corresponding to stanza distance. Menninghaus et al. (2018) used two measures to quantify the autocorrelation representation. The first measure is relatively straightforward and is the correlation coefficient at the syllable lag that corresponds the (mean) distance between stanzas, measured in syllables. The second measure takes into account all correlation coefficients and emphasizes those that are "significant". Significance is determined by a resampling procedure, involving 10000 permutations of the original F0 series and subsequent autocorrelation analyses of the resampled series. For each syllable lag, it is calculated how often the autocorrelation coefficient is equal or larger than the autocorrelation coefficient of the original series. If this condition holds in 5% or less, the corresponding correlation coefficient is considered significant. Subsequently, the proportion of significant autocorrelations (PSA) of a syllable- or tone-based F0 time series is the amount of significant autocorrelation coefficients divided by the total number of syllables of this time series. It is a quantitative measure of the time series' repetition structure: the higher the value, the more repetitive the time series. Note that the measure does not only capture the number of time lags at which repetitions occur, but also the consistency with which these repetitions are observable.

Menninghaus et al. (2018) demonstrated that both measures, i.e., stanza-based autocorrelation coefficients and PSA, positively correlate with several aesthetic ratings that were given by participants listening to spoken renditions of a set of stanza-based poems. Notably, the autocorrelation structure was based on poetic features such as rhyme and meter; eliminating those features led to a decrease of the stanza-based autocorrelation coefficient. Moreover, the stanza-based autocorrelation coefficient was predictive for subsequent musical settings of the respective poems. If a poem had a high stanza-based autocorrelation coefficient, it was more likely to be set to music at a later time. The authors concluded that the autocorrelation measures ideally capture the F0-based repetition structure of spoken poems and are thus good approximations to the poems' melody.

Repetition structure is indeed a property that has been claimed to be central to melodies (Bradley, 1971; Margulis, 2013; Nunes et al., 2015). It seems to increase memorability, but may also be central to aesthetic processing insofar as repetitions generate expectations, the latter of which interact with surprise during aesthetic processing (Cheung et al., 2019). Since not all examples displayed in Figure 3B have strophic structure, quantifying the autocorrelation structure is only possible by referring to PSA. If doing so, the PSA for the spoken rendition is 0.29. The musical setting by Kreutzer yields a PSA of 0.27, while the musical setting by Strauss shows a PSA of 0.53. Again, the similarity of Kreutzer's composition to the textual origin is reflected in this value, while the higher PSA for Strauss seems to be driven by stronger repetitions at shorter lags and by negative autocorrelation coefficients at intermediate lags.

3.4 Comparing speech and music by means of the PSA

After having established the measure of PSA (Menninghaus et al., 2018), a further question was whether it would be sensitive to potential differences between music and speech. I therefore selected 8 exemplary pieces from different musical and literary genres. Musical genres were pop songs (due to the high relevance of melody and stanza-structure, Nunes et al., 2015), arias and romantic songs. Romantic songs were based on musical settings of 8 poems from the larger poem corpus described in Menninghaus et al. (2018). Literary genres included the same 8 selected poems and their modified counterparts from which poetic properties such as rhyme and meter were removed. Finally, I included 8 excerpts from 4 German short stories.

The speech material was analyzed as describe above: After automatic annotation into syllables, the recorded data underwent manual correction of syllable boundaries, extraction of syllable-based F0 values, quantization of F0 and syllable durations and subsequent autocorrelation analyses. The musical pieces were obtained from freely available MIDI-files in the internet, most of which from the Choral Public Domain Library (CPDL, www.cpdl.org). Musical analyses were based on the extracted melody line of the respective piece (i.e., the voice-part). Importantly, the underlying data therefore corresponded to the musical notation, and not to individually different performances. The calculation of the F0-based autocorrelations followed the steps illustrated above.

When looking at the average PSA values across the different genres, a remarkable gradient emerges (Figure 4).

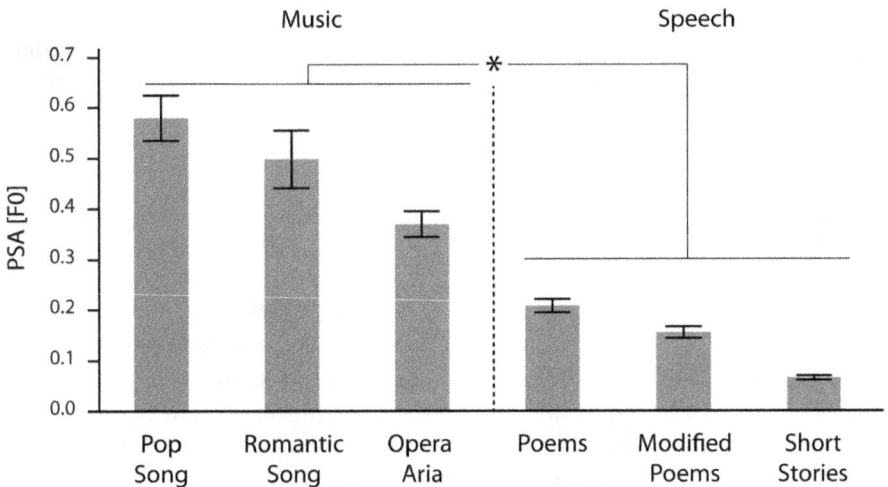

Figure 4: Differences of F0-based PSA values across different musical and literary genres. Each category is based on 8 exemplary pieces that were analyzed as quantized F0-time series, either derived from musical notation (music) or from spoken recordings (speech). Importantly, poems and their modified counterpart were produced by the same professional speaker described in greater detail in Menninghaus et al. (2018), while the short stories were produced by different speakers. The asterisk indicates a significant difference in mean PSA values between music and speech.

The PSA gradient spans from pop songs with highest PSAs and thus strongest repetition structure to short stories with lowest PSAs and thus lowest repetition structure (based on F0). The decrease of PSA from pop songs through romantic songs and opera arias correlates with their musical structure. Most romantic songs showed strophic structure, resulting in relatively high PSAs, while not all opera arias showed a da capo form. Poems, on the other hand, showed a close affinity to musical pieces regarding their F0-based PSAs. This is in accordance with impressionistic evidence that poems sound "melodious" and substantiated by the study of Menninghaus et al. (2018). Finally, when removing poetic properties such as rhyme and meter, the PSA decreases further and approaches the value of spoken prose (short stories). This is remarkable, too, since the PSA for short stories is not equal to 0. This would be expected if F0 values were randomly distributed over syllables. Thus, we find evidence for a small degree of melodiousness even in prose, a topic that is very promising for future research (see e.g., Breiss & Hayes, 2020).

Althogether, the PSA of quantized F0 is a promising measure for quantifying melodic repetition structure in speech and music. The observed gradient suggests that differences between speech and music are not necessarily dichotomous. The measure is thus able to acount for categorical endpoints in either domain, perhaps representing prototypical melodies for music and speech, but also for a certain transition zones where speech and music percepts oscillate and cannot be attribute to either domain, akin to Schönberg's "Pierrot Lunaire" (Rapoport, 2004).

4 Discussion and summary

Affinities between language and music have been observed for a very long time. A central level of comparing aspects of language and music is the acoustic level on which sensory information of spoken language and performed or (re)played music converges. At this level, speech and music seem to share the construct of melody. Melodic properties of speech have been discussed in several linguistic and musical approaches to speech prosody, but unifying frameworks for quantifying melodies in speech and music are rare (but see Chow & Brown, 2018). I have proposed that an ideal strategy to capture essential aspects of melodic structure in both speech and music is based on autocorrelation analyses of quantized F0- or tone information. The approach has several advantages that can recapitulated as follows:

(a) F0 information is derived from every syllable. This advantage is further discussed in Chow & Brown (2018)
(b) F0 information and syllable durations are represented on the same level. Again, this advantage is highlighted in Chow & Brown (2018)
(c) F0 is derived following suggestions by Hirst (2011), attempting to minimize octave-jumps
(d) F0 extraction is comparable to the approach used with Prosograms (Hart, 1981; Mertens, 2004). Research at the interface of language and music has been based on Prosogram-approaches (e.g., Patel, 2006), therefore ensuring a solid methodological basis.
(e) Autocorrelation analyses can either derive one repetition structure quantification for an entire time series (spoken poem, musical song) or one repetition structure quantification for a specific melody-relevant position (rhyme, stanza). Autocorrelation analyses thus capture an essential higher-order property of melodies: Repetitions of F0 or tones (Bradley, 1971; Margulis, 2013; Nunes et al., 2015).
(f) Autocorrelation analyses can be conducted on large corpora of digital music in the MIDI format. Such MIDI corpora have been used previously e.g., for the analysis of rhythm (e.g., Levitin et al., 2012)

Autocorrelations or the PSA measure are predominantly means of describing the repetition structure of information in time. What is the advantage of such measures beyond descriptive elegance? The most important aspect of these measures is (a) that they may provide an ecologically valid index of predictive and aesthetic processing and (b) that they may provide the shared descriptive basis for accounting for structural similarities in speech and music.

4.1 Perception is based on predictions

Current theories of brain function capitalize on the theory of "unconscious inference" by Hermann Helmholtz from the 19th century, culminating in Predictive Coding frameworks (Friston, 2005; Friston, 2012) that are also applied to auditory perception (Winkler et al., 2009). In essence, Predictive Coding holds that the brain constantly predicts the future states of its sensory surrounding and attempts to minimize the difference between sensory predictions and actual sensory information. Only this difference is actively processed and used to update the internal predictions.

This is considered a computationally optimal principle, because the amount of sensory information to be processed is reduced to the difference between what is predicted and what is actually perceived. Predictive Coding is also applied to speech perception, in part due to the fact that speech has quasi-regular structure. Regular sensory input is beneficial for updating predictions (e.g., Tavano et al., 2014), for which reason any repetitive stimulus (i.e., also musical pieces or poetic recitals) is an "ideal" stimulus in Predictive Coding frameworks, in that is should tax processing resources only to small degrees. This assumption is reminiscent of a cognitive approach to aesthetic theory, namely, Processing Fluency (Babel & McGuire, 2015; Reber et al., 2004).

Processing Fluency describes facilitated perceptual and cognitive processing of sensory events by which these events are perceived aesthetically. That is, aesthetic pleasure comes about by a certain ease of processing. A potential explanation for this claim is provided by Menninghaus et al. (2015) who showed that rhetorical features such as repetitions (in rhyming words or assonances) facilitate prosodic processing and in turn increase aesthetic perception. Importantly, the aforementioned study on F0/pitch autocorrelations in spoken poems is also in accordance with Processing Fluency accounts. In Menninghaus et al. (2018), autocorrelations of pitch as well as the PSA measure positively correlated with aesthetic ratings of spoken poems these repetition measures were derived from. Put differently, increased repetition structure of pitch (akin to speech melody) co-varied with increased aesthetic pleasure. Among the aesthetic measures were also melodiousness ratings. Theses ratings correlated in a particularly strong way with the repetitions measures, ascribing them perceptual reality beyond merely describing repetition structures.

Finally, Predictive Coding frameworks are increasingly applied to aesthetics (e.g., Van de Cruys & Wagemans, 2011). Lately, Cheung et al. (2019) showed that musical pleasure derives from an interplay of prediction and surprise. Prediction in this study was operationalized as uncertainty, with high uncertainty corresponding to low predictability and low uncertainty corresponding to high predictability. The authors found that chords with low uncertainty and high surprise and chors with high uncertainty and low surprise elicited high pleasure. Both effects modulated brain activity in auditory cortex, the primary region for perceiving and processing auditory stimuli in speech and music. Thus, autocorrelation and PSA measures seem ideally suited to link descriptive analyses of speech and music stimuli to current theories of processing and aesthetics.

4.2 Melodic repetition is shared between speech and music

The descriptive advantage of the autocorrelation and PSA measures is that it can equally be applied to music and speech. It does not suffer from some of the shortcomings of the aforementioned notational systems that have attempted to illustrate commonalities between language and music (e.g., MOMEL or Prosogram-approaches). Importantly, in Menninghaus et al. (2018), we could demonstrate that the autocorrelation measures capture inherent properties of recited poems that allow predictions regarding subsequent musical renditions of these poems. More precisely, spoken poems with high autocorrelation values of pitch between stanzas were more likely to be set to music than spoken poems with lower autocorrelation values. Note that poems with high autocorrelation values may be those with a very consistent strophic, metric and rhyming structure. As alluded to in the beginning of the chapter, vowels (as primary pitch-bearing units) have intrinsic pitch (i.e., intrinsically sound higher or lower and bear intrinsically different F0s). Rhyming pairs but also stanzas with rhyming relations between them are characterized by similar intrinsic pitches on their respective vowels. If the poem has a very consistent strophic, metric and rhyming structure, its intrinsic pitches should therefore be regularly distributed in time. This regular distribution causes high autocorrelation values. It thus seems that a guiding principle of composition and text-setting refers to the repetition structure of the (silent or actual) prosodic structure of texts to be put to music.

The advantage of the autocorrelation measure is that it can directly express this correlation; it is furthermore not only applicable to both speech and music, but also able to differentiate between the discreteness of tonal events. In Western music, tonal events are commonly discrete, while in speech, even if quantized as described here, (non-lexical) pitches are less discrete and may differ by one or more semitones between renditions. This accounts for the gradient structure of the PSA when comparing pop songs on the one hand with spoken prose on the other hand.

4.3 Future directions

The account presented here suffers from three obvious shortcomings that need to be dealt with in future research and in future modifications. First, glissando thresholds are somewhat ignored; at least to the degree that a syllable can only carry one tone in speech, while it can carry several tones in music. It is, however, possible, to treat speech and music alike and to derive mean F0's of syllables that span across several tones. Second, it is apparent from research in music theory and music cognition that melodic properties extend beyond repetition structures (Hüschen, 1961; Müllensiefen & Frieler, 2007; Müllensiefen & Halpern, 2014). For instance, musical melodies have a tonal center, while such a tonal center (in its strict sense) does not exist in speech melodies. Third, rhythmical and metrical structure has not been explicitly looked at. In the study by Menninghaus et al. (2018), autocorrelation of quantized syllable durations also explained variance regarding aesthethic ratings, in particular, melodiousness ratings. Furthermore, removal of rhyme, meter and further poetic text properties also effected the autocorrelation structure of syllable duration. However, overall, F0-based autocorrelation yielded stronger effects and seem to suggest the primacy of tone-based information over rhythm-based information. Again, a closer examination of the tone-rhythm relationship as expressed in autocorrelation analyses needs to be focused at in future research.

Notwithstanding these critical aspects, melody in speech and music can be described within a unified account as presented here. Given the possibilities of quantification resulting from autocorrelation coefficients, this account crucially extends similar approaches (e.g., the musical approach to speech melody by Chow & Brown (2018) towards having a stronger empirical basis.

References

Alkon, Paul P. 1959. Joshua Steele and the melody of speech. *Language and Speech* 2(3). 154–174.
Babel, Molly & Grant McGuire. 2015. Perceptual fluency and judgments of vocal aesthetics and stereotypicality. *Cognitive Science* 39(4). 766–787.
Bachem, A. 1950. Tone height and tone chroma as two different pitch qualities. *Acta Psychologica* 7. 80–88.
Beckman, Mary E., Julia Hirschberg & Stefanie Shattuck-Hufnagel. 2004. The original ToBI system and the evolution of the ToBI framework. In: Sun-Ah Jun, editor. *Prosodic models and transcription: Towards prosodic typology*, 9–54. Oxford: Oxford University Press.
Boersma, Paul & David Weenink. 2019. PRAAT: Doing Phonetics by Computer (ver. 6.0.50). Amsterdam: Institut for Phonetic Sciences.
Bonds, Mark Evan. 2003. *A history of music in Western Culture*. Upper Saddle River, NJ: Prentice Hall.
Bowling, Daniel L. 2013. A vocal basis for the affective character of musical mode in melody. *Frontiers in Psychology* 4.
Bradley, Ian L. 1971. Repetition as a factor in the development of musical preferences. *Journal of Research in Music Education* 19(3). 295–298.
Breen, Mara, Laura C. Dilley, J. Kraemer & Edward Gibson. 2012. Inter-transcriber reliability for two systems of prosodic annotation: ToBI (Tones and Break Indices) and RaP (Rhythm and Pitch). *Corpus Linguistics and Linguistic Theory* 8. 277–312.
Breiss, Canaan & Bruce Hayes. 2020. Phonological markedness effects in sentence formation. *Language* 96. 338–370.
Brown, Judith C. 1993. Determination of the meter of musical scores by autocorrelation. *The Journal of the Acoustical Society of America* 94(4). 1953–1957.

Cheung, Vincent K. M., Peter M. C. Harrison, Lars Meyer, Marcus T. Pearce, John-Dylan Haynes & Stefan Koelsch. 2019. Uncertainty and surprise jointly predict musical pleasure and Amygdala, Hippocampus, and Auditory Cortex activity. *Current Biology* 29(23). 4084–4092.
Cheveigné, Alain de & Hideki Kawahara. 2002. Yin, a fundamental frequency estimator for speech and music. *The Journal of the Acoustical Society of America* 111(4). 1917–1930.
Chow, Ivan & Steven Brown. 2018. A musical approach to speech melody. *Frontiers in Psychology* 9. 247.
Christiansen, Paul. 2004. The meaning of speech melody for Leoš Janáček. *Journal of Musicological Research* 23(3–4). 241–263.
Cocco, Christelle & Francois Bavaud. 2015. Correspondence analysis, cross-autocorrelation and clustering in polyphonic music. In: B. Lausen, editor. *Data Science, learning by latent structures, and knowledge discovery*, 401–410. Heidelberg: Springer.
Colley, Ian D. & Roger T. Dean. 2019. Origins of 1/f noise in human music. *Plos One* 14(5). e0216088.
Cruttenden, Alan. 1997. *Intonation*. Cambridge: Cambridge University Press.
Cutler, A., D. Dahan & W. van Donselaar. 1997. Prosody in the comprehension of spoken language: A literature review. *Language and Speech* 40 (Pt 2). 141–201.
D'Alessandro, C., S. Rosset & J. P. Rossi. 1998. The pitch of short-duration fundamental frequency glissandos. *Journal of the Acoustical Society of America* 104(4). 2239–2348.
Dahan, Delphine. 2015. Prosody and language comprehension. *Wiley Interdisciplinary Reviews. Cognitive Science* 6(5). 441–452.
Deliege, Irene. 1987. Grouping conditions in listening to music: An approach to Lerdahl & Jackendoff's grouping preference rules. *Music Perception: An Interdisciplinary Journal* 4(4). 325–359.
Diehl, Randy L. 1991. *On the Relation between Phonetics and Phonology*. Basel: Karger.
Dilley, Laura C. & Meredith Brown. 2005. *The RAP (Rhythm and Pitch) labeling system*. Cambridge, MA: The MIT Press.
Dowling, W. J. 1978. Scale and contour: Two components of a theory of memory for melodies. *Psychological Review* 85(4). 341–354.
Dowling, W. J. & D. L. Harwood. 1986. *Music cognition*. Orlando, CA: Academic Press.
Eck, Douglas. 2006. Identifying metrical and temporal structure with an autocorrelation phase matrix. *Music Perception* 24(2). 167–176.
Fant, Gunnar. 1956. *On the predictability of formant levels and spectrum envelopes from formant frequencies*. The Hague: De Gruyter.
Fant, Gunnar. 1960. *Acoustic theory of speech production*. The Hague: De Gruyter.
Fischer, Peter-Michael. 1993. *Die Stimme des Sängers*. Stuttgart: Metzeler.
Friston, K. 2005. A theory of cortical responses. *Philosophical Transactions of the Royal Society of London B: Biological Sciences* 360(1456). 815–815.
Friston, Karl. 2012. Prediction, perception and agency. *International Journal of Psychophysiology* 83(2). 248–252.
Gill, Kamraan Z. & Dale Purves. 2009. A biological rationale for musical scales. *Plos One* 4(12). e8144.
Hart, Johan't. 1981. Differential sensivity to pitch distance, particularly in speech. *Journal of the Acoustical Society of America* 69(3). 811–821.

Hart, Johan 't, René Collier & Antonie Cohen. 1990. *A perceptual study of intonation: An experimental-phonetic approach to speech melody.* Cambridge: Cambridge University Press.
Hirst, D. J. 2005. Form and function in the representation of speech prosody. *Speech Communication* 46(3). 334–347.
Hirst, Daniel. 2011. The analysis by synthesis of speech melody: From data to models. *Journal of Speech Sciences* 1(1). 55–83.
Hirst, Daniel, A. Di Cristo & Robert Espesser. 2000. Levels of representation and levels of analysis for the description of intonation systems. In: Merle Horne, editor. *Prosody: Theory and experiment. Studies presented to Gösta Bruce*, 51–87. Dordrecht: Kluwer Academic Publishers.
Hirst, Daniel & Robert Espesser. 1993. Automatic modelling of fundamental frequency curves using a quadratic spline function. *Travaux de l'institut de phonétique d'Aix* 15. 71–85.
Holleran, S., M. R. Jones & D. Butler. 1995. Perceiving implied harmony: The influence of melodic and harmonic context. *Journal of Experimental Psychology. Learning, Memory, and Cognition* 21(3). 737–753.
Hsü, K. J. & A. Hsü. 1991. Self-similarity of the "1/f noise" called music. *Proceedings of the National Academy of Sciences of the United States of America* 88(8). 3507–3509.
Hüschen, Heinrich. 1961. Melodie. In: F. Blume, editor. *Die Musik in Geschichte und Gegenwart*, 19–25. Kassel: Bärenreiter.
Jacewicz, Ewa & Robert Allen Fox. 2015. Intrinsic fundamental frequency of vowels is moderated by regional dialect. *The Journal of the Acoustical Society of America* 138(4). EL405–EL410.
Jones, Mari Riess. 1987. Dynamic pattern structure in music: Recent theory and research. *Perception & Psychophysics* 41(6). 621–634.
Kassler, J. C. 2005. Representing speech through musical notation. *Journal of Musicological Research* 24. 227–239.
Kingston, John. 1992. The phonetics and phonology of perceptually motivated articulatory covariation. *Language and Speech* 35(1–2). 99–113.
Kisler, Thomas, Uwe D. Reichel & Florian Schiel. 2017. Multilingual processing of speech view web services. *Computer Speech and Language* 45. 326–347.
Korotkov, E. V., M. A. Korotkova, F. E. Frenkel & N. A. Kudriashov. 2003. The informational concept of searching for periodicity in symbol sequences. *Molekuliarnaia Biologiia* 37(3). 436–451.
Krumhansl, Carol L. 1990. *Cognitive foundations of musical pitch.* New York: Oxford University Press.
Krumhansl, Carol L. 2000. Rhythm and pitch in music cognition. *Psychological Bulletin* 126(1). 159–179.
Ladd, Robert & Kim E. A. Silverman. 1984. Vowel intrinsic pitch in connected speech. *Phonetica* 41(1). 31–40.
Leben, William R. 1973. Suprasegmental phonology [Ph.D. dissertation]. Cambridge, MA: MIT.
Lee, Hweeling & Uta Noppeney. 2014. Music expertise shapes audiovisual temporal integration windows for speech, sinewave speech, and music. *Frontiers in Psychology* 5. 868.
Lee, Yune-Sang, Petr Janata, Carlton Frost, Zachary Martinez & Richard Granger. 2015. Melody recognition revisited: influence of melodic Gestalt on the encoding of relational pitch information. *Psychonomic Bulletin & Review* 22(1). 163–169.

Lehiste, I. & G. E. Peterson. 1961. Some basic considerations in the analysis of intonation. *The Journal of the Acoustical Society of America* 33. 419–419.

Lerdahl, F. & Ray Jackendoff. 1977. Toward a formal theory of tonal music. *Journal of Music Theory* 21. 111–171.

Lerdahl, F. & Ray Jackendoff. 1983. *A generative theory of tonal music*. Cambridge, MA: MIT Press.

Levitin, Daniel J., Parag Chordia & Vinod Menon. 2012. Musical rhythm spectra from Bach to Joplin obey a 1/f power law. *Proceedings of the National Academy of Sciences* 109(10). 3716–3720.

Liu, Lu, Jianrong Wei, Huishu Zhang, Jianhong Xin & Jiping Huang. 2013. A statistical physics view of pitch fluctuations in the classical music from bach to chopin: Evidence for scaling. *Plos One* 8(3). e58710.

Magdics, Klára. 1963. From the melody of speech to the melody of music. *Studia Musicologica Academiae Scientiarum Hungaricae* 3. 325–346.

Margulis, Elizabeth Hellmuth. 2013. Repetition and emotive communication in music versus speech. *Frontiers in Psychology* 4. 167.

McAdams, Stephen & Kai Siedenburg. 2019. Perception and cognition of musical timbre. In: Peter J. Rentfrow, Daniel J. Levitin, editors. *Foundations in music psychology. Theory and research*, 71–120. Cambridge, MA: The MIT Press.

Meddis, R. & L. O'Mard. 1997. A unitary model of pitch perception. *The Journal of the Acoustical Society of America* 102(3). 1811–1820.

Menninghaus, W., V. Wagner, C. A. Knoop & M. Scharinger. 2018. Poetic speech melody: A crucial link between music and language. *PLoS One* 13(11). e0205980.

Menninghaus, W., V. Wagner, E. Wassiliwizky, T. Jacobsen & C. A. Knoop. 2017. The emotional and aesthetic powers of parallelistic diction. *Poetics* doi: 10.1016/j.poetic.2016.12.001.

Menninghaus, Winfried, I. C. Bohrn, Christine Knoop, S. A. Kotz, W. Schlotz & Arthur M. Jacobs. 2015. Rhetorical features facilitate prosodic processing while handicapping ease of semantic comprehension. *Cognition* 143. 48–60.

Mertens, Piet. Semi-automatic transcription of prosody based on a tonal perception model. In: B. Bel, I. Marlien editors,. Proceedings of Speech Prosody; 2004; Nara, Japan.

Miller, G. A. 1956. The magical number seven, plus or minus two. Some limits on our capacity for processing information. *Psychological Review* 63. 81–97.

Müllensiefen, Daniel. 2009. FANTASTIC: Feature ANalysis Technology Accessing STatistics (in a corpus). Goldsmiths, University of London.

Müllensiefen, Daniel & Klaus Frieler. 2007. Modelling experts notions of melodic similarity. *Musicae Scientiae, Discussion Forum* 4A. 183–210.

Müllensiefen, Daniel & Andrea R. Halpern. 2014. The role of features and context in recognition of novel melodies. *Music Perception: An Interdisciplinary Journal* 31(5). 418–435.

Nadel, Siegfried & Theodore Baker. 1930. The origins of music. *The Musical Quarterly* 16(4). 531–546.

Narmour, Eugene. 1989. The "genetic code" of melody: Cognitive structures generated by the implication-realization model. *Contemporary Music Review* 4. 45–64.

Narmour, Eugene. 1990. *The analysis and cognition of basic melodic structures: The implication-realization model*. Chicago, IL, US: University of Chicago Press.

Nespor, Marina & Irene Vogel. 1986. *Prosodic Phonology*. Dordrecht: Foris.

Nunes, Joseph C., Andrea Ordanini & Francesca Valsesia. 2015. The power of repetition: Repetitive lyrics in a song increase processing fluency and drive market success. *Journal of Consumer Psychology* 25(2). 187–199.

Nygaard, Lynne C. & Jennifer S. Queen. 2008. Communicating emotion: Linking affective prosody and word meaning. *Journal of Experimental Psychology: Human Perception and Performance* 34(4). 1017–1030.

Oxenham, Andrew J. 2012. Pitch perception. *The Journal of Neuroscience* 32(39). 13335–13338.

Oxenham, Andrew J. 2018. How we hear: The perception and neural coding of sound. *Annual Review of Psychology* 69. 27–50.

Oxenham, Andrew J. 2019. Pitch: Perception and neural coding. In: Peter Jason Rentfrow, Daniel J. Levitin, editors. *Foundations in Music* Psychology. *Theory and Research*, 3–33. Cambridge, MA: The MIT Press.

Paliwal, Kuldip K. & Paranandi Venkata S. Rao. 1981. A modified autocorrelation method of linear prediction for pitch-synchronous analysis of voiced speech. *Signal Processing* 3(2). 181–185.

Palmer, Caroline & Sean Hutchins. 2006. What is musical prosody? *Psychology of Learning and Motivation* 46. 245–278.

Patel, Aniruddh D. 2005. The relationship of music to the melody of speech and to syntactic processing disorders in aphasia. *Annals of the New York Academy of Sciences* 1060. 59–70.

Patel, Aniruddh D. 2006. An empirical method for comparing pitch patterns in spoken and musical melodies: A comment on J.G.S. Pearl's "eavesdropping with a master: Leos Janáček and the music of speech.". *Empirical Musicology Review* 1(3). 166–169.

Patel, Aniruddh D. 2010. *Music, language, and the brain.* New York: Oxford University Press.

Patel, Aniruddh D. & Joseph R. Daniele. 2003. An empirical comparison of rhythm in language and music. *Cognition* 87. B35–B45.

Patel, Aniruddh D., John R. Iversen & Jason C. Rosenberg. 2006. Comparing the rhythm and melody of speech and music: The case of British English and French. *The Journal of the Acoustical Society of America* 119(5). 3034–3047.

Pearl, Jonathan. 2006. Eavesdropping with a master: Leos Janácek and the music of speech. *Empirical Musicology Review* 1.

Poon, Matthew & Michael Schutz. 2015. Cueing musical emotions: An empirical analysis of 24-piece sets by Bach and Chopin documents parallels with emotional speech. *Frontiers in Psychology* 6. 1419.

Prieto, Eric. 2002. Speech melody and the evolution of the minimalist aesthetic in Steve Reich's "The Cave". *Circuit. Musiques contemporaines* 12(2). 21–44.

Pulleyblank, Douglas G. 1986. *Tone in Lexical Phonology.* Dordrecht: Reidel.

Randel, Don. 2003. *The Harvard Dictionary of music.* Cambridge, MA.: Harvard University Press.

Rapoport, Eliezer. 2004. Schoenberg-Hartleben's Pierrot Lunaire: Speech – poem – melody – vocal performance. *Journal of New Music Research* 33(1). 71–111.

Reber, Rolf, Norbert Schwarz & Piotr Winkielman. 2004. Processing fluency and aesthetic pleasure: is beauty in the perceiver's processing experience? *Personality and Social Psychology Review* 8(4). 364–382.

Rousseau, Jean-Jacques. 1768. *Dictionnaire de musique.* Paris: Veuve Duchesne.

Schellenberg, E. Glenn & Peter Habashi. 2015. Remembering the melody and timbre, forgetting the key and tempo. *Memory & Cognition* 43(7). 1021–1031.

Schmidt, Jürgen E. 1986. *Die mittelfränkischen Tonakzente*. Stuttgart: Steiner.
Schönberg, Arnold. 1911. *Harmonielehre*. Wien: Universal Edition.
Selkirk, Elisabeth O. 1984. *Phonology and syntax: The relation between sound and structure*. Cambridge, MA: The MIT Press.
Sievers, Eduard. 1912. *Rhythmisch-melodische Studien*. Heidelberg: C. Winter.
Steele, Joshua. 1775. *An essay towards establishing the melody and measure of speech to be expressed and perpetuated by peculiar symbols*. London: Bowyer and Nichols.
Stevens, Kenneth N. 1998. *Acoustic phonetics*. Cambridge, MA; London, England: The MIT Press.
Sundberg, J. 1977. The acoustics of the singing voice. *Scientific American* 236(3). 82–91.
Tavano, Alessandro, Andreas Widmann, Alexandra Bendixen, Nelson Trujillo-Barreto & Erich Schröger. 2014. Temporal regularity facilitates higher-order sensory predictions in fast auditory sequences. *European Journal of Neuroscience* 39(2). 308–318.
Toiviainen, Petri & Tuomas Eerola. 2006. Autocorrelation in meter induction: The role of accent structure. *The Journal of the Acoustical Society of America* 119(2). 1164–1170.
Van de Cruys, Sander & Johan Wagemans. 2011. Putting reward in art: A tentative prediction error account of visual art. *i-Perception* 2(9). 1035–1062.
Vos, P. G., A. van Dijk & L. Schomaker. 1994. Melodic cues for metre. *Perception* 23(8). 965–976.
Voss, Richard F. & John Clarke. 1975. '1/ f noise' in music and speech. *Nature* 258(5533). 317.
Voss, Richard F. & John Clarke. 1998. "1/f noise" in music: Music from 1/f noise. *The Journal of the Acoustical Society of America* 63(1). 258.
Wertheimer, M. 1924. *Gestalt Theory*. Raleigh, NC: Hayes Barton.
Whalen, D. H., Bryan Gick, Masanobu Kumada & Kiyoshi Honda. 1999. Cricothyroid activity in high and low vowels: Exploring the automaticity of intrinsic F0. *Journal of Phonetics* 27(2). 125–142.
Whalen, D. H. & Andrea G. Levitt. 1995. The universality of intrinsic F0 of vowels. *Journal of Phonetics* 23(3). 349–366.
Wingfield, Paul. 1992. Janacek's speech-melody theory in concept and practice. *Cambridge Opera Journal* 4(3). 281–301.
Winkler, István, Susan L. Denham & Israel Nelken. 2009. Modeling the auditory scene: Predictive regularity representations and perceptual objects. *Trends in Cognitive Sciences* 13(12). 532–540.
Wu, Dan, Keith M. Kendrick, Daniel J. Levitin, Chaoyi Li & Dezhong Yao. 2015. Bach is the father of harmony: Revealed by a 1/f fluctuation analysis across musical genres. *Plos One* 10(11). e0142431.
Xu, Yi. 2005. Speech melody as articulatorily implemented communicative functions. *Speech Communication* 46(3–4). 220–251.
Yip, Moira. 2002. *Tone*. Cambridge: Cambridge University Press.
Yip, Moira Jean Winsland. 1980. *The tonal phonology of Chinese*. Bloomington, IND: Indiana University Linguistics Club.
Yost, William A. 2009. Pitch perception. *Attention, Perception & Psychophysics* 71(8). 1701–1715.
Zatorre, Robert J. & Shari R. Baum. 2012. Musical melody and speech intonation: Singing a different tune. *PLoS Biology* 10(7). e1001372.
Zimmermann, Gerhard. 1998. Die 'singende' Sprechmelodie im Deutschen. *Zeitschrift für Germanistische Linguistik* 26. 1–26.

Dicky Gilbers & Teja Rebernik
A constraint-based approach to structuring language and music: Towards a roadmap for comparing language and music cross-culturally

Abstract: We pursue the hypothesis that musical differences between cultures are based on linguistic, especially phonological, properties of the culture's spoken language. To study this hypothesis, we present a general constraint-based framework for describing the structural similarities between music and language. Music and language are structured by the fact that some sounds are more important than others, based on cognitive strategies which we present here as universal well-formedness conditions. However, which sounds are considered to be most salient differs across cultures, as evidenced by the world's many linguistic and musical typologies. The first goal of our research approach is to identify these universal well-formedness conditions (e.g. prominence of strong elements based on the syllable/chord structure and domain marking based on intonation/melody patterns, pauses) for speech and music. The second goal is to assess how cultures differ from each other in terms of the relative salience assigned to these conditions (i.e. how these conditions are "ranked"). The current paper is meant to be an introduction to a new approach with focus on the identification of general well-formedness conditions. We introduce similar conditions for the description of language and music in order to make comparison of the two disciplines more fruitful. The goal of our research approach is to create a theoretical and methodological map to aid more detailed culture-specific comparisons. The ultimate aim is to provide a comprehensive typological overview for which we will start with a selection of culture families following the World Atlas of Language Structures online (Dryer & Haspelmath, 2013) for language and the Global Jukebox (Wood & Arèvalo, 2018) for music.

Acknowledgements: We would like to thank Matt Coler, Steven Gilbers and the participants of the Workshop "Prosody from a cross-domain perspective: How language speaks to music (and vice versa)", 41st Annual Conference of the German Linguistic Society, Bremen, March 2019, for comments and input. We would also like to thank two anonymous reviewers who significantly contributed to improvements on the earlier version of the manuscript.

Dicky Gilbers, Teja Rebernik, University of Groningen, The Netherlands

https://doi.org/10.1515/9783110770186-004

Keywords: linguistic and musical typology, optimality theory, universality and variation

1 Introduction

Similarities between music and language can be found at various levels and defined in different ways. In his book *Music, Language, and the Brain* (Patel, 2010), the author proposes that the comparison can be done on six levels: *sound elements* (pitch in music and timbre in language) serve as the organizing force; *rhythm*, as the systematic patterning of sound, shows that both domains group smaller sounds into higher-level units;[1] spoken and musical *melody* can be directly compared in terms of pitch patterning or contour; *syntax* binds both language and music in terms of a hierarchical, logical structure (i.e. words form sentences, tones form chords); *meaning* can be conveyed by both language and music, although musical meaning is a lot more difficult to define; finally, the domains of language and music can be compared from an evolutionary perspective (i.e. to what extent humans evolved their musical and linguistic abilities by natural selection). In this paper, we focus especially on the more structural levels of rhythm, melody, and syntax.

Others, such as Jackendoff (2009), propose a different way of looking at the language-music connection: for processing language and music, individuals must have the memory capacity for storing representations, integrate these representations in different combinations, create expectations, possess fine-scale control of vocal production, express desire to imitate others, invent new items, and join in with others to produce something together. The general idea, linking different views, is that language and music are uniquely human.[2] Both language and music are highly systematic particular sound systems that are innately perceived and occur in all cultures. This observation raises a compelling question: what are the common (universal) cognitive strategies that are used to process the stream of sounds in order to structure language and music?

The idea that there are structural similarities between language and music did not start with Patel's aforementioned book nor did it end there. Fenk-Oczlon and Fenk (2009), for example, discuss parallels between the musical and linguistic

---

[1] However, temporal periodicity plays a significantly smaller role in speech than it does in musical meter, where it serves "as a mental framework for sound perception" (Patel, 2010).
[2] Comparatively, in holistic sound systems, like those used by many animals, each sound is associated with a particular meaning, but sounds are not recombined to form new meanings.

building blocks (namely, musical intervals and vowels) or the length and size of utterances (clauses in language and phrases in music, respectively). They find that both linguistic and musical utterances typically have a duration of about 2 seconds and 5–10 "pulses". Likewise, sound inventories consist of between 3 and 12 elements (most frequently 5) for both notes and vowels. Other researchers take a more experimental approach, for example by comparing speech rhythm and (classical) music rhythm of different European languages using the nPVI index[3] (see e.g., Patel & Daniele, 2003; Daniele & Patel, 2004; VanHandel & Song, 2009; Jekiel, 2015). Temperley & Temperley (2011) go into more detail by comparing the prevalence of a certain rhythmic type and vowel length in several languages, finding that the prevalence of the rhythmic pattern "Scotch snap" (short accented note followed by a longer one) in Scottish and English songs but not in German or Italian songs is potentially related to the fact that British English song lyrics have many more very short stressed syllables compared to German or Italian song lyrics. The study of musical and linguistic structure gets even more complicated when one considers regional variation of one country's or culture's languages and musics. Gilbers et al. (2020) show that regional variation in African American English prosody and rap flows make patterns in similar ways, suggesting a connection between rhythm and melody in language and music. Furthermore, studies on both English dialects and folk music (McGowan & Levitt, 2011) and Slovenian dialects and folk music (Rebernik & Gilbers, 2017) have shown that undeniable regional differences exist in the speech and folk music across the countries. For example, in Slovenia, the speech and folk music of border regions show unique characteristics (Rebernik & Gilbers, 2017).

These comparative approaches, no matter how informative, fail to consider the breadth of languages and musics, also seen in the fact that they mostly focus on a single level (e.g. rhythm) and on a limited set of cultures (predominantly Western). They also face the fact that despite intriguing similarities between language and music, such as metrical structures and mechanisms processing pitch, there are also important differences. For example, music does not possess a lexicon with a conceptual system that gives rise to compositional meaning as language does. With a musical instrument you cannot communicate a sentence such as "let us convince you this is a very interesting research approach". Therefore, musical syntactic structures cannot be perfectly aligned with linguistic ones in a one-to-one manner. Hierarchical structures in language have referential,

---

[3] nPVI or the "normalized pairwise variability index" is a measure of the "degree of contrast between successive durations in an utterance" (Patel, 2010). Due to its nature, it can be used either for measuring durations in speech utterances or measuring durations in musical segments.

propositional meaning, whereas the relationship between essential and ornamental elements in music defines tension-relaxation patterns that encode affect. When studying music and language from a structural perspective, we must start seeing the forest as opposed to just individual trees. In this case, we must shift our efforts towards creating a comprehensive framework that could explain the structure of both linguistic and musical sounds.

Indeed, Asano & Boeckx (2015) suggest that a fruitful comparison of music and language needs to incorporate action-related components such as goal of action, action planning, motor control and sensory-motor integration. Language has a conceptual goal, i.e. organizing thought, and a pragmatic goal, i.e. communication. Music, on the other hand, has an affective-gestural goal, i.e. inducing emotion, and a socio-intentional goal, i.e. performing an enjoyable activity in a group. What they have in common is that they are temporally structured sequences. Hierarchical structures are considered as linking action and syntax. In this view, music and language share a planning component as an interface, adapting stored representations to achieve various domain-specific goals. Music and language use the same computation for these hierarchical structures, defining head and dependent elements in different domains. Accordingly, differences between language and music can be explained in terms of different goals reflected in the hierarchical plans. For example, in Western tonal music, the cadence can be seen as a kind of structural goal in the dynamics of tension and relaxation. However, the intended affect depends on the conventionally acquired knowledge of the musical idiom of the listener. We argue that this makes a constraint-based approach particularly suitable to study it.

The aim of this chapter is to discuss structure in terms of well-formedness conditions or constraints that identify essential and ornamental elements in the processing of music and language. We lean on and combine two constraint-based approaches: *Optimality Theory* (Prince & Smolensky, 1993), which has predominantly been used to explain linguistic structure, and the *Generative Theory of Tonal Music* (Lerdahl & Jackendoff, 1983), which was created to explain (Western tonal) music. We wish to quantify linguistic and musical characteristics in terms of the cognitive strategies that help people structure these two phenomena. While this chapter presents the early stages of our approach, mostly explaining it in terms of constraints that can be used for classifying inventories, harmony, rhythm and melody/intonation, the ultimate goal of the present research is to generate an account of the way language and music are structured across cultures and the degree to which differences in musical styles and languages can be explained by differently ordering general well-formedness conditions on structure depending on the culture. In other words, culture-specific differences are reflected in the relative salience of the well-formedness conditions for each culture.

In the next section, we briefly introduce Optimality Theory and the Generative Theory of Tonal Music. We follow by discussing the typology of universal well-formedness conditions. Subsequently, we discuss constraints on chord complexity and rhythm by presenting Optimality Theory-inspired tableaus. Finally, we conclude by considering the implications of our approach and the problems of describing two phenomena that are so similar yet differ to such a great extent across cultures.

2 Similarities between language and music

2.1 Constraint-based frameworks

Optimality Theory (OT) aims to explain structure in language. OT is an output-oriented theory of language and grammar that became a popular trend in linguistics after its introduction by phonologist Alan Prince and cognitive scientist Paul Smolensky (Prince & Smolensky, 1993). In OT a grammar consists of a set of well-formedness constraints on possible outputs, i.e. realizations of phonological forms. These constraints apply simultaneously to representations of structures, and they are soft, which means violable.

OT introduces several types of constraints. First, so-called "markedness" constraints ensure simple structures, as exemplified in, for example, a constraint on clusters of consonants within a syllable. Second, markedness constraints interact with so-called "correspondence" constraints, which establish relations between underlying, i.e. mentally stored (input) forms and the actually realized (output) forms. This is in line with Boersma (1998), who quotes Passy (1891), asserting that speakers will try to get their message across as *quickly* and *clearly* as possible. In a functionally oriented OT account of morpho-phonological processes, therefore, markedness constraints, which ensure articulatory easiness (*quickly*) for the speaker, are potentially in conflict with correspondence constraints, which ensure diversity of forms and meaning (*clearly*), which makes communication easier for the listener. Finally, OT also contains so-called "alignment" constraints, which function as domain boundary markers. They require that the edges of different domains, for example of morphological units and phonological units, coincide.

In OT, different constraints may lay down opposite requirements on the preferred structure. If so, conflicts are solved by assuming differences in weight between the different constraints. An optimal output may violate a certain constraint as long as this violation leads to the satisfaction of a more important constraint.

This can be likened to traffic rules: the constraint to wait for a red traffic light has more weight than having precedence on the main road, although both constraints are defined strictly. Eventually, the whole set of hierarchically ranked constraints determines the optimal realization of phonological forms.

Possible variations attested in the world's languages can be accounted for with reference to the different hierarchical ranking of the universal set of these constraints. In other words, not all universal constraints are equally important in each language. Indeed, individual languages rank the universal constraints in such a way that higher ranked constraints have total dominance over lower ranked constraints. By analysing the results arising from ranking the universal constraints in all possible dominance hierarchies, one can predict and explain which surface patterns are possible in natural languages (Gilbers & de Hoop, 1998).[4]

OT owes the idea of ranking soft constraints to the Generative Theory of Tonal Music (GTTM), introduced in 1983 by musicologist Fred Lerdahl and linguist Ray Jackendoff, who sought to explain structure in (Western) music. Lerdahl and Jackendoff describe how a listener constructs connections between different parts of a musical piece. In their music theory, the musical stream of sounds is hierarchically divided into domains. Each domain (e.g. a verse) contains some smaller domains (e.g. a phrase), which in turn contain smaller domains (e.g. a motif). In each domain, head and dependent parts are defined by the application of preference rules, comparable to constraints in OT. As in OT, the preference rules are not strict claims on the interpretation of a musical piece. It is possible for a head constituent to violate a certain preference rule as long as this violation leads to the satisfaction of a more important preference rule. By imposing this hierarchical structure on the entire piece and by distinguishing between important and ornamental parts by means of applying preference rules that are ranked for importance, the listener is able to understand the piece of music (Gilbers & Schreuder, 2000; 2002; Schreuder, 2006).

Gilbers & Schreuder (2002) mention that within existing theories of music and language structure, there is only one mentioned ranking of preference rules for music (in GTTM), whereas there are several rankings for language, as the ranking of universal constraints (which in themselves are unranked) has to be established for every individual language (in OT). Although Lerdahl & Jackendoff (1983) only offer one ranking, namely for tonal Western music, one can imagine that the dominance hierarchy of preference rules is different for, for example, Eastern music. The ultimate question in the current research approach is whether

---

[4] The appendix shows a summary table of all OT-constraints used in this chapter.

there is a relation between the relative importance of similar well-formedness conditions in the language and music of the same culture. For example, in the assignment of stress in most stress-timed languages, such as Dutch, syllable weight plays an important role, just like harmonic consonance (see description of the latter in section 2.2) in the culture's music.[5] In a tonal language, such as Sino-Tibetan Hmong, on the other hand, syllable weight is less important. The syllables in this language are less complex than in e.g. Dutch. Diversity in linguistic meaning is established by means of tonal differences in Hmong. Similarly, in the culture's music, prolongation of the melody line is more important than its harmonic consonance.

2.2 General well-formedness conditions

How can we use the two approaches introduced above in order to find musico-linguistic similarities? Both GTTM and OT are underlined by a simple fact: listeners construct connections between the sounds they perceive. Mostly subconsciously, the listener is capable of recognizing the construction of a piece of music by considering some notes/chords as more prominent than others. If listeners cannot recognize what is essential and what is ornamental, they will "lose contact" with the piece, and it will become a meaningless sequence of unrelated sounds to them. Similarly, with language, if listeners, for example those learning a second language, cannot recognize how the stream of sounds is structured, they will have problems with comprehension. Well-formedness conditions, defined as, respectively, preference rules or constraints, identify prominent elements in music and language, e.g. in terms of "prominence of strong elements" or "domain marking". These conditions in turn can help us explain the structure of both language and music.

According to Ball (2010), the brain is a pattern-seeking organ; it looks for patterns in sound to make sense of what we hear.[6] Consider two examples of well-formedness conditions in music and language. First, one that refers to the differences in weight between syllables in language and between chords in music.

---

[5] Harmonic consonant intervals in music are characterized by ratios of frequencies of lower integers: 2:1 (octave), 3:2 (fifth), 4:3 (fourth). The lower these integers are, the less tension there is in the music. Musical preference rules are based on harmonic stability, following Lerdahl & Jackendoff, 1983.
[6] Some modernist composers, such as Schönberg, intentionally undermine this cognitive aid for making music easier to understand, which makes it harder for the brain to find structure.

In language, syllables may differ in weight, which may be an important cue in order to find out which syllable is the stressed one, i.e. the prominent one, in a word. Prominent parts may be characterized acoustically by a higher pitch, a longer duration and/or more intensity, which makes perception of the structure of the message and thereby communication easier for the listener.

For example, in Hindi, the strongest, i.e. most complex, syllable available in the word is stressed (Hayes, 1995). In the word *kidhar*, the closed syllable *dhar* is heavy and the open syllable *ki* is light. Accordingly, *dhar* will be stressed. Likewise, in the word *reezgarii*, the syllable *reez* (tense vowel and closed) is super heavy, *ga* (lax vowel and open) is light and *rii* (long vowel and open) is heavy, hence *reez* will be stressed.

Similar to the way the smallest linguistic building blocks, phonemes, can be combined into a next higher domain, syllables, the smallest musical building blocks, tones, can be combined with each other into a next higher domain, chords. Similar to syllables in language, chords in music can also be ranked according to differences in weight. In GTTM, the preference rule specifies that the head of a domain is the chord (or the note) which is relatively harmonically consonant. This preference rule is connected to a hierarchy of chords based on harmonic stability. A triad tonic-tierce-fifth (c-e-g) is more stable than a diminished chord C0 (c-e_b-g_b). The latter chord is to be used ornamentally as a transition from one prominent chord to another. The preference rule indicates that a chord C is preferred to C0 as the head of a domain. Just compare the notes c and g in a tonic-fifth combination of a triad tonic-(tierce)-fifth to the combination of c and g flat in a diminished chord C0 (c-(e_b)-g_b). The upper picture in Figure 1 (below) shows that two cycles of the sound wave c have the same duration as three cycles of the sound wave g (ratio 3:2). At the point indicated by the arrow the pattern repeats itself. These waves harmonize in such a way that the combination is easy to process for us. On the other hand, the lower picture in Figure 1 (below) shows that the waves of c and g_b (ratio 64:45) do not easily coincide in a periodic pattern: tension remains and needs to be solved for listeners in a combination of waves that harmonize better.

Therefore, a diminished chord is perceived as a chord building up tension, as a transition chord. This is not a matter of taste: c and g are strongly related. The fact that c and g harmonize better than c and g_b follows from physical principles. The combination of frequencies as in Figure 1 (upper) will be preferred to the combination of frequencies as in Figure 1 (lower). The universal cognitive strategy in structuring language and music we identify is prominence of strong elements. Humans focus on strong elements in order to detect structure in a sequence of different sound events.

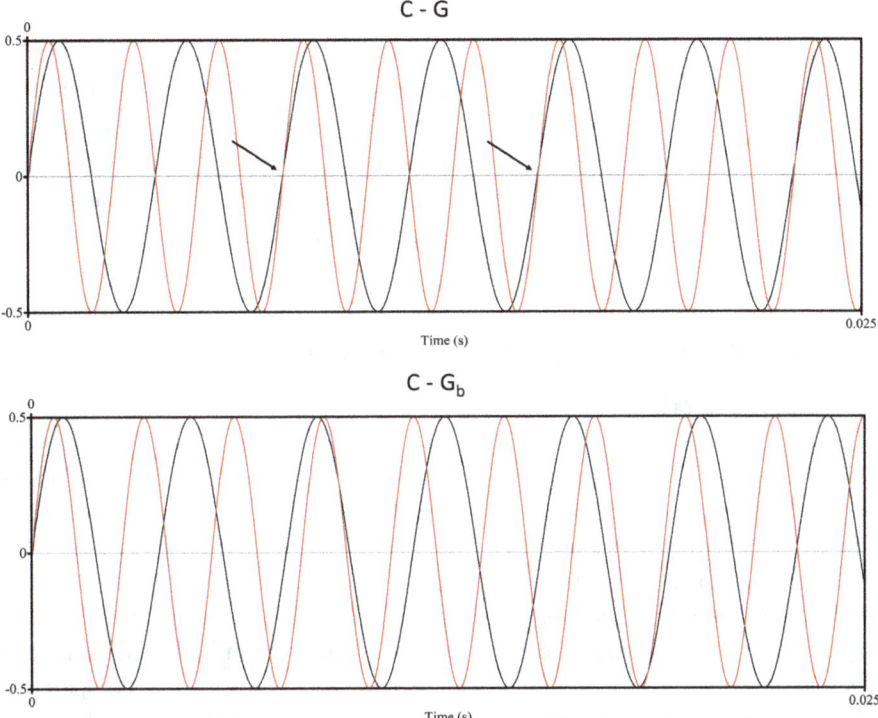

Figure 1: Sound waves of two note combinations.

As a second example of well-formedness conditions, boundary marking effects can be observed in both language and music. Prosodic cues such as intonation contours, pitch accents, stress shifts, pauses and rhythm patterns help listeners to detect the structure, to understand where a domain begins and ends. As we have seen in the previous section, OT makes use of alignment constraints to account for this effect of boundary marking. In music, not all chords are suitable for domain boundary marking. Just as there is a hierarchy in strength of chords, not all chord combinations are equal; a logical sequence of chords is predictable. Usually, the optimal chord is the final chord, a chord which generally is built on the tonic, preceded by a dominant chord. In the key of C, the dominant chord is G. This chord is suitable for a cadence: G7 creates a kind of tension in music that has to be solved by a subsequent tonic chord (see Figure 2). The cadence chord often concludes a phrase or section.

This preference of a harmonically more consonant chord in the chord sequence marking the boundary of a domain is defined as a GTTM-preference rule which chooses the chord which emphasizes the end of a group as a cadence as the

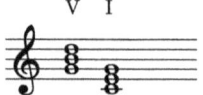

Figure 2: C major perfect authentic cadence (dominant to tonic).

head of the domain. We hypothesize domain marking to be an important universal cognitive strategy in structuring both language and music. This is where our search for universal cognitive well-formedness conditions begins.

3 Typology of universal well-formedness conditions

The typology of universal well-formedness conditions in language is based on the phonological parameters in Dryer and Haspelmath (2013). They include parameters such as "vowel and consonant inventory" (small, average, large), "syllable structure" (simple, moderately complex, complex), "stress system" (unbounded, fixed stress, weight-sensitive, weight-insensitive) "location stress" (left-edge, right-edge), "rhythm type" (trochaic, iambic), "tone system" (no tone, simple or complex tone system). These linguistic parameters, in turn, can be compared to music characteristics such as melodic shape, interval range, rhythm, and more.

The typology of musical universals is based on Alan Lomax's ambitious Cantometrics project (Brown & Jordania, 2011). It includes parameters on pitch (e.g. discrete pitches vs. portamentos, musical scales, intervals), rhythm (e.g. predominance of isometric rhythms, metre types such as duple or triple, use of few durational values), melodic structure and texture (organization into phrases, melodic archetypes: descending, ascending, undulating contours, small or large intervals, harmonizing), form (beginning, middle, end, internal repetition), vocal style (predominance of syllabic singing, use of embellishment: melisma, vibrato, glides), expressive devices (tempo, amplitude, mode/emotion association).[7] Although the

---

[7] Musical universals can be split into five different categories: tautological universals that are true for every culture's music (i.e. music as a system with its physical and sensory properties); conserved universals that are governed by biology and are true for every musical utterance (e.g. every utterance uses discrete pitches); predominant patterns that are true for every musical system but can have outliers in individual utterances (e.g. every scale has seven or fewer pitches per octave); common patterns that appear in many cultures but not all (e.g. singing is syllabic); and, finally, range universals that refer to the diversity in different categories (e.g. a culture with a free rhythm vs. a metric one, monophony or polyphony) (Brown & Jordania, 2011).

Cantometrics project has been criticised heavily with respect to, e.g., song sample, classification scheme and statistical analysis (see Savage, 2018, for a critical review), we agree with Savage that Lomax's map and song coding provides a useful starting point, keeping in mind that no method of cross-cultural comparison will be completely perfect.

Below we show exemplary analyses of how language and music characteristics can be described in a constraint-based OT manner. We can compare intonation patterns in a language, with long or short (descending or undulating) melodies in the culture's music, for example. Using similar constraints/well-formedness conditions makes comparison between music and language easier. The first example concerns variation in tone and segment inventories between cultures. Cultures may differ in the number of categories they display in the language as phonemes or in their music as note differences. In our approach comparing bigger units is done by using similar well-formedness conditions for language and music. It enables us to compare large or small inventories of phonemes in a language with the number of tone categories in the culture's music (3.1). The second example concerns cross-cultural variation in the way tones and segments can be combined to bigger units, such as, chords and syllables, respectively (3.2). The third example concerns the prosodic difference between descending and undulating melodies in music and in intonation patterns in language (3.3) and the fourth example concerns rhythmic variation in language and music (3.4).

3.1 Segment inventories in language and music

> *Music and language are 'particulate' sound systems, in which a set of discrete elements of little inherent meaning (such as tones or phonemes) are combined to form structures with a great diversity of meanings.* (Patel, 2010)

In this section we will introduce similar conditions for the description of language and music in order to make comparison of the two disciplines more fruitful. In language, the biggest contrast in 'particles', speech sounds, is between those produced with "mouth closed", e.g. plosives like /p/, versus those produced with "mouth open", e.g. vowels like /a/. No language lacks the contrast of voiceless plosives and vowels (see WALS, Dryer & Haspelmath, 2013; Jakobson, 1972). While this contrast is necessary, it is not sufficient. Segment inventories of languages need to be more complex in order to be an adequate vehicle of communication.[8]

---

[8] There are indeed various ways to couple enough differences in meaning to sound events. Some languages exhibit complexity in the structure of syllables (e.g. English), whereas others

This complexity can be achieved in different ways, e.g. through recourse to classes of segments between the extreme plosives and vowels in the segment inventory. Dryer & Haspelmath (2013) describe segment inventories in languages ranging from small to large. For example, the number of steps in sonority between voiceless plosives and full vowels varies in the world's languages.[9] Indeed, not every language exhibits a meaningful contrast between the so-called liquid speech sounds /l/ and /r/. In Japanese, [l] and [r] are variants of the same segment category, whereas they are contrastive in Indo-European languages. We can observe that Japanese monolinguals have difficulty perceiving and producing a distinction between those two sounds. For them, 'lake' and 'rake' may seem identical. Put differently, while the contrast between plosives and vowels is universal, the meaningful distinction between different categories of speech sounds is, broadly speaking, language-specific.

Table 1 depicts the acoustic differences of liquids /l,r/ and glides /j,w/ schematically. These differences can be related to their relative second and third formant locus frequencies. Ainsworth & Paliwal (1984) found that in a perceptual-identification experiment sounds having a mid F2 locus frequency were classified as /r/ if they had a relatively low F3 locus frequency and as /l/ if they had a relatively high F3 locus frequency. The sounds were identified as /w/ if they had a low F2 locus frequency and as /j/ if they had a high F2 locus frequency.

In our constraint-based framework, "Parse as category (PARSECAT)" is a correspondence constraint that classifies acoustically available features into a category and is in conflict with markedness constraints such as MaxContrast, which establishes dispersion, and "No category (*CAT)". Since children can learn to perceive any category, they start with constraints against acquired categories (Boersma, 1998).[10] The number of perceptual dimensions increases with the number of categories. With respect to /l/ and /r/, the *CAT constraints are ranked gradually for

---

keep syllables simple and exhibit complexity in e.g. the tone system (e.g. Mandarin Chinese) or in morphological operations such as reduplication (e.g. Hawaiian).
9 Sonority is a challenged concept because there are languages that exhibit counter-examples. Nevertheless, satisfaction of sonority slopes in syllable structures is attested in most languages. This is where the merits of a constraint-based approach are evident. The OT-constraints are soft, which means violable. Satisfying the constraints describes unmarked structures, violating the constraints results in marked structures and counter-examples.
10 However, children are quick to lose this flexibility, as perceptual categories for a particular native language are formed before one year of age and it might be that universal perception of speech sound occurs even before birth (see review article by Chládková & Paillereau, 2020).

Table 1: Typical set of responses obtained from listening to glide/liquid-vowel synthetic stimuli (adapted from Ainsworth & Paliwal, 1984).

3160 Hz	w	w	w	l	l	l	l	j	j	j
↑	w	w	w	l	l	l	l	j	j	j
F3 locus freq.	w	w	w	r	r	r	r	j	j	j
↓	w	w	w	r	r	r	r	j	j	j
1540 Hz	w	w	w	r	r	r	r	j	j	j
	760	Hz		←	F2	locus	freq.	→	2380	Hz

the locus frequency of the third formant given the value of F2 as shown in Table 1: *CAT (F3 1500 Hz – 1700 Hz) >> ... >> *CAT (F3 1500 Hz – 2200 Hz) >> ... >> *CAT (F3 1500 Hz – 3200 Hz). If PARSECAT is dominated by *CAT (F3 1500 Hz – 1700 Hz) and *CAT (F3 1500 Hz – 2200 Hz), [l] and [r] will be allophones as in Japanese. If PARSECAT intervenes between *CAT (F3 1500 Hz – 2200 Hz) and *CAT (F3 1500 Hz – 3200 Hz), /l/ and /r/ are contrastive in the language system as in English. In other words, the position of PARSECAT is determined by the number of categories, i.e. the phonemes that the language displays in this frequency range.

Table 2 shows an OT-table of /r/-categorization. Assume the input sound, the perceived sound segment, has all the acoustic characteristics liquids and glides share and a third formant of 2000Hz, shown in the highest-leftmost cell. The constraints are depicted horizontally in dominating order from left to right and the candidate outputs are depicted vertically. "*" indicates violation of a constraint and "*!" means the violation is fatal, i.e. there is a better candidate given the ranking of constraints.

Table 2: /r/ as phoneme, a contrastive category (English system).

F3 2000 Hz	*CAT (F3 1500 Hz – 1700 Hz)	PARSECAT	*CAT (F3 1500 Hz – 2200 Hz)	*CAT (F3 1500 Hz – 3200 Hz)
/r/1 (F3 1500–1700Hz) and /r/2 (F3 1700–2200Hz)	*!			
☞ /r/ (phoneme) (F3 1500–2200Hz)			*	
[r] (allophone) (F3 1500–3200Hz)		*!		

Table 3: [r] as allophone (in the same category with [l]) (Japanese system).

F3 2000 Hz	*CAT (F3 1500 Hz – 1700 Hz)	*CAT (F3 1500 Hz – 2200 Hz)	PARSECAT	*CAT (F3 1500 Hz – 3200 Hz)
/r/1 and /r/2	*!			
/r/ (phoneme)		*!		
☞ [r] (allophone)				*

In Table 2 the dominating constraint *CAT (F3 1500 Hz – 1700 Hz) is satisfied by both /r/ as a phoneme, which has a range of approximately 1500–2200 Hz, and [r] as an allophone, because it falls within the range of 1500–3200 Hz. The first candidate violates the dominating constraint since the input F3 = 2000 Hz falls outside the range of 1500–1700 Hz. The candidate [r] as an allophone violates PARSECAT because this candidate is not categorized and although the candidate violates *CAT (F3 1500–2200 Hz), it is the optimal candidate given the constraint ranking of English. Reranking the constraints, as in Table 3, shows the dominance hierarchy of a different language system, as in Japanese. Another reranking could establish a system with two r-like sounds as separate categories. The constraints are universal, but the ranking is culture-specific. The number of categories is of course limited by undominated physical constraints that indicate so-called "just noticeable differences" humans can perceive.[11]

Similar to phonemes as building blocks in language, the building blocks in music are notes and tones. A musical universal is the octave, a doubling of frequencies between tones (Brown & Jordania, 2011). Comparable to the way in which languages divide the scale between plosives and full vowels into categories of segments differently, the way in which the octave is divided into different steps is also culture-specific. In Western music the octave is divided into 12 equal-sized pitch intervals, whereas e.g. Javanese Gamelan music divides the octave into 7 pitch intervals (Perlman & Krumhansl, 1996; Patel, 2010). Just as it was difficult for a Japanese native speaker to discriminate between /l/ and /r/ in a Western language, leading to difficulties with semantic processing, it may be difficult for someone who is only familiar with Western music to process a Javanese song, for example. Previous research has shown that adults detect mistuned tones for familiar (major, unequal-step) scales more easily than for unfamiliar

---

[11] For more elaborated functionally-oriented OT-accounts of segment inventories, see Flemming, 1995 and Boersma, 1998.

scales (e.g., Lynch et al., 1990; Trehub et al., 1999). Furthermore, aesthetic *preferences* in music perception are not purely biologically conditioned: McDermott et al. (2016), for example, reported that consonance and dissonance were perceived equally aesthetically pleasing by members of a native Amazonian society compared to individuals living in the city who found consonance more pleasing (even though both groups could discriminate between the sounds themselves).

We assume the octave to be present in all musical cultures. In the key of A, for example, intervals with a ratio 1:2 (440Hz:880Hz) can be observed. MAX-CONTRAST is a constraint that evaluates the harmonic value of intervals with a 1:2 ratio as optimal. The second-best interval has a ratio 2:3 adding E (660Hz; the fifth in the key of A) to the possible intervals. Similar to the linguistic constraints, *CAT constraints are ranked gradually for the fundamental frequency, F0: *CAT (F0 440–441 Hz) >> ... >> *CAT (F0 440Hz – 660 Hz) *CAT (F0 440–880 Hz). If a correspondence constraint PARSECAT intervenes between *CAT (F0 440Hz – 660 Hz) and *CAT (F0 440–880 Hz), only octaves and intervals of fifths exist in the music system.[12] The position of PARSECAT in the gradually ranked, acoustically defined *CAT constraint determines the number of categories in the segment inventory, similar to linguistic categories as depicted in Tables 2 and 3.

Once the number of segments in the octave is defined this way, different musical scales can be described by different positions of PARSECAT within a gradually ranked series of *CAT constraints for semitone steps. For example, given a 12 steps division of the octave, (1a) shows the chromatic scale (see notation in Figure 3), with PARSECAT dominating all *CAT constraints. (1b) shows the constraint ranking for a pentatonic scale (see notation in Figure 4) with steps of two semitones within the octave.

Figure 3: Ascending chromatic scale, starting on C.

---

12 As in language systems, the number of categories in music is of course also limited by undominated physical constraints that indicate the "just noticeable differences" humans can perceive in order to identify frequency differences as belonging to different categories.

Figure 4: Minor pentatonic scale, starting on A.

The constraint ranking in (1) is comparable to the constraint ranking in the top row of Tables 2 and 3. The different positions of PARSECAT in (1a) and (1b) can be compared to the different positions of PARSECAT in Tables 2 and 3. The different positions describe different inventories of phonemes in language and different tone steps within an octave in music.

(1)   a. Chromatic scale in OT:
      PARSECAT >> *CAT 1 semitone >> * CAT 2 semitones, etc.
  b. Pentatonic scale in OT (simplified):
      *CAT 1 semitone >> PARSECAT >> *CAT 2 semitones, etc.

3.2 Syllables and chords

Linguistic segments, phonemes, are combined in units called syllables and musical particles, notes, can be combined in units called chords. In (2) some exemplary OT-markedness constraints for syllable structure are shown (Prince & Smolensky, 1993; Archangeli, 1997).

(2)   Markedness constraints on syllable structure
        ONSET: syllables begin with a consonant
        *CODA: syllables end with a vowel
        *COMPLEX: syllables have at most one consonant at an edge
        PEAK: syllables have one vowel as nucleus

These markedness constraints ensure simple structures. If all constraints are satisfied, the result will be a syllable that consists of a consonant followed by a vowel (CV), the optimal syllable that is attested in all languages. These markedness constraints interact with correspondence constraints that warrant diversity in structure and thereby in meaning. Different rankings of the same set of constraints describe the possible variations attested in the world's languages. For example, Hawaiian does not allow consonant clusters or codas, as exemplified in words such as *kanaka* "man" and *wahine* "woman". In other words, *COMPLEX and *CODA are high-ranked constraints in that language. In English, *COMPLEX and *CODA are low-ranked as exemplified in words such as *sprint* with an initial complex CCC-cluster and a CC-coda. The differences between the systems can be seen in loan words from English in Hawaiian, such as *weleweka* "velvet" which is adapted to the Hawaiian system satisfying *COMPLEX and *CODA by inserting vowels.

Archangeli (1997) nicely shows that languages solve conflicts between these constraints after morphological operations differently. In Yawelmani, syllables cannot be more complex than CVC (consonant-vowel-consonant). Therefore, the morphologically complex form *logwen* (*logw + en*) "will pulverize" is not problematic: *log.wen* (with the dot indicating the syllable boundary), but *logw + hin* "pulverized" is problematic. In Yawelmani the attested word is *lo.giw.hin*, indicating that the correspondence constraint DEP-IO, "no insertion", is violated in order to satisfy the dominant markedness constraint *COMPLEX, "no clusters of consonants within a syllable". In Spanish, a similar conflict is solved differently. In Spanish *absorber* is unproblematic since it can be syllabified as *ab.sor.ber*. However, suffixation with *to* instead of *er* leads to a violation of the dominant syllable constraint *COMPLEX within a syllable: neither **ab.sorb.to* nor *ab.sor.bto* satisfies *COMPLEX. Spanish solves the conflict by means of violation of the correspondence constraint MAX-IO, "no deletion". The attested form is *ab.sor.to* in which the root ends with the single consonant /r/. In English, the combination *limp + ness* results in *limp.ness*, indicating that the markedness constraint *COMPLEX, which is so dominant in Yawelmani and Spanish, is violable and thus less important in the ranking of universal constraints for this language. In other words, the universal constraints can be ranked differently in different languages constituting variability between language systems.

Complexity in musical chords can be described in a similar way. The notes of a musical system can be combined horizontally, as in a melody, or vertically as in chords or harmony. Just like linguistic differences in syllable structure, musical cultures may differ in the complexity of chords and chord sequences that is used in the music. The notes in triads harmonize better than in a 7th chord, which is more harmonic than e.g. sus4 or diminished chords. This can be described as a parse note combination correspondence constraint, which interacts with an intervening set of ordered *Combi markedness constraints on parsing note combinations. The ordering of these constraints on note combinations is based on (Krumhansl, 1979), who describes relatedness between tones as obtained from a perception task using multidimensional scaling. The closer the perceived relatedness, the closer the tones are in the graph in Figure 5. The possible combinations of tones are also dependent of the tone inventory, of course. In other words, the inventory constraints mentioned in section 3.1 dominate the constraints introduced in this section.

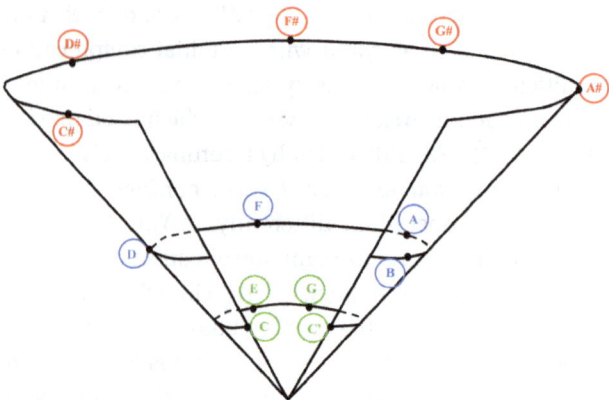

Figure 5: Tone distances in the key of C (adapted from Krumhansl, 1979).

The markedness constraint *Combi in (3) is defined as restrictions on combinations of frequencies in an octave of 12 equal-sized pitch intervals. *Combi is a gradually violable constraint in a similar way sonority constraints in language are. Therefore, *Combi is split up into a set of restrictions on combinations of fundamental frequency ratios. For example, *Combi 2:1 means no combination of notes that form an octave are allowed, e.g. 440 Hz (A_4) plus 220 Hz (A_3). The order of ratios in (3) is strict. *Combi 16:15 (diminished 2nd) is always higher ranked than *Combi 3:2 (perfect 5th), just as /r/ is always less sonorous than /a/ in language. The order in (3) reflects the observation by Pythagoras: ratios of lower simple numbers are more consonant than those that are higher.[13] The chords in question are depicted in Figure 6.

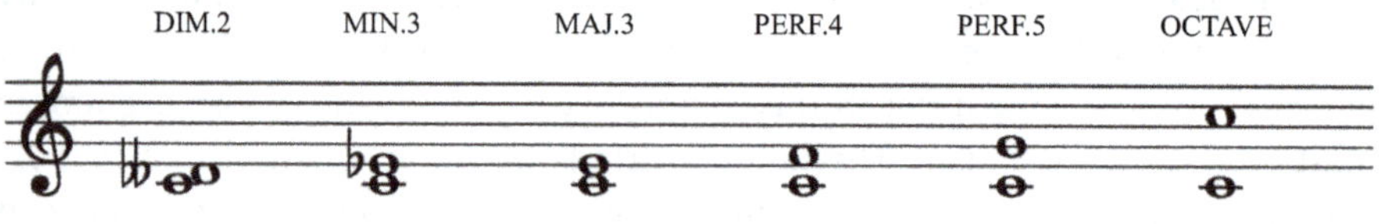

Figure 6: Chords mentioned in example (3), in C major.

---

[13] There is no general consensus on the distinction between consonance and dissonance in the history of music. Unisons, octaves, perfect fifths and perfect fourths are often regarded as perfect consonances; major and minor thirds as examples of imperfect consonances and diminished seconds and diminished fifths as examples of dissonance, but this categorisation varies in time. The order in (3) depicts a gradual change from dissonance to consonance, similar to the gradual change in sonority between segments in language.

(3) Combinations of notes
*Combi 16:15 (dim. 2nd) >> . . . >> *Combi 6:5 (min. 3rd) >> *Combi 5:4 (maj. 3rd) >> *Combi 4:3 (perfect 4th) >> *Comb 3:2 (perfect 5th) >> *Combi 2:1 (octave)

The position of the correspondence constraint PARSE COMBI MAX(imally) determines the complexity of harmonic structures that appear in the music. For example, if PARSE COMBI MAX intervenes between *Combi 2:1, e.g. C8 – C, and *Combi 3:2, e.g. G – C, only octaves are allowed in the music culture, characterized in Brown and Jordania (2011) as a lack of polyphony. The position of PARSE COMBI MAX is culture-specific and determines whether or not certain note combinations are used. The higher the ranking of an intervening PARSE COMBI MAX in the sequence in (3), the more complex harmony can be observed in the music culture. Low-ranked PARSE COMBI MAX describes a music culture of simple harmonic structures which might of course be accompanied by more complex melodies or rhythms, resembling a language with simple syllable structure which might be characterized by a more complex tone system.

In Table 4, PARSE COMBI MAX is ranked between *Combi 6:5 and *Combi 5:4, which means that the culture only allows for monophony, octave combinations, power chords, e.g. C-G combinations, perfect fourths and major triads. The output candidate monophony shows the most violations of PARSE COMBI MAX, given the possible output candidates presented here, whereas a diminished 2nd shows the least violations, because monophony rules out all possible combinations and a diminished 2nd, being the least harmonic combination with the tonic within an octave, allows for all note combinations in Table 4.

On the other hand, Table 5 depicts a more complex system in which PARSE COMBI MAX is promoted one step, which reflects a system with minor and major chords, but e.g. no diminished second. Notice that this account implies that a culture that allows for minor and major chords also allows power chords, perfect fourths and octave combinations, similar to language: if a language system allows for consonant clusters in syllables, it also allows for lesser complex CV-combinations.

The relation between chords as in chord progressions can be described in a similar way. The tonic I (e.g. C) is the most central chord, followed by the dominant V (G) and the subdominant IV (F). Krumhansl et al. (1982) investigated perceived relatedness between chords, as shown in Figure 7. Indeed, chords V and IV are most closely related to chord I, the tonic.

Table 4: Chord complexity (simplified) (tableau of a simple harmonic system).

Input: All possible fundamental frequency combinations	*Combi 16:15	...	*Combi 6:5	PARSE COMBI MAX	*Combi 5:4	*Combi 4:3	*Combi 3:2	*Combi 2:1
Monophony				***!***				
≤Octave				***!**				*
≤Power Chord				***!*			*	*
≤Perfect Fourth				***!		*	*	*
☞≤Triad/Major 3rd				**	*	*	*	*
≤Minor 3rd			*!	*	*	*	*	*
...								
≤Diminished 2nd	*!		*		*	*	*	*

Table 5: Chord complexity (simplified) (tableau of a slightly more complex harmonic system).

Input: All possible fundamental frequency combinations	*Combi 16:15	...	PARSE COMBI MAX	*Combi 6:5	*Combi 5:4	*Combi 4:3	*Combi 3:2	*Combi 2:1
Monophony			**!****					
≤Octave			**!***					*
≤Power Chord			**!**				*	*
≤Perfect Fourth			**!			*	*	*
≤Triad/Major 3rd			**!		*	*	*	*
☞≤Minor 3rd			*	*	*	*	*	*
...								
≤Diminished 2nd	*!			*	*	*	*	*

If a music culture only makes use of the three most related chords I, V and IV (tonic, dominant, subdominant), it can be described as in (4), in which the high ranked restrictions on combinations define the less related chord combinations and the low-ranked restrictions on combinations the closest relatedness between chords.

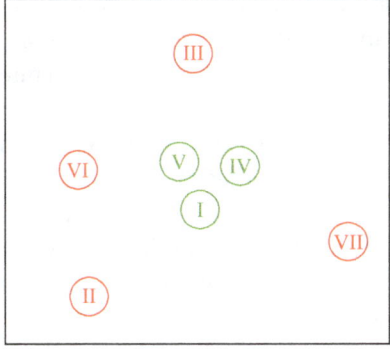

Figure 7: Psychological relatedness of different chords (adapted from Krumhansl et al., 1982).

(4) Combinations of chords (simplified). Ranking for a culture in which the music isn't more complex than tonic dominant subdominant harmonically, as in most blues and country music
*Combi I-II >> *Combi<I-III >> PARSE COMBI >> *Combi<I-IV >> *Combi< I-V >> *Combi

Again, low-ranked PARSE COMBI describes a music culture of simple chord progressions which might be accompanied by more complex melodies or rhythms. Our research approach is interested in these kinds of correlations. The more markedness (*COMBI) constraints are dominated by the correspondence PARSE COMBI constraint, the more complex chord progressions can be found in the music of a certain culture, just like the more linguistic markedness constraints, such as *COMPLEX, are dominated by linguistic correspondence constraints, such as MAX-IO, the more complex syllables can be attested in the language of the culture. Therefore, this constraint-based approach makes comparison of the music and language within a certain culture or between cultures possible in a straight-forward way.

3.3 Intonation/melody

In section 2, we mentioned "prominence of strong elements" and "domain marking" as important well-formedness conditions in structuring music and language. The latter becomes especially prominent in the constraint-based account of intonation and melody patterns. Prosodic phrasing is described in (Selkirk, 1995;

2000; Truckenbrodt, 1999; Eisenberg, 1991; Antilla & Bodomo, 1996; Lacy, 2002; Zhang, 2004; Ghamdi, 2006; and Gussenhoven, 2004), among others. In these approaches, edges of prosodic domains need to be aligned with morpho-syntactic constituents, new information needs to be associated with a prosodic constituent, and the length of the prosodic domains is variable. All these characteristics of prosodic constituents can be captured in OT by the interaction of prosodic structure constraints.

For our comparison of intonation patterns in language and melody in music, alignment constraints are in conflict with a so-called WRAP-constraint. Alignment constraints function as phrase boundary markers, they require that the edge of a phrase coincides with a tone. For example, satisfying ALIGN-L (High tone) and ALIGN-R (Low tone) constitutes a descending pattern for each intonation phrase (IP). WRAP requires that a minor phrase, e.g. a preposition phrase is contained in a single major phrase, e.g. an intonation phrase (IP), as illustrated in (5) below.

In (5), two possible intonation patterns of the sentence *Deep Purple stole the melody from Bombay's calling* are depicted. We recorded, respectively, a descending and an undulating intonation pattern of the same sentence. If WRAP dominates ALIGN, all phonological phrases, e.g. the verbal phrase (VP), the noun phrase (NP) and the preposition phrase (PP) in (5a) are incorporated in one IP, creating a descending pattern. If, on the other hand, ALIGN dominates WRAP, all phrases constitute their own IP (5b), creating an undulating intonation pattern. The different, simplified intonation patterns (only H- and L-marks for tone) are also depicted visually in Figures 8 and 9.

(5) Different intonation patterns based on the position of an Alignment constraint
[[Deep Purple]$_{NP}$ [[stole]$_{V,\text{ in focus}}$ [the melody]$_{NP}$ [from Bombay's calling]$_{PP}$]$_{VP}$]$_S$
a. WRAP Phrase >> ALIGN-R:
(Deep Purple stole the melody from Bombay's calling)$_{IP}$
b. ALIGN-R >> WRAP Phrase
(Deep Purple)$_{IP}$ (stole)$_{IP}$ (the melody)$_{IP}$ (from Bombay's calling)$_{IP}$

As in language, in music alignment constraints parse boundary tones that mark the beginning and end of musical phrases and as in language various melodic patterns can be obtained by ranking the association constraints: WRAP >> ALIGN describes descending melodies and ALIGN >> WRAP describes undulating melodies. Of course, there is much variation in the shape, range and length of melodies in each culture, but the Global Jukebox (Wood & Arèvalo, 2018) – an online repository of music from all over the world based on Alan Lomax's field recordings, collected for his Cantometrics project (Lomax, 1976) – describes the dominating

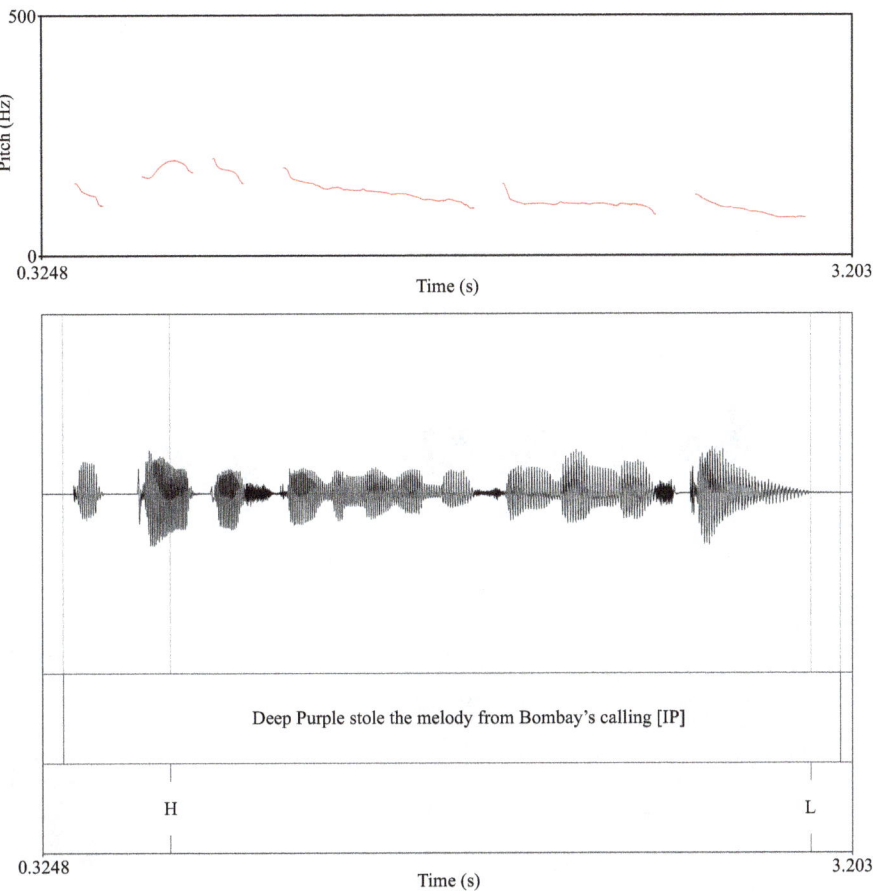

Figure 8: Descending intonation pattern (based on the ranking in 5a).

patterns in each culture as characteristic for its music, e.g. undulating short melodies are dominant in African Shilha music (cf. the ranking in 5b), whereas Southern American Kalina music is characterized by predominance of descending medium length melody lines (cf. the ranking in 5a).

3.4 Linguistic and musical rhythm

As a final example of our constraint-based approach, we consider variation in rhythm types. Over again, we introduce similar conditions for the description of language and music in order to make comparison of the two disciplines possible.

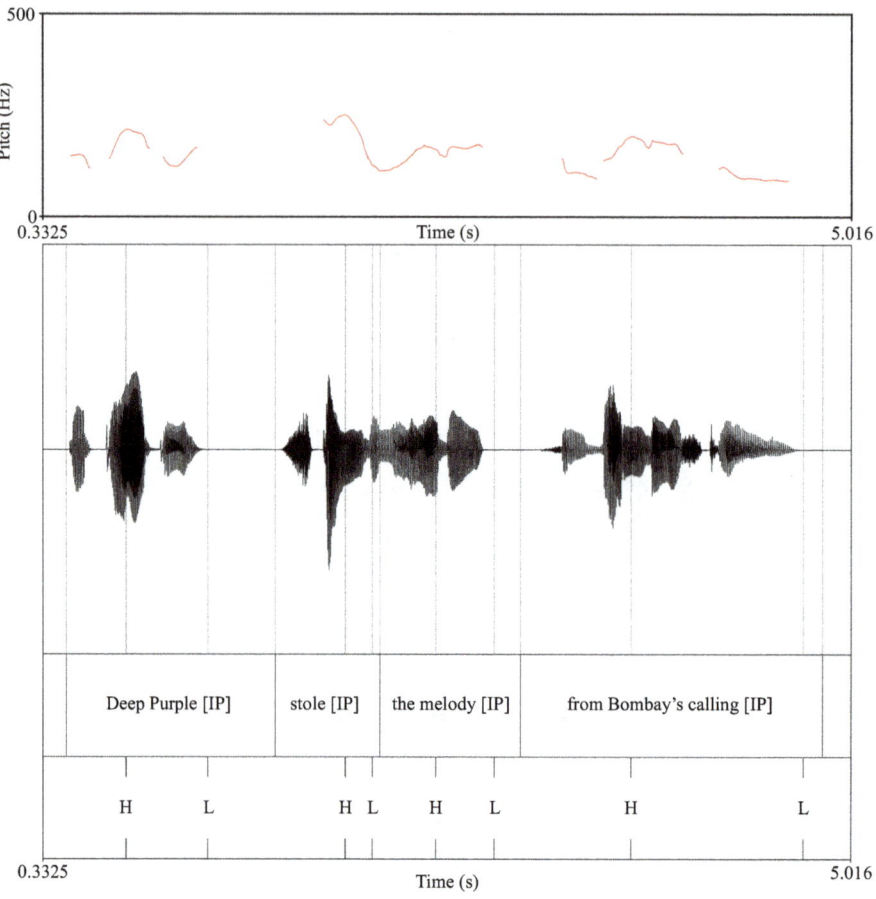

Figure 9: Undulating intonation pattern (based on the ranking in 5b).

This means that we define our music constraints similar to already established constraints in linguistics. In (6) some exemplary linguistic constraints on rhythm types are shown (Hayes, 1984; Prince & Smolensky, 1993; McCarthy & Prince, 1993; Nouveau, 1994; Gilbers & Jansen, 1996).

(6)   Some constraints on linguistic rhythm structure
         PARSE-σ: syllables are footed
         ALIGN-L/ALIGN-R: The left/right edge of every foot is aligned with the left/right edge of a Prosodic Word (PrWd) (it forces all feet to be adjacent at an edge)
         PEAK PROMINENCE: the heaviest syllable in a PrWd has main stress

FOOT BINARITY (FtBIN): a foot consists of two syllables
RHYTHM TYPE = TROCHAIC/IAMBIC: the first/last syllable in a foot is stressed

Again, different rankings of the universal constraints in (6) describe culture-specific variation in rhythmic structures. For example, if PARSE-σ dominates ALIGN the optimal pattern will be a bounded stress system as in stress-timed languages, such as English: (σ σ)(σ σ). If, on the other hand, ALIGN dominates PARSE-σ, unbounded systems are preferred as in syllable-timed languages such as French: (σ σ σ σ). If ALIGN-L dominates PARSE-σ the pattern of leftmost systems such as Khalkha Mongolian is optimal, if ALIGN-R is dominant, the rightmost system of e.g. Yawelmani is optimal (McCarthy & Prince, 1993; Prince & Smolensky, 1993). Furthermore, the interaction of ALIGN and PEAK PROMINENCE enables us to describe the difference between fixed stress systems as in Yawelmani (ALIGN-R dominates PEAK PROMINENCE) and weight-sensitive systems as in Hindi (PEAK PROMINENCE dominates ALIGN-R).

Possibly the most striking characteristic of rhythm is alternation, formulated in linguistics as the Obligatory Contour Principle (OCP; Leben, 1973), which prohibits two adjacent unstressed syllables (*LAPSE) or two adjacent stressed syllables (*CLASH) in (7). If these constraints are dominant, alternating rhythm patterns of strong (s) and weak (w) syllables occur: (s w)(s w)(s w). (Hayes, 1984) introduces eurithmicity rules for optimally alternating patterns: the disyllabic rule ensures (s w)-patterns and the quadrisyllabic rule (S w)(s w)-patterns in which S is the head of a larger domain. The former is captured in OT with the combination of FtBIN and RHYTHM TYPE = TROCHAIC, the latter is reformulated here as a constraint that requires alternation of strong and weak feet. ALIGN forces all feet to be adjacent at the left or right edge.

(7) OCP-markedness constraints on linguistic rhythm structure
     ALTERNATE (OBLIGATORY CONTOUR PRINCIPLE) (OCP)
     Examples: *LAPSE: two adjacent weak syllables are forbidden
        *CLASH: two adjacent stressed syllables are forbidden
        *FtFt: feet must not be adjacent
        QUADRI-SYLLABIC constraint: alternate strong and weak feet:
        (S-w) (s-w)

These constraints enable us to describe rather complex systems as well. In a ternary rhythm system, as in Estonian, *FtFt dominates ALIGN-L and *LAPSE is ranked low in the hierarchy of constraints allowing for (s w) w (s w) w-patterns (Kager, 1994).

Musical preferences on rhythmic structure can be formulated as OT-like well-formedness conditions as well, including alignment constraints, OCP-constraints. In order to make comparison with language easier, we introduce the musical domain "unit" as a combination of two beats, analogous to two syllables united into a linguistic foot.

(8) Some similar constraints on musical rhythm structure
 PARSE-BEAT: every beat is united
 UNIT BINARITY (UnitBIN): a unit consists of two beats
 RHYTHM TYPE = TROCHAIC: the first beat in a unit is stressed
 PARSE-UNIT (PARSE-UNIT): every input unit is parsed equally strong in a phrase
 ALIGN-L: The left edge of every unit is aligned with the left edge of a phrase
 ALTERNATE (OBLIGATORY CONTOUR PRINCIPLE) (OCP)
 Examples: *LAPSE: two adjacent weak beats are forbidden
  *CLASH: two adjacent stressed beats are forbidden
  *UnitUnit: units must not be adjacent
  QUADRI-BEAT: alternate strong and weak units: (S-w) (s-w)

The constraints in (8) enable us to describe musical metre. Just like FtBIN in language, UnitBIN is an undominated constraint with respect to the description of the most common metre patterns, such as 3/4 and 4/4. Just as in the ternary rhythm patterns in Estonian, musical odd metres can be described by ranking *UnitUnit above ALIGN-L. Dominant ALIGN-L, on the other hand, is satisfied in even metres. The correspondence constraint PARSE-UNIT demands all feet to be equally strong, whereas the markedness constraint QUADRI-BEAT requires alternation between strong and weak feet. If PARSE-UNIT dominates QUADRI-beat, 2/4 will be optimal. If QUADRI-beat dominates PARSE-UNIT, 4/4 will be optimal. Some examples of isometric, regular rhythm types are given in (9). The ternary pattern in (9) consist of binary feet followed by a stray beat: (s w) w (s w) w, etc. With respect to language prosody, Selkirk (1984) describes these combinations as superfeet.

(9) Typology of metre based on re-ranking constraints
 3/4: *UnitUnit >> Align-L >> PARSE-UNIT >> QUADRI-beat
 2/4: Align-L >> * UnitUnit >> PARSE-UNIT >> QUADRI-beat
 4/4: Align-L >> * UnitUnit >> QUADRI-beat >> PARSE-UNIT

If the constraints in (9) are low-ranked, rhythmic stability may be overruled by e.g. the influence of dominant melodic or harmonic conditions. If, for example, in a certain music culture parsing long notes of unequal length in a melody is more important than the rhythm constraints, the rhythm might become irregular or free.

Keep in mind that we might have to add a caveat to the description of rhythm in this section. Despite the attempt to speak of universal language and music characteristics, the focus is Western-centric, based on distances between beats. In other music cultures, e.g. in Indian Raga music, the idea of what rhythm is might be different. With "Western ears" we might fail to perceive a rhythm in the sequence of tones as a repetitive pattern of beats, but with "Eastern ears" the differences in note density in the melody structure may possibly be perceived as the rhythm of the song. For example, a sequence of predominant quarter notes in the melody followed by predominant sixteenth notes followed by predominant quarter notes again can be felt as a rhythmic flow without isochronic accented events.

In this section, we provided examples of universal cognitive strategies formulated as well-formedness conditions that can be ranked for importance culture-specifically. Identification of these conditions enables us to describe the language and music of different cultures and their mutual relation. We now turn to broader implications of the constraints and approaches we discussed in section 3.

4 Conclusion and perspective

The research approach presented in this chapter concerns the cognitive mechanisms underlying the human capacities to learn and structure language and music (universal well-formedness conditions) and the possible variations in languages and music cultures (the ranking for importance of these conditions). The first aim of the framework we suggest is to find out what kind of musical features can be matched with linguistic ones. The well-formedness conditions identified in this chapter will make it possible to relate typologically different languages to their matching musical cultures. This part of the research is aided in its aim by two freely available databases. For language, Dryer & Haspelmath (2013) present the World Atlas of Language Structures, including linguistic analyses of the sound systems of more than two thousand languages and language varieties, belonging to different language families. For music, ethnomusicologist Alan Lomax's field recordings, collected for his Cantometrics project (discussed above), served as the basis for the Global Jukebox (Wood & Arèvalo, 2018), a survey of the world's music styles including structural analyses. Both databases are meant to show similarities and differences between cultures with respect to, on the one hand, the inventories of distinctive sound systems in both music and language, and, on the other hand, temporal ordering in both disciplines for harmony, melody and rhythm, as discussed in the previous section.

In our approach, similar well-formedness conditions for music and language enable us to answer questions such as: are the rhythm patterns in the music of a certain culture related to the rhythm type of its language? Does the complexity in harmonic patterns in music relate to the complexity in syllable structure in language? And what are the relevant correlates? Indeed, the second aim of our approach is the culture-specific ranking of the universal conditions on rhythm, melody, harmony and delivery. Lerdahl & Jackendoff (1983) show that in Western tonal music harmonically optimal conditions dominate metrical ones, i.e., harmony is more important than rhythm. Our first analysis of the data gives birth to the hypothesis that rhythmic conditions are more important in African music and language, whereas in Asian music and language melodic conditions predominate. For example, a preliminary analysis of Vietnamese music in South-East Asia in the Global Jukebox reveals that it is predominantly characterized as monophonic, the overall rhythm of the music is one-beat rhythm (meaning all notes are of the same length) or free rhythm, the melodic shape is arched or undulating, the phrases are long and the intervals between tones are narrow. The tempo of the music is quite slow or very slow and the singing is characterized by much melisma, maximal glissando, and extreme embellishment in general. Interestingly, the languages of the related cultures exhibit a complex tone system (Dryer & Haspelmath, 2013). Hausa music in West Africa, on the other hand, is predominantly characterized as polyphonic and very rhythmic. A common melodic shape is descending and very short phrases predominate. The intervals are wide or very wide and the tempo of the music is fast or very fast. The singing shows little or no embellishment nor glissando. We can see, then, that African music shows quite the opposite characteristics to Asian music. Similarly, if we compare African languages to Asian languages, African languages in general have a simple tone system, and Asian languages have a complex tone system. We intend to study patterns of this kind in the language and music families within the context of one general constraint-based framework for analysing linguistic and musical structure.

Liberman (1975) already assumed every form of temporally ordered behaviour to be structured the same way. The findings from our investigations will reveal 1) to what extent language and music are structurally similar, and 2) whether the world's musical typologies and the corresponding regions' linguistic typologies are related to each other on a structural level. If it is found that the rankings of universal well-formedness conditions in both the language and the music of a particular culture are related, this research will provide fundamental insight into the cognitive mechanisms that underlie the way people learn and structure language and music (i.e. universal well-formedness conditions) and provide basic insight into the possible variation in language and music of different cultures (i.e. the ranking of these conditions).

Appendix: OT-Constraints used in this chapter

A. Markedness constraints (all these constraints ensure simple forms)
*COMPLEX: consonant clusters in syllables are forbidden
*Coda: a coda segment in a syllable is forbidden
ONS: every syllable begins with a consonant
Hnuc: the most sonorant segment is chosen as nucleus of a syllable
Hons/Hmar: the least sonorant segment is chosen syllable-initially
MaxContrast: establishes dispersion in a segment inventory
*CAT (no category)/*Combi, etc: prohibits new categories in the inventory, combinations of chords or notes in a chord, etc. that make inventories, output structures or combinations of events more complex
WRAP (Phrase) combines different categories into one. For example, it requires that a minor phrase, e.g. a preposition phrase is contained in a single major phrase, e.g. an intonation phrase (IP)
PEAK PROMINENCE: the heaviest syllable in a PrWd has main stress
FOOT BINARITY (FtBIN): a foot consists of two syllables
UNIT BINARITY (UnitBIN): a unit consists of two beats (musical equivalent of FtBIN)
ALTERNATE (OBLIGATORY CONTOUR PRINCIPLE) (OCP), examples:
RHYTHM TYPE = TROCHAIC/IAMBIC: the first/last syllable in a foot is stressed
RHYTHM TYPE = TROCHAIC: the first beat in a unit is stressed (musical equivalent)
*LAPSE: two adjacent weak syllables are forbidden
*LAPSE: two adjacent weak beats are forbidden (musical equivalent)
*CLASH: two adjacent stressed syllables are forbidden
*CLASH: two adjacent stressed beats are forbidden (musical equivalent)
*FtFt: feet must not be adjacent
*UnitUnit: units must not be adjacent (musical equivalent of *FtFt)
QUADRI-SYLLABIC constraint: alternate strong and weak feet: (S-w) (s-w)
QUADRI-BEAT: alternate strong and weak units: (S-w) (s-w) (musical equivalent)

B. Correspondence/Faithfulness constraints (ensure diversity by linking segments on different strings, e.g. a segment in the underlying form and the realized form)

MAX-IO: every (underlying) input segment/feature has a correspondent in the output (no deletion) (cf. PARSE in earlier OT-literature: prohibits underparsing)

DEP-IO: every (realized) output segment/feature has a correspondent in the input (no insertion/epenthesis) (cf. FILL in earlier OT-literature: prohibits overparsing)

PARSECAT (Parse as category): classifies acoustically available features into a phoneme category

PARSE COMBI MAX(imally): determines the complexity of harmonic structures that appear in the music

PARSE-σ: all syllables are footed in the prosodic structure

PARSE-BEAT: every beat is united (musical equivalent of PARSE- σ)

PARSE-UNIT: every input unit is parsed equally strong in a phrase

C. Alignment constraints (function as domain boundary markers, they require e.g. that the edge of a phrase coincides with a high or low tone).

ALIGN-L (High tone): aligns the left boundary of the domain with a H-tone

ALIGN-R (Low tone): aligns the right boundary of the domain with a L-tone

ALIGN-L/ALIGN-R: the left/right edge of every foot is aligned with the left/right edge of a Prosodic Word (PrWd) (it forces all feet to be adjacent at an edge of the directly higher prosodic domain)

ALIGN-L: The left edge of every unit is aligned with the left edge of a phrase (musical equivalent)

References

Ainsworth, William A. & Kuldip K. Paliwal. 1984. Correlation between the production and perception of the English glides /w, r, l, j/. *Journal of Phonetics* 12(3). 237–243.

Antilla, Arto & Adams Bodomo. 1996. Stress and tone in Dagaare. Ms. Stanford University and Norwegian University of Science and Technology.

Archangeli, Diana. 1997. *Optimality Theory: An introduction to linguistics*. Oxford: Blackwell.

Asano, Rie & Cedric Boeckx. 2015. Syntax in language and music: What is the right level of comparison? *Frontiers in Psychology* 6. 942.

Ball, Philip. 2010. *The music instinct: How music works and why we can't do without It*. Oxford: Oxford University Press.

Boersma, Paul. 1998. Functional phonology: Formalizing the interaction between articulatory and perceptual drives. [Doctoral Dissertation]: University of Amsterdam.

Brown, Steven & Joseph Jordania. 2011. Universals in the world's musics. *Psychology of Music* 41(2). 229–248.
Chládková, Katerina & Nikola Paillereau. 2020. The what and when of universal perception: A review of early speech sound acquisition. *Language Learning: A Journal of Research in Language Studies* 70(4). 1136–1182.
Daniele, Joseph R. & Aniruddh D. Patel. The interplay of linguistic and historical influences on musical rhythm in different cultures. Proceedings of the 8th International Conference on Music Perception and Cognition; 2004; Sydney, Australia. Causal Productions. p 759–762.
Dryer, Matthew S. & Martin Haspelmath. 2013. The world atlas of language structures online. Leipzig: Max Planck Institute for Evolutionary Anthropology.
Eisenberg, Peter. 1991. Syllabische Struktur und Wortakzent: Prinzipien der Prosodik deutscher Wörter. *Zeitschrift für Sprachwissenschaft* 10(1). 37–64.
Fenk-Oczlon, Gertraud & August Fenk. 2009. Some parallels between language and music from a cognitive and evolutionary perspective. *Musicae Scientiae* 13(2). 201–226.
Flemming, Edward S. 1995. Auditory representations in phonology [Doctoral Dissertation]: UCLA.
Ghamdi, Ahmed Al. 2006. A preliminary analysis of the intonation of Riyadh Saudi Arabic. Rutgers Optimality Archive. [#812 – 0306].
Gilbers, Dicky & Helen de Hoop. 1998. Conflicting constraints: An introduction to Optimality Theory. *Lingua* 104(1–2). 1–12.
Gilbers, Dicky & Wouter Jansen. 1996. Klemtoon en ritme in Optimality Theory, deel 1: Hoofd-, neven-, samenstellings- en woordgroepsklemtoon in het Nederlands. *Tabu* 26. 53–101.
Gilbers, Dicky & Maartje Schreuder. 2000. Taal en muziek in Optimaliteitstheorie. *Tabu* 1–2. 1–27.
Gilbers, Dicky & Maartje Schreuder. 2002. Language and music in Optimality Theory. Rutgers Optimality Archive [#571–0103].
Gilbers, Steven, Nienke Hoeksema, Kees de Bot & Wander Lowie. 2020. Regional variation in West and East Coast African-American English prosody and rap flows. *Language and Speech* 63(4). 713–745.
Gussenhoven, Carlos. 2004. *The phonology of tone and intonation.* Cambridge: Cambridge University Press.
Hayes, Bruce. 1984. The phonology of rhythm in English. *Linguistic Inquiry* 15(1). 33–74.
Hayes, Bruce. 1995. *Metrical stress theory: Principles and case studies.* Chicago, IL: The University of Chicago Press.
Jackendoff, Ray. 2009. Parallels and nonparallels between language and music. *Music Perception* 26(3). 195–204.
Jakobson, Roman. 1972. Why 'mama' and 'papa'? In: Bertil Malmberg, editor. *Readings in modern linguistics*, 313–320. The Hague: De Gruyter.
Jekiel, Mateusz. 2015. Comparing rhythm in speech and music: The case of English and Polish. *Yearbook of the Poznan Linguistic Meeting* 1. 55–71.
Kager, René. 1994. Ternary rhythm in alignment theory. Utrecht University.
Krumhansl, Carol L. 1979. The psychological representation of musical pitch in a tonal context. *Cognitive Psychology* 11(3). 346–374.
Krumhansl, Carol L., Jamshed J. Bharucha & Edward J. Kessler. 1982. Perceived harmonic structure of chords in three related musical keys. *Journal of Experimental Psychology: Human Perception and Performance* 8(1). 24–36.

Lacy, Paul de. 2002. The interaction of tone and stress in optimality theory. *Phonology* 19(1). 1–32.
Leben, William R. 1973. Suprasegmental phonology [Doctoral Dissertation]. Cambridge, MA.
Lerdahl, Fred & Ray Jackendoff. 1983. *A generative theory of tonal music*. Cambridge, MA: The MIT Press.
Liberman, Mark. 1975. *The intonational system of English*. New York: Garland Publishing Inc.
Lomax, Alan. 1976. Cantometrics: An approach to the anthropology of music [Doctoral Dissertation]. Berkeley: University of California Extension Media Center.
Lynch, Michael P., Rebecca E. Eilers, D. Kimbrough Oller & Richard C. Urbano. 1990. Innateness, experience, and music perception. *Psychological Science* 1(4). 272–276.
McCarthy, John J. & Alan S. Prince. 1993. *Prosodic Morphology I: Constraint interaction and satisfaction*. New Brunswick, NW: Rutgers University Center for Cognitive Science.
McDermott, Josh H., Alan F. Schultz, Eduardo A. Undurraga & Ricardo A. Godoy. 2016. Indifference to dissonance in native Amazonians reveals cultural variation in music perception. *Nature* 535. 547–550.
McGowan, Rebecca W. & Andrea Levitt. 2011. A comparison of rhythm in English dialects and music. *Music Perception* 28(3). 307–314.
Nouveau, Dominique. 1994. Language acquisition, metrical theory, and optimality: A study of Dutch word stress [Doctoral Dissertation]: Rijksuniversiteit Utrecht.
Passy, Paul. 1891. *Étude sur les changements phonétiques et leurs caractères généraux*. Paris: Librairie Firmin – Didot.
Patel, Aniruddh D. 2010. *Music, language, and the brain*. Oxford: Oxford University Press.
Patel, Aniruddh D. & Joseph R. Daniele. 2003. An empirical comparison of rhythm in language and music. *Cognition* 87. B35–B45.
Perlman, Marc & Carol L. Krumhansl. 1996. An experimental study of internal interval standards in Javanese and Western musicians. *Music Perception* 14. 95–116.
Prince, Alan S. & Paul Smolensky. 1993. *Optimality Theory. Constraint interaction in Generative Grammar*. Malden, MA: Blackwell.
Rebernik, Teja & Dicky Gilbers. 2017. Morebitni medsebojni vpliv prozodije slovenskega govora in slovenske ljudske pesmi. *Slavistična Revija* 65(4). 577–952.
Savage, Patrick E. 2018. Alan Lomax's cantometrics project: A comprehensive review. *Music & Science* 1. 1–19.
Schreuder, Maartje. 2006. Prosodic processes in speech and music [Doctoral Dissertation]: University of Groningen.
Selkirk, Elisabeth O. (1984). *Phonology and syntax: The relation between sound and structure*. Cambridge, MA: The MIT Press.
Selkirk, Elisabeth O. 1995. Sentence prosody: Intonation, stress, and phrasing. In: John A. Goldsmith, editor. *The handbook of phonological theory*, 550–569. Cambridge, MA: Blackwell.
Selkirk, Elisabeth O. 2000. The interaction of constraints on prosodic phrasing. In: Merle Horne, editor. *Prosody: Theory and experiment*, 231–261. Dordrecht: Kluwer Academic Publishers.
Temperley, Nicholas & David Temperley. 2011. Music-language correlations and the "scotch snap". *Music Perception* 29(1). 51–63.
Trehub, Sandra R., E. Glenn Schellenberg & Stuart B. Kamenetzky. 1999. Infants' and adults' perception of scale structure. *Journal of Experimental Psychology: Human Perception and Performance* 25(4). 965–975.

Truckenbrodt, Hubert. 1999. On the relation between syntactic phrases and phonological phrases. *Linguistic Inquiry* 30(2). 219–255.
VanHandel, Leigh & Tian Song. Influence of linguistic rhythm on individual compositional style in 19th century French and German art song. Proceedings of the 7th Triennial Conference of European Society for the Cognitive Sciences of Music; 2009; Jyväskylä, Finland. p 553–557.
Wood, Anna L. & M. Jorge Arèvalo. 2018. The global jukebox.
Zhang, Jie. 2004. *The role of contrast-specific and language-specific phonetics in contour tone distribution*. In: Bruce Hayes, Robert Kirchner, Donca Steriade, editors. *Phonetically-based phonology*, 157–190. Cambridge: Cambridge University Press.

Jasmin Pfeifer, Silke Hamann
Word stress perception by congenital amusics

Abstract: Congenital Amusia is a developmental disorder that is defined by difficulties with the perception of pitch and rhythm. While it used to be described as a disorder of musical pitch perception, recent publications have shown that congenital amusia also affects linguistic pitch perception. In this chapter we report the first study of word stress processing by congenital amusics. We designed a behavioral identification task and a mismatch negativity study using German minimal stress pairs as basis for our stimuli. We considered the acoustic parameters fundamental frequency (pitch), duration, intensity and spectral slope. Behavioral results surprisingly revealed no pitch processing difficulties for word stress in the amusic group in comparison to controls, and amusics also showed a better usage of durational cues. The electrophysiological results revealed that amusics consistently have an MMN, though it is smaller than that of controls. The present results warrant further investigation of the use of linguistic cues by congenital amusics.

Keywords: Congenital Amusia, Word Stress, Pitch, Duration, MMN

1 Introduction

1.1 What is congenital amusia?

Congenital amusia (henceforth: amusia) is a neuro-developmental disorder that has a negative influence on pitch perception and partly also on rhythm perception (Peretz et al., 2002; Foxton et al., 2004; Stewart, 2008). People with amusia (in the following called amusics) face lifelong impairments in the musical domain. Their symptoms can range from an inability to discriminate notes of

---

Acknowledgements: This work was supported by the *Netherlands Organisation for Scientific Research* (NWO; grant number 322-75-004) to the first author.
  We thank Dirk Vet for helping us writing the Praat and E-Prime script used in the EEG study.

Jasmin Pfeifer, Institute for English Language and Linguistics, Heinrich-Heine-University, Germany, e-mail: pfeifer@phil.hhu.de
Silke Hamann, Amsterdam Center for Language and Communication, University of Amsterdam, Amsterdam, The Netherlands, e-mail: silke.hamann@uva.nl

https://doi.org/10.1515/9783110770186-005

different pitches, an inability to recognize well-known songs without lyrics or an inability to recognize out of tune singing, to an inability to recognize music as such. In the most extreme cases, their symptoms can be so severe that music causes discomfort to them (Peretz et al., 2002; Foxton et al., 2004; Stewart, 2008). Most likely due to those more apparent symptoms, early research has mostly been focused on the influence of amusia on music. Hence, amusia has long been characterized as a music-specific disorder (Ayotte et al., 2002; Peretz et al., 2002; Peretz et al., 2001). Different aspects of musical engagement have been assessed and found impaired in amusia, such as pitch perception (Peretz et al., 2002), pitch production (Dalla Bella et al., 2011), rhythm perception (Foxton et al., 2006), beat synchronization (Sowiński & Dalla Bella, 2013), timbre perception (Marin et al., 2012a), consonance rating (Ayotte et al., 2002), and musical emotion perception (Marin et al., 2012b).

Amusia is neither caused by insufficient exposure to music, nor by a hearing deficiency, brain damage or intellectual impairment (Ayotte et al., 2002), and the disorder is considered innate (e.g. Peretz et al., 2002; Ayotte et al., 2002). The underlying cause of this multi-faceted disorder has been hypothesized to be a fine-grained pitch processing deficit (Ayotte et al., 2002; Foxton et al., 2004; Hutchins et al., 2010; Hyde & Peretz, 2004), a pitch memory deficit (Gosselin et al., 2009; Tillmann et al., 2009; Williamson & Stewart, 2010; Tillmann et al., 2016), a statistical learning deficit (Peretz et al., 2012) or a rapid-auditory processing deficit (Williamson et al., 2010; Albouy et al., 2016) and partly also a rhythm/beat perception deficit (Phillips-Silver et al., 2013; Launay et al., 2014). However, there is no consensus yet on the cause, and it is likely a multi-causal deficit that is responsible for the different symptoms exhibited by amusics. The exact neural underpinnings are also still unknown and various studies implicated different brain areas as having structural or functional abnormalities: less white matter in the left and right inferior frontal gyrus (IFG; Hyde et al., 2006); more grey matter in the right inferior frontal gyrus and right superior temporal gyrus (STG) and other brain areas (Hyde et al., 2007); less grey matter in the left IFG (Broca's area) and left STG (Wernicke's area; Mandell et al., 2007); less white matter in the arcuate fasciculus (AF; a fiber bundle connecting IFG and STG; Loui & Schlaug, 2009); abnormal deactivation and reduced connectivity in the right IFG (Hyde et al., 2011); more grey matter and less white matter in the right IFG and less grey matter in the right STG (Albouy et al., 2013b); decreased magnetic amplitude in the left and right STG and the left and right IFG, and decreased activation in the right dorsolateral prefrontal cortex (DLPFC) for memory tasks (Albouy et al., 2013a); and abnormal white matter structural connectivity in the right AF (Chen & Yuan, 2016). However, Chen et al. (2014) showed that the findings concerning the detection of the AF might be questionable as they strongly depended on the tracking algorithm that was used.

Due to these mixed and not yet fully substantiated findings, no neurological markers can be used to diagnose amusia. Instead, the behavioral markers mentioned above are currently used to screen for amusics. The most widely used tool for amusia screening is the *Montreal Battery of Evaluation of Amusia* (MBEA; Peretz et al., 2003), a series of tests that was originally devised to assess the musical abilities of brain-damaged patients. Nowadays, it is the main tool used to screen for and diagnose congenital amusia, in combination with questionnaires. It consists of six subtests, namely a scale, contour, interval, rhythm, meter, and memory test. A repeated score of 22 or below out of 30 (22 corresponding to two standard deviations below the mean scores of Peretz et al.'s normal participant group) on at least two of the first four subtests, and a self-reported history of problems with music perception used to be utilized to diagnose amusia (e.g. Foxton et al., 2004; Peretz et al., 2003; Tillmann et al., 2009). However, the cut-off scores, scoring procedures and the use of parametric statistics has recently been criticized (Wise, 2009; Henry & McAuley, 2010, 2013; Pfeifer & Hamann, 2015) which has led to the use of Signal Detection Theory (SDT; Green & Swets, 1966) for the evaluation of MBEA results, see section 2.2 below.

1.2 Congenital amusia and speech perception

While early research on amusia focused on musical impairments, more recent work also investigated the impact of amusia on language perception, since pitch also plays an important role in speech. In intonation, pitch is, for example, used to disambiguate questions from statements or to mark focus; while on the word level, pitch (among other things) is used to distinguish words with similar segmental structure but different stress pattern (e.g. English pre*sent* vs. *present*, where underscore denotes the stressed syllable) or to distinguish words with identical segments but different tones (e.g. in tone languages such as Mandarin Chinese). Other linguistic information such as conveying emotion or irony also makes use of pitch. Some of these areas of speech perception have been shown to be affected by amusia, i.e. intonation perception (Patel et al., 2008; Liu et al., 2010; Hamann et al., 2012), tone language perception (Liu et al., 2015a; Liu et al., 2015b; Liu et al., 2012; Tillmann et al., 2011) emotional prosody in language (Lolli et al., 2015; Thompson et al., 2012) and vowel perception in tonal languages (Huang et al., 2016; Zhang et al., 2017; Tang et al., 2018). Due to these findings, amusia has more recently been described as a domain-general disorder affecting pitch processing in general (Hamann et al., 2012; Liu et al., 2010; Zhang et al., 2017).

The speech perception studies with most relevance to the present study are on the one hand studies about intonation and on the other studies about the usage of durational cues by amusics. The first to systematically research intonation perception impairments were Patel et al. (2008), who investigated the pitch perception of British English and Canadian French amusics in an AX discrimination task. They utilized statement-question pairs that were edited to acoustically differ only in the final region of the intonation contour. In addition, Patel et al. used tonal analogs of the statement-question pairs. They found that 30% of the amusics had difficulties discriminating statements from questions based on intonation, while they were able to discriminate the tone analogs based on these sentences well (Patel et al., 2008). These findings were in contrast to all previous studies (such as Ayotte et al., 2002) claiming that linguistic pitch perception was unaffected by amusia.

Liu et al. (2010) investigated the pitch processing of British English amusics in an AX discrimination task using statement-question pairs, nonsense speech analogs and tone analogs. As in the study by Patel et al. (2008), the stimuli retained the final pitch of naturally produced statements or questions. The amusics performed significantly worse than controls on all three stimuli types. Furthermore, amusics performed significantly better on gliding tones than on natural speech, while their discrimination of nonsense-speech was worst, thus showing that amusics have an impaired intonation perception. This result differs from Patel et al.'s (2008) insofar as Liu et al. found an impairment of intonation perception for a subgroup of amusics only.

Hamann et al. (2012) investigated the intonation perception of German amusics in an AX discrimination task. They looked at pitch processing as well, including two tonal analogs. However, they were the first to also consider other linguistic factors such as the length of the stimuli, and the continuity of the pitch curve. Their stimuli consisted of short (3–6 syllables) and long (7–10 syllables) statement-question pairs and were also varied concerning the segmental material. Sentences either contained only vowels and voiced consonants (resulting in a continuous pitch), or they also contained voiceless consonants (resulting in a discontinuous intonation contour). Amusics were again shown to be impaired in the discrimination of speech as well as non-speech material. It was also found that amusics as well as controls performed worse for continuous intonation contours; however, the length of the stimuli was not found to have an influence.

The speech perception studies with amusics up to now have almost exclusively focused on intonation and on pitch as a perceptual cue, probably due to the fact that most hypotheses on the underlying deficit of amusia are based on some form of pitch perception deficit. However, there are two recent studies that also investigate the perception and usage of durational cues by amusics. The study by Huang et al. (2015) considered durational differences and linguistic tone at the same time, and was conducted with native speakers of a tonal language. They found that at least the speech tone deficit in Mandarin amusics is independent of duration. However, there is no evidence that the same holds true for the durational cue in word stress perception. The other study, by Jasmin et al. (2019), investigated the cue weighting of durational versus pitch cues of amusics. They investigated phonetic cue weighting using the English minimal pairs *beer* and *pier*, for which they identified voice onset time (VOT) as the durational and primary cue and the fundamental frequency of the following vowel as the secondary cue of pitch. In addition, they also used a prosodic cue weighting paradigm in which two phrases with different stress patterns were used. In this paradigm, pitch was regarded as primary cue and durational differences as secondary cue. Jasmin et al. (2019) found no differences between amusics and controls in the phonetic cue weighting. In the prosodic cue weighting, however, amusics placed greater emphasis on the durational VOT cues than on the vowel-inherent pitch cues.

Contrastive word stress is an area that has not yet been explored in amusia. However, it seems ideally suited to explore the different speech cues and participants' sensitivity to them. Weber et al. (2004) showed, for example, that German infants were sensitive to the predominant strong-weak stress pattern of their native language at an age as young as 5 months. In addition, the perception (and production) of word stress and its different perceptual correlates have been assessed and found impaired in many other populations such as children at risk of dyslexia (e.g. De Bree et al., 2006; Leong et al., 2011; Goswami et al., 2013), children at risk of SLI (e.g. Gallon et al., 2007; Haake et al., 2013; Fikkert & Penner, 1998) and people with Down syndrome (e.g. Pettinato & Verhoeven, 2008). In addition to these behavioral findings, electrophysiological evidence concerning word stress perception in clinical populations is also available, as discussed in the following section.

1.3 The electrophysiology of congenital amusia

The mismatch negativity (MMN), an early event-related potential (ERP) component, is especially useful for studies on the electrophysiology of word stress perception. It reflects the neural responses of automatic change detection and its recording does not require attentive action from the participant (Näätänen et al., 1978), for reviews, see Näätänen (2001); Näätänen et al. (2007); Picton et al. (2000). The MMN is generated as the brain's automatic, unconscious response to auditory changes but it also indexes behavioral accuracy e.g. Näätänen et al. (2007). Large MMN amplitudes are elicited by accurate stimulus discrimination, and small MMN amplitudes have been shown to be associated with inaccurate discrimination (Kujala & Näätänen, 2001) in various healthy groups and patients. It peaks at around 100 to 250 ms if the auditory system has formed a representation of the repetitive aspect of the standard stimulus and then a deviant occurs (Näätänen, 2001).

MMN paradigms have widely been used in general auditory but also speech perception research (e.g. Chládková et al., 2013; Kirmse et al., 2008; Näätänen, 2001; Partanen et al., 2011; Ylinen et al., 2006). The linguistic MMN is hypothesized to arise not only from auditory change detection but also from the representation of speech sounds in long term memory that facilitate the discrimination process (e.g. Näätänen, 2001; Partanen et al., 2011), and it has been shown to be more left lateralized (Shtyrov et al., 2000; Sorokin et al., 2010). Partanen et al. (2011) have shown that the MMN in linguistic research can be used to establish an auditory discrimination profile, taking into account duration, intensity, pitch and vowel differences. A reduced MMN amplitude is thought to reflect poorer representations of the phonetic categories, which is hypothesized to possibly result from poor language-specific learning of relevant phonetic cues (e.g. Näätänen et al., 2014). Weber et al. (2005) investigated ERP responses of 5-month-old German infants at risk of SLI, finding a significantly reduced MMN to changes in stress patterns. These were interpreted as indicating a less effective processing of word stress and thereby leading to a delay in language acquisition. A reduced mismatch negativity was also found in schizophrenia, when investigating stimuli that deviated in frequency, duration and intensity (Hay et al., 2015).

The MMN has been shown to originate in the auditory cortex and the fronto-central scalp areas (for a review see Näätänen et al., 2007), and in a lesion study (Alain et al., 1998) specifically the dorsolateral prefrontal cortices were implicated. These are also the regions that are affected by amusia, as shown by Albouy et al. (2013a) and Hyde et al. (2011). The MMN therefore seems well suited to investigate the neurophysiological processes underlying congenital amusia.

Numerous studies on pitch perception by amusics have utilized the MMN already, however with widely differing findings: The first to use it were Braun et al. (2008), who found the MMN to be absent in amusics (for melodies containing altered notes). Studies by Moreau et al. (2009), testing adults with melodies, and Mignault Goulet et al. (2012), testing children with tonal sequences, on the other hand, found normal MMNs in amusics. The same holds for the study by Moreau et al. (2013), testing amusics with piano tone sequences.

Reduced, abnormal MMNs were found by Lebrun et al. (2012) for one child to small tonal changes of 25 per cent and by Nan et al. (2016) for the responses of tone-language speaking amusics to lexical tones. The latter found a reduced MMN only for a subgroup of amusics, namely for tone agnosics. Taken together, the aforementioned findings seem to show absent or reduced MMNs to tonal sequences in at least some amusics.

Based on this, the present study looks at a fairly homogeneous group of amusics showing both a pitch and a rhythm deficit of a non-tonal language, German, with a contrastive stress difference. We hypothesize that these amusics will perform behaviorally worse in identifying carefully controlled stimuli based on stress minimal pairs and will show reduced MMNs in comparison to controls. To test these hypotheses, we designed a behavioral study and an electrophysiological one. Before we present the details of these studies, we briefly describe the perceptual cues to contrastive word stress in German.

1.4 Perceptual cues to word stress in German

The primary perceptual cue for word stress in German is the length of the vowel or syllable, with stressed vowels and syllables having longer duration than their unstressed counterparts, as shown by Dogil (1995), Jessen et al. (1995) and Haake et al. (2013), amongst others. Secondary cues are pitch, loudness and spectral slope (Lintfert, 2010): Stressed syllables are usually produced with higher pitch than unstressed syllables (Dogil, 1995; Jessen et al., 1995) and they usually are louder (have a higher intensity) than unstressed syllables; however, this strongly correlates with the slope of the frequency spectrum: In stressed syllables, higher frequencies are also produced with a higher intensity, resulting in a less tilted spectrum than in unstressed syllables (Jessen et al., 1995). As unstressed vowels are usually also more reduced than stressed vowels, even in a language like German, where vowel reduction is minimal, the formant values of unstressed values are more centralized than that of stressed vowels (Lintfert, 2010). As mentioned by Haake et al. (2013), all of these cues are quite variable within and across speakers.

With respect to where the word stress is positioned and therefore expected in German, the penultimate syllable is considered the default stress position (Eisenberg, 1991; Wiese, 2000: 180–182).

1.5 Cue weighting and the relation between speech and music

The perception of speech and that of music involves the integration of several acoustic characteristics as perceptual cues – as indicated above for the case of word stress in German: mainly duration (perceived as length), fundamental frequency (perceived as pitch), intensity (perceived as loudness) and spectral slope (perceived as a combination of vowel quality and loudness). These cues have to be weighted and integrated in order to be mapped onto a categorical representation. For speech perception, spectral and temporal variations are mapped onto linguistic units, whereas in music, tonal and rhythmical variation are mapped onto musical units (e.g. Patel, 2003). This mapping and categorizing is no easy feat as it requires a very precise and rapid detection and integration of a number of acoustic cues. Lisker (1986), for example, lists 16 acoustic properties that can be used as cues to differentiate between voiced and voiceless sounds alone, i.e., the difference between e.g. /b/ and /p/. While this means that a great level of redundant information is present that needs to be integrated, those redundant cues can also ensure that a selective perceptual deficit does not make speech perception impossible, thereby making it more robust (Patel et al., 2008). Congenital amusia, with its very specific perceptual deficits and yet seemingly unimpaired overall language perception and production, offers a unique window into possible different cue weighting and integration strategies that the redundancy in the acoustic signal affords. And as detailed in the previous subsections, stress assignment in German seems to be an ideal testing ground for examining general auditory deficits and potential speech perception deficits of amusics, as it involves not only individual perceptual cues (such as pitch, length, loudness, and vowel quality) but also higher-order processes of cue weighting and integration.

2 Materials and methods

In the following subsections, we describe the stimuli (section 2.1), participants (section 2.2) and the procedure (section 2.3) of our behavioral and MMN experiment.

2.1 Stimuli

In order to test the role of duration, which was found to be the most important cue for stress perception in German (recall section 1.4), and the role of pitch, which should pose the greatest difficulty to amusics due to their pitch perception impairment (recall sections 1.1 and 1.2) on stress perception in German, we need to manipulate real speech. Natural speech always includes all potential cues, and in order to systematically test the weight of one or two of them, all other cues need to be changed to intermediate values between a stressed and an unstressed syllable, which can only be achieved by manipulation.

For the creation of the stimuli for both our experiments, we recorded a native speaker of German producing several repetitions of the stress minimal pair *umstellen* ['ʊmʃtɛln] "to reposition" vs. *umstellen* "to surround" [ʊm'ʃtɛln] in isolation (where underscore denotes the syllable with main stress). We then picked the productions that were pronounced the clearest. Though we had many more stress minimal pairs with two distinct meanings (e.g. *untergraben*, *durchreisen*) included in our recordings and the pilot, we had to restrict the actual experiment to one pair as it would have been much too long otherwise.

For the acoustic analysis and manipulation, we considered each word as consisting of two parts: the first being the verbal prefix, i.e. the first syllable [ʊm] (which in the unstressed cases was mostly realized as a nasalized vowel [ʊ̃]), and the second part being the stem, i.e. the second and third syllable together, excluding the initial fricative, thus the sequence [tɛln]. For each part of each word, we measured the acoustic parameters duration, fundamental frequency (which we will call by its perceptual correlate pitch in the following), spectral slope and intensity, as given in Table 1. Spectral slope (or tilt) was calculated as the slope between the low frequency band (below 1 kHz) and the high frequency band (from 1 to 4 kHz). The realization of the fricative [ʃ] did not differ in any of the parameters between the two words and is therefore not reported here.

Table 1: Acoustic parameters of the first and second part of the two words.

	umstellen		*umstellen*	
	first part	second part	first part	second part
duration (ms)	158	360	98	386
pitch (Hz)	170 to 153	110 to 82	101	165 to 82
spectral slope (dB)	−30	−22	−29	−17
intensity (dB)	78	69	70	75

As a starting point for the manipulations that we performed in Praat (Boersma & Weenink, 2016), we took the first part plus fricative from the original *umstellen* and the second part from the original *umstellen*, so both parts had stress and clearly articulated segments, and we adjusted this combined sound file to the parameters given below. The vowel quality was not manipulated, but corresponded to the formant values of both stressed vowels in natural speech.

Since **duration** was found to be the main cue to stress perception in German, we used the duration of the original initial word parts (158 ms for stressed and 98 ms for unstressed) as the two end values on our duration scale, and created a third, middle value at a fractional step of 1.2697, i.e. at 124.4 ms, see the first and second row in Table 2. In the second word part (measured from release of the [t]), the two original durations were too close to each other (with less than 20% noticeable difference between them), probably due to phrase-final lengthening. We therefore decided not to vary the duration of the second part but to employ an in-between value of 378 ms for all stimuli.

Table 2: Parameters of the manipulation. First rows: actual values, second rows: labels used in the following descriptions. The values in the left column correspond to realizations with stress on the first part, the values in the right column to those with stress on the second part, while the values in the middle column correspond to ambiguous realizations.

Duration of first part	158 ms	124.4 ms	98 ms
	= long	= mid	= short
Pitch contour of first and second part	170 to 153 Hz 110 to 82 Hz	131 to 124 Hz 135 to 82 Hz	101 Hz 165 to 82 Hz
	= early peak	= two peaks	= late peak
Spectral slope of second part	−22	−19.5	−17
	= high slope	= mid slope	= low slope
Intensity of first and second part	78 dB 69 dB	74 dB 72 dB	70 dB 75 dB
	= falling	= level	= rising

Of major importance for amusics is their possible impaired perception of **pitch** in speech. We therefore manipulated the pitch of our stimuli by using the natural contours of the two words and creating an in-between pitch contour with a slight fall from 131 Hz (9.01/2 semitones) to 124 Hz (7.19/2 semitones) for the first word part, and a slight fall from 135 Hz (7.02/2 semitones) to the 82 Hz that both words shared for the second word part. This yielded in total three pitch contours, see Table 2, rows three to five.

With respect to the secondary stress cue **spectral slope**, the original unstressed and stressed first parts differed only marginally, and therefore only one intermediate value was taken. For the second word part, we used the values of the original recordings and created an intermediate middle value, resulting in three spectral slope patterns, see Table 2, rows six and seven.

Intensity is mentioned as another relevant secondary cue of German stress perception in the literature. We therefore manipulated the intensity of the two parts of our stimuli, based again on the measures of the original recordings. In addition to these two, we also created an in-between intensity contour; see the last three rows in Table 2.

The above-described manipulation in duration, pitch, slope and intensity resulted in a total of 81 stimuli (= 3 duration values * 3 pitch contours * 3 slope patterns * 3 intensity contours).

The two re-synthesized endpoint stimuli were tested in a pilot study with 5 native listeners, to check whether they were consistently categorized as having stress either on the first or on the second word part, which was the case. A task similar to the main study (described below in 2.3) was used for this pilot.

For the EEG experiment, only four of the stimuli from the behavioral task were used: due to the experimental constraints of an oddball task. Two of these were the two re-synthesized endpoint stimuli with a contrast in all cues. The choice of the other two was based on the expected pitch-deficit in speech of our amusic group. For the EEG study, we therefore chose two further stimuli that contained a contradiction between pitch and all other cues: the first had an ambiguous pitch contour (two peaks) whereas all other parameters corresponded to those for stress on the first word part, and the second had an early peak pitch contour (corresponding to stress on the first part) whereas all other parameter settings corresponded to stress on the second part.

2.2 Participants

Amusics and controls were matched for age, gender, handedness, education and musical training in both studies. All participants were native speakers of German, right-handed and had no self-reported psychological or neurological disorders. They had normal hearing defined as a mean hearing level of 20 dB or less in both ears, assessed by a pure tone audiometry at 250, 500, 1000, 2000, 3000, 4000, 6000 and 8000 Hz. The participants were recruited from an existing pool of amusics. Congenital amusia was diagnosed based on the three pitch-based subtests and the rhythm subtest of the MBEA and a detailed questionnaire about their educational and musical background. Only amusics exhibiting both a pitch perception and a rhythm perception deficit were included in this study to ensure homogeneity as much as possible. MBEA scores as the proportion correct out of 30 and d' scores on the four subtests that we employed are given for each study separately in the subsections below. The difference between the two groups was calculated based on d' values. Our amusic group falls below traditional proportion correct cut-off scores from Peretz et al. (2003) on all but the memory subtest.

All participants were tested in a sound-attenuated chamber in the phonetics laboratory at the University of Düsseldorf. The Ethical Committee of the Medical Faculty at the University of Düsseldorf approved the study protocol, and each participant signed an informed consent form before the experiment, and received a small monetary reimbursement for their participation afterwards.

2.2.1 Behavioral experiment

10 controls and 7 amusics were included in the behavioral study. Their characteristics can be found in Table 3, and their MBEA scores for the four relevant subtests in Table 4. The discriminatory ability of the two groups is significantly different, as shown by the t-test values in Table 4.

Table 3: Subject characteristics of behavioral study: Descriptive statistics and results of t-tests comparing amusic (N=7) and control (N=10) participants characteristics. t: test statistic of the independent samples t-test; p: probability value.

Group		Age	Years of education	Years of music education	Gender
Amusics	Mean	27.43	18.86	3.00	2 male
Controls	Mean	29.00	19.50	2.60	3 male
t-test (df 15)	t	−1.179	−0.541	0.398	
	p	0.257	0.297	0.696	

Table 4: Montreal Battery of Evaluation of Amusia scores for behavioral study: Means and standard deviations of proportion correct scores (number of correct responses, out of 30), and d' scores for amusics (N = 7) and controls (N = 10). The t-test was calculated on d'- values. t: test statistic of the independent samples t-test; p: probability value.

			Scale	Contour	Interval	Rhythm	Meter	Memory
Proportion Correct	control	Mean	27.50	28.40	28.70	28.50	28.60	28.90
		SD	1.72	1.07	1.25	0.71	1.96	1.20
	amusic	Mean	20.29	20.86	19.71	22.43	22.00	25.57
		SD	3.04	1.21	2.81	2.51	3.06	2.82
d'	control	Mean	3.34	3.67	3.78	3.59	3.84	3.99
		SD	0.83	0.45	0.63	0.39	1.01	0.62
	amusic	Mean	1.23	1.43	1.00	1.60	1.32	2.20
		SD	0.71	0.47	0.43	0.76	0.66	1.07
t-test (df 15)		t	−5.497	−9.946	−10.077	−7.104	−5.746	−4.378
		p	0.000	0.000	0.000	0.000	0.000	0.001

2.2.2 MMN experiment

10 controls and 10 amusics were included in the MMN study. Their characteristics can be found in Table 5, and their MBEA scores for the four relevant subtests in Table 6. Again, the discriminatory ability of the two groups is significantly different, as shown by the t-test values in Table 6. The seven amusics who participated in the behavioral study also participated in the MMN study with three additional amusics. As both studies were conducted more than 12 months apart, we do not

Table 5: Subject characteristics of MMN study: Descriptive statistics and results of t-tests comparing amusic and control participants (N= 10 per group) characteristics. t: test statistic of the independent samples t-test; p: probability value.

Group		Age	Years of education	Years of music education	Gender
Amusics	Mean	36.70	19.10	2.40	3 male
Controls	Mean	33.50	19.00	2.10	3 male
t-test (df 18)	t	0.496	0.074	0.252	
	p	0.626	0.942	0.804	

Table 6: Montreal Battery of Evaluation of Amusia scores for MMN study: Means and standard deviations of proportion correct scores (number of correct responses, out of 30), and *d'* scores for amusics and controls (N= 10 per group). The *t*-test was calculated on *d'*- values. *t*: test statistic of the independent samples *t*-test; *p*: probability value.

			Scale	Contour	Interval	Rhythm	Meter	Memory
Pro-portion Correct	control	Mean	27.50	28.30	28.50	28.60	28.50	29.00
		SD	1.72	1.16	1.35	0.84	1.90	1.25
	amusic	Mean	21.60	20.10	19.30	23.50	21.70	24.70
		SD	1.96	2.60	1.34	3.44	4.32	3.06
d'	control	Mean	3.40	3.58	3.66	3.67	3.76	4.07
		SD	0.77	0.56	0.73	0.51	0.97	0.65
	amusic	Mean	1.33	1.10	0.97	1.96	1.45	2.44
		SD	0.48	0.50	0.36	0.93	1.12	1.05
t-test (df 18)		*t*	−7.253	−10.542	−10.453	−5.094	−4.924	−4.177
		p	0.000	0.000	0.000	0.000	0.000	0.001

think that there were any carryover effects for the seven participants who participated in both studies.

2.3 Procedure

2.3.1 Behavioral paradigm

In the behavioral experiment, the 81 stimuli were presented in isolation, as the original recordings on which the stimuli were based on were also words in isolation. The stimuli consisted of three syllables, and therefore provided enough information for the listeners to normalize for speech rate and speaker (see Summerfield, 1981). Participants were presented with a forced-choice identification task in three blocks (of 81 stimuli each) with two pictures as answer choices. They heard one stimulus at a time and had to click on one of two pictures in order to indicate the meaning of the word. The two pictures that were used as answer categories were introduced to the participants with two sentences before the start of the experiment. They were hand-drawn scenes depicting typical situations for both meanings and they were piloted before the experiment. The order of these two pictures was counterbalanced between blocks and participants. Each stimulus was repeated three times and occurred once per block, and the presentation was pseudo-randomized. Participants took a break after each block. The behavioral task lasted approximately 45 to 60 minutes.

2.3.2 EEG paradigm

The EEG session was recorded approximately twelve months after the behavioral session. Each session lasted about 3.5 hours in total, of which about 100 minutes were EEG recording time. Each session consisted of four approximately 25-minute recording blocks with short breaks in between. Participants were watching a silenced nature documentary without subtitles or visible lip movements, while completing a passive listening task. We used nature documentaries to avoid having lip movements of a different language than the one being tested in the video material, as this has been shown to distort EEG results (Kang et al., 2016; Shinozaki et al., 2016). Participants listened passively to the stimuli as they were instructed to disregard the sounds and to focus their attention on the movie. The auditory stimuli were presented at 60 dB via two loudspeakers placed in front of the participant at a distance of approximately 1 m.

The auditory stimuli were presented in a multi-deviant oddball paradigm with two different blocks. Each block contained 1800: (tokens) auditory stimuli. Each block was repeated once, resulting in four blocks in total, which were counterbalanced across participants.

The standard in each block was one of the two stimuli in line with the natural distribution of cues, with all cues indicating stress either on the first word part or on the second word part. The three deviants consisted of the other stimulus with naturally distributed cues and two further stimuli that contained a contradiction between pitch and all other cues, as described in detail in section 2.1 above: This means 4 different stimuli (types) were used.

As is usual in a multi-deviant oddball paradigm, the standard occurred 85 % of the time and each deviant occurred 5 % of the time. Each block started with 20 standards, followed by the oddball sequence, and each deviant was separated from the next by at least 4 and at most 8 standards. The inter-stimulus interval was varied randomly between 300 ms and 500 ms. A variable inter-stimulus interval was chosen to avoid entrainment effects to the stimulus chain (Repp & Su, 2013; Tal et al., 2017). The combination of 2 standards and 6 deviants yielded a total of 8 event-related potentials (ERPs) per participant. These 8 ERPs were used to calculate MMNs for 6 different conditions, as the MMN is derived by subtracting the average ERP of the standard from each of the three deviants.

The most negative peak in the 100 to 275 ms post stimulus onset was determined per condition. Each MMN amplitude was calculated as the mean voltage over a 40 ms time window centered at the most negative peak.

2.3.3 EEG parameters and preprocessing

The EEG was recorded using a BioSemi Active Two system (Biosemi Instrumentation BV, Amsterdam, The Netherlands) with 64 Ag-AgCl electrodes that were placed according to the international 10/20-system in a cap fitting the participant's head size. 7 further electrodes were placed on the tip of the nose, the left and right mastoid, below and above the left eye and the outer canthi of the left and right eyes (recording the electro-oculogram; EOG). The EEG signal was recorded at 8192 Hz and later down-sampled to 512 Hz. The subsequent analyses were performed in Praat (Boersma & Weenink, 2019). The data were offline referenced to the average of the two mastoid channels. Slow drifts were removed by subtracting a line from each channel so that the first and the last sample become zero. The data were bandpass filtered in the frequency domain with a low cut-off of 1 Hz (0.5 Hz bandwidth) and a high cut-off of 25 Hz (12.5 Hz bandwidth). The EEG was segmented into epochs of 500 ms, from 110 ms before to 390 ms after stimulus onset. For baseline correction, the mean voltage of the 110 ms pre-stimulus served as a baseline for amplitude measurement and was subtracted from each sample in this epoch. Artifact correction was done automatically and epochs with an EEG or EOG change exceeding +/−75 mV were excluded. Participants with more than 50% of artifact-contaminated epochs would have been excluded from analysis. No participant exceeded this limit. This way at least 90 deviants per type remained in the analysis.

3 Results

3.1 Behavioral

A generalized linear mixed effects model with subjects and stimulus item as random effects and everything else as fixed effects (i.e. the complete model) was calculated. The number of answers "stress on the first word part" was taken as the dependent variable. Following established modeling practices (Baayen et al., 2008), a full model that included all variables and interactions was used as a starting point. Stimuli were contrast coded and only explicit contrasts were used, i.e. variables were centered around zero. The regression models were then simplified by the stepwise exclusion of non-significant fixed effects. A fixed effect was considered non-significant if its *p*-value was higher than 0.05, if there were no significant interactions including it and if the Akaike Information Criterion of the model including the predictor was higher than when the predictor was not included. The final model only contained group, pitch and duration as fixed effects, as intensity and slope did not yield any significant results. We found main effects of duration and of pitch and an interaction between duration and group. The model specifics can be found in Table 7. To understand the Group by Duration interaction, separate models with only duration as fixed factor were performed for each group separately. This revealed an effect of duration in the amusic group (B = –1.75, SE = 0.79, z = 2.20, p = 0.028), but not in the control group (B = 0.74, SE = 0.76, z = 0.98, p = 0.33).

Table 7: Final generalized linear mixed model fit by maximum likelihood. Asterisks indicate significance levels: * p < 0.05; ** p < 0.01; *** p < 0.001.

	Estimate	Std. Error	z-value	Pr(>|z|)
(Intercept)	–0.76	0.16	–4.73	2.22e-06 ***
Group	–0.25	0.18	–1.35	0.17774
Duration	1.15	0.36	3.24	0.00118 **
Pitch	5.37	0.36	14.99	< 2e-16 ***
Group by Duration	–0.85	0.28	–3.01	0.00217 **
Group by Pitch	–0.17	0.30	–0.57	0.56916
Duration by Pitch	0.42	0.88	0.48	0.63341
Group x Duration by Pitch	–0.31	0.74	–0.42	0.67724

A visualization of the observed data can be found in Figures 1 and 2. Figure 1 depicts a clear effect of pitch: Both amusics and controls identified an early pitch rise (the first two bars in each plot) as stress on the first word part (the blue bar is higher than the green one), and a late pitch rise (the last two bars in each plot) as stress on the second part (the green bar is higher than the blue one). The ambiguous stimuli with two pitch peaks (the two bars in the middle of each plot) were mainly identified as having stress on the second part.

Figure 2 depicts the effect of duration of the first vowel. All participants showed a preference to identify all stimuli as being stressed on the second word part. However, while the responses of the control group (upper panel) are

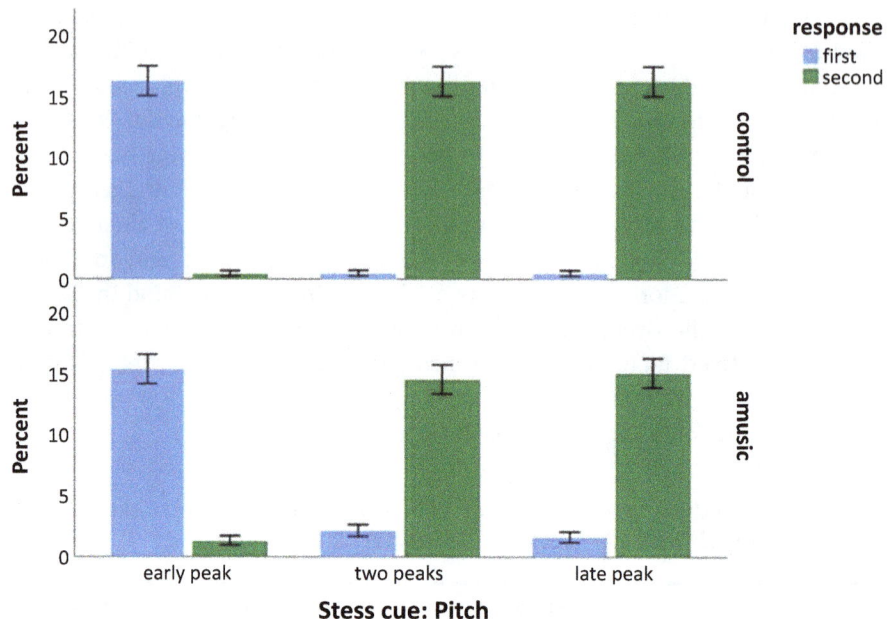

Figure 1: Responses to pitch cue split by group. Response first (blue) or second word part (green) in percent (grand total) to stimuli where pitch has an early peak (left), two peaks (middle), or a late peak (right). Top: control group, bottom: amusic group. Error bars show 95% CI.

not influenced by the duration of the first vowel (the ratio of their answers stays the same across all three vowel durations), the responses by the amusic group (lower panel) depend on the duration of the vowel, with far more "stress on first part" identifications for stimuli with a long than with a mid or short first vowel. The amusics thus use durational cues more reliably than controls to identify stress.

3.2 EEG

The EEG analysis was run on the MMN amplitude measured at 9 channels (Fz, FCz, Cz, F3, F4, FC3, FC4, C3, C4).

Visual analysis of the scalp topography confirms the negative polarity, the expected latency and fronto-central scalp distribution of the MMN for the controls, cf. Figure 3. Amusics overall do not show a strong negativity, as indicated by the lighter blue color compared to the control group in the left panel. The right panel shows the average difference waveform (i.e., the waveform of the

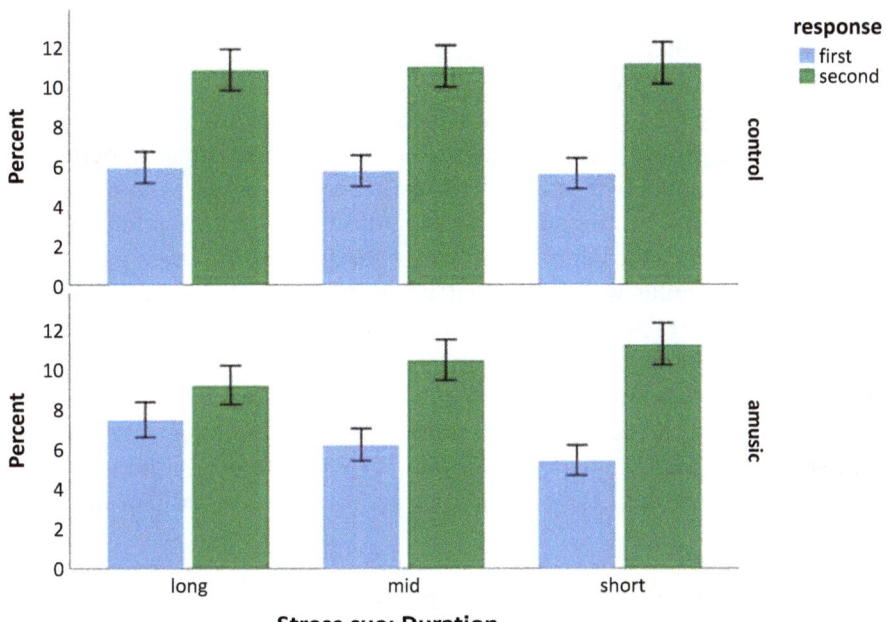

Figure 2: Responses to duration cue split by group. Response first (blue) or second word part (green) in percent (grand total) to long (left), mid (middle) or short duration (right) of the first vowel. Top: control group, bottom: amusic group. Error bars show 95% CI.

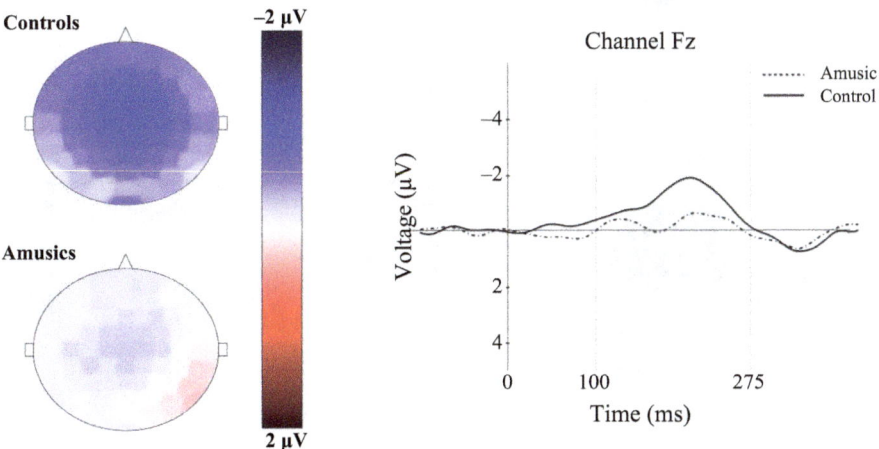

Figure 3: Difference between amusics and controls in a time window between 100 and 275 ms averaged across all conditions. Left panel are the topographical maps and right panel the grand average difference waves plotted at Fz.

deviant minus the waveform of the standard) averaged across all conditions for amusics (dotted line) and controls (solid line).

Figure 4 shows the topographical plot per condition and group. As explained in section 2.1 and 2.3.2, the standards are the two stimuli in line with the natural distribution of cues, with all cues indicating stress either on the first word part (upper two panels; <u>um</u>stellen) or on the second word part (lower two panels; ums<u>tel</u>len). Deviant 1 is the stimulus that was standard in the other condition, i.e. with all congruent stress cues for the opposite stress pattern. Deviant 2 is the stimulus with an ambiguous pitch but all other cues for stress on the first word part. Deviant 3 has a pitch pattern that indicates stress on the first word part but all other cues are in line with stress on the second word part. The dark blue color for the topographical plot on the upper left indicates that the deviant with all cues for stress on the second word part and the standard stressed on the first elicited the strongest MMN in controls. A similar pattern (though far less strong) can be found for amusics, see second plot in the left

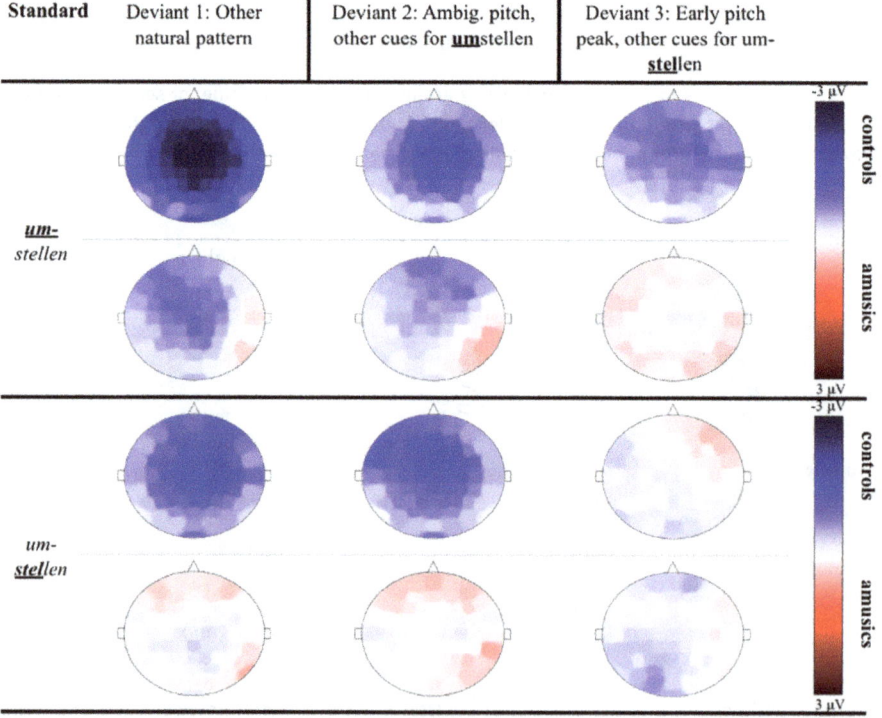

Figure 4: Topographical maps of amusics and controls averaged in a time window between 100 and 275 ms per condition. Controls at the top and amusics at the bottom per condition.

column. The reverse condition, with deviant stressed on the first and standard on the second word part, elicited quite a strong MMN again in controls, but not so in amusics (cf. plot 3 and 4 left column).

After visual analysis, we performed two-tailed t-tests against zero separately for each group to determine whether the difference waveform response was present in every condition, all of which were significant, see Table 8.

Table 8: Mean voltage at electrode Fz measured in µV. Top value is that of the control group, bottom value that of the amusic group. * indicate significance levels in t-tests against zero: * $p < 0.05$; ** $p < 0.01$; *** $p < 0.001$.

Standard	Deviant 1: other natural pattern	Deviant 2: ambiguous pitch, other cues for um*stellen*	Deviant 3: early pitch peak, other cues for um*stellen*
um*stellen*	−4.51***	−2.67***	−2.81***
	−2.79***	−1.73***	−1.96***
*um*stellen	−2.34***	−2.09***	−1.05***
	−1.97***	−1.84 ***	−1.28***

Table 9: Summary of the model.

	Estimate	Std. Error	t-value	p-value
(Intercept)	−3.23	0.19	−17.37	<0.001
Group	−1.68	0.37	−4.52	<0.001
Condition	0.32	0.02	15.56	<0.001
Group by Condition	0.34	0.04	8.21	<0.001

A laterality analysis was carried out but revealed no significant differences between conditions or groups.

As we were interested in the differences between amusics and controls in every condition, we calculated a linear mixed model (lmer) in R with subject as random effect and group and condition as fixed factors. Coding and modeling were carried out as described in section 3.1:, a summary of the model can be found in Table 9. We found a main effect for group with amusics (M = −1.93) overall having a smaller MMN than controls (M = −2.58), a main effect for condition, and an interaction between group and condition. To understand the Group by Condition Interaction, separate models with only group as fixed factor were performed for each condition separately. They all yielded significant results, except in one case: When the standard was stressed on the second word part and Deviant 3 from Table 8 was used, then there was no significant effect, also depicted in similar patterns for controls and amusics the bottom right topographical maps in Figure 4.

4 Discussion

Our experiments tested the identification of word stress by amusics and controls based on the acoustic cues of fundamental frequency (pitch), duration, intensity and spectral slope.

Spectral slope and intensity did not have a significant effect on identification. The differences in both cues are based on the naturally produced minimal stress word pair. For spectral slope, it is rather small (a difference of 5). For intensity, the difference is noticeable (8 dB in the first word part and 6 dB in the second). It is possible that taken together the two are still too small and not salient enough to override the more salient acoustic information of duration and pitch contour. Recall also from section 1.4. that loudness and spectral slope, together with pitch, form secondary cues to word stress in German (Lintfert, 2010) while duration has been shown to be the primary perceptual cue (Dogil, 1995; Jessen et al., 1995; Haake et al., 2013).

To our surprise, both controls and amusics used pitch in a very similar way for the identification of word stress: unambiguous pitch cues were used to identify the corresponding word stress patterns, while the ambiguous stimuli with two pitch peaks were mainly identified as having stress on the second word part (as expected, since default stress is on the penultimate syllable in German; cf. Eisenberg, 1991; Wiese, 2000). Though there were small differences in the behavior of the two groups, these were not significant. This finding is unexpected as amusics were expected to show difficulties in their pitch perception.

Even more surprising was the finding that amusics seemed to use durational cues more reliably than controls to identify stress on the first word part. This finding could hint at compensation strategies that amusics may have developed to compensate for their pitch perception deficits.

In addition, amusics did display a significantly reduced MMN in comparison to controls in all but one condition. The exception is the condition where the standard has stress on the second part, while the deviant had only pitch cues for stress on the first part, while all other cues indicated stress on the second part. For this condition, controls showed the least strong MNN, presumably because the deviant did not differ from the standard with respect to any cues but pitch. Amusics had a very similar MNN for this condition, and therefore the two groups did not show a significant difference.

Despite the difference in amplitude, the MMNs were present in both groups.

These findings taken together are surprising, as amusics seem to be able to identify something in the behavioral task to which they show an at least reduced early neural response. It seems to stand to reason that amusics might compensate for their reduced early change detection responses at later processing stages. Our findings are somewhat comparable to those by Jasmin et al. (2019) who found no differences between amusics and controls in their phonetic cue weighting but did find that amusics placed greater emphasis on durational cues than on pitch cues in their prosodic cue weighting task. Further investigations are needed to untangle whether Jasmin et al.'s findings of no difference in the cue usage between amusics and controls in consonants (VOT) also hold for vowels, or whether vowel duration would be more comparable to their and our findings concerning word stress, i.e. that amusics placed greater emphasis on durational cues than on pitch cues. Regardless of this, their findings also point to a possible compensation strategy of amusics.

Our ERP results show that the auditory system of amusics has formed a representation of the repetitive aspect of the standard stimulus as represented by the MMN that they exhibit. However, their MMN is significantly reduced in comparison to our control population and might therefore represent a more inaccurate discrimination of the stimuli than the controls' larger MMN does (Kujala & Näätänen, 2001). This finding is in line with Weber et al.'s (2005) finding of infants at risk of SLI showing a significantly reduced MMN to changes in stress patterns. A further comparison of amusia to other developmental disorders and their behavioral and neurophysiological markers seems warranted.

The general finding that amusics did indeed display an MMN response is in direct opposition to that by Braun et al. (2008), who did not find an MMN in amusics at all. Furthermore, the fact that the response of our amusics was significantly reduced is in opposition to the findings by Moreau et al. (2009; 2013) and Mignault Goulet et al. (2012) who found that amusics displayed completely normal MMNs. All these findings utilized musical stimuli, however. Our study supports the results by Nan et al. (2016), who found a reduced MMN for tone-language speaking amusics in response to lexical tones.

Our study can be criticized for its small sample size, which can be seen as problematic for an ERP study. A small sample size is a pitfall that all studies with amusics face, as the population is a rather small one. Compared to other ERP studies with amusics, however, the size of our sample is fairly large.

5 Conclusion

Our study is the first to investigate word stress processing in congenital amusia. By employing a behavioral and an electrophysiological paradigm, we were able to assess both in relation to each other. Our results surprisingly show that in the behavioral task amusics utilize durational cues more than controls and that they did not struggle with pitch cues when it comes to the identification of word stress.

We were also able to demonstrate that amusics did indeed show an MMN, as an automatic reaction to auditory change detection to different word stress patterns. However, this MMN was significantly reduced in comparison to our control population, indicating abnormal neural processes even at this very early stage of processing.

Taken together, these findings show that amusics exhibit some difficulties when it comes to word stress cued by pitch, but that these difficulties do not lead to overall processing differences between amusics and controls: While the MMN results indicate deficits in central auditory processing and/or representations, the behavioural results demonstrate that amusics use other cues than pitch and a different weighting of cues than we saw in the control group to compensate for their deficits.

The difficulties of amusics in the perception of word stress that we found in the present study are similar to their previously reported impairment in musical pitch, supporting the accumulating evidence for an impairment that is not specific to the domain of music.

Further studies investigating later ERP components, as well as different cues and cue weightings, and a comparison to other developmental disorders are warranted.

References

Alain, Claude, David L. Woods & Robert T. Knight. 1998. A distributed cortical network for auditory sensory memory in humans. *Brain Research* 812(1–2). 23–37.

Albouy, Philippe, Marion Cousineau, Anne Caclin, Barbara Tillmann & Isabelle Peretz. 2016. Impaired encoding of rapid pitch information underlies perception and memory deficits in congenital amusia. *Scientific Reports* 6. 18861.

Albouy, Philippe, Jérémie Mattout, Romain Bouet, Emmanuel Maby, Gaëtan Sanchez, Pierre-Emmanuel Aguera, Sébastien Daligault, Claude Delpuech, Olivier Bertrand, Anne Caclin & Barbara Tillmann. 2013a. Impaired pitch perception and memory in congenital amusia: The deficit starts in the auditory cortex. *Brain* 136(5). 1639–1661.

Albouy, Philippe, Katrin Schulze, Anne Caclin & Barbara Tillmann. 2013b. Does tonality boost short-term memory in congenital amusia? *Brain Research* 1537. 224–232.

Ayotte, Julie, Isabelle Peretz & Krista Hyde. 2002. Congenital amusia: A group study of adults afflicted with a music-specific disorder. *Brain* 125(2). 238–251.

Baayen, R. Harald, Douglas J. Davidson & Douglas M. Bates. 2008. Mixed-effects modeling with crossed random effects for subjects and items. *Journal of Memory and Language* 59. 390–412.

Boersma, Paul & David Weenink. 2016. Praat: Doing phonetics by computer (version 6.0.15). Retrieved from http://www.praat.org/.

Braun, Allen, Joe McArdle, Jennifer L. Jones, Vladimir Nechaev, Christopher Zalewski, Carmen Brewer & Dennis Drayna. 2008. Tune deafness: Processing melodic errors outside of conscious awareness as reflected by components of the auditory ERP. *Plos One* 3(6). 1–6.

Chen, Jian & Jie Yuan. 2016. The neural causes of congenital amusia. *The Journal of Neuroscience* 36(30). 7803–7804.

Chen, Joyce L., Sukhbinder Kumar, Victoria Wiliamson, Jan Scholz, Timothy Grifiths & Lauren Stewart. 2014. Detection of the arcuate fasciculus in congenital amusia is dependent on tractography algorithm. *The 20th Annual Meeting of the Organization for Human Brain Mapping* 6. 1–11.

Chládková, Katerina, Paola Escudero & Silvia C. Lipski. 2013. Pre-attentive sensitivity to vowel duration reveals native phonology and predicts learning of second-language sounds. *Brain and Language* 126(3). 243–252.

Dalla Bella, Simone, Magdalena Berkowska & Jakub Sowiński. 2011. Disorders of pitch production in tone deafness. *Frontiers in Psychology* 2. 164.

De Bree, Elise, Frank Wijnen & Wim Zonneveld. 2006. Word stress production in three- year- old children at risk of dyslexia. *Journal of Research in Reading* 29(3). 304–317.

Dogil, Gregorz. 1995. The phonetic manifestation of stress. *Arbeitspapiere des Instituts für Maschinelle Sprachverarbeitung (Universität Stuttgart)* 2. 3–51.

Eisenberg, Peter. 1991. Syllabische Struktur und Wortakzent: Prinzipien der Prosodik deutscher Wörter. *Zeitschrift für Sprachwissenschaft* 10(1). 37–64.

Fikkert, Paula & Zvi Penner. 1998. Stagnation in prosodic development of language- disordered children. Proceedings of the Boston University Conference on Language Acquisition; p 201–212.

Foxton, Jessica M., Jennifer L. Dean, Rosemary Gee, Isabelle Peretz & Timothy D. Griffiths. 2004. Characterization of deficits in pitch perception underlying "tone deafness". *Brain* 127(4). 801–810.

Foxton, Jessica M., Rachel K. Nandy & Timothy D. Griffiths. 2006. Rhythm deficits in 'tone deafness'. *Brain and Cognition* 62(1). 24–29.

Gallon, Nichola, John Harris & Heather Van der Lely. 2007. Non-word repetition: An investigation of phonological complexity in children with grammatical SLI. *Clinical Linguistics & Phonetics* 21(6). 435–455.

Gosselin, Nathalie, Pierre Jolicœur & Isabelle Peretz. 2009. Impaired memory for pitch in congenital amusia. *Annals of the New York Academy of Sciences* 1169(1). 270–272.

Goswami, Usha, Natasha Mead, Tim Fosker, Martina Huss, Lisa Barnes & Leong Victoria. 2013. Impaired perception of syllable stress in children with dyslexia: A longitudinal study. *Journal of Memory and Language* 69(1). 1–17.

Green, David M. & John A. Swets. 1966. *Signal Detection Theory and Psychophysics*. New York: Wiley.

Haake, Caroline, Malte Kob, Klaus Willmes & Frank Domahs. 2013. Word stress processing in specific language impairment: Auditory or representational deficits? *Clinical Linguistics & Phonetics* 27(8). 594–615.

Hamann, Silke, Mats Exter, Jasmin Pfeifer & Marion Krause-Burmester. 2012. Perceiving differences in linguistic and non-linguistic pitch: A pilot study with German congenital amusics. In: Emilios Cambouropoulos, Costas Tsougras, Panayotis Mavromatis, Konstantinos Pastiadis, editors. Proceedings of The 12th International Conference On Music Perception And Cognition (ICMPC *and 8th Triennial Conference of the European Society for the Cognitive Sciences of Music (ESCOM).*); Thessaloniki, Greece. School of Music Studies, Aristotle University of Thessaloniki. 398–405.

Hay, Rachel A., Brian J. Roach, Vinod H. Srihari, Scott W. Woods, Judith M. Ford & Daniel H. Mathalon. 2015. Equivalent mismatch negativity deficits across deviant types in early illness schizophrenia-spectrum patients. *Biological Psychology* 105. 130–137.

Henry, Molly J. & J. Devin McAuley. 2010. On the prevalence of congenital amusia. *Music Perception* 27(5). 413–418.

Henry, Molly J. & J. Devin McAuley. 2013. Failure to apply signal detection theory to the montreal battery of evaluation of amusia may misdiagnose amusia. *Music Perception* 30 (5). 480–496.

Huang, Wan-Ting, Chang Liu, Qi Dong Dong & Yun Nan. 2015. Categorical perception of lexical tones in Mandarin-speaking congenital amusics. *Frontiers in Psychology* 6. 829.

Huang, Xunan, Caicai Zhang, Feng Shi, Nan Yan & Lan Wang. 2016. Impaired vowel discrimination in Mandarin-speaking congenital amusics. Proceedings of The 5th International Symposium on Tonal Aspects of Languages (Tal 2016); Buffalo, NY. 138–141.

Hutchins, Sean, Nathalie Gosselin & Isabelle Peretz. 2010. Identification of changes along a continuum of speech intonation is impaired in congenital amusia. *Frontiers in Psychology* 1. 236.

Hyde, Krista L., Jason P. Lerch, Robert J. Zatorre, Timothy D. Griffiths, Alan Evans & Isabelle Peretz. 2007. Cortical thickness in congenital amusia: When less is better than more. *The Journal of Neuroscience* 27(47). 13028–13032.

Hyde, Krista & Isabelle Peretz. 2004. Brains that are out of tune but in time. *Psychological Science* 15(5). 356–360.

Hyde, Krista, Robert J. Zatorre, Timothy D. Griffiths, Jason P. Lerch & Isabelle Peretz. 2006. Morphometry of the amusic brain: A two-site study. *Brain* 129(10). 2562–2570.

Hyde, Krista, Robert J. Zatorre & Isabelle Peretz. 2011. Functional MRI evidence of an abnormal neural network for pitch processing in congenital amusia. *Cerebral Cortex* 21(2). 292–299.

Jasmin, Kyle, Fred Dick, Lori L. Holt & Adam Tierney. 2019. Tailored perception: Individuals' speech and music perception strategies fit their perceptual abilities. *Journal of Experimental Psychology: General* 149(5). 914–934.

Jessen, Michael, Krzysztof Marasek, Katrin Schneider & Kathrin Claßen. 1995. Acoustic correlates of word stress and the tense/lax opposition in the vowel system of German. Proceedings of The International Congress Of Phonetic Sciences; Stockholm University, Stockholm. 428–431.

Kang, Shinae, Keith Johnson & Gregory Finley. 2016. Effects of native language on compensation for coarticulation. *Speech Communication* 77. 84–100.

Kirmse, Ursula, Sari Ylinen, Mari Tervaniemi, Martti Vainio, Erich Schröger & Thomas Jacobsen. 2008. Modulation of the Mismatch Negativity (MMN) to vowel duration changes in native speakers of Finnish and German as a result of language experience. *International Journal of Psychophysiology* 67(2). 131–143.

Kujala, Teija & Risto Näätänen. 2001. The mismatch negativity in evaluating central auditory dysfunction in dyslexia. *Neuroscience & Biobehavioral Reviews* 25(6). 535–543.

Launay, Jacques, Manon Grube & Lauren Stewart. 2014. Dysrhythmia: A specific congenital rhythm perception deficit. *Frontiers in Psychology* 5. 18.

Lebrun, Marie-Andrée, Patricia Moreau, Andréane McNally, Geneviève Mignault Goulet & Isabelle Peretz. 2012. Congenital amusia in childhood: A case study. *Cortex* 48(6). 683–688.

Leong, Victoria, Jarmo Hämäläinen, Fruzsina Soltész & Usha Goswami. 2011. Rise time perception and detection of syllable stress in adults with developmental dyslexia. *Journal of Memory and Language* 64(1). 59–73.

Lintfert, Britta. 2010. Phonetic and phonological development of stress in German [Doctoral Dissertation]. Stuttgart: University of Stuttgart.

Lisker, Leigh. 1986. "Voicing" in English: A catalogue of acoustic features signaling /b/ versus /p/ in trochees. *Language and Speech* 29(1). 3–11.

Liu, Fang, Cunmei Jiang, Bei Wang, Yi Xu & Aniruddh D. Patel. 2015a. A music perception disorder (congenital amusia) influences speech comprehension. *Neuropsychologia* 66. 111–118.

Liu, Fang, Akshay R. Maggu, Joseph C. Y. Lau & Patrick C. M. Wong. 2015b. Brainstem encoding of speech and musical stimuli in congenital amusia: Evidence from Cantonese speakers. *Frontiers in Human Neuroscience* 8. 1029.

Liu, Fang, Aniruddh D. Patel, Adrian Fourcin & Lauren Stewart. 2010. Intonation processing in congenital amusia: Discrimination, identification and imitation. *Brain* 133(6). 1682–1693.

Liu, Fang, Yi Xu, Aniruddh D. Patel, Tom Francart & Cunmei Jiang. 2012. Differential recognition of pitch patterns in discrete and gliding stimuli in congenital amusia: Evidence from Mandarin speakers. *Brain and Cognition* 79(3). 209–215.

Lolli, Sydney L., Ari D. Lewenstein, Julian Basurto, Sean Winnik & Psyche Loui. 2015. Sound frequency affects speech emotion perception: Results from congenital amusia. *Frontiers in Psychology* 6. 1340.

Loui, Psyche & Gottfried Schlaug. 2009. Investigating musical disorders with diffusion tensor imaging: A comparison of imaging parameters. *Annals of the New York Academy of Sciences* 1169(1). 121–125.

Mandell, Jake, Katrin Schulze & Gottfried Schlaug. 2007. Congenital amusia: An auditory-motor feedback disorder? *Restorative Neurology and Neuroscience* 25(3–4). 323–334.

Marin, Manuela M., Bruno Gingras & Lauren Stewart. 2012a. Perception of musical timbre in congenital amusia: Categorization, discrimination and short-term memory. *Neuropsychologia* 50(3). 367–378.

Marin, Manuela M., William F. Thompson & L. Stewart. 2012b. Emotion perception of dyads and triads in congenital amusia. In: Emilios Cambouropoulus, Costas Tsougras, Panayotis Mavromatis, Konstantinos Pastiadis, editors. Proceedings of The 12th International Conference on Music Perception and Cognition (ICMPC *and 8th Triennial Conference of the European Society for the Cognitive Sciences of Music (ESCOM)*.); Thessaloniki, Greece. School of Music Studies, Aristotle University of Thessaloniki. 652–653.

Mignault Goulet, Geneviève, Patricia Moreau, Nicolas Robitaille & Isabelle Peretz. 2012. Congenital amusia persists in the developing brain after daily music listening. *Plos One* 7(5). e36860.
Moreau, Patricia, Pierre Jolicœur & Isabelle Peretz. 2009. Automatic brain responses to pitch changes in congenital amusia. *Annals of the New York Academy of Sciences* 1169(1). 191–194.
Moreau, Patricia, Pierre Jolicœur & Isabelle Peretz. 2013. Pitch discrimination without awareness in congenital amusia: Evidence from event-related potentials. *Brain and Cognition* 81(3). 337–344.
Näätänen, Risto. 2001. The perception of speech sounds by the human brain as reflected by the Mismatch Negativity (MMN) and its magnetic equivalent (mMMN). *Psychophysiology* 38(1). 1–21.
Näätänen, Risto, A. W. K. Gaillard & S. Mäntysalo. 1978. Early selective-attention effect on evoked potential reinterpreted. *Acta Psychologica* 42(4). 313–329.
Näätänen, Risto, Pekka Paavilainen, Tehu Rinne & Kimmo Alho. 2007. The Mismatch Negativity (MMN) in basic research of central auditory processing: A review. *Clinical Neurophysiology* 118(12). 2544–2590.
Näätänen, Risto, Elyse Sussman, Dean Salisbury & Valerie L. Shafer. 2014. Mismatch Negativity (MMN) as an index of cognitive dysfunction. *Brain Topography* 27(4). 451–466.
Nan, Yun, Wan-ting Huang, Wen-jing Wang, Chang Liu & Qi Dong. 2016. Subgroup differences in the lexical tone Mismatch Negativity (MMN) among Mandarin speakers with congenital amusia. *Biological Psychology* 113. 59–67.
Partanen, Eino, Martti Vainio, Teija Kujala & Minna Huotilainen. 2011. Linguistic multifeature MMN paradigm for extensive recording of auditory discrimination. *Psychophysiology* 48(10). 1372–1380.
Patel, Aniruddh D. 2003. Rhythm in language and music: Parallels and differences. *Annals of the New York Academy of Sciences* 999(1). 140–143.
Patel, Aniruddh D., Meredith Wong, Jessica Foxton, Aliette Lochy & Isabelle Peretz. 2008. Speech intonation perception deficits in musical tone deafness (congenital amusia). *Music Perception* 25(4). 357–368.
Peretz, Isabelle, Julie Ayotte, Robert J. Zatorre, Jacques Mehler, Pierre Ahad, Virginia B. Penhune & Benoît Jutras. 2002. Congenital amusia: A disorder of fine-grained pitch discrimination. *Neuron* 33(2). 185–191.
Peretz, Isabelle, Anne J. Blood, Virginia B. Penhune & Robert J. Zatorre. 2001. Cortical deafness to dissonance. *Brain* 124(5). 928–940.
Peretz, Isabelle, Anne Sophie Champod & Krista Hyde. 2003. Varieties of musical disorders: The Montreal Battery of Evaluation of Amusia. *Annals of the New York Academy of Sciences* 999(1). 58–75.
Peretz, Isabelle, Jenny Saffran, Daniele Schön & Nathalie Gosselin. 2012. Statistical learning of speech, not music, in congenital amusia. *Annals of the New York Academy of Sciences* 1252(1). 361–366.
Pettinato, Michèle & Jo Verhoeven. 2008. Production and perception of word stress in children and adolescents with Down syndrome. *Down Syndrome Research and Practice* 13. 48–61.
Pfeifer, Jasmin & Silke Hamann. 2015. Revising the diagnosis of congenital amusia with the Montreal Battery of Evaluation of Amusia. *Frontiers in Human Neuroscience* 9. 161.

Phillips-Silver, Jessica, Petri Toiviainen, Nathalie Gosselin & Isabelle Peretz. 2013. Amusic does not mean unmusical: Beat perception and synchronization ability despite pitch deafness. *Cognitive Neuropsychology* 30(5). 311–331.

Picton, Terence W., Claude Alain, Leun Otten, Walter Ritter & André Achim. 2000. Mismatch Negativity: Different water in the same river. *Audiology and Neurotology* 5(3–4). 111–139.

Repp, Bruno H. & Yi-Huang Su. 2013. Sensorimotor synchronization: A review of recent research (2006–2012). *Psychonomic Bulletin & Review* 20(3). 403–452.

Shinozaki, Jun, Nobuo Hiroe, Masa-aki Sato, Takashi Nagamine & Kaoru Sekiyama. 2016. Impact of language on functional connectivity for audiovisual speech integration. *Scientific Reports* 6(1). 31388.

Shtyrov, Yury, Teija Kujala, Satu Palva, Risto J. Ilmoniemi & Risto Näätänen. 2000. Discrimination of speech and of complex nonspeech sounds of different temporal structure in the left and right cerebral hemispheres. *Neuroimage* 12(6). 657–663.

Sorokin, Alexander, Paavo Alku & Teija Kujala. 2010. Change and novelty detection in speech and non-speech sound streams. *Brain Research* 1327. 77–90.

Sowiński, Jakub & Simone Dalla Bella. 2013. Poor synchronization to the beat may result from deficient auditory-motor mapping. *Neuropsychologia* 51(10). 1952–1963.

Stewart, Lauren. 2008. Fractionating the musical mind: Insights from congenital amusia. *Current Opinion in Neurobiology* 18(2). 127–130.

Summerfield, Quentin. 1981. Articulatory rate and perceptual constancy in phonetic perception. *Journal of Experimental Psychology: Human Perception and Performance* 7(5). 1074–1095.

Tal, Idan, Edward W. Large, Eshed Rabinovitch, Yi Wei, Charles E. Schroeder, David Poeppel & Elana Zion Golumbic. 2017. Neural entrainment to the beat: The "missing-pulse" phenomenon. *The Journal of Neuroscience* 37(26). 6331–6341.

Tang, Wei, Xi-jian Wang, Jia-qi Li, Chang Liu, Qi Dong & Yun Nan. 2018. Vowel and tone recognition in quiet and in noise among Mandarin-speaking amusics. *Hearing Research* 363. 62–69.

Thompson, William F., Manuela M. Marin & Lauren Stewart. 2012. Reduced sensitivity to emotional prosody in congenital amusia rekindles the musical protolanguage hypothesis. *Proceedings of the National Academy of Sciences of the United States of America* 109(46). 19027–19032.

Tillmann, Barbara, Denis Burnham, Sebastien Nguyen, Nicolas Grimault, Nathalie Gosselin & Isabelle Peretz. 2011. Congenital amusia (or tone-deafness) interferes with pitch processing in tone languages. *Frontiers in Psychology* 2. 120.

Tillmann, Barbara, Philippe Lalitte, Philippe Albouy, Anne Caclin & Emmanuel Bigand. 2016. Discrimination of tonal and atonal music in congenital amusia: The advantage of implicit tasks. *Neuropsychologia* 85. 10–18.

Tillmann, Barbara, Katrin Schulze & Jessica M. Foxton. 2009. Congenital amusia: A short-term memory deficit for non-verbal, but not verbal sounds. *Brain and Cognition* 71(3). 259–264.

Weber, Christiane, Anja Hahne, Manuela Friedrich & Angela D. Friederici. 2004. Discrimination of word stress in early infant perception: Electrophysiological evidence. *Cognitive Brain Research* 18(2). 149–161.

Weber, Christiane, Anja Hahne, Manuela Friedrich & Angela D. Friederici. 2005. Reduced stress pattern discrimination in 5-month-olds as a marker of risk for later language impairment: Neurophysiologial evidence. *Cognitive Brain Research* 25(1). 180–187.

Wiese, Richard. 2000. *The phonology of German*. Oxford: Oxford University Press.
Williamson, Victoria J., Claire McDonald, Diana Deutsch, Timothy D. Griffiths & Lauren Stewart. 2010. Faster decline of pitch memory over time in congenital amusia. *Advances in Cognitive Psychology* 6(1). 15–22.
Williamson, Victoria Jane & Lauren Stewart. 2010. Memory for pitch in congenital amusia: Beyond a fine-grained pitch discrimination problem. *Memory* 18(6). 657–669.
Wise, Karen. 2009. Understanding "tone deafness": A multi-componential analysis of perception, cognition, singing and self-perception in adults reporting musical difficulties [Doctoral Dissertation]: Keele University.
Ylinen, Sari, Anna Shestakova, Minna Huotilainen, Paavo Alku & Risto Näätänen. 2006. Mismatch Negativity (MMN) elicited by changes in phoneme length: A cross-linguistic study. *Brain Research* 1072(1). 175–185.
Zhang, Caicai, Jing Shao & Xunan Huang. 2017. Deficits of congenital amusia beyond pitch: Evidence from impaired categorical perception of vowels in Cantonese-speaking congenital amusics. *Plos One* 12(8).e0183151.

Richard Wiese
Rhythmic structure – parallels between language and music

Abstract: Rhythm is a phenomenon which is obviously present for both language and music. However, it is unclear whether the term "rhythm" has the same meaning in these two domains, and both musicologists and cognitive scientists have disputed this. In the present paper, I argue that there are central aspects of rhythm which are indeed shared between language and music. Formally, the metrical grid provides the necessary tool to represent rhythm in both domains. Empirical evidence for similarities across the two domains comes from a series of studies (neurolinguistic-experimental and corpus-based) demonstrating that regular alternation, a prominent feature of rhythm in music, is the preferred option in the production and perception of language, analogous to music and in contrast to obvious appearances to the contrary. This observation makes rhythm in language more akin to rhythm in music than is sometimes thought.

Keywords: rhythm, stress clash, music, prosody, EEG

1 Introduction

Relations between music and language have been studied on several levels, such as their structural properties on various levels, their (co-)evolution, or their potential to convey meaning. The present paper is thus focused on the following question: how domain-specific is rhythm? This question has been discussed widely in recent years, and with different conclusions, as we will see. One way of re-formulating the question is by reference to the *Metrical Organization Hypothesis*. As proposed by Liberman (1975), this hypothesis claims that "All temporally ordered behavior is metrically organized." If true, this hypothesis leads to the question what the commonalities and differences of metrical organization across different domains of behavior are. This contribution will discuss this question for language and music.

Acknowledgements: I am grateful for the advice and help by a number of colleagues. In particular, Pauline Larrouy-Maestri, Ingo Plag and Mathias Scharinger helped to improve the present article.

Richard Wiese, Philipps-Universität Marburg, Pilgrimstein 16, D-35032, Marburg, e-mail: wiese@uni-marburg.de

https://doi.org/10.1515/9783110770186-006

In particular, a number of studies on the role of rhythm in the processing of language will be presented. The interpretation will then focus on the comparison of linguistic and musical rhythm and will pursue the claim that the properties of rhythm of language and music are more similar to each other than has sometimes been proposed. The similarity consists largely in the emphasis on *regularity of rhythm*, a dimension often called "meter" in both language and music (see next section). Another conclusion of this paper will be that rhythm is part of a *predictive structure*, largely comparable for both language and music, in spite of appearances to the contrary.

2 Grid representation of rhythm

Rhythm can be defined, quite generally, as a property of a sequence of events with durational structure and with distinctive differences in prominence. That is, based on some conception of time, events unfold in time, and some of them are relatively prominent compared to other events in their proximity. Under this view, rhythm can be represented as a layered structure of events in time as in (1), taking the German five-syllable word *Universität* 'university' as an example. This structural view was first proposed by Liberman & Prince (1977), Prince (1983), and Lerdahl & Jackendoff (1983).

(1) Grid representation of German word *Universität* 'university'

```
                x
x               x
x       x       x
x   x   x   x   x
U   ni  ver si  tät
```

The grid represents recurrent individual events as columns, succession of events in left-to-right order, and different levels of scansion as rows. For the linguistic example considered here, syllables are considered to constitute basic events. Each cell in a row may be marked as a bearer of prominence by a grid entry 'x', or not. Such a "bearer of prominence" constitutes a beat. Thus, grids allow to represent multiple grades of stress levels, as the number of rows is not limited, in theory. For the example word, four levels of prominence ranging from primary stress on the final syllable to unstressed syllables two and four seem to provide an adequate description. An alternative notation, the simpler strong–weak notation (¯ vs.˘) often used in descriptions of poetic meter or music does not allow for such more numerous degrees of prominence.

The formal theory of rhythm in music has taken a step forward by the analyses provided by Lerdahl & Jackendoff (1983). In their grid theory of rhythm, taken from linguistic analysis, beats receive a formal representation by marks on layered levels, while alternations on some level of rhythmical organization are represented by beats on this level which are accompanied by intervening beats on the next lower level. Rhythm in music has similar properties to that of language: a sequence of events in time and an alternating structure of strong(er) and weak(er) such events. This is demonstrated by the following example (2) in the grid analysis of rhythm in Lerdahl & Jackendoff (1983). The metrical analysis as illustrated here is only one of several structural dimensions postulated by the authors for music. Grouping structure, time-span reduction and prolongational reduction are additional formal dimensions of music not covered here.

(2) W. A. Mozart, *Sinfonie g-moll*, KV 550.

Here, in the piano transcription of the first bars of Mozart's *g-minor symphony*, a grid representation is added for which the eighth note is the basic unit on the first grid level, one which allows for prominence to each alternating beat on each higher level (notated downwards here). Three points are noteworthy: first, for the first four levels layered on top of the basic one (the eighth note), there is a completely regular alternation between a strong event (the first one) and an immediately following weak event (one without a grid entry). Secondly, the highest level proposed, consisting of two wholes, is marked as having optional grid entries on the second possible position. optional grid entries. That is, a strongest beat may be either on the first beat of the section, on the second strong beat (as indicated), or be completely absent. Finally, there may be a level of a basic, perceptually most prominent, the beat (also called *tactus* or *pulse* in musicology). For the present piece this may be the beat on the half note level, but decisions by performers and conductor may lead the audience to a different perception of what the basic beat is.

Finally, we note that in this example there are relatively strong positions over pauses, that is, without any notes to be played, as for the third beat in bars three, five, and seven, respectively. These cases provide evidence for the role of meter in music: perceived rhythm depends not only on acoustic prominence, but also on a conceptual unit, the regular meter. For the role of duration in this network of concepts, see Arjava & Kentner (2022).

More generally, the near-complete regularity in rhythm displayed in (2) illustrates that, for rhythm in music, there is a prominent role of an additional factor, that of meter. Meter is defined as a high degree of regularity in rhythmic alternation. The regularity comes about by an abstract-cognitive unit, that of the four-quarter time signature in the present case. Its grid representation is given in (3).

(3) The meter of the 4/4-time signature in grid notation

```
x
x       x
x   x   x   x
♩   ♩   ♩   ♩
```

Let us also have a brief look at the 3/4 signature, as in a waltz. In (4), the meter for bars 1 to 6 reveal that a strong bar-initial beat is followed by not one, but two, weak beats.

(4) The meter of the 3/4-time signature in grid notation (Johann Strauß, op. 314, *An der schönen blauen Donau*)

The highest level of the grid, as proposed by the present author, has the same kind of optional grid entries as those given in (2), to which alternative placements are available. Rhythm in the sense introduced here is not strictly tied to its acoustic realization. In (4), this is again obvious from those beats in which there is no melodic note, as for the second beat in bars 2, 3, and 4.

Beats, rhythm and meter may thus be acoustically prominent (and measurable), but not necessarily so. The difficulties in measuring rhythm have tempted some researchers to characterize rhythm as a "collective hallucination"; Liberman, 1975. But as there is comprehensive evidence for a role of rhythm in the acquisition, perception, and change of language, there is reason to argue that rhythm is a phonological structuring of linguistic expressions, grounded in both phonetic preferences as well as rhythmical principles; see also Mołczanow & Wiese (2014). Phonetic preferences might arise, e.g., by the fact that periodic muscle activity for lung contraction generates temporal patterns of syllables or feet; Abercrombie, 1992. As for the metrical grid, Jackendoff (2009) stresses that "in the rhythmic domain, the metrical grid may well be a genuine capacity unique to language and music", but also emphasizes that the degree of regularity is different for these two domains.

3 Rhythm in music and in language

We have seen that rhythm in music (at least of the type considered) displays two fundamental ingredients, namely repetition and alternation. Lerdahl's & Jackendoff's account of regular repetition (1983) is stated as a wellformedness rule as in (5). (In the second edition of their work, the authors note that such wellformedness rules show the properties of constraints in the sense of Optimality Theory: they may be violated so that other, higher ranked, constraints are fulfilled.) For the examples in (2) and (4), this rule is fulfilled without exception.

(5)   *Metrical Wellformedness Rule*
      Each metrical level must consist of equally spaced beats.

In Western tonal music, such alternating rhythms are (nearly) completely regular. The influence of meter in the sense discussed above is strong, as expressed by the rule/constraint in (5) and illustrated by the previous examples. Western music thus strongly follows the two fundamental ingredients of regular rhythm (meter), repetition and alternation. We will discuss other types of music shortly.

3.1 Differences between music and language

It is obvious that this highly constrained rhythmical organization just illustrated for music cannot hold for linguistic utterances in general. Rhythm in speech is not regular to the same extent. The ultimate reason for this lies in the fact that syntax and lexicon conspire to prevent regular alternation. Linguistic expressions do not follow a metrical pattern in a perfect manner because language conveys meaning by concatenating meaningful lexical units (the arbitrary Saussurean signs) in a way dictated by morphology and syntax. This is not to say that prosody plays no role in the formation of utterances. Evidence for prosody and other phonological factors co-determining the make-up of sentences has been accumulating (see, e.g., Agbayani & Golston, 2010 or Breiss & Hayes, 2020). The latter demonstrate that the build-up of English sentences is strongly influenced by a specific set of phonological constraints, among them stress clash constraints. Their study is based on both written and spoken texts. However, grammar and lexicon inevitably conspire to prevent completely regular alternation, as the speaker chooses lexical and phrasal units and their language-specific concatenation in order to perform the speech act s/he wants to perform at the particular moment. This is also a fundamental difference to the performance of a musical expression or even the composition of a piece of music.

Accordingly, some of the pertinent literature assumes that there are substantial differences between the properties of rhythm in these two domains, as the following excerpts demonstrate. Lerdahl & Jackendoff (1983) argue: "The major difference between music and language in this respect is that musical events are organized around a fixed and regular metrical structure that must be maintained throughout. In language, by contrast, the rhythm is flexible and is not required to conform to any particular pattern." Probably on the basis of similar considerations, Kotz et al. (2018) argue that "compared to music, rhythm in speech is more difficult to define and commonalities across the two domains remain elusive".

In German musicology, Kühn (1987) makes an analogous claim: "Poetry rests upon verse, meter, rhyme and stanza; from this, it gains regularity, symmetry, correspondence. The linguistic form of prose does not recognize such means and correspondence; it claims freedom of speech."[1]

Finally, Patel, 2010 gives the metrical grid as introduced above for language an interpretation different from music by arguing that "linguistic metrical grids

---

[1] Present author's translation. Original: "Poesie beruht auf Vers, Metrum, Reim, Strophe; daraus gewinnt sie Regelmaß, Symmetrie, Entsprechung. Die Sprachform der Prosa kennt solche Mittel und Korrespondenzen nicht; sie meint Ungebundenheit der Rede."

are not abstract mental patterns (like musical metrical grids) but are simply maps of heard prominences, full of temporal irregularities." Furthermore, Patel (2010) downgrades the parallelism between language and music in terms of its regularity as such: „The notion that rhythm in language is primarily *consequence* rather than *construct* stands in sharp contrast to rhythm in music, in which patterns of timing and accent are a focus of conscious design".

In contrast to these views, there is recent evidence for the view that rhythm in music and language are in fact based on similar or identical mechanisms. For example, Chern et al. (2018) argue that linguistic skills in children can be enhanced by training in the musical domain. Furthermore, the sensitivity towards linguistic and musical rhythm can be transferred from one domain to the other, as demonstrated in (Magne et al., 2016). Thus, at least for children there is a transfer of effects of rhythm from one domain to the other. And Kotz et al. (2018), who are skeptical with respect to the similarity of rhythm in music and language (see above), also note: "The fact that neural coupling to the acoustic stream occurs in both music and speech implies that shared mechanisms might underlie this process."

3.2 The role of rhythm in language and music

The role of rhythm in music and language must also be approached with the question of the functions of rhythm in these domains, because if the functions of rhythm would be largely identical, it is plausible that it will operate analogously in the two domains. Previous studies have identified a number of plausible functions of rhythm in language and music, which can be summarized as follows.

The functions of rhythm in language relate to all the major cognitive domains of language, namely perception, production and acquisition. For perception, rhythm has been demonstrated to support the segmentation of the speech stream into words and phrases by means of a *Metrical Segmentation Strategy* Cutler & Norris, 1988, Cutler, 1990, according to which prosodic prominence marks the beginning of new lexical units. In languages such as English, Dutch, or German, the hearer may expect a new word to begin when perceiving a stressed syllable. Similar expectations arise for the beginnings or endings of syntactic units. That is, rhythm creates predictions in perception, because segmentation into relevant units facilitates the prediction of upcoming material. A further function of rhythm, in its relation to stress, is to highlight information, in particular as new information.

In production, linguistic rhythm facilitates synchronization of linguistic units with other periodic movements, such as breathing, gestures and limb movement.

Conversely, neural entrainment, the modification of brain oscillations in accordance with temporal fluctuations of speech, would be made virtually impossible without a reasonably steady beat frequency. Furthermore, rhythmical structure in production interacts with perception by means of neural entrainment, see Assaneo et al., 2021.

In language acquisition, one of the tasks for the child is to separate out meaningful units from the speech stream. Again, there is evidence that children make use of rhythm to achieve this task (Hay & Saffran, 2012; Ommen et al., 2020). They are guided by rhythm to achieve both word recognition as well as word learning.

The functions of rhythm in music are even more obvious but differ from those in language. First, rhythm is part of the aesthetic impression of a piece; and musical styles are often identified by their specific rhythm type – compare marches to jazz or waltzes. In addition, rhythm also serves the memorability of pieces of music; Snyder, 2000. This may be a function more important for the performer than for the listener. Also, the experience of pleasing music is related to stronger neural entrainment via the perception of rhythm; Trost et al., 2014. On a more social level, Mehr et al. (2019) argue that rhythmic behavior reinforces social bonding, and was therefore evolutionary advantageous.

There is a further function of rhythm in music that is more crucially important to music performance than it is to linguistic performance, namely the synchronization between actors. While verbal utterances are usually performed by a single actor/speaker, and with little or no overlap between speakers who are usually aligned in a consecutive mode, music is far more often a common and simultaneous enterprise by a group of co-present actors, as in a band, a choir, or an orchestra, with the size of such ensembles to vary between two and several hundred. For this reason, synchronization between actors within an ensemble is of utmost importance in musical performance. Rhythm is a crucial element here, because, as mentioned above, rhythm strongly facilitates prediction, and thus synchronization. On the other hand, there is also evidence for synchronization in verbal communication, for turn-taking in particular (see Wilson & Wilson, 2005). However, synchronization between consecutive actors is to be distinguished from synchronization of simultaneous actors. If the role of synchronization in both music and language can be corroborated, this would strengthen the case for the parallelism between music and language.

While these considerations may give the impression that the functions of rhythm in language and music are primarily different, there is an overarching concept which gives an important unity to the function of rhythm in these domains: the function of rhythm can be subsumed under the notion of prediction. The view that prediction is a crucial mechanism in language processing is proposed by Kutas et al. (2011) who propose a "strong form" of prediction in which "features are pre-activated at some time point prior to encountering the confirmatory bottom-up input" (p. 196). Expecting metrical beats with or without the corresponding acoustic signal seems to fulfill this patterning. Prediction as an important factor in the processing of music is also demonstrated by Vuust et al. (2009).

4 Back to music: Additive and other types of rhythm

The observation that language is less regular in terms of rhythmical alternations than music leads to a reconsideration of a distinction established in studies of musical rhythm: that of divisive vs. additive types of rhythm, as proposed by Sachs (1952). In divisive (or multiplicative) rhythm, beats at each level can be divided by a simple digit such as two or three. This leads to time signatures such as 2/4, 3/4, 4/4, or others (see illustrations (2) and (4)). In contrast, additive rhythm *adds* simple rhythmic patterns which need not be identical, leading to time signatures such as 5/8 or even 8/8 if partitioned as 3+3+2. Such agglomerations of small rhythmic parts cannot be analyzed by division (or multiplication) of integers. The latter type has been found (in various varieties) in European medieval music, Balkan music and in African styles of music. So-called additive rhythm seems like a good candidate for the type of rhythm present in language. But in additive rhythm, there is still a metrical regularity within and across phrases which cannot be achieved perfectly in language.

A third type of rhythm completely refrains from such identity of a sequence of bars (each instantiating a metrical pattern) within a piece or a larger part thereof. To illustrate this type of rhythm in music, consider the piece *Three Pieces for Solo Clarinet, first movement,* by Igor Stravinsky, with the first bars given in (6). As can be seen, bars bearing different time signatures ranging from 3/8 to 7/8 are concatenated here in a completely unpredictable manner. Furthermore, strong beats are not predictably to be realized on the first beat, as indicated by means of breath marks and accents in the score.[2] This rhythm type (called "numerical" by Sachs, 1952) then illustrates the "third group of verses

---

[2] The heading to the score of this piece says: "The breath marks, accents and metronome marks indicated in the 3 pieces should be strictly adhered to." A recording can be found here: https://en.wikipedia.org/wiki/File:Igor_Stravinsky_-_3_Pieces_for_Clarinet_Alone.ogg

and melodies in which no metric organization and hardly any recurrence of accents are considered" (Sachs, 1952).

(6) Three Pieces for Solo Clarinet, first movement, bar 1–9, by Igor Stravinsky (1919)

A preliminary conclusion of these considerations might be that music and language share the less regulated types of musical rhythm of the type illustrated in (6). However, in the following I will try to show that there is more to say on this issue.

5 Five studies on rhythm in language

In the following, I will present evidence for regular rhythmic alternation in the perception and production of language. This provides the empirical basis for the claim that rhythm in language is indeed more similar to rhythm in music than some authors have claimed it to be. The evidence for rhythmic alternation in language comes from two types of studies which have been conducted over a number of years in Marburg. The present focus is on their common theme of providing evidence for metrically regular rhythm.

Three of these studies (sections 5.1.1 to 5.1.3) address the perception of rhythm in language and have been conducted by making use of the paradigm of electroencephalography (EEG): (Bohn et al., 2013) on the Rhythm Rule in German particle verbs, (Henrich et al., 2014) on the Rhythm Rule in English compounds, and (Knaus et al., 2011) on the Rhythm Rule in German compounds. The Rhythm Rule describes an alternation of stressed and unstressed syllables in particular linguistic contexts and will be illustrated shortly.

A second group of studies, presented in section 5.2., are corpus studies, which can thus shed some light not on the perception, but the production of rhythmically regulated structures: (Wiese & Speyer, 2015) on a phenomenon called *Prosodic Parallelism* in written German, and (Wiese, 2016) on evidence for such Prosodic Parallelism in spoken German. All these studies thus address the question of rhythmic regularity in language. Note that all studies discussed here refer to two languages (German, English) which have been considered to represent the stress-timed type of rhythm, and not the syllable-timed type of rhythm.

5.1 Electrophysiology – event-related potential paradigm

One important approach to the study of cognition and language processing consists in the recording and analysis of electroencephalography, based on the measurement of miniscule fluctuations in the electric activity of the neocortex (voltage changes over short periods of time, typically 1 to 1.5 sec.), as measured on the surface of the scalp. Such EEG measurements, especially within the paradigm of event-related potentials (ERPs), have provided valuable access to on-line brain (or at least cortex) activity in recent decades with very fine-grained temporal resolution (see, e.g., Luck, 2014).

5.1.1 EEG study on the *Rhythm Rule* in German particle verbs

The *Rhythm Rule* is a formalization of a widely observed phenomenon, although disputed, in which a stress is "moved" from its original place such that an alternation of stresses is achieved. The phenomenon is often illustrated by the English example of *thir'teen* changed to *'thirteen* in a phrasal context such as *'thirteen "men*. Note that stress on *men* is stronger than stress on the preceding adjective. The secondary stress is moved from the immediately following primary stress within the phrase. In other words, a clash of two adjacent stresses is resolved by a shift, moving the secondary stress away from the primary stress. This may be regarded as an informal statement of the Rhythm Rule. More formal statements of the rule can be found in (Liberman & Prince, 1977) for English; and in (Kiparsky, 1973, Giegerich, 1985, Wiese, 2000) for German. An alternative analysis sees the stress change not as a shift, but as a stress deletion, again for the secondary of the two clashing stresses (Gussenhoven, 1991). However, under this analysis the result is the same: a stress clash is resolved in favor of alternation. Other issues discussed for this rule are its context conditions, its optionality and perceptibility.

Bohn et al., 2013, presented an EEG study with the explicit intention of testing the reality of the Rhythm Rule in German. In German, a potential stress clash or, alternatively, a rhythmically conditioned shift can be found in particle verbs as right-hand members of a phrase, as in: *den Ter"min 'absagen* 'cancel the appointment'. Particle verbs carry main stress on the particle, while preceding object nouns (bisyllabic in the present case) carry stronger stress than the verbs. Therefore, a stress clash in the phrase can be resolved by moving stress onto the particle verb, resulting in *den Ter"min ab'sagen*. In the experiment, German adult speakers listened to sentences as in Table 1. Note that the shift in condition 1 creates alternating stress, while this is already the case in condition 2. If stress is shifted here, the result is a stress lapse, condition 4, with more than one unstressed syllable between two stressed ones. Note also that condition 4 is "incorrect" in two ways: shift causes a deviation from the stress patterning of particle verbs, and the shift results in a lapse, a non-preferred pattern with two unstressed syllables. This is different in condition 3, where the stress clash co-occurs with correct lexical stresses.

Table 1: Experimental conditions and filler conditions of EEG experiment, (Bohn et al., 2013).

Condition	Example
1) Correct SHIFT	Sie soll den **Ter'min ab'sagen**, wie besprochen. *She is supposed to cancel the appointment, as discussed.*
2) Correct NO SHIFT	Sie soll die **'Feier 'absagen**, wie besprochen. *She is supposed to cancel the party, as discussed.*
3) CLASH	Sie soll den **Ter'min 'absagen**, wie besprochen. *She is supposed to cancel the appointment, as discussed.*
4) LAPSE	Sie soll die **'Feier ab'sagen**, wie besprochen. *She is supposed to cancel the party, as discussed.*
5) Filler correct	Sie soll die **'Preise redu'zieren**, wie immer. *She is supposed to reduce the prices, as usual.*
6) Filler incorrect	Sie soll die **'Preise re'duzieren**, wie immer. *She is supposed to reduce the prices, as usual.*

Comparing the experimental conditions of Table 1 with each other involved primarily analyzing the differences between mean EEG responses over time. Participants listened to sentences as in Table 1, while ERPs were recorded. The results are summarized in Table 2 below. For purposes of illustration, the first of the relevant comparisons, that between Clash and Shift, is given in (7). Here, the mean voltage changes over nine electrodes are given. There are two differences between the clash condition (*Ter'min 'absagen*) and the shift condition (*Ter'min ab'sagen*): For the first condition we find an early negativity around 200 ms, followed by a late positive component (LPC) around 1000 ms., as indicated in figure (7) on electrode FZ.

(7) Grand averages of event-related potentials for the conditions Clash and control condition Shift measured from 200 ms prior the verb onset up to 1500 ms, (Bohn et al., 2013)

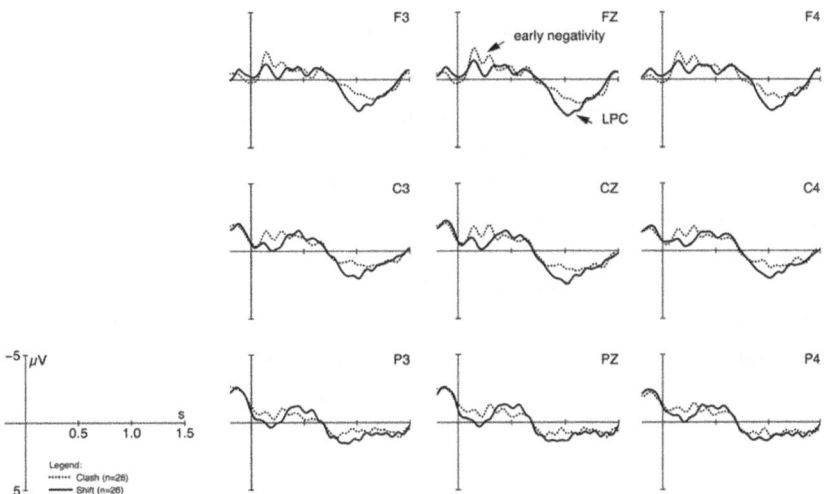

Similar biphasic EEG patterns are found if conditions Lapse vs. Noshift are compared, where we find again an N400 and a later positivity around 1200 ms, as shown in the second line of Table 2. More generally, biphasic patterns of negativity and later positivity are revealed by comparing rhythmical irregularities to contrasting conditions with alternating rhythms.

The EEG responses of participants (adult German speakers with no particular musical background) react to irregular rhythm, as shown by an early negativity and an N400, a negative-going deflection around 400 ms. Such an interaction of lexical stress and rhythmical wellformedness was also found in a follow-up study by Kandylaki et al., 2017, who identified brain structures between brain stem and cerebellum sensitive to these beat shifts. The paradigm used here was

Table 2: Comparisons between experimental conditions; (Bohn et al., 2013).

Comparison	Negativity	Positivity	Critical phrases
CLASH and SHIFT	100–320 ms **	850–1150 ms	Termín *àbsagen* vs. Termín *absàgen*
LAPSE and NO SHIFT	400–750 ms ***	1050–1280 ms **	Féier *absàgen* vs. Féier *àbsagen*
CLASH and NO SHIFT	250–320 ms * (right anterior)	960–1080 ms *	Termín *àbsagen* vs. Féier *àbsagen*
LAPSE and SHIFT	380–560 ms **	1000–1140 ms *	Féier *absàgen* vs. Termìn *absàgen*

Statistical significance is indicated by * ($p<.05$); **($p<.01$); *** ($p<.001$). Words in italic (*àbsagen*) indicate the critical word's onset for average calculation.

that of functional magnetic resonance imaging (fMRI), complementing the time-sensitive ERP analyses by location-sensitive results.

We may conclude that rhythmic irregularities are perceived as different from regular rhythm, and that rhythmically induced stress shifts play a role in the processing of words. The *Rhythm Rule* as discussed above is real in the sense that both stress shifts as well as rhythmic irregularities are perceived on the neural level. Note that the study looked at stress clashes (two or more stressed syllables adjacent to each other) as well as stress lapses (two or more unstressed syllables adjacent to each other). It is those configurations that should be avoided, because avoiding them increases the regularity of rhythm.

5.1.2 EEG study on English compounds

A further EEG study on the Rhythm Rule was presented by Henrich et al. (2014), in this case on English compounds. The rhythmical shifts discussed for compounds in English are the mirror image to the German case, as in English it is the left-hand element, and not the right-hand element, which is affected by the shift. The rule is not only operative in phrases such as *four'teen* → *'fourteen "women*, but also in compounds as in *Tennes"see* → *"Tennessee "waltz*. Therefore, the study by Henrich et al. (2014) operated with the set of conditions given in Table 3, in which primary stress on the right-hand element of a compound caused (or did not cause) stress shift on the preceding word within the compound. Participants were asked to evaluate the stimuli heard (embedded in appropriate sentences) w. r.t. their naturalness.

Table 3: Experimental and filler conditions, (Henrich et al., 2014).

Condition	Example
Correct SHIFT	The **'champagne 'cocktails** are very pricey.
Correct NO SHIFT	The **cham'pagne de'sserts** are very delicious.
CLASH	The **cham'pagne 'cocktails** are very pricey.
LAPSE	The **'champagne de'sserts** are very delicious.
Filler correct	I like to **in'vite** good friends.
Filler incorrect	*I like to **'invite** good friends.

Overall, the online brain reactions of British English listeners, as measured in ERP analyses, demonstrated a sensitivity to both the lexically given stress patterns as well as the rhythmical irregularities, both clashes and lapses. This is shown in Table 4, summarizing the comparisons between three relevant stimulus conditions.

Table 4: Comparisons of ERP effects, from (Henrich et al., 2014).

Comparison	Early Positivity	Negativity	Late Positivity	Critical phrases
SHIFT & NO SHIFT	120–220 ms* (frontal) 280–360 ms**	500–750 ms***	–	chàmpagne vs. champàgne
CLASH & SHIFT	30–180 ms ***	250–330 ms n.s.	450–850 ms**	champàgne cócktails vs. chàmpagne cócktails
LAPSE & NO SHIFT	–	120–220 ms**	900–1100 ms**	chàmpagne dessérts vs. champàgne dessérts

Underlined words (chàmpagne) indicate the onset of plotting and averaging processes.
*Statistical significance is indicated by p < .05.
**Statistical significance is indicated by p < .01.
***Statistical significance is indicated by p < .001.

Simplifying somewhat, any rhythmically licensed deviance from lexical stress causes a negative deflection of the EEG signal (N400). A deviance not rhythmically licensed shows a further, different, EEG effect. Rhythmical regularity is part of predictive computations during perception, and stress clash and lapse are deviations from these predictions which are immediately picked up by the brain. The authors also interpret the processing of rhythmical irregularities as causing additional processing costs.

5.1.3 EEG study on German compounds

As with English compounds, stress shift can also be found for compounds of German, but in a different fashion compared to English. Knaus et al., 2011 studied stress shifts within pentasyllabic words such as *Universi'tät* 'university' (see (1)) or *Enthusi'asmus* 'enthusiasm'. Such words with either final stress or penultimate stress were embedded as right-hand elements into compounds with a variety of left-hand elements bearing primary stress, see *Eu"ropa-Enthusi'asmus* 'enthusiasm for Europe' in (8). Stress shifts in the right-hand elements were recorded to the first (*'Enthusiasmus*) and, alternatively, the second syllable (*En'thusiasmus*) of the pentasyllabic items. 22 adult German participants had to judge correctness of stress while ERPs were recorded.

(8) ERPs recorded at midline electrodes for pentasyllabic words with final or penultimate stress, stress shift to first and second syllable, (Knaus et al., 2011)

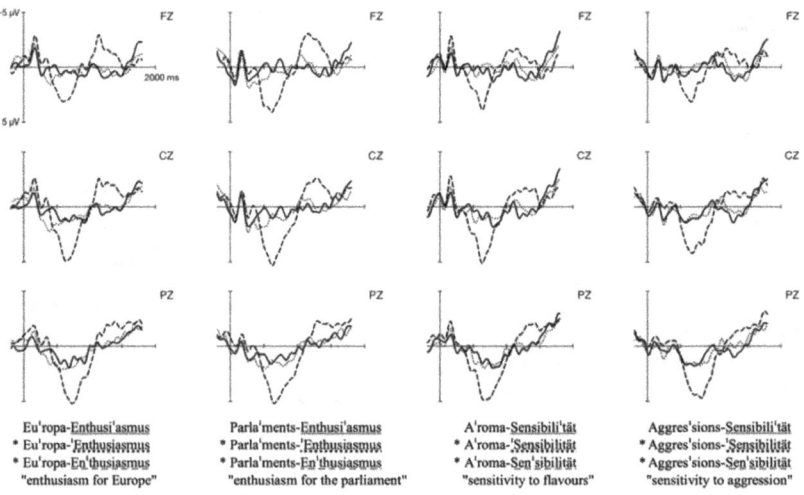

The analysis first revealed that the stress pattern of the left-hand member of the compounds did not show an effect: reactions to stress shifts on the second member were independent of stress patterning on the first member. Second, deviations in ERPs were found with stress shift to the second, but not the first, syllable of the word. Thus, a shift of the type *Aggres"sions-Sensibili'tät* → *Aggres"sions-'Sensibilität* received different reactions than those from a shift of the type *Aggres"sions-Sensibili'tät* → *Aggres"sions-Sen'sibilität*. For the latter shift, a positive deflection after 300 ms was found; see ERPs in (8).

The relevance of these observations for the present discussion is that a preferred initial strong beat (prosodically: a left-strong foot) within a particular domain (prosodically: the word) is another instance of the metrically regular beat structure which we have seen throughout the present discussion, starting with the metrical grid describing example in (1).

5.2 Corpus studies on *Prosodic Parallelism* in German

Another domain in which regular rhythm in language reveals its status is based on a phenomenon in the production, not the perception, of words. The regularity consists in so-called *Prosodic Parallelism,* as proposed by Wiese & Speyer (2015): there is a tendency in German for adjacent words to display identical prosodic structure. This is related to the variable presence or absence of the vowel schwa [ə] in German. For a large number of different grammatical configurations, schwa may either be present in the final syllable of a word or be absent. To illustrate: German adverb *gern(e)* 'gladly' may appear, as indicated in the orthography, with or without final schwa, that is, with or without a final weak syllable. This alternation seems to be a case of free variation, but the hypothesis of Prosodic Parallelism claims that the variability may depend on the shape of the neighboring item: in *sehr gern* 'very willingly' the adverb tends to be monosyllabic, just like the preceding word, while in *wirklich gerne* 'really willingly' the bisyllabic form is preferred.

Prosodic structures obeying Prosodic Parallelism are relevant in the present context as they follow the principle requiring identity from one metrical unit to an adjacent one. This is analogous to the metrical regularity of music in which one bar is identical in meter to the neighboring one (see section 2.). Binarity of alternating structures (strong – weak) is thus complemented by a repetition of the structures built up for good reasons, usually the dictate of specific lexical items, such as monosyllabic *sehr* 'very' in the case just mentioned.

The number of such cases is surprisingly large in German, ranging from genitive singular forms of nouns (*des/eines Tag(e)s* 'the/a day') over verb plus adverb combination: *wär(e) gern(e)* 'would gladly' to some adverbs such as *nah (e)* 'near' with preceding verbs. Additionally, the study by Wiese & Speyer

(2015) also looked at historically older stages of German, such as stem-final schwa in nouns from Early New High German (14th to 17th century). The evidence for Prosodic Parallelism comes from a comprehensive corpus search over two-word phrases as the ones just given, containing the alternating word as a first and/or second member. To illustrate the hypothesis in quantitative terms, for the noun *Tag* 'day' in its genitive singular form, in combination with the definite (monosyllabic) article *des* or the indefinite (bisyllabic) article *eines*, the possible combinations are presented in (9), with the combinations preferred according to Prosodic Parallelism bolded.

(9) Article-noun combinations for *des/eines Tag(e)s*, (Wiese & Speyer, 2015)

		Trochaic noun	
		no	yes
Trochaic article	no	**des Tags**	des Tages
	yes	eines Tags	**eines Tages**

For these combinations, frequencies of occurrence were identified on the basis of the *DeReKo*, (*Deutsches Referenzkorpus/Archiv der Korpora Geschriebener Gegenwartssprache*).[3] The corpus represents present-day written German mostly from newspaper texts, with approximately 25 bn. orthographic word forms at the time of search (2014). For the four word combinations of (9) the resulting frequencies are given in the contingency table (10). For each cell, actual frequency of occurrence is given in the first line, followed by percentages and sums of rows/columns. Expected frequencies are found in the second line of each cell. In total, 113,781 tokens were found and entered the statistical analysis.

(10) Observed (top) and expected (bottom) frequencies for article-noun combinations for *des/eines Tag(e)s* 'of the day', (Wiese & Speyer, 2015)

		Trochaic noun		∑
		no	yes	
Trochaic article	no	1682 (1.7)	96,202 (98.3)	97,884
		1430.42	96,453.58	
	yes	273 (0.8)	35,624 (99.2)	35,897
		524.58	35,372.42	
∑		1955	131,826	133,781

---

3 http://www.ids-mannheim.de/cosmas2/

Deviations between observed and expected counts form the basis of the statistical analysis. To put it simply, for the case considered in (9) observed numbers were higher than expected on the basis of sums of rows and columns for *des Tags* ("no/no") and *eines Tages* ("yes/yes"). These differences were significant using a chi-square test with *Pearson's* χ^2 (1) = 167.34; p < 0.0001. Altogether, 15 different constructions across the grammatical categories of present-day German, plus three constructions from Early New High German, were the object of the study. Except for two cases, the hypothesis of Prosodic Parallelism, the metrical identity of two successive words, was confirmed, although Kentner (2015) raises some open questions and points out possible extensions involving other prosodic levels.

Note that these results were obtained on the basis of texts of *written* German (simply because of the availability of very large corpora of written, but not spoken, German). Finding effects of rhythm in written productions may seem surprising, but there has been various evidence for the role of prosody in writing (see, e.g., Fodor, 2002, Ashby & Clifton Jr., 2005, Schlüter, 2015, and Kentner & Vasishth, 2016).

Wiese (2016) extended the search for Prosodic Parallelism to spoken German. A similar, but not identical, set of constructions on the basis of a corpus of spoken German (*Database for Spoken German*, described by Schmidt (2014) was analyzed. Similar results were obtained, as summarized in (11). Since the conditions for chi-square testing were not met because of smaller numbers of cases in the corpus, Fisher's exact test was used to compute P-values representing probabilities of a non-association between variables.

(11) Constructions analyzed effects of Prosodic Parallelism with results of statistical tests; (Wiese, 2016)

Search items	Results for Fisher's exact test
die, der/eine, einer + Tür(e)	P = 0.396, n.s.
des/eines + Tag(e)s	P = 0.033*
des/eines + Jahr(e)s	numbers too small, test not applicable
(un) + gern(e)	P = 0.000***
bin, war, ist, sind, seid / waren, seien, werden, wurde, wurden + nah(e)	numbers too small, test not applicable
heut(e) + früh/morgen	P = 0.041*
nah(e) + bin, war, ist, sind, seid / waren, seien, werden, wurde, wurden	numbers too small, test not applicable

dem/einem + Tag(e)	P = 0.027*
sehr/wirklich + gern(e)	P = 0.724, n.s.

The results presented in table (11) demonstrate that this study was able to replicate some of the results from (Wiese & Speyer, 2015), although the small numbers of cases prevented a full-scale replication. Prosodic Parallelism exists as a tendency in written and spoken German, while it is necessarily constrained by syntax and lexicon. Whether this metrical regularity is more prominent in writing than in speech, because of the larger degree of advance planning in the former mode, must remain an open question; however, see (Breiss & Hayes, 2020) on this point. They provide large-scale evidence that there are larger phonological effects in writing, presumably due to amplified advance planning also of phonological wellformedness. Parallelism eases prediction (within a phrase, the hearer can expect the next word to bear the same prosodic structure as the present one), but it may even lead to non-optimal rhythmical structure: if a monosyllabic non-alternating word is chosen from the lexicon, the likelihood for another such word increases.

6 Conclusions

Various types of evidence presented above demonstrate that a number of processes are operative in language to increase the amount of metrical regularity and thereby approach (though not achieve) the regular metrical structure of music. Arguably, there are no processes to be found which directly *decrease* the amount of regularity, although those would not be totally dysfunctional: they would heighten the degree of variability in language. On the basis of the studies discussed in the previous section, it is obvious that rhythmic patterns with regular alternations are a preferred option in German and English, with alternation and repetition to be as regular as possible under the dictate of a particular message. To take up the views formulated in section 3.1, Kotz et al. (2018) state that "The isochrony typical of music, and its relative absence in speech, represents the most obvious difference between these two domains."[4]

---

[4] It is only fair to acknowledge that the same authors also state in their conclusion: "Interestingly, at both neural and cognitive levels, current data suggest more overlap than separation for facets of rhythm across cognitive domains, suggesting that shared resources may be deployed in the perception of any signal with some regular temporal structure." (Kotz et al., 2018)

The present paper has attempted to show that this claim has to be taken with some caution, without committing itself to the view that the notion of isochrony is the underlying force behind the similarity.

In addition to the studies presented, there is more evidence from other languages or prosodic domains pointing in the same direction. For example, Kukhto & Piperski (2020) argue that variation in lexical stress in Russian (which is considered to be a fixed-stress language, but does show some variation) is shaped by a preference for alternating stresses. On the sentence level, Franz et al. (2020) present some evidence for an influence of rhythmic regularity on word order in German. A strong tie between rhythm in language and music is also provided by the fact that humans from all societies put words to their music (one of the results established in (Mehr et al., 2019). This coupling alone would make it difficult to base rhythm in language on principles different from those in music.

Additionally, there is evidence that musical rhythm may depend on the language of the respective culture: Iversen et al. (2008) and Patel (2003) demonstrated that the rhythmical patterning in music as evidenced in Baroque national styles depended on the prosodies of the languages in which the respective music originated. The close relation between rhythm in language and music may thus derive from an influence of the rhythmical patterning of a particular language on the properties of a musical idiom (see also Gilbers & Rebernik, 2022). Such shaping of musical idioms is well documented (Patel et al., 2006). On a more general level, Asaridou & McQueen (2013) review the body of evidence that the experience of musicians influences their processing of speech; conversely, experience with tonal properties of language also exerts an influence on the processing of music.

The overall picture leads to the conclusion that it is true that language "is not required to conform to any particular pattern" (Lerdahl & Jackendoff, 1983), but that there is a strong preference for linguistic expressions to achieve such patterning, both in perception as well as in production. Rhythm in language and music may thus a stronger coupling than has sometimes been suspected, as the comparison of music and language reveals that they share identical patterns of regularity. Arguably, this is more than a coincidental similarity, especially if it is expressed in terms of metrical principles.

The rhythm as studied here has been labeled as "abstract-cognitive", but this does not mean that it has no base in physical realization (acoustics). Perceived rhythm depends on both the bottom-up analysis of acoustic events as well as the expected rhythmical structure. Differences in the acoustic realization of prominence do not necessarily provide counterevidence for the claim made here. For example, Ding et al. (2017) find a rather constant peak in the modulation spectrum of speech (temporal modulations in sound intensity) around 4–5 Hz, across a number of languages and speech styles. For music, they find such a peak around 0.5–3 Hz, that is, with a considerably lower modulation rate. (Differences within music relate largely to different instrumental bands and styles.) One possible explanation for both the uniformity within speech and music and the variation within music is that there is one level of a basic beat (see section 2.) valid for both domains. For language, this may be the level of the syllable (with some unstressed syllables excluded), and for music, there is a beat level which varies between musical styles, but is usually slower than the syllable rate in speech. For the present analysis, this means that the basic beat, one out of many levels of prominence, is usually not the same for speech and music.

Taken together, the results discussed here also raise the question whether rhythm in the sense of metrical regularity is primarily a question of perception or of production. This issue, also debated in the discussion of isochrony and rhythm type of languages from (Pike, 1945) to (Grabe & Low, 2002), cannot be resolved finally (see also Beier & Ferreira, 2018). The most plausible answer at present may be that there is a strong preference for rhythmic regularity supported by neural and cognitive mechanisms in both production and perception.

References

Abercrombie, David. 1992. *Elements of general phonetics*. Edinburgh: Edinburgh University Press.

Agbayani, Brian & Chris Golston. 2010. Phonological movement in Classical Greek. *Language* 86(1). 133–167.

Arjava, Heini & Gerrit Kentner. 2022. Alignment of prosodic weight and musical length in Finnish vocal music textsetting. In: Mathias Scharinger, Richard Wiese, editors. *How language speaks to music: Prosody from a cross-domain perspective*, 161–189. Berlin: De Gruyter.

Asaridou, Salomi S & James M. McQueen. 2013. Speech and music shape the listening brain: evidence for shared domain-general mechanisms. *Frontiers in Psychology* 4. 321.

Ashby, Jane & Charles Clifton Jr. 2005. The prosodic property of lexical stress affects eye movements during silent reading. *Cognition* 96(3). B89–B100.

Assaneo, M. Florencia, Johanna M. Rimmele, Yonatan Sanz Perl & David Poeppel. 2021. Speaking rhythmically can shape hearing. *Nature Human Behaviour* 5(1). 71–82.

Beier, Eleonora J. & Fernanda Ferreira. 2018. The temporal prediction of stress in speech and its relation to musical beat perception. *Frontiers in Psychology* 9. 431.

Bohn, Karen, Johannes Knaus, Richard Wiese & Ulrike Domahs. 2013. The influence of rhythmic (ir)regularities on speech processing: Evidence from an ERP study on German phrases. *Neuropsychologia* 51(4). 760–771.

Breiss, Canaan & Bruce Hayes. 2020. Phonological markedness effects in sentence formation. *Language* 96(2). 338–370.

Chern, Alexander, Barbara Tillmann, Chloe Vaughan & Reyna L. Gordon. 2018. New evidence of a rhythmic priming effect that enhances grammaticality judgments in children. *Journal of Experimental Child Psychology* 173. 371–379.
Cutler, Anne. 1990. Exploiting prosodic probabilities in speech segmentation. In: Gerry T. M. Altman, editor. *Cognitive models of speech processing*, 105–121. Cambridge, MA: The MIT Press.
Cutler, Anne & Dennis Norris. 1988. The role of strong syllables in segmentation for lexical access. *Journal of Experimental Psychology: Human Perception and Performance* 14(1). 113–121.
Ding, Nai, Aniruddh D. Patel, Lin Chen, Henry Butler, Cheng Luo & David Poeppel. 2017. Temporal modulations in speech and music. *Neuroscience & Biobehavioral Reviews* 81. 181–187.
Fodor, Janet Dean. 2002. Prosodic disambiguation in silent reading. *North East Linguistics Society*. p 8.
Franz, Isabelle, Markus Bader, Frank Domahs & Gerrit Kentner. Influences of rhythm on word order in German. Proceedings of the 10th International Conference on Speech Prosody; 2020; Tokyo. ISCA. p 385–388.
Giegerich, Heinz J. 1985. *Metrical phonology and phonological structure: German and English*. Cambridge: Cambridge University Press.
Gilbers, Dicky & Teja Rebernik. 2022. A constraint-based approach to structuring language and music. Towards a roadmap for comparing language and music cross-culturally. In: Mathias Scharinger, Richard Wiese, editors. *How language speaks to music: Prosody from a cross-domain perspective*, 72–103. Berlin: De Gruyter.
Grabe, Esther & Ee L. Low. 2002. Durational variability in speech and the rhythm class hypothesis. In: Carlos Gussenhoven, Natasha Warner, editors. *Laboratory Phonology 7*, 515–546. Berlin: De Gruyter.
Gussenhoven, Carlos. 1991. The English rhythm rule as an accent deletion rule. *Phonology* 8(1). 1–35.
Hay, Jessica F. & Jenny R. Saffran. 2012. Rhythmic grouping biases constrain infant statistical learning. *Infancy* 17(6). 610–641.
Henrich, Karen, Kai Alter, Richard Wiese & Ulrike Domahs. 2014. The relevance of rhythmical alternation in language processing: An ERP study on English compounds. *Brain and Language* 136. 19–30.
Iversen, John R., Aniruddh D. Patel & Kengo Ohgushi. 2008. Perception of rhythmic grouping depends on auditory experience. *The Journal of the Acoustical Society of America* 124(4). 2263–2271.
Jackendoff, Ray. 2009. Parallels and nonparallels between language and music. *Music Perception* 26(3). 195–204.
Kandylaki, Katerina D., Karen Henrich, Arne Nagels, Tilo Kircher, Ulrike Domahs, Matthias Schlesewsky, Ina Bornkessel-Schlesewsky & Richard Wiese. 2017. Where is the beat? The neural correlates of lexical stress and rhythmical well-formedness in auditory story comprehension. *Journal of Cognitive Neuroscience* 29(7). 1119–1131.
Kentner, Gerrit. 2015. Problems of prosodic parallelism: A reply to Wiese and Speyer (2015). *Linguistics* 53(5). 1233–1241.
Kentner, Gerrit & Shravan Vasishth. 2016. Prosodic focus marking in silent reading: Effects of discourse context and rhythm. *Frontiers in Psychology* 7. 319.

Kiparsky, Paul. 1973. "Elsewhere" in phonology. In: Stephen R. Anderson, Paul Kiparsky, editors. *A Festschrift for Morris Halle*, 93–106. New York: Holt Rinehart and Winston.

Knaus, Johannes, Richard Wiese & Ulrike Domahs. 2011. Secondary stress is distributed rhythmically within words: An EEG study on German. The 17th International Conference of the Phonetic Sciences. 1114–1117.

Kotz, Sonja A., Andrea Ravignani & W. Tecumseh Fitch. 2018. The evolution of rhythm processing. *Trends in Cognitive Sciences* 22(10). 896–910.

Kühn, Clemens. 1987. *Formenlehre der Musik*. München: Bärenreiter.

Kukhto, Anton & Alexander Piperski. 2020. Lexical stress variation and rhythmic alternation in Russian: A pilot study. *Linguistic Variation* 20(1). 33–55.

Kutas, Marta, Katherine A DeLong & Nathaniel J Smith. 2011. A look around at what lies ahead: Prediction and predictability in language processing. In: Moshe Bar, editor. *Predictions in the brain: Using our past to generate a future*, 190–207. Oxford: Oxford University Press.

Lerdahl, Fred & Ray Jackendoff. 1983. *A generative theory of tonal music*. Cambridge, MA: The MIT Press.

Liberman, Mark. 1975. *The Intonational system of English*. New York: Garland Publishing Inc.

Liberman, Mark & Alan S. Prince. 1977. On stress and linguistic rhythm. *Linguistic Inquiry* 8(2). 249–336.

Luck, Steven J. 2014. *An introduction to the event-related potential technique*. Cambridge, MA: The MIT Press.

Magne, Cyrille, Deanna K. Jordan & Reyna L. Gordon. 2016. Speech rhythm sensitivity and musical aptitude: ERPs and individual differences. *Brain and Language* 153. 13–19.

Mehr, Samuel A., Manvir Singh, Dean Knox, Daniel M. Ketter, Daniel Pickens-Jones, S. Atwood, Christopher Lucas, Nori Jacoby, Alena A. Egner, Erin J. Hopkins, Rhea M. Howard, Joshua K. Hartshorne, Mariela V. Jennings, Jan Simson, Constance M. Bainbridge, Steven Pinker, Timothy J. O'Donnell, Max M. Krasnow & Luke Glowacki. 2019. Universality and diversity in human song. *Science* 366 (6468).eaax0868.

Mołczanow, Janina & Richard Wiese. 2014. Rhythm is in the mind of the beholder. Remarks on the nature of linguistic rhythm. *Linguistica Copernicana* 11. 169–182.

Ommen, Sandrien van, Natalie Boll-Avetisyan, Saioa Larraza, Caroline Wellmann, Ranka Bijeljac-Babic, Barbara Höhle & Thierry Nazzi. 2020. Language-specific prosodic acquisition: A comparison of phrase boundary perception by French- and German-learning infants. *Journal of Memory and Language* 112. 104108.

Patel, Aniruddh D. 2003. Rhythm in language and music: Parallels and differences. *Annals of the New York Academy of Sciences* 999(1). 140–143.

Patel, Aniruddh D. 2010. *Music, Language, and the Brain*. Oxford: Oxford University Press.

Patel, Aniruddh D., John R. Iversen & Jason C. Rosenberg. 2006. Comparing the rhythm and melody of speech and music: The case of British English and French. *The Journal of the Acoustical Society of America* 119(5). 3034–3047.

Pike, Kenneth L. 1945. *The intonation of American English*. Ann Arbor, MI: The University of Michigan Press.

Prince, Alan S. 1983. Relating to the grid. *Linguistic Inquiry* 14(1). 19–100.

Sachs, Curt. 1952. Rhythm and tempo: An introduction. *The Musical Quarterly* 38(3). 384–398.

Schlüter, Julia. 2015. Rhythmic influence on grammar: Scope and limitations. In: Ralf Vogel, Ruben van de Vijver, editors. *Rhythm in cognition and grammar*, 179–206. Berlin: De Gruyter.

Schmidt, Thomas. 2014. The database for spoken German – DGD2. Proceedings of Ninth Conference on International Language Resources and Evaluation (LREC'14), Reykjavik. European Language Resources Association (ELRA). p 1451–1457.
Snyder, Bob. 2000. *Music and memory: An introduction*. Cambridge, MA: The MIT Press.
Trost, Wiebke, Sascha Frühholz, Daniele Schön, Carolina Labbé, Swann Pichon, Didier Grandjean & Patrik Vuilleumier. 2014. Getting the beat: Entrainment of brain activity by musical rhythm and pleasantness. *Neuroimage* 103. 55–64.
Vuust, Peter, Leif Ostergaard, Karen J. Pallesen, Christopher Bailey & Andreas Roepstorff. 2009. Predictive coding of music – brain responses to rhythmic incongruity. *Cortex* 45(1). 80–92.
Wiese, Richard. 2000. *The phonology of German*. Oxford: Oxford University Press.
Wiese, Richard. 2016. Prosodic parallelism – comparing spoken and written language. *Frontiers in Psychology* 7. 1598.
Wiese, Richard & Augustin Speyer. 2015. Prosodic parallelism explaining morphophonological variation in German. *Linguistics 53*(3). 525–559.
Wilson, Margaret & Thomas P. Wilson. 2005. An oscillator model of the timing of turn-taking. *Psychonomic Bulletin & Review* 12(6). 957–968.

Heini Arjava & Gerrit Kentner

Alignment of prosodic weight and musical length in Finnish vocal music textsetting

Abstract: In the study of textsetting, i.e., the alignment of lyrics to music in song writing, the rhythmic treatment of prosodic syllable weight in relation to note length has so far received less attention than other areas of prosody, such as stress prominence and pitch. This study offers an exploratory analysis of textsetting in a Finnish song corpus, focusing on the alignment of note length in music with the prosodic weight and segmental filling of the corresponding syllables. Music is rhythmically exceptionally versatile, and the present perspective on Finnish is original in that it allows to study the relationship of prosodic weight and note length in textsetting while controlling for lexical stress and musical prominence. Here, note length is conceived not only in terms of absolute note values but relative to neighbouring note values as well, with long notes considered particularly long when followed by short notes. The results of the corpus analysis suggest that song writers align prosodic weight and musical length, with light syllables particularly avoided on notes that are long both in absolute as well as in relative terms. Over and above prosodic weight, sonority and certain segmental features are shown to affect the alignment of syllables with notes. In sum, this study regarding the phonological choices in textsetting sheds light on how song writers align the durational prosody of lyrics with musical length in vocal music.

Keywords: prosody, vocal music, textsetting, quantity, length, weight, metrics, lengthening, asymmetries

1 Introduction

Consider this opening phrase of the Gloria suite of Mass C by Ludwig van Beethoven in Figure 1, the first syllable spanning the musical duration of no less than two to three seconds. This musical phrase, where notes differ greatly in length, illustrates the peculiarity of our traditions of singing: contrary to regular

---

Heini Arjava, Department of Languages, University of Helsinki, Finland
Gerrit Kentner, Department of Linguistics, Goethe-University Frankfurt, Germany, and Max Planck Institute for Empirical Aesthetics, Frankfurt, Germany

https://doi.org/10.1515/9783110770186-007

Figure 1: *L. v. Beethoven*: Gloria, Mass in C.

speech, sound segments, and especially vowels, can be held in singing for what phonetically counts as an eternity.

This article aims to examine how song writers align verbal material in the lyrics with note length in vocal music. In this task, we specifically focus on environments where length is asymmetrically distributed over regularly occurring musical boundaries, also presented by the Beethoven passage above. At the outset, a terminological clarification is in order: "length" refers to abstract duration. In the linguistic domain, length refers to the quantity of phonological units like segments or moras; in music, note length equals the note value in the notational system. Hence, with the term length, we abstract away from actual duration in speech or note durations in the musical performance.

Singing and speech are both essential for the human condition, and they share a few conspicuous characteristics of production and organization: Processes of speech and singing draw on the same neurological substrate (cf. Patel, 2003, 2010), and both domains are based on fine-grained phonetic production in the human vocal tract. Most importantly for the present discussion, they tend to share similar principles of rhythmic organization, the basis of which is a hierarchically graded accentual prominence, manifesting itself as *meters* in musical and poetic traditions. However, singing and speech also differ in some key aspects of rhythmic and vocal production, most notably in their use of length and pitch variation.

Musical and linguistic vocal production interact most clearly when the two are combined in a shared rhythmic and temporally regulated frame, a song. *Textsetting*, that is, the arrangement of lyrics into music, offers insights into the principles that govern the interaction of language and music in song composition. Here, we focus on the alignment in textsetting of musical note length with one of its linguistic counterparts, namely *prosodic weight* that is determined by the quantity of phones in the syllable, whereas *stress* refers to the increased emphasis of a syllable. One challenge regarding this length alignment lies in the fact that prosodic weight is represented on an ordinal scale with two or at most three categories (light vs heavy vs super-heavy); music, in contrast, measures note length on an interval scale, i.e., there is no a priori limit to the number of categories that can be distinguished. Therefore, the alignment cannot be fully deterministic. Still, our study reveals clear correlations suggesting that song writers consider musical length and prosodic weight together when aligning text and tune, aiming to avoid conflicts between them.

In the remainder of the introduction, we briefly review previous musico-linguistic work on textsetting and then introduce critical phonological features of the language under study, Finnish. Section 2 provides background on rhythm in metrical poetry and music with a focus on the role of length or quantity in the two systems. In Section 3, we describe the construction of the Finnish song corpus which serves as the basis for the analysis presented in Section 4. Section 5 concludes the paper.

A cornerstone in the field of rhythmic musico-linguistics was laid by Lerdahl & Jackendoff (1983), who adopted generative grammar in the metrical analysis of Western (instrumental) music. Following this tradition, the alignment of musical prominence and linguistic stress or accent has been studied in various song corpora (e.g., Palmer & Kelly, 1992, Kiparsky, 2006, Dell & Halle, 2009, Rodríguez-Vázquez, 2010a, 2010b, Temperley & Temperley, 2013, Proto & Dell, 2013, deCastro Arrazola, 2018, and Girardi & Plag, 2022). Broader literature-based reviews on musico-linguistic case-studies are provided, for instance, by Proto (2015) and McPherson (2019). Only few studies have examined the phonological length or phonetic duration of syllables in language in relation to note length in music: Temperley & Temperley (2011) investigated syllable and note durations comparing speech and corpora of music. Hayes & Kaun (1996) formulated a general preference rule for the alignment of musical and syllabic length in the vicinity of prosodic phrase boundaries; and Rodríguez-Vázquez (2010a) expanded the discussion by making important qualitative remarks on musical length in her wide-ranging volume on rhythm in English and Spanish. However, these studies investigate length as either a correlate of linguistic stress/accent or prosodic phrasing, and mostly disregard the inherent phonological length of the syllable, i.e., the prosodic weight.

The present study is one of the first empirical studies systematically exploring phonological length in textsetting in terms of prosodic weight while controlling for the influence of linguistic stress or accent.[1] In order to disentangle effects of linguistic stress/accent and prosodic weight, we study textsetting in Finnish. Finnish is a quantity language in which length or prosodic weight is relatively independent of stress. Several stress-independent properties make

---

[1] In this study, we do not discuss the role of musical pitch (melody), which is not a prosodically salient feature in Finnish (Suomi et al., 2008:76). Generally, the less important role of pitch compared to the other prosodic domains in popular tunes has been noted by Hayes & Kaun (1996) and Girardi & Plag (2022). Pitch peaks in textsetting have been treated by, for instance, Domene Moreno & Kabak (2022).

phonological quantity a clearly discernible part of the Finnish prosodic system (see, i.e., Suomi et al., 2008).

i) Quantity of both vowels and consonants is phonemic, that is, it creates semantic distinctions (cf. *tuli* 'fire', *tuuli* 'wind', *tulli* 'customs') (id: 76). Beyond underlying geminates, long consonants also arise as a common sandhi process, making geminates a particularly salient feature of the language.[2]

ii) Syllable weight is phonologically independent of stress: the primary stress is weight-independent and fixed on the first syllable (cf. *'tu.lee*, '(s)he comes') (id: 75).

iii) All segments in the syllable rhyme (i.e., nucleus vowel and coda consonant) are *moraic* (μ) and contribute equally to the prosodic weight of a syllable. Prosodic weight in turn determines wordhood: A minimal word, for instance, consists of at least two voiced moras (id: 71).

iv) The phonetic salience of sound segments varies relatively little, as unstressed segments are not heavily reduced in speech (Suomi, 2007), contrary to some weight-sensitive languages, such as English or German (Goedemans & van der Hulst, 2013).

However, prosodic weight is not wholly independent of stress in Finnish either, as evidenced by phonological quantity-based regulations on secondary stress, or the phonetic lengthening of the primary stress placed on the first two moras of a polysyllabic word, irrespective of syllabic association (Suomi et al., 2003, Suomi & Ylitalo, 2004). Length and stress also interact in metrical verse: long syllables with two or more moras are preferred on metrically strong positions in classical Finnish poetry, and there are stricter length-based rules on heavy positions and primary-stressed syllables in the archaic Kalevala meter (Ryan, 2017, 2019:147). Altogether, however, quantity is an audible and important feature in the prosodic system of Finnish, which, as the hypothesis goes, makes also the listeners of Finnish vocal music sensitive to misalignments between musical and linguistic length.

In this paper, we set out to study the alignment between musical note length and the prosodic weight of the corresponding syllable and were particularly interested in how it manifested in the comparison of durationally symmetric and asymmetric musical contexts (to be discussed in Section 2.2.). The analysis of a corpus of popular Finnish vocal music demonstrates that song writers align musical length and prosodic weight when assigning syllables in the lyrics to notes

---

[2] Note that in Finnish, a geminate actually consists of two adjacent identical phonemes straddling a syllable boundary (e.g., *kuk.ka* 'flower') (Suomi et al., 2008:40). The syllable boundary inside the geminate is perceptually arbitrary, although its phonetic nature is still partly an open question (cf. Lehiste, 1970:44).

in the tune. We also find certain segmental features of the syllables to affect the assignment to notes, although their interpretation remains more ambiguous.

2 Rhythmic conflicts between language and music

2.1 Music and spoken verse: Differences between the durational systems

The rhythmic organization of both spoken verse and vocal music of the Western tradition is built on similar metrical templates in which prominent and less prominent elements alternate systematically and combine to form metrical hierarchies of various depths (see the classic discussion in Lerdahl & Jackendoff, 1983, among others). In poetry, metrical building-blocks are traditionally called *weak* and *strong* positions, which build up the higher units of poetic feet Figure 2.[3]

Φ		Φ		Φ		Φ		Φ	
w	s	w	s	w	s	w	s	w	s
σ	σ	σ	σ	σ	σ	σ	σ	σ	σ
Which	would	be	plan-	ted	new-	ly	with	the	time

(William Shakespeare, *Macbeth*)

Figure 2: Positions and hierarchies of prominence in a poetic line in iambic pentameter (σ = syllable, w=weak position, s=strong position, Φ=poetic foot).

In traditional musical terminology, on the other hand, the analogous basic strong positions of the metrical template are called *beats*, which are grouped into *tacti*, i.e., the higher level in the prominence hierarchy. The tactus (see the note examples in 3 below) refers to the most prominent recurring beat of a musical composition, which the listener, with or without musical education, can feel as the basic 'ticking', or the *pulse* of the piece (cf. Lerdahl & Jackendoff,

---

[3] Accentual poetry is based on the alignment of metrically prominent positions and linguistic stresses, with some less strict preferences regarding syllable weight (cf. Leino, 1982:278–287). Since the prototypical Western art song and its lyrics first and foremost follow a similar accentual meter based on stress prominence, we do not expand here on the other typical determiners of poetic organization, such as syllable count, as in the French *Alexandrine*, or phonological quantity such as in the Classical *hexameter* or the Finnish *Kalevala meter*.

1983:70–74 and passim). In other words, tactus could be described as the basic perceptual unit that constitutes the rhythmic structure of a musical passage.

Determining the perceptual distinction between the basic beat unit and the tactus is notoriously challenging (cf. id.:73), but the distinction is important to make if one needs to find a common metrical ground to compare length variation within or between songs, which is the aim of this study. Musical lengths are measured in beats, but not all beats are the same because of the song-specific variation of the tactus. The *time signature* of a piece is a good but not a definite indicator of the tactus level, as will be illustrated in the examples Figure 3 below. The time signatures are expressed as fractions, the most typical ones of which include 4/4, 3/4, and 6/8. The time signature implies how many beats are included in a bar (a further musical unit above the tactus-level, visually separated by vertical lines). In a 3/4 time signature, for instance, a bar includes three quarter-note-long beats (cf. Figure 3c below), and the 6/8 time signature denotes six eighth-note beats in a bar.

In ternary time signatures, the tactus level is especially challenging to determine, as the asymmetric prominence structure does not mathematically indicate a clear secondary prominence level besides the primary musical stress of the first note. Based on the overall rhythmic structure of a song, it is sometimes necessary in ternary compositions to qualitatively determine if the tactus equals one beat as in Figure 3c, or, as for instance in the case of many waltzes, a whole three-beat bar.

As for length, unlike spoken poetry where a syllable usually fills only one or two metrical positions, syllables in songs can be lengthened to cover any number of metrical positions in music. In Figure 3a, the first syllable of the Finnish lyrics (*kuu-*) takes up three short 1/16 notes (see level 0, the first two 1/16s not marked in the grid but implied on level 1), whereas in Figure 3b, the syllable *ai* in the second bar takes up two long quarter-note beats (level 1), and one whole tactus (level 2). The metrical depiction below follows the convention of earlier musico-linguistic studies, where metrical positions have typically been presented as x-grids following Liberman (1975) and introduced to music by Lerdahl & Jackendoff (id.).

As indicated above, both music and poetry operate on positional templates. But there are differences regarding the typical principles of how these abstract musical and linguistic meters generate rhythm. This poses challenges for song writers when aligning text and tune in actual textsetting, as well as for the theoretical comparison of the durational differences between language and music. A key difficulty is that, while rules of accentual/stress prominence of verse and music tend to be similar, there are more fine-grained differences when it comes to length variation, both within and between the two domains.

Figure 3: Levels of musical prominence in a song line. (a) 4/4 time signature (tactus length = 1/4, i.e., one beat), (b) 4/4 (2/2) time signature in *alla breve* (tactus length = 2/4, i.e., two beats), (c) 3/4 time signature (tactus = 1/4).

The first general challenge of rhythm alignment comes from the requirement to take *both* the prominence and the length of notes into account in songs. In music, both musical prominence and length are regulated at the same time. In contrast, the rules of poetic meter tend to regulate only one rhythmic aspect (e.g., either stress or length, depending on the language or poetic tradition). As writers and composers of vocal music are well known to aim for both accentual alignment and, to some extent, length alignment (Hayes & Kaun, 1996, Rodriguez-Vazquez 2010a), the requirement of considering both makes textsetting particularly demanding. This area is still understudied.

What is more, poetic systems and similarly organized musical meters are not necessarily geared towards the language used in that system. For example, accentual stress-based poetry, illustrated by the Shakespeare line in Figure 2 above, is the dominant modern verse tradition of many European languages. Crucially, it is not only employed in accent-driven languages with positionally free and weight-dependent stress (such as English, German, or Russian), but also in quantity-based languages with fixed and weight-independent stress such as Finnish. The classical Finnish poetry is accent-based despite the archaic Finnish Kalevala meter being primarily based on prosodic weight (Leino, 1982).

A further complication for the comparison of musico-linguistic durations is that, in the majority of languages studied, length is dependent on, and a phonetic correlate of, linguistic stress or accent. Western music is considerably more variable. Note length may be a cue to note prominence, and it is hence often difficult to separate musical length and prominence. However, length in music may also be entirely independent of musical prominence, as exemplified in Figure 4. There are no particular musical constraints against the last long note being completely non-prominent (indicated by a single x in the grid) – if the composer so wishes.

Figure 4: Musical durations unaligned with musical prominences.

Music and language also differ in their treatment of length distinctions and categories themselves. The typical prosodic weight classification in language trades in the unit of *mora*: every segmental position in the syllable rhyme (the nucleus vowel(s) and the coda consonant(s)) corresponds to one mora. In languages that allow for fairly complex syllable structure like Finnish or English, there is a minimally ternary distinction between *monomoraic short syllables*, *bimoraic heavy syllables*, and *trimoraic* (or longer) *superheavy syllables* (Table 1).

Quantitative meters of spoken verse (which are based on these or similar syllabic length contrasts) usually regulate phonological weight even more heavily, contrasting only metrically short and long syllables (Ryan, 2019:137 ff.). In contrast to this confinement of linguistic length to binary oppositions in verse, musical notes cover a much wider scale of durational variation, as illustrated by the note examples and discussion in Figure 3. The durational tools of vocal music are thus generally much more diverse than those of poetry. All this variation needs to be considered when studying the relation between musical note length and syllabic or prosodic weight in the textsetting of vocal music. In the following,

Table 1: Some basic syllable types in English and Finnish.

Prosodic weight	Examples	English	Finnish
Light/short (1μ)	(C)V	to	jo
Heavy (2μ)	(C)VC	can	jos
	(C)V:	be	tee
	(C)VV	may	voi
Superheavy (3μ)	(C)VCC	cost	kilt.ti
	(C)V:C	seen	kuut.ti
	(C)VVC	fine	kuit.ti

we consider specific environments in which the length distinction can be studied while controlling for musical prominence or linguistic stress/accent.

2.2 Durational regulation in asymmetric musical environments

How, then, should the durations between language and music be compared, if one aims to systematically calculate linguistic and musical length correspondences? A basic comparison can naturally be made between short and long notes, and the properties of syllables assigned to them. Our special focus in this study is on the long notes because we expect these to be the rhythmic environments which can more easily trigger linguistically non-neutral prosodic choices.

Most authors have a good intuitive conception of a long note that is lengthened beyond what can be considered neutral, but it is not always clear where the line between 'short' and 'long' notes should be drawn. Various definitions and approaches used for the definition of musical duration, such as by Hayes & Kaun (1996), or Temperley & Temperley (2011), differ in precision and method, but typically determine musical length in beats, the smallest prominent unit in music (see 2.1.).

For practical reasons stated in 2.1., we define note length based on the tactus. Long notes, in our conception, are those that exceed half a tactus in tacti with an even number of beats, or one third of a tactus in ternary musical meters. All other notes are considered durationally neutral or 'short'.

Still, defining note length as a simple function of the absolute number of beats per tactus disregards that length, by its nature, is a relative concept. A long

Figure 5: Puusydän/Muss i denn, *Trad. Ger.*

note is not felt as being particularly long when it is surrounded by other long notes (as on the words *huokuu vain*, in the second and third bars of Figure 5).

Conversely, note length is particularly salient when a long note is surrounded by shorter notes. Such a context is found in the asymmetrically distributed rhythms, illustrated by the first note of the first bar of Figure 5 above, or our first example, the Beethoven opening in Figure 1, revisited below in (?) Figure 6. In these examples the long note is followed by a shorter note within the same metrical unit and it is therefore perceived as very long. This lengthening does not depend on the note's absolute length. That is why it is important to look at the length relations within the whole group or pair of notes.

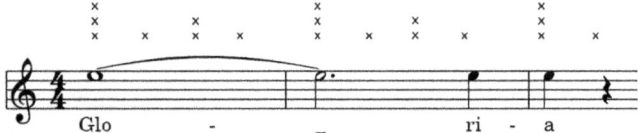

Figure 6: [1] *L. v. Beethoven*: Gloria, Mass in C.

We hypothesize that, in the context of textsetting, the linguistic relevance of the asymmetric durational ratios manifests itself particularly clearly in beat- and tactus-internal asymmetries, as beats and tacti are the most closely comparable musical units to the metrical feet or larger units such as hemistitches (half-lines) in poetic verse.

We call any two notes in asymmetrically distributed tacti *Asymmetric Durational Pairs* (ADP), modifying and expanding on the term used for the traditional note pair with a 3:1 length ratio, the *Regular dotted pair* (RDP) by Temperley & Temperley (2011). The widely used term "dotted" comes from musical notation but overlooks the very common similar asymmetries in ternary meters, which is why we refrain from its use in this more general concept of asymmetry. The ADP, and its symmetric counterpart, the *Symmetric Durational Pair* (SDP) can be defined as follows:

- SDP (Symmetric Durational Pair) = Pair of notes within a beat or tactus, starting with a musical beat with equal or greater metrical prominence than the following note, and with durations distributed in a 1:1 ratio, as in Figure 7.

Figure 7: Symmetric Durational Pairs (SDP).

- ADP (Asymmetric Durational Pair) = Pair of notes within a beat or tactus, starting with a prominent beat and with durations distributed in an asymmetric 3:1 or 2:1 ratio, as in Figure 8, depending on the binarity (Figure 8a) or ternarity (Figure 8b) of the musical meter.

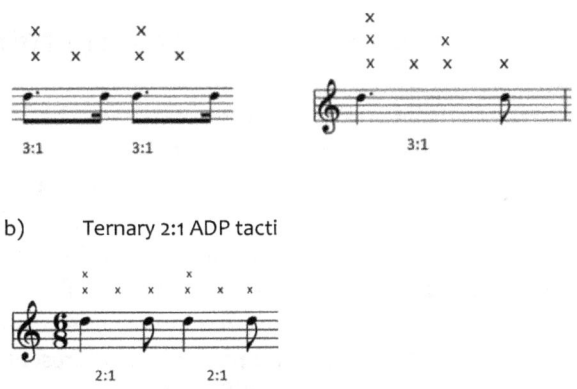

Figure 8: Asymmetric Durational Pairs (ADP).

A long first (i.e., prominent) note in an ADP is not only long but lengthened, as it were. The perceptual duration of ADPs is particularly strictly connected to the following note, as both notes participate in the realization of the asymmetric durational distribution within the same metrical unit. This interdependence and extra lengthening make the long note of the ADP different from other long notes, which, as pointed out by Hayes & Kaun (1996:245), tend to serve for articulation and phrasing rather than rhythmic purposes. In this study, we therefore examined how syllable quantity in terms of prosodic weight relates to the durationally regulated musical environment by comparing the prosodic weight and structure of syllables on the long notes of Asymmetric Durational Pairs to corresponding long notes of Symmetric Durational Pairs.

To conclude, the main hypotheses of this study are:
- In Finnish textsetting, musical length is correlated with prosodic weight (a feature that is functionally loaded in the phonological system of the language): long notes are preferably assigned to heavy syllables (and vice versa), and short notes to light syllables.
- The correlation between prosodic weight and note length is stronger for long notes in asymmetric contexts, reflecting their especially lengthened nature.

Apart from examining these hypotheses concerning the relation of prosodic weight and note length, we explore whether the durational asymmetry engenders segmental length-related effects over and above prosodic weight, such as the nature of the nucleus (short or long vowel, diphthong), the sonority profile of the syllable, and gemination of coda consonants.

3 Methods of sampling and corpus construction

The songs used in this study represent original and translated vocal music in the Finnish language, and we focused on music that can be considered mainstream, prototypical and generally accepted as metrically and rhythmically neutral by Finnish listeners. For these purposes, we used as the basis of our song corpus the iconic 23-volume Finnish song collection *Suuri toivelaulukirja* ('The Great Song Book of Popular Tunes'). The sample consisted of 27 songs mainly from the volumes 2, 3, 4, 6, and 7; the beginning in the series contains many of the most well-known songs in Finnish, and presumably represent prosodic choices that are generally appreciated. In addition, a few similar songs were randomly selected from an earlier pilot corpus.

It should be noted that our sample does not make a strict distinction between the three main variants of the text-to-tune relationship in the musical creation process. First, in many cases, the lyric writer worked on an existing melody. This includes the pieces where a foreign song was translated or otherwise provided with Finnish lyrics. There is also at least one clear reverse case in the sample of a composer writing music to an existing poem. Finally, it would also be possible that the music and text were created simultaneously. In such cases, such as in traditional Finnish songs, it is impossible to reconstruct the creation process.

Although the direction of the process is a potentially relevant factor in the analysis, a systematic comparison was beyond the scope of this study. Different scholars have approached this question with varying sampling methods (cf. e.g., Temperley & Temperley, 2013, and Girardi & Plag, 2022), and different theoretical perspectives on whether song lyrics are inherently set to linguistic or musical metrical templates (see Dell, 2015:183–185). It is therefore not always easy to compare the results of such studies.

The songs were selected according to some parameters that aimed for an adequate stylistic and rhythmic representation of Finnish popular vocal music: they include variation in genres (e.g., popular songs, folk music, hymns, film music, and Christmas songs), source languages, Finnish lyric writers, and the rhythmic organization of songs, including different time signatures and the presence or absence of ADPs. The data was collected in a spreadsheet database with each syllable annotated for musical and linguistic features related to rhythm (e.g., musical prominence on a scale from 0–2, 2=tactus, and note lengths in ratios of beats and tacti). Of every song, the first 70 to 100 syllables were included (approximately following strophic boundaries), refrains and other longer repetitions were excluded, and ADPs and SDPs were coded in the corpus. The key features of the corpus are summarized in Table 2.

To examine the effect of asymmetric length relations while controlling for effects of linguistic stress and musical prominence, we compared syllable features on the long first[4] (metrically prominent) notes of ADPs with the first (metrically prominent) notes of SDPs, distinguishing between long SDPs and durationally neutral, or 'short' SDPs. Melismas, the distribution of a syllable on several notes, were extremely rare in the data, and if included, were counted for the total duration of the notes.

Another reason for the focus being on the first notes of the SDPs was the need to exclude phrase-final long notes from the comparison. In both language and music, there is a well-known overarching tendency of constituent-final elements to be treated differently from other positions in a phrase or a meter. (e.g., Hayes & Kaun, 1996:259, Ryan, 2019:139). Phrase-final notes are also more prone to repetition of previous syllabic features because of rhyming.

Linguistic parameters compared included syllable lengths in moras, as well as their segmental rhyme types (e.g., V:, VV, and VC), which will be discussed in more detail in the following analysis section. In addition to phonological

---

4 It should be noted that ADPs of the opposite relationship with short-long ratios of 1:3 and 1:2 (the so-called 'Scotch Snap' pattern, see Temperley & Temperley 2011) were marginal in the vocal music of the corpus and are ignored in this study.

Table 2: Details of the song corpus.

Parameter	Examples in corpus
Time signatures	2/4, 4/4, 4/4 (*alla breve*), 3/4, 6/8
Original languages	Finnish, English, French, German, Italian, Russian, Swedish
Genres	hymns, Christmas songs, film music, trad., var. popular tunes
Songs	27
Writers	25
Prominent notes	914
ADPs	347
SDPs (long)	304
SDPs (short)	263

weight classification, we also took into account the so-called boundary lengthening, a morphophonetic rule in Finnish (Karlsson, 1983:349, Suomi et al., 2008:44–46), which is triggered by some final vowels and morphemes and adds a pre-boundary lengthening to the following onset (e.g., /tule tänne/ [tulet:änne]; /anna se/ [annas:e]). In the song data, light syllables that triggered the boundary lengthening were thus analysed as bimoraic, and the syllable boundary as including a geminate. The inclusion of the phonetic lengthening is justified as it is perceptually prominent in Finnish and plays a key role in the flow of singing, in which notes are usually bound together without breaks by continuously resonant phonation, or in musical terms, *legato*.

4 Results and discussion

4.1 Results

4.1.1 Syllable weight and the assignment of syllables to prominent first members of note pairs

In a first step, we compare the assignment of prosodic weights to the prominent first notes of all the SDPs (long and short) and ADPs (inherently long) identified in the corpus. These notes are linguistically comparable owing to their typical alignment with word-initial and hence stressed syllables.

The plot in Figure 9 shows the distribution of prosodic weights of the syllables on the prominent note categories (long ADP notes and long as well as short SDPs; only notes that are not phrase-final were considered although including them did not affect the significance and interpretation of the results). The left panel shows the raw numbers from the corpus (ADP-L, n=347; SDP-L, n=304; SDP-S, n=263, total n=914). Conspicuously, the percentage of monomoraic or light syllables increases as the relative note length decreases, i.e., from ADP-L (18%) through SDP-L (32%) to SDP-S notes (50%). Conversely, the percentage of both heavy and super-heavy syllables decreases along the same scale (for bimoraic syllables: 41% on ADP-L, 33% on SDP-L, and 26% on SDP-S; for super-heavy syllables: 39% on ADP-L, 36% on SDP-L, and 26% on SDP-S). Correspondingly, a Chi square test leads us to reject the assumption of independence of note category and prosodic weight (Chi squared=34.11, df=4, p<0.001), conforming instead that note category and prosodic weight are significantly correlated. The second panel of Figure 9 shows the standardized residuals from this Chi square distribution. Positive residuals indicate overrepresentation, i.e., more observed cases than expected under the null hypothesis (which would predict a uniform distribution), and negative residuals indicate underrepresentation.[5] The residuals show that monomoraic or light syllables are significantly underrepresented on long ADP notes, and, conversely, significantly overrepresented on short SDP notes.

The comparison underlying this comprehensive Chi square test, however, confounds two factors of interest, namely note length and symmetric vs asymmetric context. To disentangle these factors, we considered two subset comparisons. First, we isolated the note length contrast by comparing the distribution of moras to only prominent long SDP notes vs prominent short SDP notes (ADP-L notes discarded). The Chi square test again confirms a deviance from a homogeneous distribution (Chi squared=9.39, df=2, p=0.009). The third panel in Figure 9 shows the corresponding Chi square residuals, attesting to underrepresentation of monomoraic syllables on long SDP notes and, conversely, overrepresentation of these syllables on short SDP notes.

Secondly, we pitted long ADP notes against long SDP notes (Chi squared=8.08, df=2, p=0.0176), ignoring the short SDP-S notes. The significant deviance from a homogeneous distribution suggests that the assignment of prosodic weight differs between asymmetrically long and symmetrically long notes. The corresponding

---

5 The standardized residuals can be interpreted like standard scores: residuals exceeding a value of |2| can be considered significant contributors to the deviance from the even distribution that would be expected under the null hypothesis.

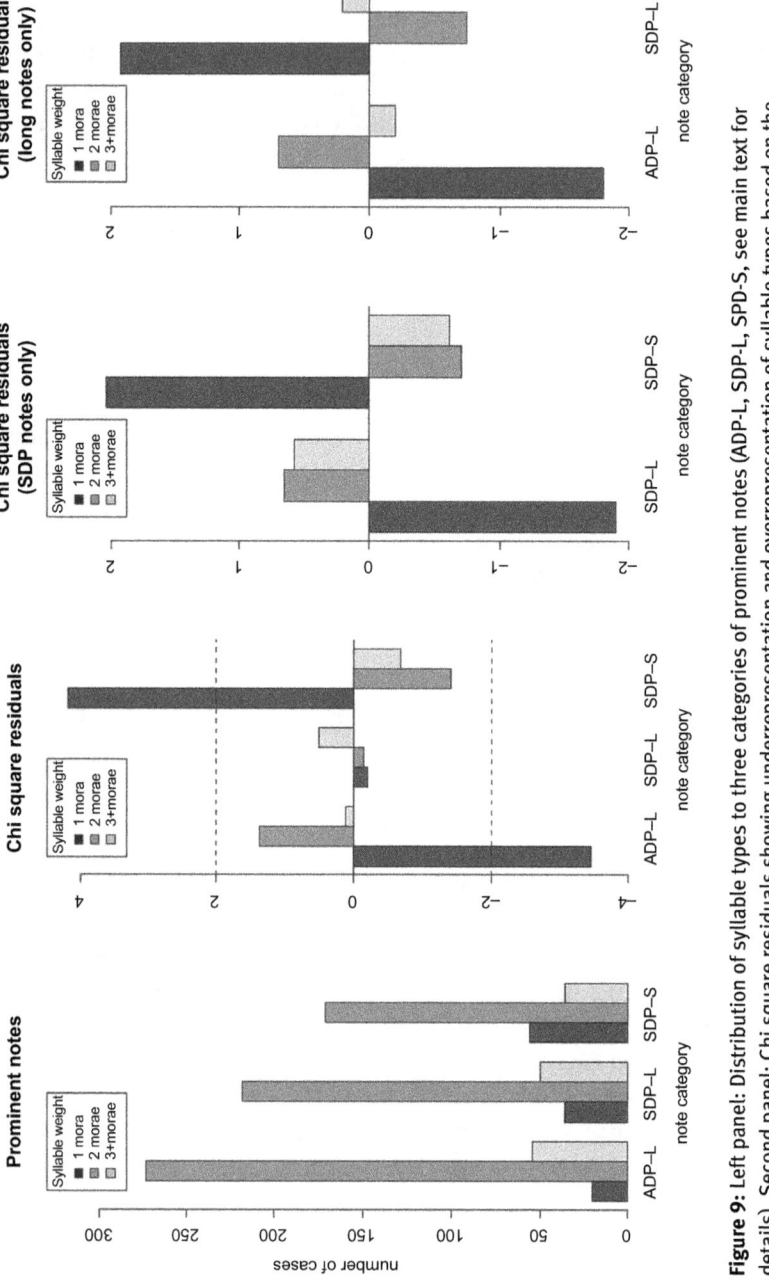

Figure 9: Left panel: Distribution of syllable types to three categories of prominent notes (ADP-L, SDP-L, SPD-S, see main text for details). Second panel: Chi square residuals showing underrepresentation and overrepresentation of syllable types based on the distribution in the first panel. Third panel: Chi square residuals on a subset regarding the length contrast (long vs short notes, only symmetric durational pairs). Fourth panel: Chi square residuals on a subset regarding the symmetry contrast (asymmetric vs symmetric durational pairs; long notes only).

residuals are plotted in the fourth panel of Figure 9. In this comparison, monomoraic syllables are overrepresented on long SDP notes when compared to long ADP notes. That is, irrespective of length, the symmetry distinction has a role to play in the assignment of syllable weights to note types.

In sum, this analysis suggests that both note length and the symmetry of the relationship to the following note in a note pair contribute to the assignment of the different syllable weights to the note categories.

4.1.2 Segmental makeup of the syllables

The distribution of the heavy syllables (grey and light grey bars in Figure 9) does not immediately suggest a significant difference regarding their assignment to the different note categories. However, there are various types of heavy syllables with differences regarding the distribution of consonantal and vocalic segments and their respective lengthening. We therefore explore whether the distribution of segmental content is contingent on the note type the syllable is set to in music (long vs short note, asymmetric long vs symmetric long). We were especially interested in whether segmental length (short vs long nuclei vs diphthongs; geminate vs non-geminate codas), is related to length and symmetry/asymmetry in music. We also explored whether sonorant versus obstruent codas differ regarding their assignment to the different note categories.

Figure 10 juxtaposes nine different types of syllable rhyme with short, long, and diphthongized nuclei and different types of codas (no coda, non-geminate coda consonants, geminate coda consonants), broken down by affiliation to asymmetrically long (ADP-L, black), symmetrically long (SDP-L, dark grey) and symmetrically short (SDP-S, light grey) prominent notes.

First, the numbers in Figure 10 reproduce the results of the first part of this study, that is the particular avoidance of monomoraic syllables on long ADP notes and the overrepresentation of the monomoraic type on the short SDP notes (left triplet of bars). Conversely, the numbers suggest that long ADP notes are preferably filled with simple -VC syllable rhymes featuring a non-geminate coda consonant after short vowels (second triplet of bars). Short SDP notes are underrepresented on all syllable types with bimoraic vowels (4th to 9th triplet of bars), irrespective of coda type. The two types of long notes (ADP-L vs SDP-L) do not appear to differ greatly in their assignment to syllables with bimoraic nuclei, apart from one observation regarding the geminate codas: Syllables with geminates after long vowels are rare, and they seem to be especially avoided on long SDP notes 6th pair of bars). Syllables with geminates after diphthongs, on the other hand, are slightly preferred on long SDP notes (last or

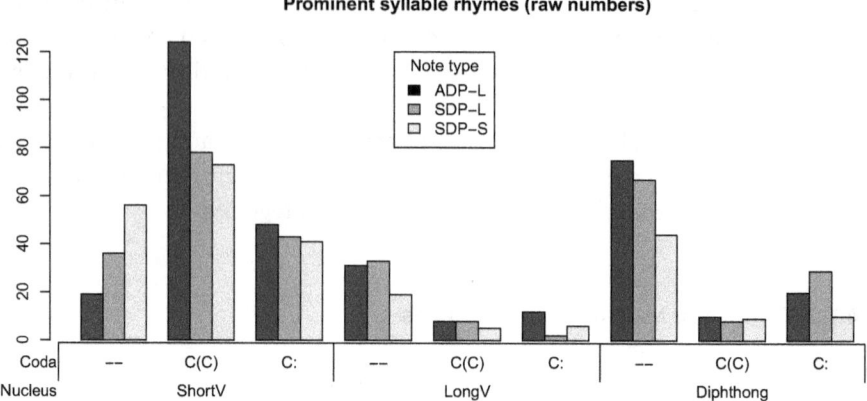

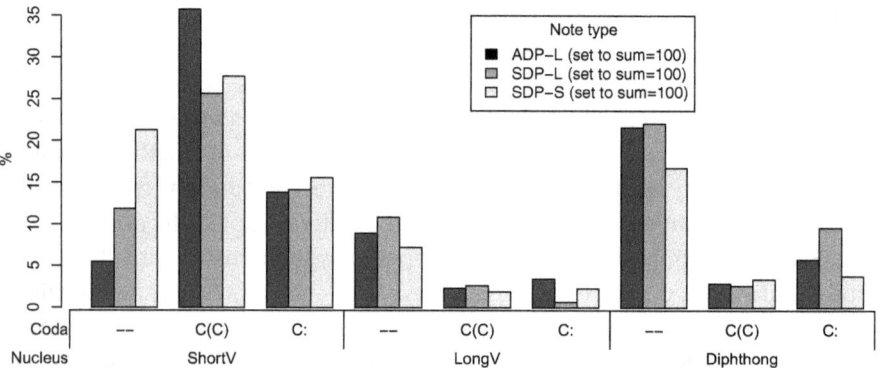

Figure 10: Distribution of nine different syllable types (broken down by type of nucleus und type of coda) over the prominent notes of asymmetric (ADP, black bars) and symmetric durational pairs (SDP-L and SDP-S, dark and light grey bars, respectively). The upper panel depicts the raw number of syllables, with percentages per vowel category for each note type shown in the bottom panel.

9th pair of bars). This suggests that the type of nucleus (short, long, diphthong) and the type of coda status (no coda, geminate or non-geminate) interact regarding the assignment of the syllables to the prominent notes of symmetric or asymmetric durational pairs.

A second explorative analysis concerns the distinction between sonorant versus obstruent coda consonants. Comparing the raw number of sonorant and obstruent coda consonants shows that sonorant codas are generally more frequent (298 codas with sonorant consonants vs. 236 obstruent codas). At first sight, there does not appear to be a significant difference regarding the distribution of sonorant vs obstruent codas among the three prominent note categories (ADP-L: 101 obstruents, 121 sonorants; SDP-L: 71 obstruents, 97 sonorants; SDP-S: 64 obstruents, 80 sonorants; Chi-squared=0.41, df=2, p-value=0.815). However, closer inspection reveals that, in the subset of songs that feature both short and long SDP notes (13 of 27 songs), the ratio of sonorant codas is in most songs higher on long notes than on short notes (see Figure 11). In fact, in only two of the 13 songs (*Kertokaa se hänelle* and *Pohjolan maa*), the ratio of sonorant codas on short notes is higher than on long notes, and this reverse tendency has relatively little weight as it is due to only very few observations in these songs (three syllables).

A comparable analysis for the symmetry contrast does not reveal a systematic relationship between symmetric versus asymmetric long notes on the one hand, and the ratio of sonorant versus obstruent codas on the other (see Figure 1 in the appendix).

To ascertain the general validity of these observations, we used R statistical software (R Core Team, 2020) to fit two hierarchical generalized linear models (Bates et al., 2014) to the data set.

To operationalize the effects of syllabic structure on syllable-to-note association, various syllabic features were determined as independent variables. These features were coded as binary orthogonal sum contrasts as follows:

1. Nucleus weight contrast: short monomoraic nuclei (–1) vs bimoraic nuclei (+1)
2. Bimoraic vowel type contrast: Diphthongs (–1) vs long vowels (+1); short vowels (irrelevant for this contrast) were set to 0
3. Coda contrast: open syllables (–1) vs closed syllables (+1)
4. Gemination: Non-Geminate (–1) vs Geminate (+1) coda; open syllables set to 0
5. Coda sonority: Obstruent (–1) vs Sonorant (+1) coda; open syllables set to 0

Along with these main effects, the full model included the set of all possible two-way interactions, namely
6. Nucleus weight : Coda contrast
7. Nucleus weight : Geminate
8. Nucleus weight : Coda sonority
9. Bimoraic vowel type : Coda contrast
10. Bimoraic vowel type : Geminate
11. Bimoraic vowel type : Coda sonority
12. Geminate : Coda sonority

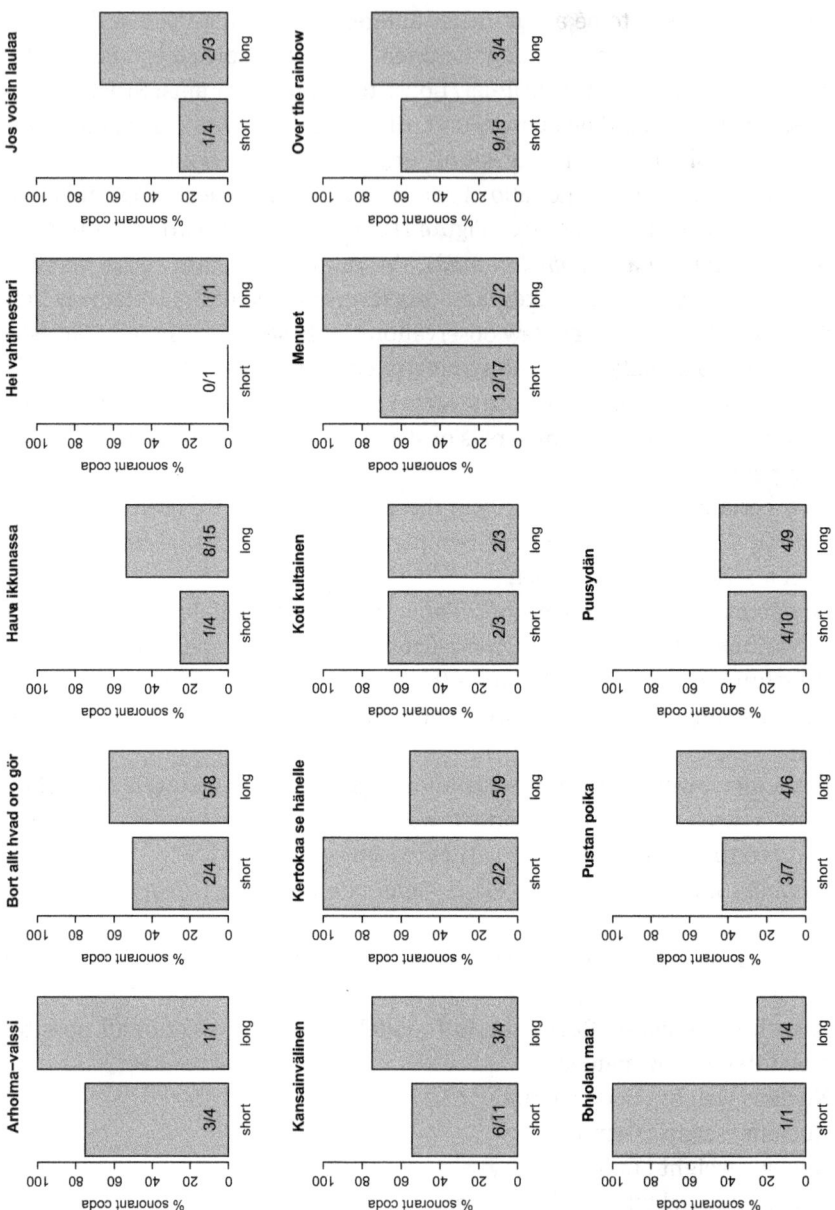

Figure 11: Percentage of sonorant coda consonants by note length (left bar: short SDP notes, right bar: long SDP notes) in syllables featuring coda consonants. Values are broken down by songs (with the ratio sonorant / all coda consonants superimposed on each bar). Only those songs that exhibit the length contrast, i.e., feature both long and short SDPs, are considered (ADP-L notes disregarded).

We included Song (n=27) as the grouping variable (random intercept only, as models with slopes did not converge, probably due to a lack of statistical power).

Given that note length is confounded with note symmetry in our data set, we fit separate models on two different subsets of the data. The first subset model considers the binary distinction between long symmetric (SDP-L) vs short symmetric notes (SDP-S) as binary dependent variable. That is, it tests whether note length per se is correlated with the syllabic features of interest. For the purpose of this model, long ADP notes were discarded. For model selection, we reduced the full model (which includes all possible two-way interaction terms), successively discarding the non-significant interaction terms with the smallest effect size unless and until further model reduction leads to deterioration of model fit, as determined by a log-likelihood test. We take the model determined this way to be the model with the best fit and report it below in Table 3.

Table 3: Summary of best fitting generalized linear mixed effects model with note length as binomial dependent variable (data from SDP notes only, ADP notes discarded).

	Estimate	Std. Error	z value	p value
Nucleus Weight	1.18	0.32	3.706	0.0002*
Coda	0.16	0.29	0.54	0.59
Coda Sonority	0.81	0.37	2.161	0.03*
Gemin-NonGemin	0.25	0.38	0.67	0.505
Diphthong-LongV	−0.005	0.41	−0.013	0.989

This model returns two significant main effects, first an effect of nucleus weight, and second, an effect of coda sonority. The coefficient estimate for the effect of nucleus weight (1.18 log odds) translates to roughly 3.2 in odds ratios and suggests that a syllable with a bimoraic vowel is about 3 times as likely to be set to a long as opposed to a short note. The effect of coda sonority (0.81 log odds, 2.24 odds ratio) suggests that it is roughly twice as likely for a syllable featuring a coda sonorant to be set to a long note compared to a syllable with a coda obstruent (cf. Figure 11). Interestingly, the effect of coda presence alone is very small and non-significant (0.16 log odds or 1.17 odds ratio). That is, the effect of syllable weight on the assignment to long vs short notes appears to be mainly an effect of the nucleus, not of the coda.

The second model tests whether the same syllabic features have an effect on the assignment of syllables to symmetrically versus asymmetrically long

Table 4: Summary of best fitting generalized linear mixed effects model with note symmetry as binomial dependent variable (data from long notes only, short SDP notes discarded).

	Estimate	Std. Error	z value	p value
Nucleus Weight	0.08	0.27	0.319	0.75
Coda	0.34	0.25	1.331	0.183
Coda Sonority	−0.16	0.26	−0.625	0.532
Gemin-NonGemin	−0.09	0.27	−0.343	0.7313
Diphthong-LongV	0.206	0.31	0.663	0.507
Gemin: DiphLongV	2.71	1.1	2.462	0.014*

notes. Consequently, for this subset, short SDP notes were discarded. Again, we report the model with the best fit, according to the above selection procedure. The output of this second model is shown in Table 4.

The second subset model yields a significant interaction between coda gemination (geminate vs non-geminate coda) and the type of bimoraic vowel (long vowel vs diphthong). This interaction reflects preferences regarding the assignment of super-heavy syllables (3+ moras, which make up roughly 15% of the data) to the prominent notes of symmetric/asymmetric durational pairs (long vowel+geminate avoided in SDP-L notes as compared to ADP-L notes, while diphthong+geminate syllables are preferably set to SDP-L, see Figure 10). This interaction suggests that over and above prosodic weight, the segmental filling of the moras has an influence on the assignment of these syllables to symmetric or asymmetric durational pairs.

4.2 Discussion

4.2.1 Prosodic weight and stress-related lengthening

This study has produced two kinds of results: those connected with the prosodic weight and those linked to the segmental makeup of the syllable rhyme. The interpretation of the former results is relatively straightforward: The statistical analysis shows that monomoraic or light syllables are preferably set to short notes and, concomitantly, particularly avoided on all prominent notes that exceed the neutral half-tactus length. A similar avoidance of light syllables on metrically strong positions has been reported by Leino for classical Finnish poems (Leino, 1982). However, while a difference between light and heavy syllables regarding note assignment is apparent in the present data, we did not find a clear difference between the assignment of heavy and super-heavy syllables to note categories (in contrast to Ryan [2019] who reports such a difference for certain strong positions in the archaic chanted Finnish Kalevala verse). Nevertheless, the present results confirm that in Finnish songs, syllable weight or quantity is a salient prosodic feature, as in Finnish speech prosody.

Beyond the contrast between musically long and short notes, the proportions of light syllables also show interesting differences between the two types of long notes (ADP-L vs SDP-L). Light syllables appear to be especially avoided on the long notes of the ADPs. Since the note values of long SDPs are often even longer than the long ADPs, which themselves are rhythmically very heterogenous, this suggests that it is not only the absolute length of a given note value but the length relationship between the adjacent notes within a prominence unit which guides the prosodic choices of the songwriters.

It has been noted that alignment in textsetting in general is mainly driven by phonological constraints (deCastro Arrazola, 2015:172), and the present results demonstrate that the inherent prosodic weight of syllables is a decisive factor in Finnish textsetting as well, as evidenced by the avoidance of light syllables on long ADP notes. Over and above the low prosodic weight, we propose that the particular avoidance of monomoraic syllables on long ADP notes may also be, in part, related to the *phonetic* consequences of the mora-based nature of word-initial stress in Finnish. Recall that stress in Finnish affects the first two moras of a word regardless of syllabic association of the moras. Therefore, if the first syllable of a word is monomoraic, stress-related lengthening extends into the second syllable (Suomi & Ylitalo, 2004). This linguistic configuration, however, is particularly misaligned in the musical context of an ADP, which emphasizes a contrast between a lengthened first note and a short second note. Instead, the musical asymmetry is rendered naturally when both of the two lengthened moras are assigned to the first syllable, making it a heavy one and, at the same time, keeping any effect of stress-related lengthening away from the short second note of this pair.

Conversely, light initial syllables appear to be tolerated on surprisingly long tacti in Symmetrical Durational Pairs. With a light first syllable, the concomitant stress-related lengthening of the following second syllable does not pose a problem in this musical context, as the second note is as long as the first: the second long note is therefore an appropriate exponent of the stress-related lengthening.

4.2.2 Analysis of the segmental syllabic features

The results concerning the segmental makeup of the syllables in our data are less clear-cut and more complicated to interpret than the results concerning prosodic weight. The segmental makeup, however, is equally relevant for the consideration of the special rhythmic and phonetic characteristics of vocal music. As discussed in the introductory sections, the lengthening potential of notes exceeds linguistic weight limits, and moreover, the continuously resonant method of *legato* singing affects the transitions between sound segments in a way that is different from speech.

Our results showed that in the basic length comparison between long and short SDP notes, it is particularly the weight of the nucleus that is decisive. This result seems natural, considering that singing long notes is aided by as resonant articulation as possible and "we sing with the vowels", as succinctly formulated by Ophaug (2015:295). We also note an effect of coda sonority: syllables with little sonority (obstruent coda) are preferably set to short SDP notes and, conversely long SDP notes attract sonorant codas (cf. Figure 11); this is probably motivated by singability as well.

As for particular segmental effects concerning the comparison between symmetric and asymmetric contexts, the picture is less clear. It seems that in ADPs, not only nucleus weight but also coda consonants may interactively contribute to the particular rhythmic effect. Among the superheavy syllables, rhymes with long vowels and a geminate coda are preferred on the particularly long and lengthened ADP notes. This might be another indication of an alignment of linguistic lengthening (concerning both nucleus and coda) with musical length.

On the other hand, as shown in Figure 10, ADP notes generally favor the simpler -VC syllables rhymes, i.e., those with a short nucleus followed by a non-geminate coda. At first sight, the potential preference of the -VC rhyme on the lengthened ADP notes seems counterintuitive. This heavy syllable is minimal on three prosodic levels: its total mora count, the separate mora counts of its nucleus and coda, and the lack of lengthening on each of its segments (i.e., lacking long or diphthongized vowel segments or a geminate). However, the aforementioned features also make this syllable type particularly clearly defined, both in terms of its acoustics and in terms of articulation. Such syllables might therefore more properly stand out as prominent syllables on the particularly prominent ADP notes.

However, there appear to be song-specific effects that blur the picture: Consider the excessive use of geminate stops after short vowels in the Finnish children's song *Magdaleena* in Figure 12. This song systematically employs ternary

ADPs combined with a salient high peak note to enforce the rhythmic salience of the geminate stops of the original poem, as illustrated by the words *makkaralla* and *päivänkakkaralla*.[6] These kinds of individual effects are evident on close inspection but are less likely to emerge as clear statistical results in the data of the present kind.

Su- kat on sil- lä mak- ka- ral- la ja   len-tää se päi- vän-kak- ka- ral- la ja

(Magdaleena, Chydenius, K., composed to a poem by Kaarina Helakisa)

Figure 12: Geminate sonorants and stops on ADPs.

Thus, although more complex nucleus-coda combinations clearly also interact with, and emphasize, musical lengthening – as in the case of *Magdaleena* – it is nevertheless possible that the most neutral way of filling an asymmetric ADP rhythm in songs could favor a simple heavy -VC syllable described above, with clear segmental transits and an unambiguous syllable boundary.

All in all, our results do not give straightforward evidence on the behavior of any particular segmental type, but do indicate that different segmental combinations play a role in the realization of length relationships in singing. The clearest sign of length alignment in Finnish textsetting based on this study is the prosodic weight of the syllables.

5 Conclusions

The analysis of the present corpus of popular vocal music of Finnish suggests that Finnish song writers are sensitive to, and consider prosodic weight and certain segmental features when setting text to musically prominent notes of varying lengths and with different length relationships to adjacent following

---

6 Note that segmental processes such as consonant lengthening connected with metrical quantitative prominence also feature in spoken verse traditions, such as Ancient Greek, where light metrically accented syllables are often connected to the following onset by gemination (Revithiadou, 2004:40).

notes. The results clearly show that song writers strive for the alignment of musical note length with prosodic weight and the overall sonority of the syllables. Effects of other segmental syllabic features on note alignment in textsetting are detectable but less clear regarding their interpretation.

The present study on Finnish demonstrates that durationally regulated musical contexts and their alignment with prosodic weight can be studied independently of linguistic stress or accent. Inspecting the interaction between musical length and prosodic weight is especially fruitful in the asymmetric durational contexts (ADPs), in which length relations between the notes concerned are more strictly regulated and which clearly behave as a particular rhythmic unit in vocal music, possibly differing from the symmetric environments also in their make-up of segmental syllabic features.

In sum, our approach extends the perspective on language-music relationships in textsetting beyond the more widely studied stress-prominence connection by focusing on the role of the prosodic weight of syllables and their alignment with musical note length in Finnish. We emphasize that the specifics of the phonological and phonetic systems of the song language and the musical context of the notes under consideration are crucial for our understanding of how phonology is put to use in the expression of rhythm in vocal music.

Appendix

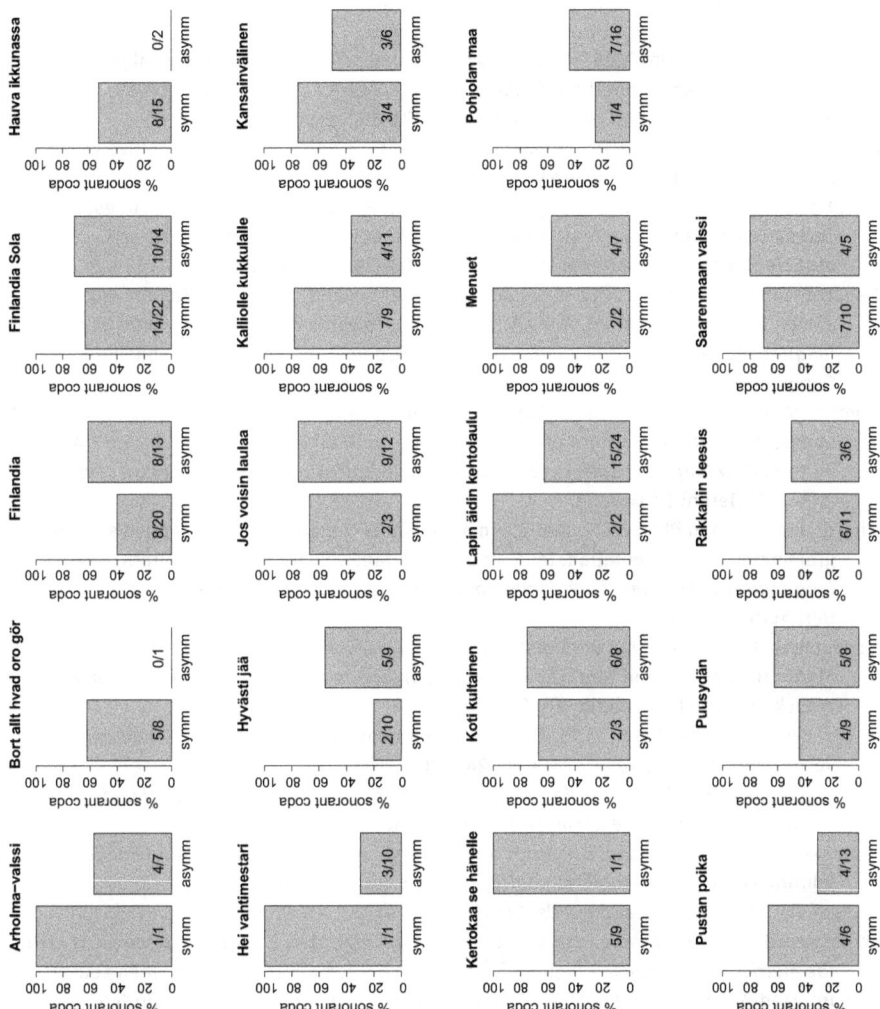

Figure 1: Percentage of sonorant coda consonants by note symmetry (left bar: symmetric SDP-L notes, right bar: asymmetric ADP-L notes) for syllables featuring coda consonants. Values are broken down by songs (with ratio sonorant / all coda consonants superimposed on each bar). Only those songs that exhibit the symmetry contrast, i.e., feature both symmetric and asymmetric long notes, are considered (SDP-S notes disregarded).

References

Bates, Douglas, Martin Mächler, Ben Bolker & Steve Walker. 2014. Fitting Linear Mixed-Effects models using lme4. *arXiv preprint arXiv:1406.5823*.
deCastro Arrazola, Varun. 2015. The prosody of Basque songs. A methodological proposal. In: Teresa Proto, Paolo Canettieri, Gianluca Valenti, editors. *Text and tune: On the association of lyrics and tune in sung verse*, 171–182. Bern: Peter Lang.
deCastro Arrazola, Varun. 2018. Typological tendencies in verse and their cognitive grounding [Doctoral Dissertation]: Leiden University.
Dell, François. 2015. Text-to-tune alignment and lineation in traditional French songs. In: Teresa Proto, Paolo Canettieri, Gianluca Valenti, editors. *Text and tune: On the association of lyrics and tune in sung verse*, 183–234. Bern: Peter Lang.
Dell, François & John Halle. 2009. Comparing musical textsetting in French and in English songs. In: Jean-Louis Aroui, Andy Arleo, editors. *Towards a typology of poetic forms: From language to metrics and beyond*, 63–78. Amsterdam: John Benjamins Publishing Company.
Domene Moreno, Christina & Bariş Kabak. 2022. Prominence alignment in English and Turkish songs: Implications for word prosodic typology. In: Mathias Scharinger, Richard Wiese, editors. *How language speaks to music: Prosody from a cross-domain perspective*, 223–258. Berlin: De Gruyter.
Girardi, Elena & Ingo Plag. 2022. Metrical mapping in text-setting: Empirical analysis and grammatical implementation. In: Mathias Scharinger, Richard Wiese, editors. *How language speaks to music: Prosody from a cross-domain perspective*, 191–221. Berlin: De Gruyter.
Goedemans, Rob & Harry van der Hulst. 2013. Weight-sensitive stress. In: Matthew S. Dryer, Martin Haspelmath, editors. *The world atlas of language structures online*. Leipzig: Max Planck Institute for Evolutionary Anthropology.
Hayes, Bruce & Abigail Kaun. 1996. The role of phonological phrasing in sung and chanted verse. *The Linguistic Review* 13(3–4). 243–303.
Karlsson, Fred. 1983. *Suomen kielen äänne-ja muotorakenne [The phonological and morphological structure of Finnish]*. Juva: WSOY.
Kiparsky, Paul. 2006. A modular metrics for folk verse. In: B. Elan Dresher, Nila Friedberg, editors. *Formal approaches to poetry*, 7–49. Berlin: De Gruyter.
Lehiste, Ilse. 1970. *Suprasegmentals*. Cambridge, MA: The MIT Press.
Leino, Pentti. 1982. *Kieli, runo ja mitta: suomen kielen metriikka [Language, poem, and meter: the metrics of the Finnish language]*. Pieksämäki: Suomalaisen kirjallisuuden seura.
Lerdahl, Fred & Ray Jackendoff. 1983. *A generative theory of tonal music*. Cambridge, MA: The MIT Press.
Liberman, Mark. 1975. *The intonational system of English*. New York: Garland Publishing Inc.
McPherson, Laura. 2019. Musical adaptation as phonological evidence: Case studies from textsetting, rhyme, and musical surrogates. *Language and Linguistics Compass* 13(12).
Ophaug, Wencke. 2015. The challenge of identifying vowel phonemes in singing. In: Teresa Proto, Paolo Canettieri, Gianluca Valenti, editors. *Text and tune: On the association of lyrics and tune in sung verse*, 287–312. Bern: Peter Lang.
Palmer, Caroline & Michael H. Kelly. 1992. Linguistic prosody and musical meter in song. *Journal of Memory and Language* 31(4). 525–542.

Patel, Aniruddh D. 2003. Rhythm in language and music: Parallels and differences. *Annals of the New York Academy of Sciences* 999(1). 140–143.
Patel, Aniruddh D. 2010. *Music, language, and the brain*. Oxford: Oxford University Press.
Proto, Teresa. 2015. Prosody, melody and rhythm in vocal music: The problem of textsetting in a linguistic perspective. *Linguistics in the Netherlands* 32. 116–129.
Proto, Teresa & François Dell. 2013. The structure of metrical patterns in tunes and in literary verse. Evidence from discrepancies between musical and linguistic rhythm in Italian songs. *Probus* 25(1). 105–138.
Revithiadou, Anthi. 2004. The Iambic/Trochaic Law revisited: Lengthening and shortening in trochaic systems. *Leiden Papers in Linguistics* 1(1). 37–62.
Rodríguez-Vázquez, Rosalía. 2010a. *The rhythm of speech, verse and vocal music: A new theory*. Bern: Peter Lang.
Rodríguez-Vázquez, Rosalía. 2010b. Text-setting constraints: A comparative perspective. *Australian Journal of Linguistics* 30(1). 19–34.
Ryan, Kevin M. 2017. The stress–weight interface in metre. *Phonology* 34(3). 581–613.
Ryan, Kevin M. 2019. *Prosodic weight: Categories and continua*. Oxford: Oxford University Press.
Suomi, Kari. 2007. On the tonal and temporal domains of accent in Finnish. *Journal of Phonetics* 35(1). 40–55.
Suomi, Kari, Juhani Toivanen & Riikka Ylitalo. 2003. Durational and tonal correlates of accent in Finnish. *Journal of Phonetics* 31(1). 113–138.
Suomi, Kari, Juhani Toivanen & Riikka Ylitalo. 2008. *Finnish sound structure: Phonetics, phonology, phonotactics and prosody*. Oulu: University of Oulu.
Suomi, Kari & Riikka Ylitalo. 2004. On durational correlates of word stress in Finnish. *Journal of Phonetics* 32(1). 35–63.
Team, R Core. 2020. R: A language and environment for statistical computing. Vienna: R Foundation for Statistical Computing.
Temperley, Nicholas & David Temperley. 2011. Music-language correlations and the "Scotch Snap". *Music Perception* 29(1). 51–63.
Temperley, Nicholas & David Temperley. 2013. Stress-meter alignment in French vocal music. *The Journal of the Acoustical Society of America* 134(1). 520–527.

Elena Girardi & Ingo Plag
Metrical mapping in text-setting: Empirical analysis and grammatical implementation

Abstract: Linguists and musicologists share a persistent interest in text-setting, that is, in how the language of a poem is matched to musical structure (e.g. Halle & Lerdahl, 1993, Kiparsky, 2006, Hayes, 2009). For example, it is generally assumed that in English vocal music, stressed syllables tend to fall on relatively strong beats of the musical meter (Palmer & Kelly, 1992, Halle & Lerdahl, 1993), but there is surprisingly little quantitative evidence for it (cf. Temperley & Temperley, 2013: 521). This paper presents a systematic quantitative investigation of how the two language-related levels poetic meter (i.e., strong (S) and weak (W) positions of a metrical template) and syllabic prominence are matched to three dimensions of musical structure: musical meter, note value, and pitch. The corpus consists of three different *Lieder* by Haydn, based on three poems by Hunter, and three different settings of the same poem (*Annabel Lee* by Poe), with 161 lines overall. Using a set of constraints that evaluate the mapping of poetic/linguistic and musical structure, we are able to establish grammars that underlie particular text-settings. Overall, the study provides solid empirical evidence about general tendencies underlying the text-setting of classical songs, and for the existence of particular type-setting grammars.

Keywords: text-setting, meter, stress, Optimality Theory, maximum entropy grammar

1 Introduction

Linguists and musicologists share a persistent interest in text-setting, that is, in how the language of a poem is matched to musical structure (e.g. Halle & Lerdahl, 1993, Kiparsky, 2006, Hayes, 2009). One domain of investigation concerns the metrical organization of language as reflected in stressed and unstressed syllables, and how this organization is mapped onto various aspects of musical organization,

---

Elena Girardi: Institut für Anglistik und Amerikanistik, Heinrich-Heine-Universität Düsseldorf, (Alumna)
Ingo Plag: Institut für Anglistik und Amerikanistik, Heinrich-Heine-Universität Düsseldorf

https://doi.org/10.1515/9783110770186-008

such as musical meter, musical phrasing, note value, musical tone pitch etc.[1] For example, it is generally assumed that in English vocal music, stressed syllables tend to fall on relatively strong beats of the musical meter (sometimes also called 'stress-matching principle', Palmer & Kelly, 1992, Halle & Lerdahl, 1993, Proto, 2015). However, there is surprisingly little quantitative evidence available for the stress-matching principle (cf. Temperley & Temperley, 2013: 521).

With regard to the language side of this matter there is a further complication. Song lyrics themselves are often metrical texts, i.e. their prosodic organization is governed by particular principles that may govern or restrict possible linguistic structures, such as the rhythmic organization of words in a line. The role of the poetic metrical structure, often called 'metrical template', in text-setting has remained under-researched so that it is unclear whether the actual stresses or the positions in the metrical template are more important for the composer.

In this paper we present a systematic quantitative investigation of how poetic meter (i.e. S and W positions of a metrical template) on the one hand and syllabic prominence on the other hand are matched to three dimensions of musical structure: musical meter, note value, and tone pitch. This means that we will not only look at the mapping of stress and musical meter, but also at the mapping of poetic meter and musical meter. And we will look at two important acoustic correlates of stress in English duration and pitch. These correlates have straightforward correspondences in music, note value and tone pitch.

To assess the range of variability possible in such mappings we created a corpus which comprised three different *Lieder* by the same composer (Haydn, based on three poems by Hunter) and three different settings of the same poem (*Annabel Lee* by Poe) to music, with 161 lines overall.

The empirical results show very clear and statistically significant tendencies in the mapping of language and music. There are, however, also differences between songs and between composers.

To get a better understanding of the observed patterns of mapping we propose an innovative approach in which we use violable constraints and maximum entropy grammars (henceforth 'maxent' grammars) to model the well-formedness of particular mappings as well as of the song-specific grammar that underlies the composer's choices in the matching of language and music. This approach is inspired on the one hand by work in generative metrics (Halle & Keyser, 1966, 1971, et seq.) and work on metrical well-formedness using maxent grammars (e.g.

---

[1] In this paper, we will use the term 'tone pitch' to unambiguously refer to the pitch of musical tones. This use of the term 'tone pitch' can also be found in the experimental or engineering literature that deals with the pitch of tones as against the pitch of other kinds of sounds, or against other properties of tones (for example duration or intensity).

Hayes et al., 2012), and on the other hand by work in Optimality Theory (Prince & Smolensky, 1993) and its application to text-setting (e.g. Hayes, 2009).[2]

We develop a set of constraints that evaluate the mapping of poetic and linguistic structure at the one end, and musical structure at the other. Using the maxent approach, we are able to establish constraint hierarchies (i.e., grammars) that underlie particular text-settings. The songs in our sample vary systematically in the probabilities with which particular constraints are violated.

Overall, our study provides solid empirical evidence about general tendencies underlying the text-setting of classical songs, and for the existence of particular type-setting strategies, which can be formalized as grammars.

In the following section, we will introduce in more detail the problems involved in the investigation of the text-setting and lay out our research questions and research strategy. Section 3 explains our methodology, which is followed by the results of the quantitative analysis in section 4. Section 5 presents the background for the constraint-based maxent analysis, and section 6 contains the results thereof. Section 7 discusses our findings.

2 Text-setting: Poetic meter, linguistic rhythm and musical organization

The general problem in text-setting is how linguistic properties and musical properties are mapped onto each other. There is a considerable amount of literature on the topic, but a number of questions have remained unanswered. In this paper we focus on the question of how the rhythmic structure of the text is mapped onto certain aspects of the music, musical meter, note value and tone pitch. With regard to stress and musical meter in English vocal music, previous research is characterized by the general assumption that stressed syllables tend to fall on relatively strong beats of the musical meter (e.g. Palmer & Kelly, 1992, Halle & Lerdahl, 1993). Quantitative evidence for such a mapping tendency is scarce, however (cf. Temperley & Temperley, 2013: 521).

In addition to stress, there is often another, more abstract level of metrical organization, the poetic meter. Many song lyrics are actually metrical texts themselves, and there is even a whole musical genre, the classical *Lied*, which takes poems, i.e., (in their majority) *metrical* texts, and adds music to them. It

---

[2] The term 'well-formedness' generally refers to the degree to which a particular structure conforms to a grammar.

is well-known, however, that there is often no one-to-one mapping of strong positions in a poetic-metrical template and stressed syllables. This is illustrated in Table 1 with a well-known line from Shakespeare's sonnet 18. The first line gives the syllables of the words of the line, and the second gives the weak ('W') and strong ('S') positions of the iambic pentameter template (see Fabb, 1997: chapter 2 for an introduction). The third line gives the strength of the stress, as coded by Hayes et al., 2012[3]. '3' and '4' indicate stressed syllables, '1' an unstressed syllable.

Table 1: Example of the mapping of stress and metrical positions in iambic pentameter.

syllables	Shall	I	com	pare	thee	to	a	sum	mer's	day?
template	(W	S)	(W	S)	(W	S)	(W	S)	(W	S)
stress	1	1	1	3	1	1	1	3	1	4

One can easily see that strong positions in the template ('S' positions) are not always matched with stressed syllables. Conversely, the stressed syllables of polysyllabic words and the strong phrasal stress at the end of the line are consistently matched with S positions. The apparent variability in the mapping of stress and metrical position raises the question whether it is the actual stresses or the strong and weak positions of the metrical template that are more important for the mapping of musical beats. Depending on whether the composer orients themself towards the stresses or towards the S positions in the template, different matchings and, consequently, different musical patterns might emerge. In the words of Fabb:

> it is an empirical question in any particular case whether the matching of text to music is a matching of prosodic phonological structure directly to musical structure, or whether it is mediated through the metrical structure of the text. (Fabb, 1997: 105f)

To our knowledge there is no quantitative empirical research available that has explicitly tackled this question. It is therefore one of our aims to clarify for a set of *Lieder* whether it is the stresses or the metrical template that is more predictive of the mapping of beats to the metrical text. This means that we need to

---

[3] Hayes et al. (2012) assume four levels of stress and provide a supplementary document that explains in great detail how the different stress levels are assigned. We followed these guidelines, which are available at https://linguistics.ucla.edu/people/hayes/ShakespeareAndMilton/TranscriptionGuidelines.pdf.

investigate two kinds of mapping. In one mapping we look at the association of stresses of various levels of strength with musical beats of varying strength, in the other mapping we look at the association of the W and S positions of the metrical template with musical beats of varying strength. We will refer to the different degrees of stress as 'stress levels', to the W and S positions in the metrical template as 'metrical positions', and to the different levels of strength of musical beats as 'musical metrical strength' or simply 'metrical strength'.

Apart from musical meter there are many other dimensions in music that may stand in a non-arbitrary relationship to the linguistic properties of the text. We have selected two parameters that seem to constitute important properties of any acoustic signal and that are shared by music and language, i.e., duration and pitch (F0 in language). These two properties of sounds are particularly interesting when investigating text-setting because they are also well-known correlates of stress (e.g., Giegerich, 1992: 179, Hammond, 1999:151).[4]

Given that in language stressed syllables tend to have higher pitch and are longer than surrounding syllables, one could venture the hypothesis that more prominent syllables in language have a tendency to be matched with relatively longer and higher tones, in addition to being in positions with stronger beats. For instance, Rodríguez-Vázquez (2010: 251) points out that there are what she calls 'mismatches', in which short syllables end up in positions with a strong beat. Hayes (2009) observes that rhythmically strong units tend to be long. Based on these considerations we can make the following empirical predictions concerning the matching of beats, note value and tone pitch on the one hand and stress and templatic positions on the other:

(1) Stress predictions
   a. Stressed syllables have a tendency to occur in positions with stronger beats
   b. Stressed syllables have a tendency to have longer notes than unstressed syllables
   c. Stressed syllables have a tendency to have higher pitch than unstressed syllables

---

[4] There are also other properties that have been shown to be acoustic correlates of stress in English, for example loudness/intensity, vowel quality, and spectral balance (Fry, 1955, 1958, Sluijter & van Heuven, 1996a, 1996b, Plag et al., 2011). We do not consider these here. Loudness has an obvious correlate in the dynamics of music but is comparatively rarely explicitly used by composers within one song.

(2) Templatic predictions
   a. Syllables in templatic S positions have a tendency to occur in positions with stronger beats
   b. Syllables in templatic S positions have a tendency to have longer notes than syllables in templatic W positions
   c. Syllables in templatic S positions have a tendency to have higher pitch than unstressed syllables

There is only scattered empirical work on the role of duration in the text-setting of English songs. Hayes & Kaun (1996) find for sung and chanted folksong lines that the number of beats allotted to a syllable corresponds to the syllable's duration in speech. In environments where one syllable can be matched to two beats, this tends to happen with longer stressed syllables (e.g. *town*), but not with shorter stressed syllables (e.g. *ci* in *city*). Conversely, the Scotch Snap (i.e. a quarter tone tactus divided 1:3 over two syllables, with the first syllable being the stressed one, the second being unstressed) tends to strongly prefer short stressed syllables (see also Temperley & Temperley, 2011). Studies focussing on pitch are usually carried out in connection to tone languages (Proto, 2015: 120), and little is known with regard to the role of pitch in English text-setting.

The present paper tests the predictions given in (1) and (2) by implementing a quantitative analysis of a corpus of six *Lieder*, three of Joseph Haydn's English canzonets (1794–95), which are text-settings of poems by the London-based poet Anne Hunter, and three rather recent settings of Edgar Allan Poe's poem *Annabel Lee* (Poe, 1997: 90), by the composers Scott Gendel, Joel B. New and Jeffrey Quick. The methodology for this empirical investigation will be described in the next section, the results will be presented in section 4.

Given the non-arbitrary distributions of linguistic and musical properties in text-settings, the obvious question is what mechanisms underlie these distributions. We will approach this question by assuming that text-setting is governed by general constraints on the mapping of linguistic and musical structure. The relative importance of these constraints, i.e., their ranking, determines how exactly the mapping plays out. In essence, we will show that certain aspects of a particular text-setting can be described by an underlying constraint hierarchy, the composer's grammar used for the given song.

A similar approach can be found in earlier work by Hayes (e.g. 2009), Rodríguez-Vázquez (2010, 2011) or Keshet (2005). We differ from previous work in three respects. First, we use different constraints, and constraint formulations, in an attempt to capture more adequately the nature of the data. Second, we model not only the mapping of linguistic stress levels and music, but also of the templatic metrical positions and music. Third, we use maximum entropy grammar (e.g. Hayes et al., 2012) to model the well-formedness of particular text-settings. The details of our approach will be discussed in section 5.

3 Methodology

3.1 The corpus

Our corpus consists of six songs varying along various dimensions. Three of them are 18th century songs by the same composer, Joseph Haydn, based on three poems by London-based poet Anne Hunter, *The Mermaid's Song*, *Fidelity*, and *The Wanderer*. The other three songs analysed are more recent (end of 19th/ beginning of 20th century) renditions of the 18th century poem *Annabel Lee* by Edgar Allan Poe by three different composers, Scott Gendel, Joel B. New, and Jeffrey Quick.

The choice of these songs is chiefly motivated by our intention to study certain kinds of variation in the mapping of language and music. The three songs based on Hunter's poetry allow for making generalizations about one composer's choices in text-setting across various compositions. The three renditions of *Annabel Lee*, in contrast, allow for comparing text-setting preferences among different composers working with the same text.[5] Finally, the poems show variation in their metrical templates. Table 2 gives an overview of the corpus.

The first row of Table 2 gives the type of feet that we found in the poems. To arrive at these kinds of feet, a metrical template was created for each line of each poem, analogous to Fabb's (1997) account of iambic pentameter. The metrical template is a series of strong (S) and weak (W) metrical positions to which syllables or feet are matched, and which are grouped into feet (e.g. Fabb, 1997: chapter 2, Hayes, 1989: 221). Each metrical template comes with instructions (i.e., a set of rules, or a kind of grammar) that regulate how the language of the poem is matched to the template. For instance, one of the most important rules Fabb (1997: 41) finds for Shakespeare's iambic pentameter is that the stressed syllables of polysyllabic words must match a strong (i.e., S) position.

---

[5] Composers may differ in their text-setting strategies for any number of reasons, one of them being the times in which they live, or the musical tradition in which they work. For instance, one could expect systematic differences between composers working in the 18th century vs. those working in the 20th century. Such considerations are outside the scope of this paper, but our results may serve as a basis for future research into the motivations for the particular text-setting strategies we have identified.

Table 2: Overview of the corpus.

Haydn			
	Mermaid	Wanderer	Fidelity
foot types in template	WS	WS, WWS	WS
time signature	2/4	3/4	4/4
# of syllables	159	130	219
# of S positions	91	47	109
# of W positions	68	79	110
Annabel Lee			
	Gendel	New	Quick
foot types in template	WS, WWS (highly variable)		
time signature	4/4, 6/4, 3/4	2/2	9/8, 6/8, 3/4
# of syllables	377	377	384
# of S positions	138	138	140
# of W positions	230	230	235

We devised a template for each line of the four poems, following established principles and procedures (see, for instance, Fabb, 1997). The aim was to devise templates that best describe all lines of a poem and are as consistent and uniform as possible across one poem. Feet were matched to lexical and phrasal stresses, minimizing the number of different foot types (trochee, iamb, dactyl, anapaest), the number of extrametrical syllables, and the number of degenerate feet.

We found highly regular and consistent metrical templates for Hunter's three poems, whereas for *Annabel Lee* we determined three different templates that in themselves are highly variable. (3) to (6) give the metrical templates for each poem. The parentheses show the grouping of positions into feet. In *Fidelity* shorter lines alternate with longer lines, so that uneven lines have an additional foot of the same kind (WS).

Annabel Lee is highly variable. There are three basic templates, which are given in (6a) to (6c). These templates are variable in themselves in the following fashion. In all three the foot type of the first foot may vary, it can be (S), (WS), (WWS). In (6a) and (6c), if the first foot is (WS) or (WWS), an optional foot may precede, again being either (S), (WS), (WWS). In (6b) and (6c), unfilled weak positions are possible at the edge of phonological phrases.

(3) *The Mermaid's Song*: (S)[6](WS) (WS) (WS)

(4) *Fidelity*: uneven lines: (WS) (WS) (WS) (WS)
    even lines: (WS) (WS) (WS)

(5) *The Wanderer*: (WS) (WWS) (WWS) (WWS)

(6) *Annabel Lee*:
    a. (WWS) (WWS)
    b. (SW) (WS) (WS) (WWS)
    c. (SW) (WS) (WS)

In total, 1646 syllables were analysed, and 952 W and 663 S positions are found.

3.2 Coding

For each syllable a number of variables was coded to capture the parameters under investigation, i.e., stress, position, musical metrical strength, note value, and tone pitch. The final coding is shown exemplarily for the first line from Anne Hunter's *The Mermaid's Song* in Figure 2 below.

The templatic positions are coded according to the metrical templates previously determined. Extrametrical syllables or the second of two syllables sharing one position were coded as "na" and are therefore excluded from the analysis (31 syllables in total). The positions are grouped into feet illustrated by the brackets. Stress was coded using four levels of stress according to the criteria developed in Hayes et al. (2012). For the subsequent quantitative analysis of the mapping of stress and beats the four stress levels were turned into a binary variable with levels 1 and 2 recoded as 'unstressed', and levels 3 and 4 recoded as 'stressed'. This allows us to compare the mapping of metrical positions (which have two values) onto musical dimensions with the mapping of stress onto these dimensions.

Musical metrical strength was assigned to the notes matching a syllable using Temperley & Temperley's (2013) method. According to Temperley & Temperley (2013: 522) the tactus level, i.e., the quarter note level in 2/4, 3/4, and 4/4 is metrical level 2. The half note level in 2/4, 3/4, and 4/4 time signatures receives

---

[6] A poetic foot of the type '(S)' can be analyzed as a variant of an iambic poetic foot (WS). This is the reason why (S) is not given in Table 2.

metrical strength 3 and the whole note level in 4/4 time signatures counts as level 4. In 6/8 and 9/8 time signatures, the tactus level is the dotted quarter note and has metrical strength 2. All other levels of metrical strength are defined accordingly. The coding is illustrated in Figure 1:

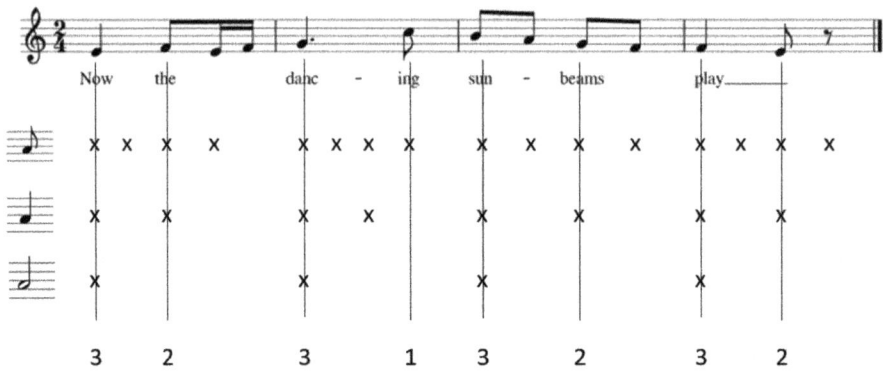

Figure 1: Coding of metrical strength, illustrated with a line from *The Mermaid's Song*.

Note value was calculated in proportion to the musical bar. For instance, a quarter note in a bar written in four quarter time signature would be assigned the value 0.25. For relative tone pitch we used three different variables. We looked at tone pitch from the preceding note to the note in question and from the note in question to the following one. Here, we coded "stay", "up", and "down" respectively. In addition, we calculated melodic peak scores (Kabak & Domene Moreno, 2017) that assign a relative pitch value to notes considering the preceding and the following note at the same time.

In those cases in which one syllable is assigned more than one note by the composer, the coding of length and pitch runs into problems. With regard to length we adopted the strategy to add up the proportional durations of all notes assigned to the syllable in question. With regard to pitch we coded the pitch of the first note assigned to the syllable in question.

syllables	now	the	dan-	cing	sun	beams	play
template / feet	(S)	(W	S)	(W	S)	(W	S)
stress level	3	1	3	1	3	2	3
stress (binary)	yes	no	yes	no	yes	no	yes
metrical strength	3	2	3	1	3	2	3
note value	0.5	0.5	0.75	0.25	0.5	0.5	0.75
pitch into	na	up	up	up	down	down	down
pitch out of	up	up	up	down	down	down	na
melodic peak score	na	4	4	6	4	4	na

Figure 2: Coding for the first line of *The Mermaid's Song*.

When a part of the poem is repeated in the musical composition, a syllable or a sequence of syllables from the poems may have more than one musical realization. In this case, the respective syllables were coded for their textual and musical characteristics for all of their musical representations. If the repetition, however, is an exact repetition of the first instance the syllable occurs in the musical representation, then it was not coded again.[7] Figure 3 below, showing bar lines 80–83 in *Fidelity*, illustrates this procedure. The first repetition of *is cast for me* is annotated again, because the word *is* is assigned a different note. The third repetition of the phrase, however, is an exact repetition of the second and is not annotated again.

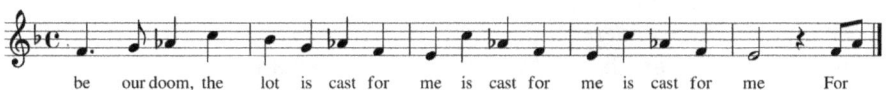

Figure 3: Bars 80–83 from *Fidelity* with repetitions of *is cast for me*.

4 Results: The mapping of language and music

We systematically tested the mapping of the musical dimensions and templatic positions, and the mapping of the musical dimensions and stress, using statistical tools provided by the statistical analysis software R (R Development Core Team,

---

[7] The examples from the music given in the present writing are our own transcriptions created with the notation software MuseScore, free for download on the respective website.

2014) and the package languageR (Baayen & Shafaei-Bajestan, 2019, version 1.5.0). The results of the two kinds of analyses are very similar, and, for reasons of space, we restrict the presentation of our quantitative results to the mapping of music and templatic positions (sections 4.1 to 4.3). In section 4.4 we will compare the matchings involving the positions in the metrical template with the matchings involving stress. This will answer the question whether composers are guided more by the stresses or by the metrical template.

For each mapping we also fitted a regression model (using the lm() function in R) that predicts the value of the musical dimension based on templatic position and stress, respectively. The aim of the regression analyses is twofold. First, it will allow us to assess whether the tendencies (if any) found in these distributional patterns are statistically significant (i.e., not due to random variation). Second, it enables us to reliably compare the predictive power of the two kinds of mappings. The regression models are summarized and discussed in section 4.4.

4.1 Musical metrical strength

The distributions of musical metrical strength by metrical position are given in Figure 4. The *x*-axes show the values for musical metrical strength. The *y*-axes give the proportion of metrical positions.

The results meet the expectations in all songs (see again prediction (2a) above). Especially Haydn's three canzonets show almost categorical distributions. In *The Mermaid's Song* metrical strength 1 is reserved for W positions, and strength 3 for S positions. Strength 2 can be frequently found in both W and S positions. In *The Wanderer* S positions are almost exclusively paired with the highest metrical strength, and W positions with strength 1 and 2. The difference in distribution between *The Mermaid's Song* and *The Wanderer* may arise from the different time signatures, which is binary in *The Mermaid's Song* and ternary in *The Wanderer*. *Fidelity* has four levels of musical metrical strength and there is a categorical binary distribution of W positions on levels 1 and 2 of musical metrical strength and of S positions on levels 3 and 4 of musical metrical strength.

Gendel's and Quick's renditions of *Annabel Lee* show the consistent tendency of increasing proportions of S positions with rising levels of musical metrical strength. In New's rendition this tendency does not hold for levels 1 and 2 of metrical strength. Overall, the three composers of *Annabel Lee* allow for more variation in the mapping than Haydn.

The regression models for all compositions show that the tendencies observed for metrical strength are significant (see section 4.4, Table 3, rows 1 and 2,

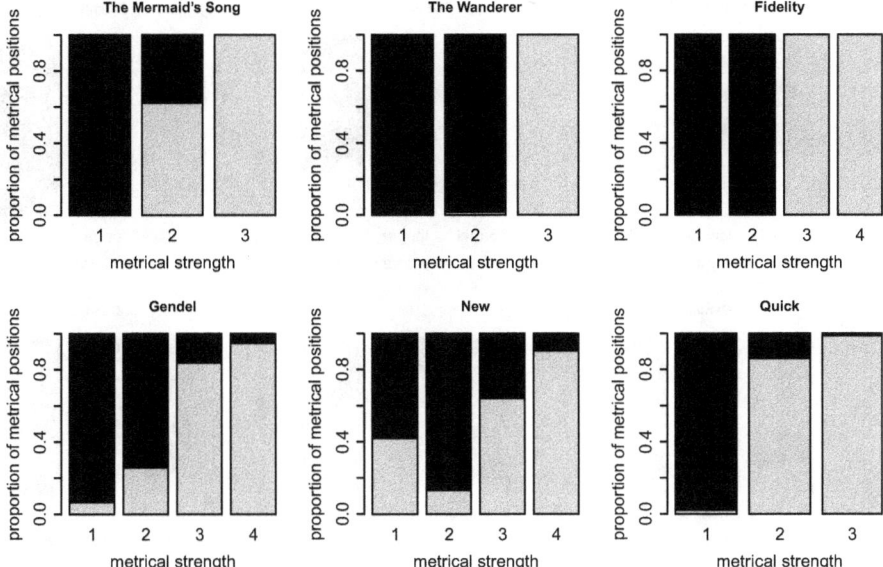

Figure 4: Metrical strength by metrical positions. Proportions for W positions are shown in black, S positions in grey.

for a more detailed documentation of the regression results). This strongly supports the stress-matching principle.

4.2 Note value

The second parameter under investigation is note value. Recall that our coding annotates for each syllable whether the note on this syllable is equal, longer or shorter than the preceding note. The results of this analysis are presented in Figure 5.

In all songs, the results largely mirror what has been found for the mapping onto musical metrical strength. Stronger musical metrical strength and S positions tend to coincide. That is, most S positions have longer notes, and longer notes tend to be reserved for syllables in S positions. W positions are mostly reserved to notes of equal or shorter durations and notes with shorter duration overwhelmingly are in syllables in W positions. Haydn's songs are more categorical in their distributions of W and S metrical positions, and the three renditions of *Annabel Lee* again show more variation.

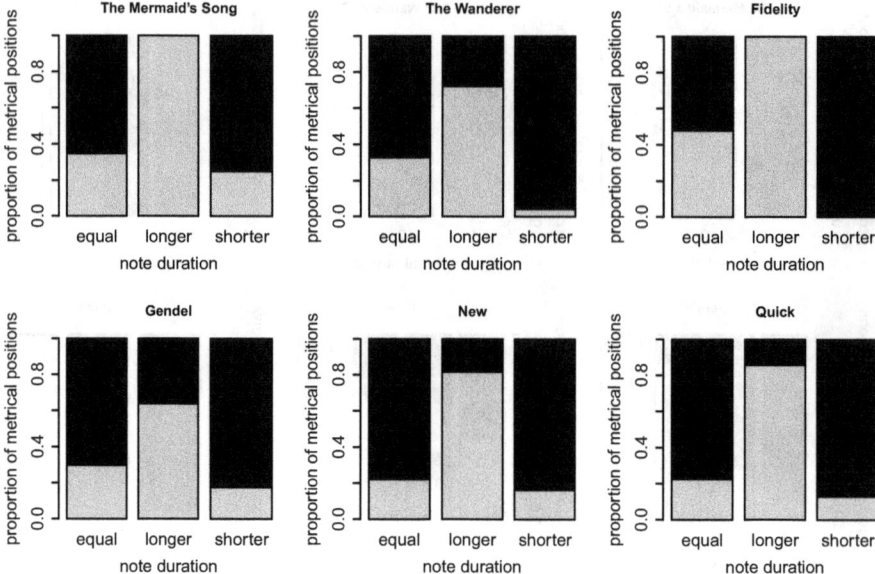

Figure 5: Note duration by metrical positions. Proportions for W positions are shown in black, S positions in grey.

The regression models for all compositions show that the tendencies observed for note value are significant (see section 4.4, Table 3, rows 3 and 4 for more detailed documentation of the regression results for note value). Overall, the results demonstrate that the mapping of note value and metrical positions is an important factor in the text-settings of all of the poems examined here.

4.3 Tone pitch

For the quantification of tone pitch we used three different variables. The first encodes pitch movement from the previous note into the note in question, the second the pitch movement from the note in question into the following note. These two variables will be used in the maxent analysis in section 5. The third variable, the so-called peak score (Kabak & Domene Moreno, 2017), gives the relative prominence of a syllable and is computed on the basis of the first two variables: If the note in question is lower than a preceding (or following, respectively) note it receives the score of 1, a level movement scores 2, and if the note in question is higher, it receives a score of 3. The peak score thus ranges from 2 to 6, with 6 indicating a melodic peak with lower notes on both sides, and 2 a melodic trough with two higher notes on each side. The results for peak scores are presented in Figure 6.

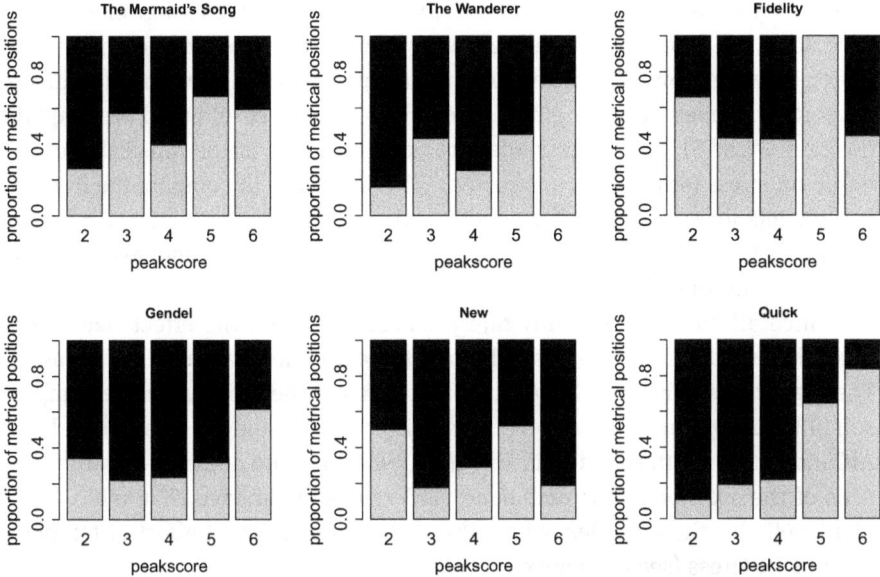

Figure 6: Peak scores by metrical positions. Proportions for W positions are shown in black, S positions in grey.

The distributions for the mapping of tone pitch and metrical position show much more random variation than the mappings discussed above. Only Quick's composition shows a strong monotonous increase in the proportions of S positions with increasing prominence, while all other compositions show a more variegated picture with relatively high proportions of S positions also for low prominence values. In the regression analyses, Quick's composition shows a strong significant effect, and *The Mermaid's Song, The Wanderer* and Gendel very weak significant effects. There are no significant effects of templatic positions on peak scores for *Fidelity* and New's setting (see section 4.4, Table 3, rows 5 and 6 for a more detailed documentation of the regression results for tone pitch). Overall, tone pitch seems to play a much less important role in the mapping of language and music than the other two dimensions.

4.4 Metrical positions vs. stresses

In order to investigate the question whether a composer relies rather on linguistic stresses or on the meter of the text, we used linear regression models. For each song, we fitted two models each for each of the three musical properties under investigation. One of the two models predicts the value of the musical property (i.e., metrical strength or note value or peak score) based on templatic position (W or S). The other model predicts the value of the musical property based on stress (stressed or unstressed). This allows us to compare the fit of the two models for each musical property, and to see whether it is the template or the stress that allows for better predictions. The regression models are documented in full in the Appendix.

Since all models have only one predictor variable, the effect size can be read off the adjusted r^2 values, which is the explained variance of the model. The higher this value, the better the predictions of the model. For the comparison of the fit of unnested models the AIC is another standard measure. A lower AIC indicates a better model fit. In Table 3 we show the adjusted r^2 values and AICs of the six models for each song. AIC values are shaded. The table shows blank cells for those models where there was no significant effect of templatic position or stress (see Appendix).

Before turning to the model comparisons, let us have a look at the size of the effects, as gauged by the r^2 values. If we compare them across the different compositions and across the three musical dimensions, we can easily see that, generally, there are large effect sizes for metrical strength (with New as an exception), somewhat smaller effects for note value, and extremely small (or no) effects for tone pitch (with the exception of Quick). For instance, *Fidelity* has an r^2 value of 0.82 for the template-based mapping of musical strength, and an r^2 value of 0.22 for the template-based mapping of note value (and no significant relation between tone pitch and metrical strength, hence the empty cell in Table 3).

The comparison of the AICs for the template-based mapping with those of the stress-based mapping reveals higher AICs with the mapping of stresses (see, for instance, the AICs of 213 vs. 476 for the mapping of metrical strength in *Fidelity*). The only exception is the model fitted to tone pitch for *The Mermaid's Song*. In this model, we have the same AIC for both models, but both models have a very poor fit (r^2 = 0.03 for the template, 0.02 for the stresses).

In sum, our data provide strong evidence that there is a greater tendency among the composers in our sample to match musical properties to templatic positions rather than to stressed and unstressed syllables.

Table 3: r^2 and AIC values of regression models for the mapping of metrical strength, note value and tone pitch onto language, based on templatic positions and stress, respectively. 'M'= *The Mermaid's Song*, 'W' = *The Wanderer*, 'F' = *Fidelity*, 'G' = Gendel, 'N' = New, 'Q' = Quick.

	M		W		F		G		N		Q	
	r^2	AIC	r^2	AIC	r^2	AIC	r^2	AIC	r^2	AIC	r^2	AIC
metrical strength												
1 template-based	0.76	183	0.74	94	0.82	213	0.59	856	0.03	970	0.79	355
2 stress-based	0.52	294	0.68	120	0.39	476	0.55	906	0.04	987	0.73	452
note value												
3 template-based	0.32	255	0.24	228	0.22	225	0.18	809	0.28	605	0.32	601
4 stress-based	0.26	267	0.22	233	0.10	255	0.18	827	0.24	641	0.34	617
tone pitch (peak score)												
5 template-based	0.03	439	0.10	377			0.04	957			0.23	877
6 stress-based	0.02	439	0.09	396			0.04	974			0.20	897

5 Constraint-based analysis: A maxent grammar of text-setting

5.1 The constraints

For our constraint-based analysis we will use constraints that address three different mapping problems: stress matching, bracket matching and contextual salience. We will discuss each in turn.

Stress matching constraints have played an important role in previous work (e.g. Hayes, 2009) as they are needed to account for the tendency of stressed syllables to coincide with strong, rather than weak, beats. Given that, as shown above, the metrical template is at least as important as the actual stresses, we will implement both the matching of stress and the matching of templatic positions to musical meter.

Hayes (2009) introduces two kinds of stress matching constraints, targeting either stressed or unstressed syllables. These constraints penalize stressed syllables in musical metrical positions that are of medium or weak strength, and they penalize unstressed syllables in strong and in weak musical metrical positions.

We differ from Hayes (2009) by taking a different direction in the coding of the constraints and by parametrizing the stress matching constraints more systematically. Given that a composer needs to map music onto an existing text, we feel that constraints regulating this mapping should be conceptualized as working in this direction, too. We therefore propose the two constraint families given in (7) and (8) for metrical positions, and the ones given in (9) and (10) for stresses. 'W' and 'S' refer to the strong and weak positions in the poetic metrical template, 'beat' refers to the positions in the musical meter. The constraint in (7) penalizes beats in W positions. The harmonic hierarchy[8] given in the second line of (7) ensures that weaker beats in W positions are more easily tolerable than stronger beats. The constraint in (8) ensures that strong beats are placed on S, with strongest beats being most desirable in this position. The constraints in (9) and (10) work analogously for the matching of stressed and unstressed syllables and beats.

(7) *BEAT IN W: Avoid beats in W positions.
     *BEAT4 IN W   >>   *BEAT3 IN W   >>
     *BEAT2 IN W   >>   *BEAT1 IN W

(8) *BEATLESS IN S: Avoid having no beats in S positions.
     *BEAT1 IN S   >>   *BEAT2 IN S   >>
     *BEAT3 IN S   >>   *BEAT4 IN S

(9) *BEAT ON UNSTRESSED: Avoid beats on stressless syllables.
     *BEAT4 ON UNSTRESSED   >>   *BEAT3 ON UNSTRESSED   >>*BEAT2
     UNSTRESSED   >>   *BEAT1 ON UNSTRESSED

(10) *BEATLESS ON STRESSED: Avoid having no beats on stressed syllables.
     *BEAT1 ON STRESSED   >>   *BEAT2 ON STRESSED   >>   *BEAT3 ON STRESSED   >>
     *BEAT4 ON STRESSED

For reasons of space, we restrict our constraint-based analyses of note value and pitch to the mapping of these parameters onto metrical positions. With

---

8 The term 'harmonic' is used in this article exclusively in its optimality-theoretical sense, and not in the musical sense. Universal preferences with regard to the well-formedness of an expression can be fomalized in terms of so-called 'harmonic' scales. Harmonic constraint rankings ensure that those candidates are optimal that best conform to harmonic scales. For a discussion of harmonic scales and constraint rankings see, for examples, Aissen (1999, 2003), Howe & Pulleyblank (2004). Harmonic Grammar was first developed by Legendre et al. (1990).

regard to note value, the most harmonic ranking would ensure that notes are longer in S positions than in surrounding W positions. This is the work of the constraints put forward in (11) and (12), which are inspired by the constraints used in to model the mapping of stress and metrical templatic positions in Shakespeare's sonnets and Milton's *Paradise Lost*. The constraints in (11b, d) and (12b, d) are stricter variants of the length constraints, as they also penalize notes of the same length, and not only notes that are longer.

(11) a. *LONGER AFTER S: Avoid longer notes after S
  b. *LONGER/EQUAL AFTER S: Avoid longer notes, or notes of equal length, after S
  c. *LONGER BEFORE S: Avoid longer notes before S
  d. *LONGER/EQUAL BEFORE S: Avoid longer notes, or notes of the same length, before S

(12) a. *SHORTER AFTER W: Avoid shorter notes after W
  b. * SHORTER/EQUAL AFTER W: Avoid shorter notes, or notes of the same length, after S
  c. *SHORTER BEFORE W: Avoid shorter notes, or notes of equal length, before W
  d. *SHORTER/EQUAL BEFORE W: Avoid shorter notes, or notes of equal length, before W

Similar constraints hold for tone pitch, as given in (13) and (14).

(13) a. *HIGHER PITCH AFTER S: Avoid higher pitch after S
  b. *HIGHER/SAME PITCH AFTER S: Avoid higher pitch, or pitch of the same height, after S
  c. *HIGHER PITCH BEFORE S: Avoid higher pitch before S
  d. *HIGHER/SAME BEFORE S: Avoid higher pitch, or pitch of the same height, before S

(14) a. *LOWER PITCH AFTER W: Avoid lower pitch after W
  b. *LOWER/SAME PITCH AFTER W: Avoid lower pitch, or pitch of the same height, after W
  c. *LOWER PITCH BEFORE W: Avoid lower pitch before W
  d. *LOWER/SAME PITCH BEFORE W: Avoid higher pitch, or pitch of the same height, before S

Let us now turn to the kind of grammar that will be used to model the text-setting.

5.2 Maximum entropy grammar

Maxent grammars emerge as the result of a learning algorithm that makes probabilistic generalizations, balancing accuracy and generality. The maximum entropy formalism has a long tradition in machine learning literature (e.g. Jaynes, 1957, Berger et al., 1996) and has recently been used in linguistics, for example in studies of phonotactics and metrics (e.g. Goldwater & Johnson, 2003, Wilson, 2006, Hayes & Wilson, 2008, Martin, 2011, Hayes et al., 2012).

A maxent grammar contains a list of numerically weighted constraints. This is different from classical Optimality, in which constraints are strictly ranked, leaving no room for variability and probability. The weight of the constraint in a maxent grammar represents its strength, which is a function of the number of times it is violated. The more violations, the lower the weight of the constraint. The constraints and their weights constitute the grammar. Given the constraints and their weight, the probability of particular potential output structures can be computed. This probability indexes the well-formedness of the structure in question.

For the implementation we make use of the maxent grammar tool hosted by Bruce Hayes (available at https://linguistics.ucla.edu/people/hayes/Maxent GrammarTool). Technical details about the algorithm and its implementation can be found in the literature referenced above and will not be discussed in detail here. In essence, the algorithm is fed a list of constraints and the number of violations of each constraint for each candidate. Based on the violations the algorithm computes the constraint weights.[9] In the next section, we will present the results of this implementation.

---

[9] For the computation of the constraint weights, it is possible to set a specific Gaussian prior for each constraint to penalize high weights. We chose $\mu=1$ and $\sigma^2=5.0E8$ for all constraints in all computations to minimize this penalization, and to obtain weights at a magnitude that makes them easy to compare.

6 Results: Constraint rankings

6.1 Musical metrical strength

The constraint weights for the mapping of musical meter and templatic positions are given in Table 4, the weights for the mapping of musical meter and stress are given in Table 5.

In all but New's text-setting we find harmonic rankings. Haydn has very clear preferences. In a ternary musical rhythm, i.e., one with three levels of strength, S positions strongly disfavor the weakest beat, and in the quarternary

Table 4: Constraint weights for the mapping of musical meter and templatic positions.

	Mermaid	Wanderer	Fidelity	Gendel	New	Quick
*BEAT1 IN S	5.00	5.00	5.00	6.60	1.25	5.72
*BEAT2 IN S	0.00	0.00	5.00	4.95	5.68	0.58
*BEAT3 IN S	0.00	0.00	0.00	1.93	6.03	0.33
*BEAT4 IN S			0.00	1.15	3.45	
*BEAT4 IN W			5.00	6.40	6.24	
*BEAT3 IN W	5.00	5.00	5.00	3.20	2.08	5.56
*BEAT2 IN W	0.00	0.00	0.00	0.56	0.17	0.70
*BEAT1 IN W	0.00	0.00	0.00	0.15	0.18	0.02

Table 5: Constraint weights for the mapping of musical meter and stress.

	Mermaid	Wanderer	Fidelity	Gendel	New	Quick
*BEAT1 ON STRESSED	5.00	5.00	5.00	6.47	1.25	5.61
*BEAT2 ON STRESSED	0.00	0.00	0.00	5.08	6.07	0.47
*BEAT3 ON STRESSED	0.00	0.00	0.00	1.78	5.69	0.27
*BEAT4 ON STRESSED			0.00	1.06	3.25	
*BEAT4 ON UNSTRESSED			1.45	6.35	6.19	
*BEAT3 ON UNSTRESSED	6.41	5.00	6.36	4.04	1.86	5.85
*BEAT2 ON UNSTRESSED	3.92	0.00	0.31	0.84	0.16	3.90
*BEAT1 ON UNSTRESSED	1.31	0.00	4.54	0.26	0.16	0.15

rhythm (with four levels of strength) S positions disfavor the two weakest beats. Gendel and Quick show very similar grammars. New's version of *Annabel Lee* shows a harmonic ranking for weak positions but a non-harmonic ranking for S positions, with S positions attracting the weakest beats (instead of the strongest, as in harmonic rankings).

The mapping of stresses, as shown in Table 5, shows a similar picture. For stressed syllables all compositions but New's have harmonic rankings, for unstressed syllables *Fidelity* shows a non-harmonic ranking that disfavors the weakest beats and favors the strongest beats on unstressed syllables.

6.2 Note values

The rankings of the constraints that are responsible for the mapping of note values onto metrical positions are given in Table 6.

Table 6: Constraint weights for the mapping of note value and templatic position.

	Mermaid	Wanderer	Fidelity	Gendel	New	Quick
*LONGER AFTER S	5.1	6.0	5.1	5.9	5.5	5.74
*LONGER/EQUAL AFTER S	0.1	1.8	0.1	3.4	0.7	1.08
*LONGER BEFORE S	5.0	5.8	5.1	5.7	5.7	5.49
*LONGER/EQUAL BEFORE S	0.0	1.3	0.1	3.9	1.0	0.62
*SHORTER AFTER W	5.9	5.2	5.0	5.9	5.9	5.77
*SHORTER/EQUAL AFTER W	1.5	0.2	0.0	3.4	1.5	1.15
*SHORTER BEFORE W	5.0	5.8	5.1	6.0	5.6	5.48
*SHORTER/EQUAL BEFORE W	0.0	1.1	0.1	3.2	0.8	0.60

All compositions are based on harmonic rankings that strongly favor S positions to have notes of longer or equal duration as the surrounding positions, and that strongly favor W positions to have notes of shorter or equal duration than its preceding and following position. The weights of the constraints vary only slightly across compositions. Only Gendel's weights are remarkably different from the others in that there is a stronger tendency for S positions to be occupied by longer notes and for W positions to be occupied by shorter than the surrounding positions.

6.3 Tone pitch

The mapping of pitch and metrical positions is much less harmonic than the previous mappings, as documented in Table 7.

Table 7: Constraint weights for the mapping of tone pitch and templatic position.

	Mermaid	Wanderer	Fidelity	Gendel	New	Quick
*HIGHER PITCH AFTER S	5.8	6.0	5.3	5.4	6.0	5.91
*HIGHER/SAME PITCH AFTER S	3.6	2.8	4.6	4.5	2.9	1.58
*HIGHER PITCH BEFORE S	5.4	5.9	5.2	5.8	6.0	5.44
*HIGHER/SAME BEFORE S	4.5	3.6	4.8	3.7	2.8	4.46
*LOWER PITCH AFTER W	5.4	5.9	5.2	5.6	6.0	5.79
*LOWER/SAME PITCH AFTER W	4.5	3.6	4.8	4.1	2.7	3.81
*LOWER PITCH BEFORE W	5.9	6.0	5.3	5.3	6.0	6.03
*LOWER/SAME PITCH BEFORE W	3.4	2.9	4.6	4.7	2.8	2.41

The Wanderer and New's version of *Annabel Lee* show harmonic patterns throughout, with S positions favoring higher pitches and W positions lower pitches than the surrounding positions. The weights of the clearly ranked constraints on the respective hierarchies (e.g. 5.8 and 3.6 in the first two cells for *The Mermaid's Song*) are, however, closer to each other than the weights in the previously discussed hierarchies for metrical strength and note value (e.g. 5.0 vs. 0.0, or 5.0 vs. 0.1 in the corresponding cells in Tables 4–6). This means that there is more variation.

The other four grammars are characterized by a mixture of weak harmonic rankings and near-ties in the constraint rankings. We use the term 'near-tie' for weights whose difference is smaller than 1. These are marked in grey in Table 7. Although the weights of these constraints are still harmonic, the weights in the grey cells are so close to each other that the grammar allows for a great number of violations with both constraints, and hence rather random variation.

Overall, the mapping of pitch and templatic positions is much less constrained than the other mappings investigated in this paper.

7 Discussion and conclusion

The present paper has investigated how poetic meter (as formalized in metrical templates) and syllabic prominence is matched to three dimensions of musical structure: musical meter, note value, and tone pitch. Based on the quantitative analysis of a corpus of three different *Lieder* by Haydn and three different musical settings of the poem *Annabel Lee*, it was possible to discern very clear tendencies in the mapping of language and music.

The strongest tendency is the matching of prosodically strong elements of the language with strong elements in the musical meter. Another strong tendency is the alignment of prosodically strong elements of the language with longer note values. Generally, there is only a weak tendency to align higher tone pitch with strong prosodic units.

The analysis also revealed that there are clear differences between songs and between composers in how they relate language and music. Composers may choose text-settings that go against the tendencies just described. For instance, New does not adhere well to the stress-matching principle, and Gendel tends to align pitch peaks with strong prosodic positions.

The quantitative analysis also allowed us to investigate a long-standing problem in the setting of metrical texts, i.e., the question of whether it is the metrical template or the stress distribution that is responsible for the mapping of linguistic prominence and musical prominence (as manifested in beats, note length and tone pitch). The comparison of both kinds of mapping using regression models yields a clear picture. There is a tighter mapping observable of musical prominence with the S and W positions of the metrical template of the poem than with the stressed and unstressed syllables in the text.

The mappings as manifested in the six songs under investigation were formally modelled using an innovative approach inspired by Optimality Theory and some recent studies on phonotactics and poetic meter. In this approach, violable constraints that mitigate against certain types of mappings of text and music are implemented in a maximum entropy grammar. Songs vary in the probabilities with which particular constraints are violated. Using the maxent approach, it is possible to establish constraint hierarchies, i.e., individual grammars, that underlie particular text-settings. This formalization allows us to make verifiable claims about the properties of the songs under consideration, but also about the nature of text-setting.

We found that in all text-settings, there is a strong tendency towards harmonic rankings in which linguistic prominence (be it via the template, or via the stresses) aligns with musical metrical prominence. Furthermore, there is a strong tendency towards harmonic rankings that regulate the mapping of templatic positions and note values. With regard to tone pitch, the alignment is much less harmonic and less strong.

Overall, in the songs investigated in this study, we find that of the three dimensions under investigation that are shared by language and music, i.e., rhythmic prominence, duration, and pitch, the first two are much more important than tone pitch in matching linguistic structure and musical dimensions.

Our maxent implementation has also demonstrated that it is possible to devise formal systems, i.e., grammars, that can bring about the particular mappings of language and music that characterize individual compositions. In this way it is possible to pin down a composer's individual strategy of dealing with particular kinds of mappings. For example, a composer may choose disharmonic rankings for some constraints and harmonic rankings for others. In sum, the maxent implementation has provided solid empirical evidence for the existence of particular type-setting strategies. The consequences of such strategies for the character of the songs may be very interesting to look at from a musicological perspective. The grammars devised in this study might thus be used as a springboard for the development of new research questions in this field.

Future work may show whether the results of this study carry over to other genres and composers, or hold also for a larger corpus of *Lieder*, representing other composers. Furthermore, the present approach could be applied to other languages and other musical traditions. Languages with different prosodic systems, different poetic traditions, and different musical genres are likely to exhibit other kinds of mappings depending on the importance of particular linguistic or musical properties in a given language or culture. The contributions by Arjava & Kentner (2022), Domene Moreno & Kabak (2022), and Gilbers & Rebernik (2022) illustrate ways of how this can be done fruitfully.

Appendix

The tables below document the regression models discussed in section 4.4. The numbers for the intercept and the predictor variables are the coefficients, the numbers in parentheses give the corresponding standard errors. The baseline value for metrical position is 'S', the baseline value for stress level is 'stressed'. Asterisks indicate significance levels: ***$p < 0.001$; **$p < 0.01$; *$p < 0.05$

Table 8: Metrical strength as dependent variable: Haydn.

	Mermaid template-based	Mermaid stress-based	Wanderer template-based	Wanderer stress-based	Fidelity template-based	Fidelity stress-based
(Intercept)	2.75***	2.75***	2.98***	2.90***	3.59***	3.49***
	(0.04)	(0.07)	(0.05)	(0.05)	(0.04)	(0.08)
metrical Position W	−1.54***		−1.21***		−1.65***	
	(0.07)		(0.06)		(0.05)	
stress Level Binary-unstressed		−1.27***		−1.13***		−1.19***
		(0.10)		(0.07)		(0.10)
R^2	0.77	0.53	0.74	0.68	0.82	0.40
Adj. R^2	0.76	0.53	0.74	0.68	0.82	0.39
Num. obs.	159	159	126	130	219	219

Table 9: Metrical strength as dependent variable: Annabel Lee.

	Gendel stress-based	Gendel template-based	New stress-based	New template-based	Quick stress-based	Quick template-based
(Intercept)	3.23***	3.21***	1.99***	1.96***	2.58***	2.58***
	(0.07)	(0.07)	(0.08)	(0.08)	(0.04)	(0.03)
stress Level Binary-unstressed	−1.84***		−0.39***		−1.50***	
	(0.09)		(0.10)		(0.05)	
metrical Position W		−1.89***		−0.36***		−1.54***
		(0.08)		(0.10)		(0.04)
R^2	0.55	0.59	0.04	0.04	0.73	0.79
Adj. R^2	0.55	0.59	0.04	0.03	0.73	0.79
Num. obs.	377	368	377	368	384	375

Table 10: Note value as dependent variable: Haydn.

	Mermaid template-based	Mermaid stress-based	Wanderer template-based	Wanderer stress-based	Fidelity template-based	Fidelity stress-based
(Intercept)	2.49***	2.51***	2.53***	2.50***	2.30***	2.28***
	(0.07)	(0.07)	(0.09)	(0.09)	(0.04)	(0.05)
metrical PositionW	−0.80***		−0.71***		−0.45***	
	(0.10)		(0.11)		(0.06)	
stress Level Binary-unstressed		−0.72***		−0.67***		−0.31***
		(0.10)		(0.11)		(0.06)
R^2	0.32	0.27	0.24	0.23	0.23	0.11
Adj. R^2	0.32	0.26	0.24	0.22	0.22	0.10
Num. obs.	144	144	121	125	206	206

Table 11: Note value as dependent variable: Annabel Lee.

	Gendel template-based	Gendel stress-based	New template-based	New stress-based	Quick template-based	Quick stress-based
(Intercept)	2.52***	2.53***	2.59***	2.59***	2.60***	2.63***
	(0.07)	(0.07)	(0.05)	(0.06)	(0.05)	(0.05)
metrical Position W	−0.80***		−0.79***		−0.83***	
	(0.09)		(0.07)		(0.07)	
stress Level Binary-unstressed		−0.80***		−0.76***		−0.87***
		(0.09)		(0.07)		(0.07)
R^2	0.19	0.18	0.28	0.25	0.32	0.34
Adj. R^2	0.18	0.18	0.28	0.24	0.32	0.34
Num. obs.	329	338	316	325	335	343

Table 12: Peak score as dependent variable: Haydn.

	Mermaid template-based	Mermaid stress-based	Wanderer template-based	Wanderer stress-based	Fidelity template-based	Fidelity stress-based
(Intercept)	4.32***	4.35***	4.58***	4.57***	3.85***	3.87***
	(0.16)	(0.18)	(0.18)	(0.18)	(0.15)	(0.17)
metrical Position W	−0.47*		−0.84***		0.38	
	(0.23)		(0.23)		(0.21)	
stress Level Binary unstressed		−0.47*		−0.84***		0.28
		(0.23)		(0.23)		(0.21)
R²	0.03	0.03	0.10	0.10	0.02	0.01
Adj. R²	0.03	0.02	0.10	0.09	0.01	0.00
Num. obs.	130	130	116	120	195	195

Table 13: Peak score as dependent variable: Annabel Lee.

	Gendel template-based	Gendel stress-based	New template-based	New stress-based	Quick template-based	Quick stress-based
(Intercept)	4.40***	4.42***	4.02***	3.99***	4.78***	4.74***
	(0.13)	(0.13)	(0.10)	(0.10)	(0.10)	(0.10)
metrical Position W	−0.54***		−0.09		−1.19***	
	(0.16)		(0.13)		(0.13)	
stress Level Binary unstressed		−0.56***		−0.04		−1.10***
		(0.15)		(0.13)		(0.13)
R^2	0.04	0.04	0.00	0.00	0.23	0.20
Adj. R^2	0.04	0.04	−0.00	−0.00	0.23	0.20
Num. obs.	290	297	268	275	300	303

References

Primary sources

Poe, Edgar Allan. 1997. *Spirits of the dead: Tales and other poems*. London: Penguin Books.

Secondary sources

Aissen, Judith. 1999. Markedness and subject choice in Optimality Theory. *Natural Language & Linguistic Theory* 17(4). 673–711.

Aissen, Judith. 2003. Differential object marking: Iconicity vs. economy. *Natural Language & Linguistic Theory* 21(3). 435–483.

Arjava, Heini & Gerrit Kentner. 2022. Alignment of prosodic weight and musical length in Finnish vocal music textsetting. In: Mathias Scharinger, Richard Wiese, editors. *How language speaks to music: Prosody from a cross-domain perspective*, 161–189. Berlin: De Gruyter.

Baayen, R. Harald & Elnaz Shafaei-Bajestan. 2019. languageR. Software package.

Berger, Adam L., Vincent J. Della Pietra & Stephen A. Della Pietra. 1996. A maximum entropy approach to natural language processing. *Computational Linguistics* 22(1). 39–71.

Domene Moreno, Christina & Barış Kabak. 2022. Prominence alignment in English and Turkish songs: Implications for word prosodic typology. In: Mathias Scharinger, Richard Wiese, editors. *How language speaks to music: Prosody from a cross-domain perspective*, 223–258. Berlin: De Gruyter.

Fabb, Nigel. 1997. *Linguistics and literature: Language in the verbal arts of the world*. Oxford, MA: Blackwell.

Fry, Dennis B. 1955. Duration and intensity as physical correlates of linguistic stress. *The Journal of the Acoustical Society of America* 27(4). 765–768.

Fry, Dennis B. 1958. Experiments in the perception of stress. *Language and Speech* 1(2). 126–152.

Giegerich, Heinz J. 1992. *English phonology: An introduction*. Cambridge: Cambridge University Press.

Gilbers, Dicky & Teja Rebernik. 2022. A constraint-based approach to structuring language and music. Towards a roadmap for comparing language and music cross-culturally. In: Mathias Scharinger, Richard Wiese, editors. *How language speaks to music: Prosody from a cross-domain perspective*, 71–103. Berlin: De Gruyter.

Goldwater, Sharon & Mark Johnson. 2003. Learning ot constraint rankings using a maximum entropy model. In: Jennifer Spenader, Anders Eriksson, Östen Dahl, editors. *Variation within Optimality Theory*, 111–120. Stockholm: University of Stockholm.

Halle, John & Fred Lerdahl. 1993. A generative textsetting model. *Current Musicology* 55. 3–23.

Halle, Morris & Samuel Jay Keyser. 1966. Chaucer and the study of prosody. *College English* 28(3). 187–219.

Halle, Morris & Samuel Jay Keyser. 1971. *English stress: Its form, its growth, and its role in verse*. New York: Harper and Row.

Hammond, Michael. 1999. *The phonology of English: A prosodic Optimality-Theoretic approach*. Oxford: Oxford University Press.

Hayes, Bruce. 1989. The prosodic hierarchiy in meter. In: Paul Kiparsky, Gilbert Youmans, editors. *Rhythm and meter*, 201–260. Orlando, CA: Academic Press.

Hayes, Bruce. 2009. Textsetting as constraint conflict. In: Jean-Louis Aroui, Andy Arleo, editors. *Towards a typology of poetic forms: From language to metrics and beyond*, 43–62. Amsterdam: John Benjamins Publishing Company.

Hayes, Bruce & Abigail Kaun. 1996. The role of phonological phrasing in sung and chanted verse. *The Linguistic Review* 13(3–4). 243–303.

Hayes, Bruce & Colin Wilson. 2008. A maximum entropy model of phonotactics and phonotactic learning. *Linguistic Inquiry* 39(3). 379–440.

Hayes, Bruce, Colin Wilson & Anne Shisko. 2012. Maxent grammars for the metrics of Shakespeare and Milton. *Language* 88(4). 691–731.

Howe, Darin & Douglas Pulleyblank. 2004. Harmonic scales as faithfulness. *Canadian Journal of Linguistics/Revue Canadienne de Linguistique* 49(1). 1–49.

Jaynes, Edwin Thompson. 1957. Information theory and statistical mechanics. *Physical Review* 106(4). 620–630.

Kabak, Barış & Christina Domene Moreno. 2017. A cross-linguistic perspective on stress-meter alignment in music: Evidence from Turkish children's songs. Poster presented at *Phonetics and Phonology in Europe 2017*. Universität Köln, Germany.

Keshet, Ezra. 2005. *Relatively optimal text-setting*. Cambridge, MA: The MIT Press.

Kiparsky, Paul. 2006. A modular metrics for folk verse. In: B. Elan Dresher, Nila Friedberg, editors. *Formal approaches to poetry*, 7–49. Berlin: De Gruyter.

Legendre, Géraldine, Yoshiro Miyata & Paul Smolensky. 1990. Harmonic grammar: A formal multi-level connectionist theory of linguistic well-formedness: Theoretical foundations. *The 12th Anual Conference of the Cognitive Science Society*, 884–891. Cambridge, MA: Lawrence Erlbaum.

Martin, Andrew. 2011. Grammars leak: Modeling how phonotactic generalizations interact within the grammar. *Language* 87(4). 751–770.

Palmer, Caroline & Michael H. Kelly. 1992. Linguistic prosody and musical meter in song. *Journal of Memory and Language* 31(4). 525–542.

Plag, Ingo, Gero Kunter & Mareile Schramm. 2011. Acoustic correlates of primary and secondary stress in North American English. *Journal of Phonetics* 39(3). 362–374.

Poe, Edgar Allan. 1997. *Spirits of the dead: Tales and other poems*. London: Penguin Books.

Prince, Alan S. & Paul Smolensky. 1993. *Optimality Theory. Constraint interaction in Generative Grammar*. Malden, MA: Blackwell.

Proto, Teresa. 2015. Prosody, melody and rhythm in vocal music: The problem of textsetting in a linguistic perspective. *Linguistics in the Netherlands* 32. 116–129.

Rodríguez-Vázquez, Rosalia. 2010. *The rhythm of speech, verse and vocal music: A new theory*. Bern: Peter Lang.

Rodríguez-Vázquez, Rosalia. 2011. Constraint ranking in English broadside ballads. In: Christoph Küper, editor. *Current trends In metrical analysis*, 197–206. Frankfurt am Main: Peter Lang.

Sluijter, Agaath M.C. & Vincent J. van Heuven. Acoustic correlates of linguistic stress and accent in Dutch and American English. Proceedings of Fourth International Conference on Spoken Language Processing; 1996a; Philadelphia, PA. IEEE. p 630–633.

Sluijter, Agaath M.C. & Vincent J. van Heuven. 1996b. Spectral balance as an acoustic correlate of linguistic stress. *The Journal of the Acoustical Society of America* 100(4). 2471–2485.

Team, R Core. 2014. R: A language and environment for statistical computing. Vienna: R Foundation for Statistical Computing.

Temperley, Nicholas & David Temperley. 2011. Music-language correlations and the "Scotch Snap". *Music Perception* 29(1). 51–63.

Temperley, Nicholas & David Temperley. 2013. Stress-meter alignment in French vocal music. *The Journal of the Acoustical Society of America* 134(1). 520–527.

Wilson, Colin. 2006. Learning phonology with substantive bias: An experimental and computational study of velar palatalization. *Cognitive Science* 30(5). 945–982.

Christina Domene Moreno & Barış Kabak
Prominence alignment in English and Turkish songs: Implications for word prosodic typology

Abstract: In vocal music, lyrics have been shown to align with musical structure on various levels, such as musical meter and melodic progressions: For instance, tonal contours in tone languages are systematically reflected in the musical melody (Wong & Diehl, 2002; Wee, 2007; Kirby & Ladd, 2016) and relatively stressed syllables have a tendency to fall on strong positions in musical meter (Halle & Lerdahl, 1993; Palmer & Kelly, 1992). Assuming the latter alignment to be possible only in languages with word-level stress such as English, stress-meter alignment has been used as a tool to determine the status of accentual prominence in languages such as French (Temperley & Temperley, 2013), where word-level stress is debatable. In order to shed light on the nature of the Turkish stress system and to test the influence of musical genre on music-prosody alignment, we measured the mean metrical weight as well as melodic peak scores of syllables in words with final and non-final stress in Turkish children's songs composed in Western music and in Makam music. We additionally investigated the degree of melodic alignment in English children's songs to lay the grounds for a much-needed typological account of how prosodic phenomena align with musical structures crosslinguistically. Our analyses revealed significant stress-meter alignment for both word-finally and non-finally stressed syllables in Turkish songs in Western music but not in Makam music. Additionally, stress-melody alignment could be shown for Turkish, which was however absent in English. Our findings,

---

Acknowledgements: This work is a product of a long cooperative effort that the authors started at the University of Würzburg in 2016. Its earlier versions were delivered on several occasions as talks or posters: GLOW 42 in Oslo in May 2019, DGfS 41 in Bremen in March 2019, DGfS 40 in Stuttgart in March 2018, PaPE 2017 in Köln in June 2017, and Seminar on General Metrics at Meertens Instituut in Amsterdam in January 2017. We would like to thank the audiences at these venues for their valuable feedback, as well as the anonymous reviewers and the editors of this volume for their constructive comments and suggestions. We are grateful to Alin Aylin Yağcıoğlu for her help with finding the musical scores of some of the Turkish children's songs in our corpus as well as to Janne Lorenzen for assistance in the meticulous melodic coding of the English songs and for her thoughtful comments on an earlier draft of the paper. The authors' names appear in alphabetical order. Needless to say, all errors are our own.

Christina Domene Moreno, Barış Kabak, University of Würzburg

https://doi.org/10.1515/9783110770186-009

combined with previous findings on tone languages, Tokyo Japanese, and French, suggest a gradient system of prosody-music mapping that takes place in different degrees that are commensurate with the phonetic and functional concomitants of word-level accentual prominence in the respective language.

Keywords: textsetting, typology, prominence

1 Introduction

Music and spoken language have long been known to share common properties. On the most fundamental level, their basic domain is sound. In both speech and music, this sound is manipulated and structured to form meaningful patterns, primarily in the case of spoken language, or aesthetically pleasing ones, primarily in the case of music. The patterns of both spoken language and music entail phonetic aspects like pitch, duration, and loudness, and they are subject to a number of wellformedness rules/constraints. When language and music meet in vocal music, the phonetic and phonological aspects of both domains interact. One way in which this interaction of language and music surfaces is the tendency for language and music to be isomorphic in terms of phonetic features like musical pitch, and phonological features like the distribution of prominence patterns. The most straightforward type of this mapping is the alignment of tone contours, i.e., the shift of one pitch level to another over the course of a syllable, in tone languages with the melodic progressions in vocal music (see, for instance, Wong & Diehl, 2002; Wee, 2007; Kirby & Ladd, 2016). In this case, two very similar features are aligned with each other, i.e., prosodic melody with musical melody. A less studied and more complex type of correspondence is the alignment between musical meter (i.e., anticipated regularities in the recursion of beats as music unfolds in time) and word accentual prominence (e.g., Halle & Lerdahl, 1993; Palmer & Kelly, 1992) realized as stress accent or pitch accent (see Section 3 for a discussion of these notions). In this type of alignment, prominent positions in linguistic domains (e.g., a stressed syllable within a word) and musical domains (e.g., a strong beat within a bar) are expected to map onto each other. Needless to say, while both domains share the notion of prominence, the conceptualizations of prominence differ across domains.

Prominence alignment is, however, not exclusive to the alignment of word accent with musical meter. Instead, accentual prominence is also likely to align with other corresponding features in music since the physical concomitants of accent are acoustic and temporal properties such as relative pitch height (e.g., stressed syllables are higher in pitch than unstressed syllables) and relative duration (e.g., stressed syllables are longer in duration than unstressed syllables) which roughly correspond to melodic structure, i.e., note transitions and note duration in music (Nichols et al., 2009). By the same logic, one expects to also observe a significantly higher degree of correspondence between, for instance, a stressed syllable and a relatively higher note, or a stressed syllable and a longer note, crucially in comparison to the degree of correspondence between unstressed syllables and the same musical features. It should be noted that, while prominence alignment may share physical properties with pattern alignment, as is the case, for instance, when stress is aligned with musical pitch, the layer on which this mapping takes place differs, and prominence and pattern alignment need to be viewed as different types of mapping.

Crucially, in order for a linguistic entity to align with any of these musical features, it must possess a physical reality in the language under scrutiny. In other words, and perhaps unsurprisingly, tone contours can only be expected to align with melodic contours if tones actually exist in the language under consideration. By the same reasoning, those syllables that are assumed to be stressed within a word should align with prominent positions in music only if the language in question employs accentual prominence such as stress or pitch accents. This fact, while perhaps trivial by itself, provides a firm link between language and music that allows researchers to use music for studying prosodic systems from a different point of view and thus to gain new insights especially into those languages where word-level accentual phenomena are inert, in that they bear no clear contrastive or grammatical function for the language user.

The first study to introduce this line of thinking and take advantage of this cross-domain link between music and language was the seminal paper by Temperley & Temperley (2013). Based on what is known about prosody-music alignment in languages such as English, whose word-level accentual system is relatively well documented and whose alignment with music has also been widely discussed (e.g., Palmer & Kelly, 1992), they extended the concept of prosody-music alignment to French in order to test the status of "stress" in this language, where the existence of word-level stress (as opposed to phrasal stress) has been disputed. Temperley & Temperley (2013) assumed that those syllables that allegedly receive word-level stress should align with metrically strong positions in the music if, and only if, word-level stress has a psycholinguistic reality in French. As such, they systematically employed the prosody-music alignment as a diagnostic for word prosodic typology.

In this chapter, we adopt this diagnostic approach and apply it to Turkish, another language for which the presence and nature of word-level stress has been controversial. Our research objective is twofold: First, we provide additional evidence for the nature of word-level prosody in general and the psycho-acoustic manifestation of stress in Turkish through the lens of music. Secondly, we extend the approach suggested by Temperley & Temperley (2013) to another musical entity that we hypothesize to correspond to prominence, i.e., melodic pitch. Specifically, we test whether (i) the alignment of meter (i.e., the strongest beats of a meter) with stress and (ii) the alignment of melodic peaks in music with stress are present in the same language system. Thus, our objective is to find the relative degree of their co-existence within the same language, which might bring insights into the psycho-acoustic concomitants of stress in the language. We achieve this on the basis of a systematic comparison between English and Turkish in our study. Another empirical contribution of our chapter stems from the necessity to tease apart the role of *musical genres* in determining the degree of prominence alignment since prominence alignment has hitherto been studied exclusively in Western European music, even in languages that are not Western European (e.g., Tokyo Japanese, Cho, 2017). To that end, we will test our predictions for Turkish in two very different musical genres: Western European[1] vs. traditional Makam music (see Section 4 below). Based on our findings and those from previous studies, we propose an explanatory model of linguistic prominence that is informed by a domain that manifests grammars through music, i.e., songs, which can then allow researchers to test a multitude of languages to gain crosslinguistic insights. This approach adds an additional, cross-disciplinary angle to the discussions surrounding prosodic typology, both in individual languages and globally, since it departs from the sometimes circular logic in the field that expediently lumps together the lack of systematic evidence for stress (in perceptual and phonetic terms) with its formal description. This way, general assumptions about stress typology can be tested using a distinct type of evidence, one that is outside the domain of its subject matter, but one that is remarkably similar.

In a first step towards a comprehensive typological account of prosody-music alignment, we examine English, a language whose prosodic properties, as has been stated above, have been explored extensively and about which there is, consequently, a large body of knowledge to form a baseline for prosody-music alignment. We then test the alignment of music and prosody in Turkish, where the status of stress is much less clear in comparison to English. Results are then compared to those from other languages in previously published studies to present a preliminary typological account of the prosody-music interface.

---

[1] Note that this is a description of the musical tradition a song or piece is composed in. A song does not have to be from a Western European background (culturally or linguistically) to be considered musically Western European.

Furthermore, we aim to resolve some language-specific issues. In particular, we will explore whether the position of stress within a word in Turkish modulates the degree of alignment since some accounts of Turkish distinguish regular word-final stress from non-final stress on phonetic and phonological grounds (see Section 3.2 below for a discussion and references).

This chapter is structured as follows: First, in light of previous research, we discuss the interface of linguistic prosody and music, which entails interactions of the two domains on different levels (meter, melody). Next, we provide a description of the word prosodic systems of Turkish and English, the two languages under investigation. Our empirical studies are presented in Section 4, followed by a discussion of the consequences of our results for word prosodic typology. Based on our findings, we introduce a typological prominence framework which makes testable cross-linguistic predictions for both the degree and type of prosody-music alignment.

2 Prosody-music alignment

There is a growing number of studies that have shown that prosodic properties of language, like stress and intonation, are likely to align with corresponding musical properties. For instance, distinctive pitch contours found in words of tone languages will correspond to the melodic movements of a vocal piece of music. The degree to which prosody is mapped onto music in this way differs across languages, however. In a perceptual experiment, Wong and Diehl (2002), for instance, report that tone contours are preserved in Cantonese (in terms of alignment between tone contours and note transitions, albeit not in terms of absolute ration, i.e. concrete change of f_0). The degree of match is at 77% in Vietnamese (Kirby & Ladd, 2016). It is likely that this type of alignment promotes and enhances (and is, in fact, a necessary precondition for) the comprehensibility of the lyrics in tone languages where (relative) pitch height and pitch progression are lexically contrastive. Consequently, a modification of the tonal pattern of words to fit it into musical melody would run the risk of jeopardizing lexical meanings.

In non-tonal languages in which stress has a lexical function such as English, word-level linguistic prominence (i.e., stress) has been shown to align strongly with prominent positions in a musical bar (see, for instance, Chen & Mok, 2014, as well as Girardi & Plag, 2022, for English, deCastro Arrazola, 2015, for Dutch). In fact, Gordon et al. (2011) have found that comprehensibility improves when the degree of this type of alignment is high. The notion of this type of alignment hinges on the hierarchical nature of musical meter (Lerdahl

& Jackendoff, 1983). Linguistically prominent positions (e.g., stressed syllables) are then more likely to fall on stronger musical beats, i.e., on the first or third full beat in a 4/4 meter (see Section 4.1), than on less strong ones (Palmer & Kelly, 1992). Figure 1, for instance, shows the two beginning bars from the song *Yesterday* by The Beatles. The first bar aligns the stressed syllable of each of the three-syllable words, **yes***terday* and **sud***denly*, with the first beat of the bar, which is the most prominent position in a 4/4 meter. In the second bar, this most prominent position is left empty, but the stressed syllable of *troubles* as well as the content word *half* fall on the third beat of the bar, which is the beat with the second highest musical prominence in 4/4. In addition, none of the content words, i.e., those words that are not subject to reduction and can thus be considered to be stressed, fall between beats. The two bars in question, then, are perfectly aligned and can thus be regarded as well-formed on the music-language interface.

1. Yes - ter-day -   all my trou-bles seemed so
2. Sud - den- ly,___   I'm not half the man I

Figure 1: First two bars of "Yesterday" by The Beatles.

This type of alignment, like the pattern alignment described above, is gradient and by no means obligatory. Lyrics can be more or less aligned with the musical material. Misalignment, i.e., the lack of correspondence between musical and linguistic prominence, can occur, for example, due to sheer compositional necessity (when, for instance, too many syllables need to be distributed across the available musical material), due to stylistic considerations, or simply as a result of carelessness. All of these, however, boil down to a lower weighting of alignment, which can be construed as a constraint, in relation to other linguistic, musical, or interface constraints (see, for instance, Hayes, 2009; Gilbers & Rebernik, 2022; and Girardi & Plag, 2022, for constraint-based approaches to textsetting).

The types of rhythmic structures that this has been demonstrated for so far have had a clear cultural bias. Indeed, music that has been analyzed in the light of prosody-music alignment could, for the most part, be formalized in the Western European metrical system (as demonstrated above). This, however, is problematic for any potential cross-linguistic or typological account of alignment since musical traditions that structure their rhythmic units differently from the canonical Western European one are likely to function differently on the prosody-music interface. In fact, Tait et al. (2014) examined prosody-music alignment in American Hip Hop music and found that, even within one single genre in one single language, there is a high degree of variation in the degree of prosody-music alignment due to stylistic differences across different artists. They mostly attributed these strong differences to the way in which syncopation, i.e., the intentional displacement of musical accent, is variably used by different rap artists. In addition, and across artists, the second beat of each bar was most likely to align with stressed syllables due to this syncopation which is rooted in African music. This demonstrates that other musical traditions have to be introduced, understood, and utilized especially in cross-linguistic inquiries in order to have a reliable comparison between alignment in different languages.

As there are multiple acoustic correlates of linguistic prominence, such as pitch, duration, and vowel quality, linguistically prominent positions are unlikely to align randomly with any of musical positions. Instead, the degree of correspondence we expect between a linguistic entity x and a musical entity y should be commensurate with phonetic similarity between x and y. In fact, one and the same language can exhibit different types of alignment, reflecting the different phonetic dimensions of prominence. As discussed above, the relationship between note transitions and tonal transitions (i.e., pattern alignment) has long been studied in tone languages. Recently, this type of alignment has been extended to Tokyo Japanese, a pitch accent language. Analyzing Japanese children's songs, Cho (2017) showed that the overall degree of correspondence between tonal and melodic transitions (in terms of similar motion) was about 54%, which, according to Cho (2017), is less than the values found for Cantonese and Vietnamese in previous studies. Furthermore, in the same study, it was shown that Tokyo Japanese also exhibits prominence alignment. In particular, in comparison to unaccented morae, accented morae were more likely to align with stronger beats of the meter, although the degree of prominence-meter alignment turned out to be much weaker than that of English and French (as tested in Temperley & Temperley, 2013). Cho (2017) took this to suggest that prominence is a gradient phenomenon.

Furthermore, along with metrical positions in music, melodic peaks and note durations have also been shown to correlate with stress in English in a study by Nichols et al. (2009). While this suggests that pitch level and syllable duration also matter for English stress, it needs to be noted that the authors use a binary categorization of musical notes into peak and non-peak, where a peak note is a note that is higher than both adjacent notes. Thomassen (1982) found that it is not only these "strict" peaks that are perceived as particularly prominent by listeners. Thus, it needs to be questioned whether the scoring system utilized by Nichols et al. indeed captures the perceptual reality of musical prominence. Furthermore, it is unclear to what extent the different types of alignment for stress are common in other languages and how the relative degree of alignment in these distinct types of alignment is a function of the suprasegmental system of the language in question. The following section will briefly present the notion of word accentual prominence and highlight crosslinguistic variation and theoretical issues therein, followed by a comparison of the word prosodic characteristics of Turkish and English to form a basis for a more comprehensive and typologically informed account of music-prosody alignment.

3 Word accentual prominence

As a relative concept, accentual prominence at the level of the word relates to the perceived salience of certain word portions (e.g., the penultimate syllables, the left edge of a word, etc.) relative to others. This salience is emanated by a number of well-known acoustic and articulatory cues. The relative importance of these phonetic cues for perception and production, and their precise realization, as well as the extent to which these covary with other aspects of phonology and/or interact with other areas of grammar (e.g., word formation rules) differ considerably across the languages of the world. These differences also have consequences for the mental representation of accentual prominence by language users. As the interaction between accentual prominence and musical prominence may reflect such crosslinguistic differences, it is necessary to clarify some terminological distinctions below and compare the test languages under investigation, Turkish and English, on these premises.

3.1 Crosslinguistic variation and issues

Broadly, whether differences in prominence are rooted in pitch-based lexical contrasts or not has traditionally led to the classification of word prosodic systems into roughly two categories: "tone" languages vs. "stress" languages, respectively. Many researchers however agree that not all languages can be neatly fitted into these categories, which has recently given way to a hybrid category known as a "pitch accent" system (see Hyman, 2009; 2014, and Gordon, 2014, for an extensive discussion). The most well-known example for a pitch accent language is Tokyo Japanese (but see Hyman, 2009, for different interpretations of word accentual prominence in Tokyo Japanese). Leaving aside the intonationally anchored usage of the term "pitch accent" in the literature, what some researchers call pitch accent systems in the sense of a hybrid word accentual system is based on the hypothesis that such languages use invariant tonal contours primarily realized as pitch contours lexically associated with accented syllables. In stress accent languages, however, stress is cued "rather by other properties such as increased duration, greater intensity (particularly at higher frequencies), and/or hyperarticulation" (Gordon, 2014), giving the pitch contours associated with accented syllables the freedom to vary (or even reduce) depending on phrase level intonational properties. This distinction is of crucial importance to the present study as one of the languages tested, Turkish, has been claimed to employ pitch-accents at the word level (e.g., Levi, 2005), as we will further discuss in Section 3.2 below.

It should be noted that stress-accent languages are not monolithic systems as they do not employ the prototypical "stress" cues and properties in the same degree and manner. We also find significant crosslinguistic differences in the functional load of stress accents. For example, accentual prominence within the word may not be relevant for the identification of lexemes in some languages since prominence may regularly fall on a fixed position within a word with no obvious consequence for lexical contrasts (e.g., Polish and French). Due to this regularity, prominence cues may nevertheless be used to identify word boundaries in running speech. On top of its lexical and culminative function, stress may exert an influence on the way grammar operates, for example, by enforcing prosodic constraints on the surfacing of certain patterns in the prosodic morphology of some languages (e.g., word formation processes relying on clipping in English), but not in others. Such variation in the phonetic, formal and functional properties of stress across the languages of the world entails that it may be more of an abstract property, on a par with some decades-old observations, such as those of Lehiste (1970), that "stress" is a word accentual phenomenon that refers to the *capacity* of a syllable to be acoustically and articulatorily enhanced.

3.2 Stress in Turkish vs. English

In this section, we highlight the most important phonetic, phonological and distributional characteristics of word level accentual prominence in Turkish and English insofar as they may be relevant for the isomorphism between prosody and music and discuss their functional relevance for the language user. Based on these language-specific observations and comparisons, we will postulate a number of predictions for music-prosody alignment in Section 4.

The canonical position of accent within Turkish words is assumed to be the rightmost syllable of a word irrespective of its weight (e.g., Lees, 1961; Inkelas,

1999; Kabak & Vogel, 2001). In compliance with the most frequently used label in the literature, and also on a par with the conclusion by Ladd (2008), we will use the term "stress" to refer to accented syllables in Turkish words in this section although this label has been put under scrutiny (see below). Examples in (1) illustrate finally stressed morphologically simplex (a-b) as well as complex (c-d) words:

(1) a. *melék* 'angel'
　　b. *pará* 'money'
　　c. *melek-ler-dén* 'from angels'
　　d. *para-sız-lík* 'lack of money, pennilessness'

Deviations from this pattern exist in both morphologically simplex (2a-c) and complex word forms, forming word prosodic patterns of non-final stress in Turkish (2 d-e):

(2) a. *tiyátro* 'theatre'
　　b. *sinéma* 'cinema'
　　c. *Belçíka* 'Belgium'
　　d. *melék-le* 'with an/the angel'
　　e. *para-síz-dı-lar* 'they lacked money'

Morphologically simplex forms that exhibit non-final stress are typically loan words (2a-b) or place names (2c), and they may be assumed to bear lexically pre-specified stress thus forming exceptions to the regular word-final stress (e.g., Kabak & Vogel, 2001; 2011). In morphologically complex forms, most suffixes and other bound morphemes are subject to regular final stress (1c-d). Non-final stress in complex words (2d-e), however, emerges typically in the thrall of so-called *stress-affecting* suffixes. These are bound morphemes that are either lexically prespecified to be *unstressable*, thereby, all else being equal, docking stress onto a previous syllable (thus also known as *pre-stressing* suffixes) or *stress-bearing* suffixes that claim stress on a prespecified position within the suffix (see Göksel & Kerslake, 2004). It should be noted that free variation in stress location may be observed in morphologically complex cases especially when they carry certain types of stress-affecting suffixes (e.g., Özçelik, 2014, see also Kabak & Lorenzen, 2020, for quantitative data).

　　From a theoretical perspective, precise mechanisms to compute stress in finally stressed words in comparison to non-finally stressed words, and the way it is represented in the phonological grammar of Turkish have been widely debated in the literature (e.g., Inkelas, 1999; Kabak & Vogel, 2001; 2011; Inkelas &

Orgun, 2003; Özçelik, 2014). What has perhaps been more controversial is the *type* of word accentual prominence that Turkish employs. As opposed to *stress* accent, Turkish has also been argued to have *pitch* accents, either instead of stress (e.g., Levi, 2005; Kamali Aknoun Azad, 2011), or in combination with it (e.g. Güneş, 2015). Since this assumption has so far primarily relied on phonetic evidence, let us briefly discuss the acoustic correlates of "stress" in Turkish. Several researchers (e.g., Konrot, 1981; Levi, 2005; Pycha, 2006; Zora et al., 2016) have shown that the most robust cue for "stress" is pitch, fo.[2]

How precisely does pitch entrain accentual prominence in Turkish? Levi (2005) shows that, while words with final prominence show a "moderate" rise in *fo* between the non-final and final syllable, words with non-final stress exhibit a falling contour, corresponding to an *fo* drop after the stressed syllable. Since no salient *fo* excursion is found in words with final prominence, Levi suggests that *fo* cannot be a robust cue for prominence in the word final position. Accordingly, accented syllables are realized with a H* + L pitch accent. When the accent is in final position, however, the pitch accent is trimmed to H* (thus no fall is realized).

Taking the phonetic arguments a step further, Levi (2005) argues that Turkish is a pitch-accent language.[3] This argument has been taken up and further corroborated by recent work on Turkish intonation, the outcome of which is of relevance to some of our research questions since they make different predictions for the representation of prominence in words with final (e.g., the items in (1) above) vs. those with non-final stress (e.g., those in (2) above). Güneş (2015), for instance, argues that non-finally stressed syllables receive an additional pitch accent via lexical association with H*L, whereas final stress is stress-accent with no pitch-accent due to the absence of any noteworthy peak in *fo* on such syllables.[4]

---

2 The phonetic foundation of this assumption is restricted, however. So far, research has investigated Turkish stress only in prosodically marked positions such as when *focus* is placed on words or phrases in sentences or in isolation. In intonation languages, such priviledged postions are marked primarily by *pitch* movements known as phrase-level accents at the utterance level. In the absence of phrase-level accents, Sluijter & van Heuven, 1996a; b show that pitch (*fo*) is the *least* reliable cue for stress in English. In Chickasaw, Gordon (2004) finds that although at the phrase level, *fo* is the most salient signal of pitch accents, it is subordinate to duration and intensity as a marker of word-level stress (see also Kochanski et al., 2005).
3 Apart from the phonetic evidence above, Levi (2005) also brings forth culminativity as an argument, which is, however, also found in both stress-accent and tone languages (Hyman 2009; 2014).
4 Albeit in the opposite direction, such a differentiation between final vs. non-final stress has also been put forward by Csató & Johanson (1998) and Johanson (1998), who argue that stress is realized by a pitch accent on the final syllable but by a stress accent on the non-final syllable.

Güneş (2015) further shows that in the pre-nuclear position, items carry a right edge tone, H-, regardless of whether they are lexically accented (i.e., non-finally stressed) or not, and takes this to suggest that H- cannot be an indication of a final accent, but a boundary tone. Similar observations have been made by Kamali Aknoun Azad (2011), who suggests that final stress is an epiphenomenon at the word level, "a perceptual elsewhere condition", since the relevant syllable bears no tonal marking. In analogy to Japanese (Pierrehumbert & Beckman, 1988) as well as some varieties of Basque Hualde et al., 2002, Kamali considers "finally stressed" words to be accentless. Similarly, for Güneş (2015), such words that are perceived to bear final stress are accentless while the ones with non-final stress are accented.

Irrespective of the theoretical controversies surrounding "stress" in Turkish, canonical final prominence can be said to have consequences for language processing, for example, by serving as a cue to word boundaries due to its regular right word-edge marking property in the language. Indeed, Turkish listeners have been shown to employ stress information in speech segmentation (e.g., Kabak et al., 2010, see van Ommen, 2016, for a replication and extension).

In contrast to Turkish, word stress in English is highly dynamic and its effects have been ubiquitous in the diachronic development of English. The presence of stress in English is not only evident in terms of its effect on segmental phonology, but also conspicuous due to the well-known interaction between metrical structure and linguistic processes outside phonology (morphology, word formation, and even, to some extent, word order). Here, we will provide only some selective examples to illustrate how dynamic stress is in English with respect to its function and effects on other parts of grammar (stressed syllables are highlighted in bold in the examples).

The phonetic effect of English stress on segmental phonology is especially evident through salient changes in vowel quality, a robust concomitant of stress in English, owing to the fact that when syllables are unstressed, they are typically reduced to schwa (e.g., *p[æ]rent* vs. *p[ə]rental*). Furthermore, the flap/tap allophony observed in some varieties such as General American English is conditioned by the position of the segment relative to the stressed syllable (e.g., *a[t] om* vs. **a[t]omic*). English stress also interacts with various morphological phenomena and word formation processes. For example, *a*-prefixing in Appalachian English is illicit with verbs carrying non-initial stress such as **a-remembering* vs. *a-talking*, and even non-Appalachian speakers have been shown to be sensitive to this constraint based on stress (e.g., Kabak & Meemann, 2013). Similarly, the expletive infix such as *bloody* or *fucking* must be inserted between two feet (e.g., *fròn-fucking-tíer*), where the primary stress falls on the second foot, but not between an unstressed syllable and a foot (e.g., **ba-fucking-nana*; see Hammond,

1999 for details). Stress can even determine the ordering of words in coordinate constructions, presumably due to the tendency to keep roughly even trochaic rhythm in English (*****sour and sweet** vs. **sweet and sour**,* e.g., Giegerich, 1992).

Although stress contributes very little to lexical contrasts in English (i.e., there are very few minimal pairs which are based on purely stress distinctions without relying on vowel quality such as ***insight*** vs. ***incite***), it has a well demonstrated effect on lexical access and spoken word recognition, especially due to the robust segmental concomitants of being stressed vs. unstressed in English (e.g., Cutler & Norris, 1988, see Cutler, 2015, for a review). It even plays a role in reading in the identification of misspellings: Misspellings are more likely to be detected in a stressed syllable than in an unstressed syllable if the misspelled word is highly predictable from context (Harris & Perfetti, 2016). To the best of our knowledge, no such unambiguously robust effects of stress within and across sub-components of English grammar have so far been attested in Turkish.

Regarding the cues for stress, English speakers are known to benefit more from the *segmental* concomitant of stress (i.e., stressed vowels are full, unstressed ones are reduced) than from the *suprasegmental* cues of stress such as pitch for lexical access and word segmentation (see Cutler, 2012, for a detailed review). Suprasegmental cues have been shown to be more efficiently used in word segmentation in other stress languages such as Spanish (e.g., Soto-Faraco et al., 2001) and Dutch (Cooper et al., 2002) in comparison to English where the same cues are ignored. In a crosslinguistic study on the perception of the stress of acoustically manipulated nonce words, Chrabaszcz et al. (2014) confirm the previous observations that the vowel quality cue is the strongest for English monolingual listeners, as well as for Mandarin (a tonal language) and Russian (a stress language) second language users of English. Pitch turned out to be the second strongest cue for the English and the Mandarin participants but not for the Russian listeners.

It is difficult to pinpoint an all-embracing canonical stress assignment rule that would reliably predict the position of stress in English words due to the interplay of several factors. Word class distinctions, a property outside the domain of phonology, as well as the presence of stress affecting morphemes that are lexically specified for certain prosodic properties determine stress placement in English, weakening the tenacity of purely phonological approaches to English stress such as an account that solely resorts to notions like syllable weight, boundaries and feet (e.g., Chomsky & Halle, 1968; Hayes, 1982; Giegerich, 1992). Descriptions get even more convoluted when one considers the extent of variation in stress placement across varieties of English (e.g., Altmann & Kabak, 2015), which altogether renders the stress system of English complex but still dynamic.

The comparison between English and Turkish above reveals a significant number of differences in the way the two languages represent word accentual prominence and how they utilize it. Broadly, in contrast to English, Turkish word prominence can be said to be inert, with no significant consequence on the grammar, not even on the phonology of the language (there are no allophonic rules sensitive to stress; no evidence for metrical phonology in the sense English stress participates in word formation; no known rhythmic adjustment based on predominant stress pattern, etc.).

4 A typological account of prosody-music alignment

When examining linguistic typology through music, an awareness of the characteristics of the other subject matter – music – is crucial. The way music itself is structured and works needs to be viewed in parallel to the organization of phonology in order to make sensible inferences for linguistics. Since a crosslinguistic approach inevitably includes working in the realm of different musical traditions with sometimes very different structural patterning systems, an influence of these patternings should also be tested and, if necessary and possible, be accounted for. The types of patterns that are of interest in this context are prominence patterns, i.e., the types of units that musical pieces are made up of and the way prominent positions are distributed within these units. Whether and to what degree such differences in the musical systems are present is dependent on the languages under scrutiny. English music largely follows the Western European musical patterning, where musical notes are patterned into bars of varying length, i.e., the meter. This will be explained in more detail below. Traditional Turkish music genres do not fall into the same category.[5] One such genre is Makam music, the "classical" music of Turkish and other adjacent cultures (Arabic, Kurdish, Persian, etc.). Makam music is rigidly structured in two domains: MELODY as far as its tonal inventory and possible melodic

---

5 Although there are several different types of traditional music genres, two different types of music can be distinguished: Turkish folk music and Turkish Makam music. The rhythmic structure of Turkish folk music is highly complex to the extent that it is said to employ not only musical prominence patterns, but also overarching polyrhythmic systems (layered patterns). Since the structural aspects of Turkish folk music have not been described in enough detail to make possible a systematic linguistic analysis based on musical structures, we do not focus on Turkish folk music in this chapter.

progressions are concerned, and RHYTHM defining a large (but restricted) set of distinct rhythmic patterns. Different tonal modes are referred to as *makams*. Makams are sets of notes built around the tonal center using strict compositional rules and conventions that determine the melodic intervals as well as the duration of tonal cycles. The rhythmic patterns are called *usuls*. There is a small set of *primary* or *simple* usuls which are each unique in the way musical prominence is distributed throughout the rhythmic unit. When combined, these simple usuls can form *complex* usuls.[6] The advantage of our focus on Makam music (on top of Western European music), a musical style that is firmly rooted in Turkish culture, stems from the fact that it has been described comprehensively concerning both its melodic and its rhythmic structure since it is formally taught. Having ensured comparability with Western European musical styles, we aim to test the effect of genre on prosody-music alignment in Turkish.

Based on the discussion on the word prosodic properties of English and Turkish and the potential differences that there may be in the nature of prosody-music isomorphism depending on the musical style, we postulate the following research questions along with some predictions for the type (stress-meter vs. stress-melody) of alignment and its relative degree. These questions will not only help us to provide cross-linguistic and cross-cultural insights into the relationship between prosody and music, but also equip us with a cross-disciplinary modus operandi to understand the nature of word-level accentual prominence in Turkish. In particular, we ask:

(1) In comparison to English, is there significant alignment of stress and meter in Turkish?
(2) Is the presence and the degree of alignment genre-specific in Turkish?
(3) In both languages, does stress align also with melody? If so, are there differences between English and Turkish in the degree of stress-melody alignment?
(4) Are there different degrees of alignment in syllables that carry default (final) stress and those that carry lexical (non-final) stress in Turkish?
(5) How does the extent of stress-meter alignment and stress-melody alignment in Turkish compare to alignment in other languages?

We predict that:
a) If there is no significant tonal marking for the canonical word-final accentual prominence in Turkish words (Levi, 2005; Kamali Aknoun Azad, 2011; Güneş, 2015), and if stress is an epiphenomenon of a perceptual illusion

---

[6] For more information on the history and structure of Makam music, see, for instance, Signell (1977).

(Kamali Aknoun Azad, 2011), Turkish should lack the kind of prominence-alignment exhibited by stress languages such as English. (RQ 1)
b) If the musical entity with which stressed syllables are aligned mirrors the dominant stress cue of the language under scrutiny, we would expect significant alignment of stress with melody (i.e., the manifestation of pitch in music) in Turkish since pitch is the most robust cue for stress. Furthermore, we would expect stress-melody alignment to be stronger in Turkish than in English. (RQ 3)
c) Being a typical property of a pitch accent language, if Turkish has both accented and accentless words in the lexicon (e.g., Kamali Aknoun Azad, 2011), we should expect to see a different degree of alignment (or the lack thereof) in words with canonical final syllable stress, so-called "accentless" words *a la* Kamali Aknoun Azad, 2011, in comparison to words that exhibit non-final stress (i.e., those with lexical pitch accents). Qualitative and quantitative differences are also expected to arise between word final syllable stress and non-final syllable stress if final stress is stress accent whereas non-final stress is realized with a co-existing pitch accent H*L, Güneş (2015). (RQ 4)

4.1 Methods

To test the degree of stress-meter and stress-melody alignment in Turkish, a total of 42 Turkish children's songs were chosen, 22 of which were written in the Makam tradition and 20 of which were composed in the Western European tradition, written by various different Turkish composers. We chose children's songs since we assume those to be relatively simple and intuitive as opposed to more sophisticated and potentially more consciously composed music aimed at adult listeners. Makam songs were taken from two collections of Turkish children's songs written in the Makam tradition, and Western European songs were taken from one collection of Turkish children's songs composed in the Western European tradition. To make a comparison with English, another 18 children's songs were collected from *The Big Book of Children's Songs* and *The Great Big Book of Children's Songs*. The time signature of all Western European songs (both Turkish and English) was 4/4 to ensure comparability in prominence patterns. The Makam corpus included songs written in 5 different *usuls*, the rhythmic structures of Makam music, or, more specifically, the "rhythmic patterns that define a sequence of strokes with varying intensity" (Holzapfel, 2015). There is a large number of different usuls in Turkish Makam music, many of them combinations of simpler usuls. Since we do not know how usuls modulate alignment in

Makam music, we chose our sample to be representative of the most common usuls.

To assess the alignment of linguistic and musical parameters, we first divided each song into individual musical phrases. Each song was subject to a linguistic analysis, where each individual word was parsed into syllables. Every syllable was then coded for whether the syllable bears stress (stressed vs. unstressed), the number of syllables in the word, and the position of the syllable in the word. Furthermore, each syllable was coded for the degree of metrical and melodic prominence in its relationship to musical parameters using the musical sheet.

For coding metrical prominence in songs written in Western European music, we followed the system commonly used in the field that assigns different scores (1–3) to the beats in each measure. Figure 2 shows the scoring pattern for the Western European 4/4 meter. Accordingly, the first beat in each measure received a score of 3 since it is the position of highest prominence. The third beat is the beat with second highest musical prominence and thus received a score of 2. Beats 2 and 4 both receive a low score of 1. All notes in between beats received a score of 0.

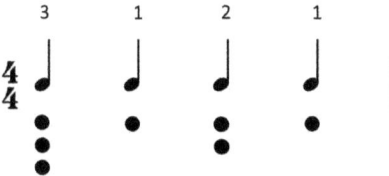

Figure 2: Prominence distribution in Western European 4/4 meter.

The coding system adapted for songs written in Makam music was based on the prominence patterns of the usuls as determined by Holzapfel (2015). The prominence distribution of the usuls used for coding prominence levels in this study can be seen in Figures 8, 9, 10, and 11 in the appendix. Like in the Western European music, scores ranged from 1 to 3, with 3 being the highest possible score per note.

For melodic prominence, we devised a bi-gram scoring system based on the pitch of each note relative to its preceding and its following note, the *melodic peak score*.[7] If a note was higher than the note immediately preceding it, it received a score of 3; if it was the same pitch, it received a score of 2; and if it was

---

[7] The melodic scoring is based on Thomassen's model of perceived melodic prominence (Thomassen 1982), whose results have since been supported by Huron & Royal (1996). Thomassen showed a change in pitch to be predictive of perceived prominence although the degree of this change, i.e., the size of the interval, was negligible.

lower it received a score of 1. The same was done relative to the following note, yielding a second score. The sum of these two sub-scores then made the melodic peak score. This way, higher relative pitch is rated higher than lower or level pitch, which corresponds to the relationship between relative prominence and relative pitch in most languages, where more prominent, i.e., stressed syllables are produced with higher pitch.

Two examples of the scoring procedure can be found in Figure 3. The melodic peak score was only calculated for songs written in Western European music. The Makam songs were excluded from this analysis due to a relatively strict inventory of pitch patterns across different Makam types (see section 4), whose influence would have been difficult to tease apart from language-triggered prosody-music alignment.

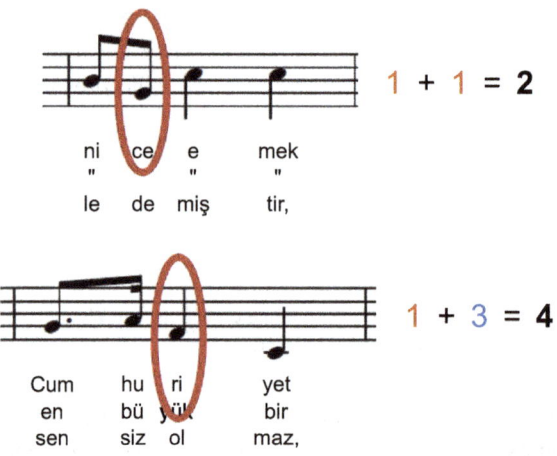

Figure 3: Melodic peak score.

Mean scores for metrical weight and melodic peak were extracted and calculated for stressed and unstressed syllables separately in each song using Regular Expressions in AntConc (Anthony, 2019). In this calculation, phrase initial and phrase final syllables were excluded due to potential edge effects in the musical material. Furthermore, we excluded monosyllabic content words from our analyses as they do not allow us to compare stressed syllables with unstressed ones. We ran mixed ANOVAs to investigate the effects and interactions of our independent variables and conducted paired t-tests with Bonferroni corrections as post-hoc tests in R (Team, 2020). If the ANOVAs and the subsequent t-tests revealed a significant difference between stressed and unstressed syllables, alignment scores were calculated by subtracting the mean score of all unstressed syllables ($w_{unstressed}$) from the mean score of all stressed syllables ($w_{stressed}$). The final metrical alignment score is called *stress-meter alignment value* (SMAV) by Temperley & Temperley (2013) and is now one of the standard alignment measures in related studies. Here we refer to its melodic equivalent (calculated in the same way) as *stress-pitch alignment value* (SPAV).

4.2 Results

A mixed ANOVA with stress (stressed vs. unstressed) and genre (Makam vs. Western European) as independent variables was run on the Turkish data with metrical weight as dependent variable. This ANOVA established a significant interaction of stress and genre ($F(1,37) = 20.23$, $p < .0001$)). Post-hoc paired t-tests with $\alpha = .025$ (Bonferroni-corrected) revealed a significant difference between stressed and unstressed syllables in Western European music ($t(17) = 4.40$, $p = .0004$)), with a higher mean metrical weight for stressed ($M = 1.875$) than for unstressed ($M = 1.176$) syllables. The difference between stressed and unstressed syllables is significant in Makam music as well ($t(21) = -2.48$, $p = .02$)), albeit with stressed syllables exhibiting significantly lower metrical weight ($M = 1.231$) than unstressed syllables ($M = 1.605$). Figure 4 shows the

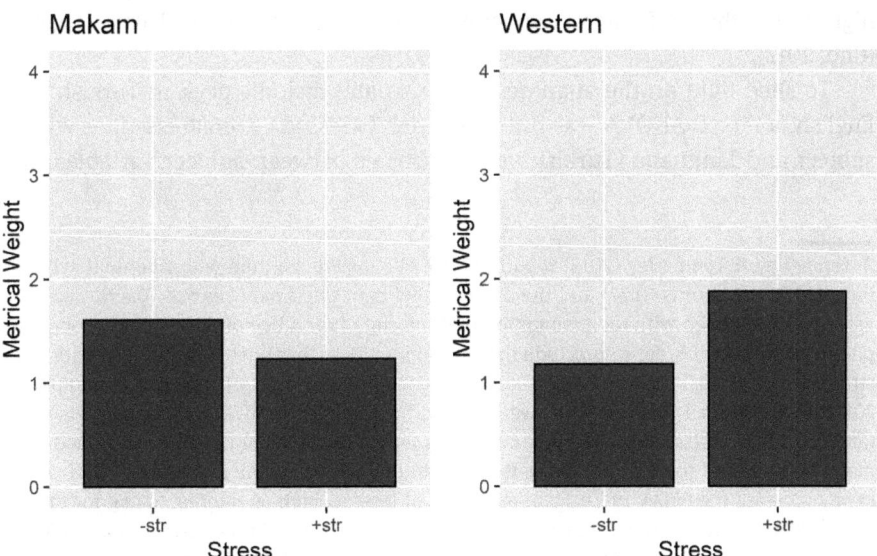

Figure 4: Mean metrical weight of stressed and unstressed syllables in Makam and Western European Turkish music.

distribution of metrical weight across stressed and unstressed syllables in Makam vs. Western European music.

In view of the unexpected results in the Turkish Makam songs, i.e., stressed syllables were shown to be less prominent metrically than unstressed syllables (in contrast to the pattern usually found in the literature with stress coinciding with higher metrical weight), we additionally checked whether any other word-level prosodic entity, such as word edges, may have a privileged status in alignment. Accordingly, we tested the metrical weight of word initial vs. word non-initial syllables in a separate analysis, which revealed a significant difference in the Makam songs ($t(21) = 9.35$, $p < .0001$) with a higher mean metrical weight for word initial ($M = 2.08$) than for word non-initial syllables ($M = 0.99$). This was however not the case in the Turkish Western European songs ($t(17) = -.24$, $p = .81$). This suggested that there was significant alignment of the *left* edge of words to metrically prominent positions in Makam music, which lacks straightforward stress-meter alignment. We will unpack the seemingly left-edge oriented alignment in Makam music in Section 5 below.

Since there was a significant difference in metrical weight between stressed and unstressed syllables, we used the mean values to calculate SMAV for Turkish, following Temperley & Temperley (2013). The Turkish SMAV was calculated on the Western European Turkish songs as 0.58, which, as can be seen in Figure 5, was lower than the SMAVs of English (Temperley & Temperley, 2013), but higher than that of French (Temperley & Temperley, 2013) and Tokyo Japanese (Cho, 2017).[8]

To shed light on the alignment of stress and melodic peak in Turkish[9] and English, a mixed ANOVA was run with stress (stressed vs. unstressed) as within-subject and language (Turkish vs. English) as between-subject variables. The

---

[8] Temperley & Temperley (2013) report two SMAVs for French: one with line-final syllables included in the counts (0.77) and the other one without line-final syllables (0.49). The latter value was calculated with the assumption that the end of each line of a song corresponds to a phrase boundary in order to preclude the confounding fact that lines typically end with fairly strong metrical positions and stressed syllables in French songs (Temperley & Temperley, 2013). As mentioned in section 4.1, we followed the latter procedure and excluded line-final (and line-initial) syllables since similar concerns regarding the potential effect of phrase edges may also be raised for Turkish. There is no doubt that including the line edges would significantly increase the SMAV of Turkish, making it at least as high as the first SMAV for French. Cho's (2017) study, however, does not take phrasal boundaries into consideration for Tokyo Japanese. As such, the comparison of French and Turkish SMAVs with that of Tokyo Japanese should be taken with caution.

[9] Remember that analyses on melodic alignment were only run on Turkish Western European music, not on Turkish Makam music.

$SMAV = w_{(stressed)} - w_{(unstressed)}$

Crosslinguistic ranking:

English	1.15
Turkish (W)	0.58
French	0.49
Japanese	0.32

Figure 5: Crosslinguistic SMAV ranking.

melodic peak score (MPS) was the dependent variable. There was a main effect of language ($F(1,34) = 11.89$, $p < .01$) and stress ($F(1,34) = 23.44$, $p < .0001$), with a significant interaction between the two ($F(1,34) = 8.31$, $p = .007$). Post-hoc analyses with paired t-tests showed a significant difference between stressed ($M = 4.656$) and unstressed syllables ($M = 3.738$) in Turkish Western European music ($t(17) = 4.59$, $p = .0003$), but not in English ($t(17) = 8.82$, $p = .09$), which can be seen in Figure 6. Analogous to SMAV à la Temperley & Temperley (2013), since the difference between the mean melodic peak score of stressed and that of unstressed syllables was significant only in Turkish Western European songs, we calculated SPAV for Turkish, which yielded a value of 0.92.

Since stressed syllables crucially aligned with both metrically strong positions and melodic peaks, the question remains as to whether there is a a

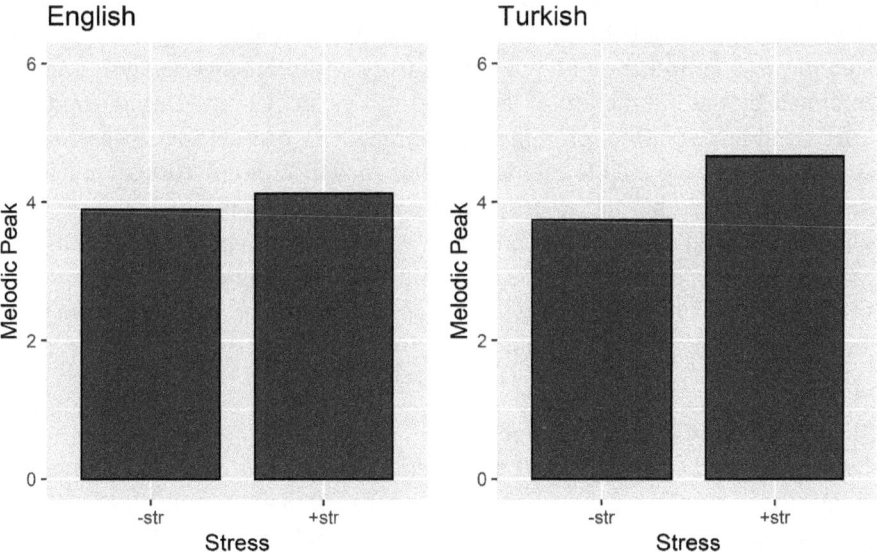

Figure 6: Melodic peak scores of stressed and unstressed syllables in Turkish (Western songs) and English.

potential connection between the two. To that end, we ran Spearman correlations on the metrical weight vs. melodic peak score of stressed syllables in Turkish Western music, which showed no significant correlation between the two values (r_s = 0.11, p = .66). We take this to suggest that the two values are two distinct phenomena, capturing rather different realizations of word-level accentual prominence in musical renditions of language.

Finally, no significant difference was found between SMAV of word finally stressed syllables, i.e., syllables with default stress, and SMAV values of non-word finally stressed syllables, i.e., syllables with non-canonical stress in Turkish. This was the case both in the Western European style ($t(17)$ = 1.72, p = .11) and the Makam music ($t(21)$ = 1.01, p = .3287). Similarly, there was no difference in alignment of default final stress vs. non-final stress with pitch (i.e., SPAV of syllables with final stress vs. SPAV of syllables with non-final stress) in the Western European Turkish music ($t(17)$ = – .69, p = .498).

5 Discussion: Towards a typology of prominence alignment

Metrical alignment in Turkish
In this chapter, we examined prosody-music alignment in Turkish to both answer questions about the Turkish prosodic system and to take a preliminary step towards an integrated typological theory of prominence in speech that is informed by the interaction of language and music. Our studies showed that Turkish indeed exhibits prominence alignment in text setting. In particular, word stress corresponds to metrical prominence in Western Turkish music. As such, Turkish can be said to generally pattern with well-researched stress languages like English. This can be taken as further evidence for the reality of stress in Turkish since stress has to be mentally represented in the composer's or singer's mind in order to trigger this sort of alignment, mirroring also what Temperley & Temperley (2013) found for French.

The role of genre in metrical alignment
Our results further showed that alignment is genre specific. Specifically, they suggest that stress and meter are significantly aligned only in Western European songs composed in 4/4 meter, but not in Makam music. This difference may be due to the very formalized nature of Makam music and its usuls, which may not leave much room for the distribution of prosodic units on the musical

material. The focus of this particular style of music is its melodic and rhythmic structure. Consequently, lyrics, and particularly their distribution, are of secondary concern and thus the interaction of language and music is likely to surface less strongly than in other musical styles. Instead, the musical material itself plays a bigger role in Makam music with the lyrics merely acting as secondary material. This finding first and foremost highlights the important role the choice of musical genre plays in studies on text-to-tune alignment, and it also indicates that, under certain circumstances, musical considerations can subdue linguistic attributes. In other words, and using terminology from constraint-based theories of phonology (e.g., Optimality Theory), at least some musical constraints can be said to be ranked higher than linguistic ones in certain musical styles. This also highlights that, on the music-language interface, both domains must essentially be taken into consideration as separate entities (and they must, of course, be analyzed in such a way) although the dynamic nature of their interaction is obvious, as the present study further corroborated in the context of a non-Indo-European language hitherto unexplored in this respect. While an in-depth analysis of these interactions is beyond the scope of the current chapter, this aspect of prosody-music alignment must urgently be studied systematically, ideally in collaboration with musicologists and musical theorists, to form a firmer grounding of linguistic-centered alignment studies in structural musicology and thus enable researchers to tease apart purely linguistic factors from interface phenomena. Purely musical constraints will have to be taken into consideration as well. For instance, White (2017) found that tonally stable notes[10] are more likely than tonally unstable ones to occur on metrically strong positions, which he interpreted as evidence for a "joint tonal-metric hierarchy".

The fact that stressed syllables unexpectedly showed *lower* metrical weight than unstressed syllables in Turkish Makam music prompted us to another inquiry to check how lyrics are then aligned with the prominence patterns of Makam music as it is unlikely that this phenomenon is simply absent or random. To that end, an analysis by word edges showed that the left edge of Turkish words finds significant alignment with metrically prominent positions in comparison to any other syllable in the word. At first sight, this may sound counter-intuitive since the right edge of words is supposed to be prosodically most prominent and in fact is known to aid listeners in word segmentation (e.g., Kabak et al., 2010, van Ommen, 2016). However, the fact that unstressed syllables turned out to

---

10 Simply, the most tonally stable notes are the first, third, fifth (and eighth) degree of a major scale, while the other scale degrees are considered tonally unstable since they are perceived as having to resolve into the stable notes.

have higher metrical weight than stressed syllables in Makam music can be said to rule out the importance of the right edge for the mapping between prosody and music in this particular musical genre. The fact that regular stress falls on the final syllable of a word does not, however, preclude the salience of word onsets for lexical access in this language, which is possibly universal. Indeed, the fact that Turkish vowel harmony, a process irrelevant to stress, is propagated from left to right from the vowel feature of the initial syllable of the word corroborates the importance of the left edge for this language. Accordingly, we suggest that, in the absence of stress as an anchor for alignment, another significant word prosodic feature takes up this role, i.e., the left edge.

Melodic alignment in Turkish and English

Another important finding in our study is that stress is not only aligned with meter but also with certain pitch events, i.e., melodic prominence, in Turkish. In our English data, on the other hand, we found no evidence for a significant alignment of stress and melodic peak, which is in line with Girardi & Plag (2022). This can be explained by the weight of prominence cues in the respective languages: As described above, the most important concomitant of stress in English is vowel quality as all unstressed vowels are reduced to schwa, and this has been shown to be the most effectively used cue for word segmentation and lexical identification (see Cutler, 2012, for a discussion and the references therein) and for identifying stress location (Chrabaszcz et al., 2014). In Turkish, on the other hand, it is pitch that has been shown to be the most reliable stress cue (e.g., Levi, 2005). These tendencies, then, are reflected in musical renditions of language where the misalignment of two similar entities is perceived as more severe and thus less likely to occur than that of dissimilar entities. We call this phenomenon *cross-domain similarity alignment*. Linguistic pitch and musical pitch are structurally more similar to each other than linguistic pitch and metrical position, which is why stress in Turkish, a language with (linguistic) pitch as its main stress cue will exhibit a higher degree of alignment with musical pitch than with metrical position. Indeed, a rendition of melodic alignment in Turkish children's songs has been explicitly formulated in various pedagogical books on vocal music through statements that prescribe the necessity of docking word accents on higher notes in music (e.g., Sun 1998). However, we find no such statements that target metrical positions (i.e., strong beats) in this kind of prescriptive work despite their focus on Western European music. We thus argue that the **musical domain** which is aligned with linguistic stress in a particular language and the degree to which stress aligns with each of these domains reflects the language-specific perceived **form** of prominence.

Word final vs. non-final prominence in Turkish

Crucially, there was no difference between syllables that carry canonical, i.e., final stress and those that carry non-canonical, i.e., non-final stress, both showing significantly higher metrical weight as well as significantly higher melodic peak score in comparison to unstressed syllables. We take this finding to suggest that, first of all, contra Kamali Aknoun Azad (2011), words with final stress in Turkish cannot be accentless. Otherwise, final syllables would not show such differences in comparison to unstressed syllables. Second, it suggests that both types of prominence, final and non-final stress, are treated the same by language users (in this case, composers and/or performers), showing that there are no reasons to assume the existence of two distinct word-level accentual systems for Turkish, contrary to what has been proposed by Csató & Johanson (1998) or Güneş (2015). This indicates that the mapping and processing of both default word final and lexically/ morphosyntactically induced non-final stress surfaces in the same way in the prosody-music alignment, suggesting that the accentual phenomena that result from the two different stress assignment mechanisms culminate in the same realizations.

Prosody-music alignment and language typology

From a typological perspective, when SMAVs available in the literature for different languages are compared, the gradient nature of prosody-music alignment becomes visible. Specifically, Turkish has been shown to exhibit alignment values lower than that of English, while Turkish values are higher than those of French and Tokyo Japanese. We suggest that this hierarchy (English > Turkish > French > Tokyo Japanese) can best be explained by the functional load of word accentual phenomena in the languages, irrespective of how they may be realized. When stress is dynamic with salient manifestations in different parts of phonology as well as in other domains of grammar, as is the case in English, SMAV is expected to be particularly high. In languages where word-level prosodic structure is irrelevant for lexical contrasts, such as in French and Turkish, accentual prominence is, beyond a reasonable doubt, in inertia with no known function or consequence other than demarcating word boundaries. The consequences of a relatively low functional load of stress in such languages, where accentual prominence is inevitably predictable for the language user, have repeatedly been demonstrated in studies on the perception of stress. In such studies, speakers of native languages with predictable stress have been shown to be "stress-deaf", i.e., unable to reliably perceive stress contrasts in another language (e.g, Dupoux et al., 2001; Altmann, 2006; Dupoux et al., 2008; Lin et al., 2014; Lukyanchenko et al., 2011).

Finally, Tokyo Japanese poses a special case since it is generally assumed to have pitch accents rather than stress. Since prominence alignment has previously been shown for this language (Cho, 2017), it could be suggested that prominence-meter alignment matrices so far used in the literature do not provide sufficient grounds to distinguish pitch accents from stress accents. In other words, metrical alignment may target word-level accents irrespective of their nature since they mark prominence in one way or another. It should be remembered that, crucially through the same modus operandi, we have ruled out the speculation that Turkish finally stressed words are accentless words, which are found in other pitch accent languages. If theories remain to refer to non-final "stress" as lexical pitch accent, then final "stress" should be construed as "canonical, default pitch accent" to match that. This position, however, turns the whole controversy into an uninteresting terminological debate, all because the primary cue for stress has so far been shown to be pitch in the language.

Figure 7 gives an overview over the multidimensional nature of the framework we propose, which is subject to further testing. Each column represents an individual language (English, French, Turkish, Tokyo Japanese, and tone languages such as Cantonese). The yellow line represents SMAV, an index of metrical alignment, while the grey line indicates SPAV, an index of melodic alignment. The lines depict in an abstract way the gradience found in the present study as well as in previous work:[11] English has a high degree of metrical alignment relative to Turkish, which has a higher degree of alignment than French, which, in turn, is aligned more robustly than Tokyo Japanese. The rightmost column, which stands for tone languages, does not indicate any degree of metrical alignment since word prosodic contrasts are not realized by stress in these languages. Like the yellow line, the grey line depicts the gradience of one alignment domain – melodic alignment. There is a high degree of tonal alignment in tone languages that use pitch transitions for word prosodic contrasts (although, as has been mentioned in Section 1, alignment in tonal languages is different in nature from prominence alignment). Based on Cho's (2017) findings, Tokyo Japanese is expected to show a lower degree of melodic alignment than tonal languages, but a higher degree of alignment than Turkish. In our study, English has been shown to lack melody alignment. These complementary hierarchies suggest that musical pitch is not the most optimal conceptual

---

11 It must be noted here that comparable SMAVs or SPAVs are available only for some of the languages included in the graph, which is due to the differences in research objectives and methodology across studies. Based on inferencing from the general facts and trends reported in these studies, however, we extrapolate abstract SPAVs and SMAVs for languages, where no corresponding data are currently available.

equivalent of stress in English. Future studies should test whether this is the case in other stress languages although "stress" may not correspond to the same entity in all such languages (see Cutler, 2012). To sum up, the intersecting hierarchies suggest a pattern of prosody-music alignment that mirrors the function and importance of phonetic stress cues across the languages of the world.

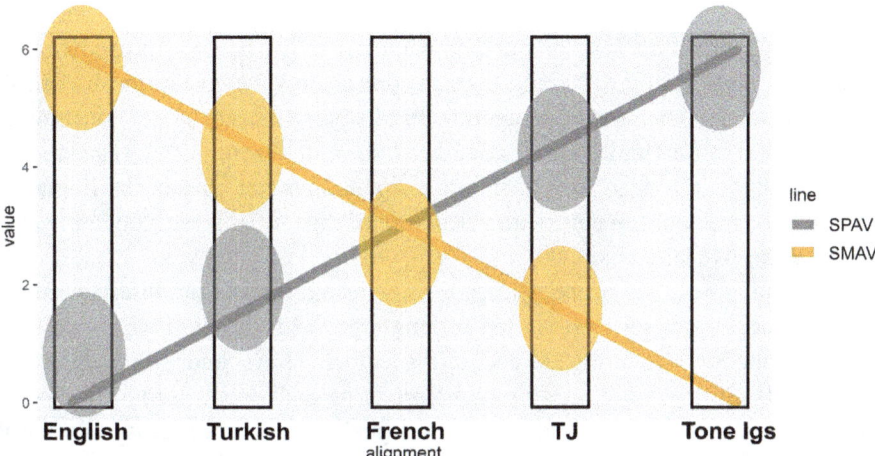

Figure 7: Cross-linguistic alignment of prosody and music.

6 Conclusions

In this chapter, we examined music-prosody alignment in Turkish songs. By making use of what is known about English prosody in general and English word-level stress in particular, our analyses have provided further evidence for the existence of word-level stress in Turkish, particularly for the much-debated reality of final stress. We arrived at these generalizations by comparing the mapping strategies that are used in Turkish compositions with those used in English music. We first showed that the well-known stress-meter alignment also exists in Turkish songs, albeit showing genre specificity and that this applies to both word final and non-final stress. Second, using a novel bi-gram scoring system based on the pitch of each note relative to the surrounding notes, we showed that Turkish maps stress, again final or non-final, also to musical melody, as operationalized by significant melodic peak values in stressed syllables in comparison to unstressed syllables. We did not find, however, such an alignment in English, suggesting that musical pitch is not a viable conceptual equivalent of stress in English. However, some of the alignment patterns, specifically the alignment of word-level stress with musical meter, have been shown to be present in both languages, showing that word-level accents are available to the users of these languages to the extent that they spill over to another cognitive domain, music. Our study further revealed this mapping takes place in different degrees that are commensurate with the phonetic and functional concomitants of word-level accentual prominence in the respective language. Furthermore, our findings indicate a decisive role of musical genre in the study of prosody-music alignment. Specifically, we found that, in contrast to Western European Turkish songs, Makam music, a musical genre with highly rigid compository constraints, does not exhibit a significant alignment of stress to strong metrical positions. This highlights the need for systematic examinations not only of the linguistic material, but also of the nature and structure of the musical tradition connected to the respective language.

The framework we proposed needs to be tested through additional empirical evidence. Crucially, text setting in languages with different word prosodic systems needs to be analyzed according to their SMAV and SPAV using the same tools. Furthermore, other parameters of prosody (e.g., duration) need to be investigated to understand how these speak to their counterparts in vocal music (e.g., note durations and their stylistic offshoots such as melismas). This necessitates a close collaboration of linguists and musicologists to account for as many linguistic and musical constraints possible.

Appendix

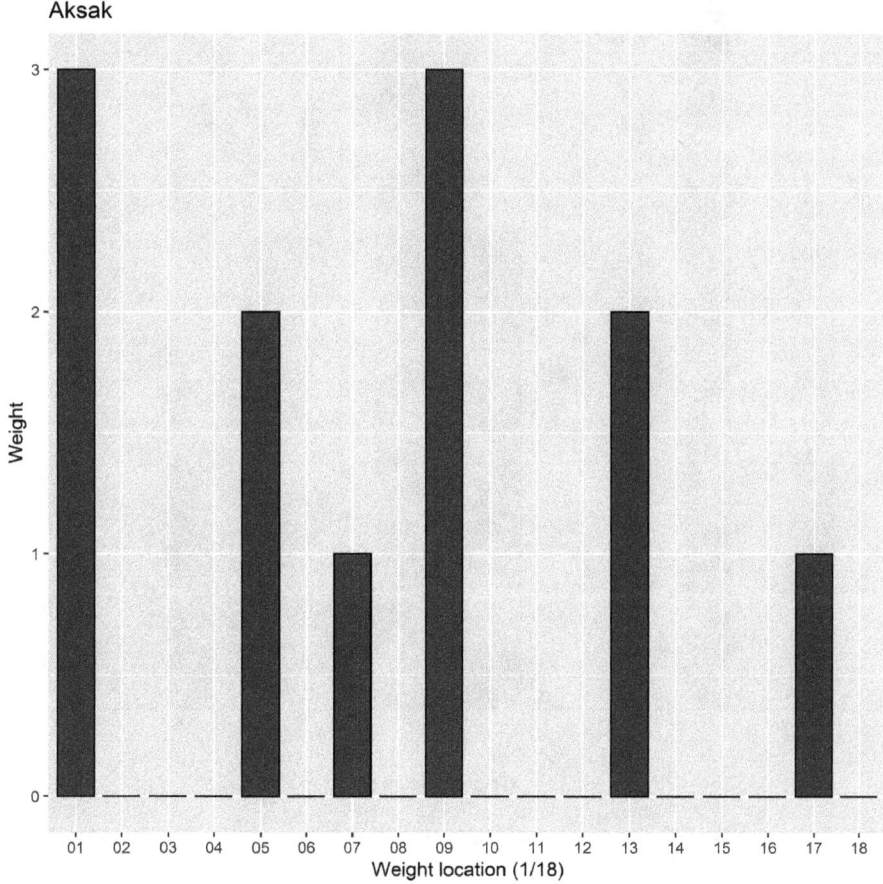

Figure 8: Prominence distribution in Turkish Usuls: Aksak (adapted from Holzapfel 2015: 28).

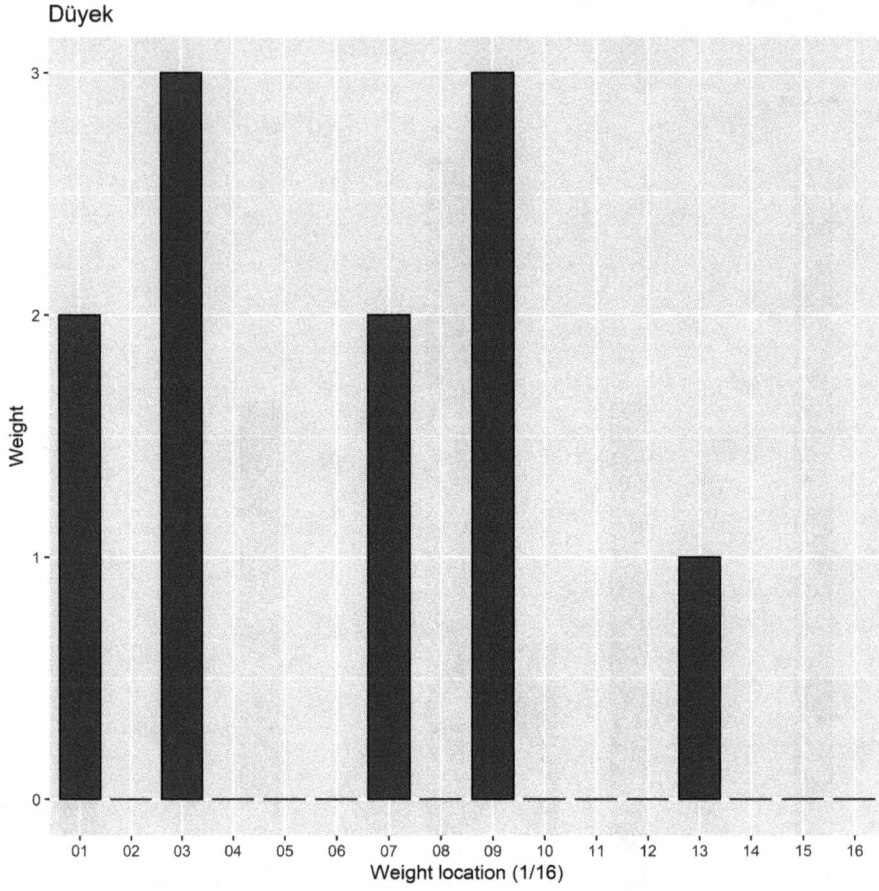

Figure 9: Prominence distribution in Turkish Usuls: Düyek (adapted from Holzapfel 2015: 28).

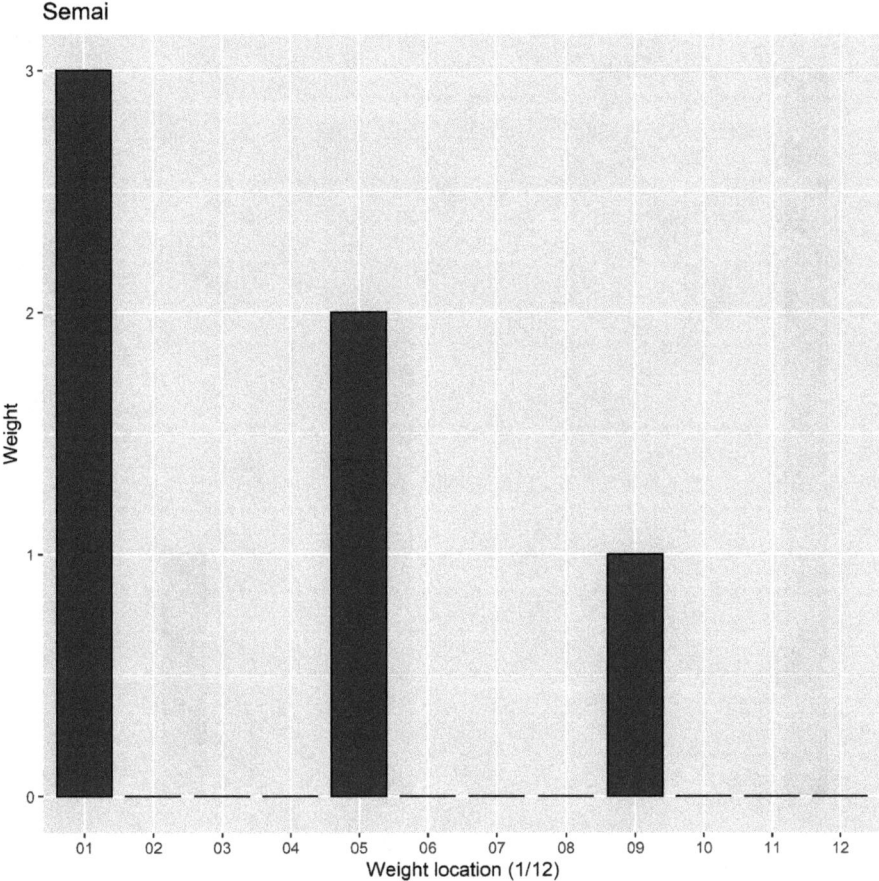

Figure 10: Prominence distribution in Turkish Usuls: Semai (adapted from Holzapfel 2015: 28).

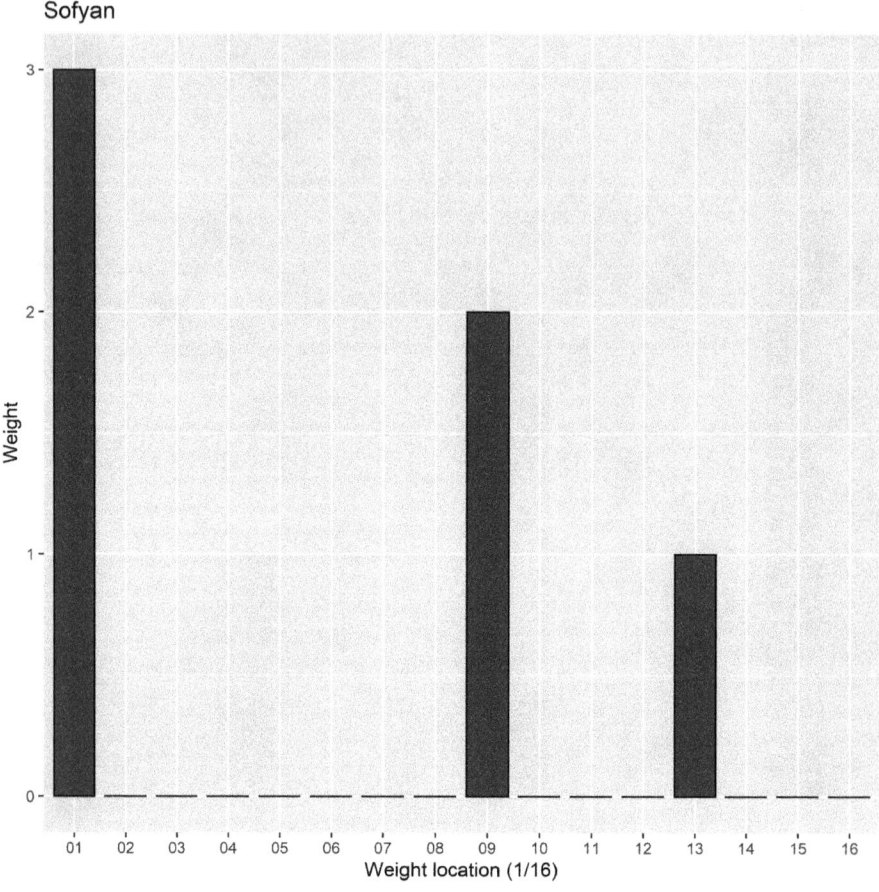

Figure 11: Prominence distribution in Turkish Usuls: Sofyan (adapted from Holzapfel 2015: 28).

References

Altmann, Heidi. 2006. *The perception and production of second language stress: A cross-linguistic experimental study*. [Doctoral Dissertation], Newark: University of Delaware.
Altmann, Heidi & Barış Kabak. 2015. English word stress in L2 and postcolonial varieties: Systematicity and variation. In: Ulrike Gut, Robert Fuchs, Eva-Maria Wunder, editors. *Universal or diverse paths to English phonology*, 185–208. Berlin: de Gruyter.
Anthony, Laurence. 2019. AntConc (Version 3.5. 8). [Computer Software]. Tokyo, Japan: Waseda University. Available from https://www.laurenceanthony.net/software.
Chen, Xi & Peggy Pik Ki Mok. Rhythmic correspondence between music and speech in English vocal music. Proceedings of Speech Prosody; 2014. 723–727.

Cho, Sunghye. 2017. Text alignment in Japanese children's song. *University of Pennsylvania Working Papers in Linguistics* 23(1, Article 5). 31–37.
Chomsky, Noam & Morris Halle. 1968. *The sound pattern of English*. New York: Harper and Row.
Chrabaszcz, Anna, Matthew Winn, Candise Y. Lin & William J. Idsardi. 2014. Acoustic cues to perception of word stress by English, Mandarin, and Russian speakers. *Journal of Speech, Language, and Hearing Research* 57(4). 1468–1479.
Cooper, Nicole, Anne Cutler & Roger Wales. 2002. Constraints of lexical stress on lexical access in English: Evidence from native and non-native listeners. *Language and Speech* 45(3). 207–228.
Csató, Éva Ágnes & Lars Johanson. 1998. Turkish. In: Lars Johanson, Éva Ágnes Csató, editors. *The Turkic languages*, 203–235. New York: Routledge.
Cutler, Anne. 2012. *Native listening: Language experience and the recognition of spoken words*. Cambridge, MA: The MIT Press.
Cutler, Anne. 2015. Lexical stress in English pronunciation. In: Marnie Reed, John M.Levis, editors. *The handbook of English pronunciation*, 106–124. Chichester, UK: Blackwell.
Cutler, Anne & Dennis Norris. 1988. The role of strong syllables in segmentation for lexical access. *Journal of Experimental Psychology: Human Perception and Performance* 14(1). 113–121.
De Castro Arrazola, Varun. 2015. The prosody of Basque songs. A methodological proposal. In: Teresa Proto, Paolo Canettieri, Gianluca Valenti, editors. *Text and tune: On the association of lyrics and tune in sung verse*, 171–182. Bern: Peter Lang.
Dupoux, Emmanuel, Sharon Peperkamp & Núria Sebastián-Gallés. 2001. A robust method to study stress "deafness". *The Journal of the Acoustical Society of America* 110(3). 1606–1618.
Dupoux, Emmanuel, Núria Sebastián-Gallés, Eduardo Navarrete & Sharon Peperkamp. 2008. Persistent stress 'deafness': The case of French learners of Spanish. *Cognition* 106(2). 682–706.
Giegerich, Heinz J. 1992. *English phonology: An introduction*. Cambridge: Cambridge University Press.
Gilbers, Dicky & Teja Rebernik. 2022. A constraint-based approach to structuring language and music. Towards a roadmap for comparing language and music cross-culturally. In: Mathias Scharinger, Richard Wiese, editors. *How language speaks to music: Prosody from a cross-domain perspective*, 71–103. Berlin: de Gruyter.
Girardi, Elena & Ingo Plag. 2022. Metrical mapping in text-setting: Empirical analysis and grammatical implementation. In: Mathias Scharinger, Richard Wiese, editors. *How language speaks to music: Prosody from a cross-domain perspective*, 191–221. Berlin: de Gruyter.
Göksel, Aslı & Celia Kerslake. 2004. *Turkish: A comprehensive grammar*. London: Routledge.
Gordon, Matthew. 2004. A phonological and phonetic study of word-level stress in Chickasaw. *International Journal of American Linguistics* 70(1). 1–32.
Gordon, Matthew. 2014. Disentangling stress and pitch-accent: A typology of prominence at different prosodic levels. In: Harry van der Hulst, editor. *Word stress: Theoretical and typological issues*, 83–118. Cambridge: Cambridge University Press.
Gordon, Reyna L., Cyrille L. Magne & Edward W. Large. 2011. EEG correlates of song prosody: A new look at the relationship between linguistic and musical rhythm. *Frontiers in Psychology* 2. 352.
Güneş, Güliz. 2015. Deriving prosodic structures: LOT, Netherlands Graduate School.

Halle, John & Fred Lerdahl. 1993. A generative textsetting model. *Current Musicology* 55. 3–23.
Hammond, Michael. 1999. *The phonology of English: A prosodic Optimality-Theoretic approach*. Oxford: Oxford University Press.
Harris, Lindsay N. & Charles A. Perfetti. 2016. Lexical stress and linguistic predictability influence proofreading behavior. *Frontiers in Psychology* 7. 96.
Hayes, Bruce. 1982. Extrametricality and English stress. *Linguistic Inquiry* 13(2). 227–276.
Hayes, Bruce. 2009. Textsetting as constraint conflict. In: Jean-Louis Aroui, Andy Arleo, editors. *Towards a typology of poetic forms: From language to metrics and beyond*, 43–62. Amsterdam: John Benjamins Publishing Company.
Holzapfel, André. 2015. Relation between surface rhythm and rhythmic modes in Turkish Makam music. *Journal of New Music Research* 44(1). 25–38.
Hualde, José Ignacio, Gorka Elordieta, Iñaki Gaminde & Rajka Smiljanic. 2002. From pitch-accent to stress-accent in Basque. In: Carlos Gussenhoven, Natasha Warner, editors. *Laboratory Phonology 7*, 547–584. Berlin: de Gruyter.
Huron, David & Matthew Royal. 1996. What is melodic accent? Converging evidence from musical practice. *Music Perception* 13(4). 489–516.
Hyman, Larry M. 2009. How (not) to do phonological typology: The case of pitch-accent. *Language Sciences* 31(2–3). 213–238.
Hyman, Larry M. 2014. Do all languages have word accent? In: Harry van der Hulst, editor. *Word stress: Theoretical and typological issues*, 56–82. Cambridge: Cambridge University Press.
Inkelas, Sharon. 1999. Exceptional stress-attracting suffixes in Turkish: Representation versus the grammar. In: René Kager, Harry van der Hulst, Wim Zonneveld, editors. *The prosody-morphology interface*, 134–187. Cambridge: Cambridge University Press.
Inkelas, Sharon & Cemil Orhan Orgun. 2003. Turkish stress: A review. *Phonology* 20(1). 139–161.
Johanson, Lars. 1998. The structure of Turkic. In: Lars Johanson, Éva Ágnes Csató, editors. *The Turkic languages*, 30–66. New York: Routledge.
Kabak, Barış & Janne Lorenzen. 2020. Paradigm leveling and regularization derive variation in stress: A corpus study on Turkish non-final stress at the morphology-phonology interface. In: Aslı Gürer, Dilek Uygun-Gökmen, Balkız Öztürk, editors. *Morphological complexity within and across boundaries: In honour of Aslı Göksel*, 194–210. Amsterdam: John Benjamins Publishing Company.
Kabak, Barış, Kazumi Maniwa & Nina Kazanina. 2010. Listeners use vowel harmony and word-final stress to spot nonsense words: A study of Turkish and French. *Laboratory Phonology* 1(1). 207–224.
Kabak, Barış & Kirsten Meemann. 2013. The role of positive vs. negative evidence in learning a novel dialect pattern: American English speakers' grammatical intuitions on a-prefixing in Appalachian English. *Zeitschrift für Anglistik und Amerikanistik* 61(3). 287–306.
Kabak, Barış & Irene Vogel. 2001. The phonological word and stress assignment in Turkish. *Phonology* 18(3). 315–360.
Kabak, Barış & Irene Vogel. 2011. Exceptions to stress and harmony in Turkish: Co-phonologies or prespecification? In: Horst J. Simon, Heike Wiese, editors. *Expecting the unexpected: Exceptions in grammar*, 59–94. Berlin: de Gruyter.
Kamali Aknoun Azad, Beste. 2011. Topics at the PF interface of Turkish [Doctoral Dissertation]: Harvard University.

Kirby, James & D. Robert Ladd. Tone-melody correspondence in Vietnamese popular song. Proceedings of the 5th International Symposium on Tonal Aspects of Languages (Tal 2016); 2016; Buffalo, NY. p 48–51.

Kochanski, Greg, Esther Grabe, John Coleman & Burton Rosner. 2005. Loudness predicts prominence: Fundamental frequency lends little. *The Journal of the Acoustical Society of America* 118(2). 1038–1054.

Konrot, Ahmet. 1981. Physical correlates of linguistic stress in Turkish. *University of Essex Language Center Occasional Papers* 24. 26–53.

Ladd, D Robert. 2008. *Intonational phonology*. Cambridge: Cambridge University Press.

Lees, Robert B. 1961. *The phonology of Modern Standard Turkish*. Bloomington, IN: Indiana University Publications.

Lehiste, Ilse. 1970. *Suprasegmentals*. Cambridge, MA: The MIT Press.

Lerdahl, Fred & Ray Jackendoff. 1983. *A generative theory of tonal music*. Cambridge, MA: The MIT Press.

Levi, Susannah V. 2005. Acoustic correlates of lexical accent in Turkish. *Journal of the International Phonetic Association* 35(1). 73–97.

Lin, Candise Y., Min Wang, William J. Idsardi & Yi Xu. 2014. Stress processing in Mandarin and Korean second language learners of English. *Bilingualism: Language and Cognition* 17(2). 316–346.

Lukyanchenko, Anna, William Idsardi & Nan Jiang. 2011. Opening your ears: The role of L1 in processing of nonnative prosodic contrasts. In: Gisela Granena, Joel Koeth, Sunyoung Lee-Ellis, Anna Lukyanchenko, Goretti Prieto Botana, Elizabeth Ann Rhoades, editors. *Selected Proceedings of the Second Language Research Forum*, 50–62. Somerville, MA: Cascadilla Press.

Nichols, Dan Morris, Sumit Basu & Christopher Raphael. Relationships between lyrics and melody in popular music. 2009. Proceedings of the 10th International Society for Music Information Retrieval Conference. Kobe, Japan.

Özçelik, Öner. 2014. Prosodic faithfulness to foot edges: The case of Turkish stress. *Phonology* 31(2). 229–269.

Palmer, Caroline & Michael H. Kelly. 1992. Linguistic prosody and musical meter in song. *Journal of Memory and Language* 31(4). 525–542.

Pierrehumbert, Janet B. & Mary E. Beckman. 1988. *Japanese tone structure*. Cambridge, MA: The MIT Press.

Pycha, Anne. 2006. A duration-based solution to the problem of stress realization in Turkish. *UC Berkeley Phonology Lab Annual Reports* 2.

Signell, Karl L. 1977. *Makam: Modal practice in Turkish art music*. Seattle, WA: University of Washington, School of Music.

Sluijter, Agaath M.C. & Vincent J. van Heuven. 1996a. Acoustic correlates of linguistic stress and accent in Dutch and American English. Proceedings of Fourth International Conference on Spoken Language Processing. Philadelphia, PA. IEEE. 630–633.

Sluijter, Agaath M.C. & Vincent J. van Heuven. 1996b. Spectral balance as an acoustic correlate of linguistic stress. *The Journal of the Acoustical Society of America* 100(4). 2471–2485.

Soto-Faraco, Salvador, Núria Sebastián-Gallés & Anne Cutler. 2001. Segmental and suprasegmental mismatch in lexical access. *Journal of Memory and Language* 45(3). 412–432.

Tait, Casey, Marija Tabain & Ingrid Sykes. 2014. Stress-meter alignment in American Hip Hop. 15th Australasian International Conference on Speech Science and Technology. Christchurch, New Zealand.

Team, R Core. 2020. R: A language and environment for statistical computing. Vienna: R Foundation for Statistical Computing.

Temperley, Nicholas & David Temperley. 2013. Stress-meter alignment in French vocal music. *The Journal of the Acoustical Society of America* 134(1). 520–527.

Thomassen, Joseph M. 1982. Melodic accent: Experiments and a tentative model. *The Journal of the Acoustical Society of America* 71(6). 1596–1605.

van Ommen, Sandrien. 2016. *Listen to the beat. A cross-linguistic perspective on the use of stress in segmentation*. Utrecht: LOT, Netherlands Graduate School.

Wee, Lian-Hee. 2007. Unraveling the relation between mandarin tones and musical melody. *Journal of Chinese Linguistics* 35(1). 128–144.

White, Christopher. 2017. Relationships between tonal stability and metrical accent in monophonic contexts. *Empirical Musicology Review* 12(1–2). 19–37.

Wong, Patrick C.M. & Randy L. Diehl. 2002. How can the lyrics of a song in a tone language be understood? *Psychology of Music* 30(2). 202–209.

Zora, Hatice, Mattias Heldner & Iris-Corinna Schwarz. 2016. Perceptual correlates of Turkish word stress and their contribution to automatic lexical access: Evidence from early ERP components. *Frontiers in Neuroscience* 10. 7.

Sonja A. Kotz
Bridging speech and music – A neural common ground perspective on prosody

Music and speech, two of the core human skills, have long captured our attention and motivated ample cross-domain research to address important questions (1) regarding the nature of their respective and possible co-evolution, and ultimately their (2) common and distinct structural and functional implementations in the human brain, shaping and facilitating these complex human behaviors.

In the present volume, Scharinger and Wiese invite the authors to focus on a possible pre-cursor of speech and music, namely that of **prosody**. Briefly, speech prosody encompasses linguistic speech elements such as intonation (e.g., the rise and fall of pitch), stress (e.g., marked by cues such as pitch, length, and loudness), and rhythm (e.g., a somewhat regular recurrence of sound events such as syllables in time), also termed the suprasegmental features of speech. Broadly speaking, they support speech comprehension (Paulmann, 2016). In social contexts, prosody can also convey a speaker's emotional state or attitude next to several other characteristics (i.e., age, sex) and therefore serves as a binding element in communication (Pell & Kotz, 2021). Comparably, music displays similar acoustic compositions as speech, but their functional implementation may differ (Kotz et al., 2018; Sammler, 2020). Emotion on the other hand may be similarly expressed and perceived while still engaging somewhat different neural correlates (Schirmer & Kotz, 2006; Frühholz et al., 2016; Koelsch, 2018; see also Scharinger & Wiese, this volume).

In their introduction to this volume, the editors draw the reader's attention to five critical aspects that they consider potential 'common ground' for prosodic features in speech and music. The obvious first one is acoustics where syllables and tones share physical properties. Second, they refer to the hierarchical structure of prosody that may be compared to the hierarchical structure in music. Third, they reflect on the evolution of speech and music as independent or co-evolving skills. Fourth, the neural correlates of speech and music prosody are considered, and lastly, the transfer between the domains (both ways) is touched upon. In the three parts of the book, the invited authors focus on ". . . underlying prosodic units based on pitch", a domain comparison of rhythm and stress, elucidating their underlying and potentially shared mechanisms, and 'text-setting', which refers to putting words to music or vice versa. Together, the editors'

Sonja A. Kotz, Maastricht University, NPPP, Universiteitssingel 40, 6200MD, Maastricht, The Netherlands

https://doi.org/10.1515/9783110770186-010

introduction and the authors' contributions to this volume provide a comprehensive account and detailed empirical and conceptual insight into why the scientifically rather undervalued phenomenon of prosody must be reckoned with in future cross-domain research, as prosody has the immense potential to consolidate commonalities between speech and music.

If prosody should be considered as a binding element for speech and music, we need to start formulating an integrative cognitive and neural perspective that allows defining how the brain encodes and decodes prosody from these dynamic sound signals. Why would such an integrative perspective be informative? First, offering an integrative perspective for prosody across domains would help to understand how acoustic and suprasegmental features of complex sound are integrated over time and generate 'relevance' for the listener. Second, such a network perspective would potentially also allow integrating different functional processes underlying speech and music prosody beyond the mere acoustic analysis of the signals. Third, a convergent network perspective might critically extend a corticocentric and an exclusively lateralized view of prosody across domains by integrating current models of prosodic and rhythmic brain networks.

The starting point taken here is a stepwise extension of lateralized corticocentric network views on prosody in speech (e.g., Poeppel, 2003; Schirmer & Kotz, 2006; Wildgruber et al., 2006) and music (e.g., Zatorre et al., 2002) by merging them with temporal and rhythmic properties that emerge in speech and music (Kotz & Schwartze, 2010; Kotz et al., 2018).

Lateralization of domain-specific acoustic properties in speech (Poeppel, 2003) and music (Zatorre et al., 2002) have been formulated based on their specific acoustic (temporal and spectral) features. For example, while speech codes specific linguistic information at different time scales that modulates over time, music may be more driven by spectral fluctuation (e.g., Poeppel, 2003; Zatorre et al., 2002). However, these strong asymmetry hypotheses have been questioned (McGettigan & Scott, 2012). For example, with increasing temporal and spectral complexity in speech, hemispheric asymmetry becomes more relative and complementary (Obleser et al., 2008, but see Albouy et al., 2020; Sammler, 2020, for sung and spoken words).

In a similar vein, decades of patient and neuroimaging research on prosody have gone from right to left to both hemispheric cortical representations of linguistic and emotional prosody. To reconcile controversy in (emotional) prosody research, Schirmer & Kotz, 2006 put forward a processing stage model that ascribes bilateral acoustic analyses of temporal and spectral signal composition (mid to posterior portion of the superior temporal cortex) that allow differentiating vocal from other sound categories. This aligns with the idea of 'relative weighting' of temporal and spectral speech features that extend over a larger time window than just syllables or tones (e.g., Obleser et al., 2008). This analysis is followed by the decoding of salient vocal features that might be particularly relevant for the listener to form expectations and goals for action (i.e., how do I respond to a particular expression or statement). Regarding emotional prosody, this processing step appears right lateralized in the anterior portion of the temporal cortex, following the ventral pathway. Interestingly, this evidence somewhat compares to a ventral pathway hypothesis for intelligible speech, where sound complexity (e.g., from tone to sentence) follows a left anterio-lateral temporal gradient (Rauschecker & Scott, 2009). Thus, one could speculate that **saliency/ relevance** of information in an increasingly **complex sound signal** (that is, beyond a sound or a tone) may follow a similar gradient (posterior to anterior) in both hemispheres but may be driven by different acoustic feature compositions that engage the left and right lateralized anterior temporal activation patterns respectively. Further, by **tagging salient/relevant information in time,** the listener may be better prepared to appraise the incoming information, considering the context and the relevance the information has for a listener. This process is related to the right and left inferior frontal cortex, respectively.

Following this concept of processing stages, at least two aspects need to be further elucidated. We need to define (1) what saliency and/or relevance of a stimulus means, and (2) how saliency/relevance may keep a listener's attention in time when complex, dynamic signals such as music and speech evolve. In several chapters of the current volume, **pitch** is defined as a prosodic cue that may be operationalized similarly in speech and music (Larrouy-Maestri et al.; Gilbers & Rebernik; Pfeifer & Hamann) but may still differ in quality between the two domains (e.g., Larrouy-Maestri et al.; Scharinger). Next to pitch, prosody also entails **meter**, defined by levels of grouping of sound events into a hierarchical structure in speech (e.g., Selkirk, 1995) and music (e.g., Fitch, 2013). In its most basic form, meter comprises two sound events (the syllable foot in speech or adjacent tones in music), with one sound being perceived as stronger than the other, forming so-called strong-weak alternations. In music meter often entails groupings of three (waltz time) or four (common time) events rather than just 2. In speech, it is specifically contrastive stress (strong-weak) rather than coordinative stress (grouping of phonetic cues) that best aligns with musical meter, the alternation of strong-weak beats (Nolan & Jeon, 2014). Thus, metrical hierarchies involve pattern formation that seems to overlap between speech and music at least at the most basic level. Further, in both music and speech meter allows **anticipating** when the next stressed sound event occurs in the signal (Kotz & Schwartze, 2010; Beier & Ferreira, 2018), and consequently facilitates how we **focus attention to salient/relevant events in time** (Kotz et al., 2018).

As noted above, stimulus complexity does not only refer to an increase in temporal and spectral properties that mark saliency/relevance of information for the listener, but also how sound dynamically evolves in time. Here we refer to this aspect as forming **auditory temporal sequences**. Acoustically marked salient/relevant sounds need to be continuously integrated, evaluated, and updated (Koelsch, 2018; Pell & Kotz, 2011). The posterior-anterior gradient in the superior temporal cortices, with relative left and right hemispheric anterior temporal weighting of saliency/relevance in speech and music may therefore support the integration of this information and the forming of auditory objects (percepts) (Boemio et al., 2005; Schönwiesner et al., 2005). This information is also shared with other brain regions including the frontal cortex (Morris et al., 1999; Schirmer & Kotz, 2006; Kotz & Schwartze, 2010), the amygdala when a stimulus is particularly relevant for the listener (Kumar et al., 2012), and subcortical regions such as the basal ganglia (Pell & Leonard, 2003; Kotz & Schwartze, 2010) and the cerebellum (Schwartze & Kotz, 2013), see also Figure 1.

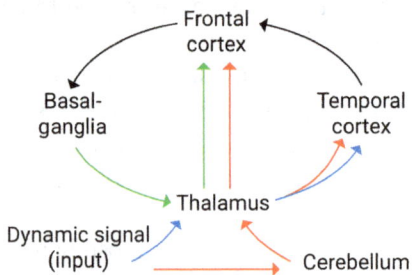

Figure 1: Schematic neural network composition underlying prosody across domains.

Dynamic signals are transferred via the thalamus along the classical pathway to the temporal cortex (blue) where decoding of acoustic properties as well as the scaling of saliency/relevance takes place (posterior-anterior gradient) before information is transferred to the frontal cortex for the evaluation of signal quality and relevance. The keeping up of attention to salient/relevant information in time engages the basal ganglia (black=input; green=output) that are sensitive to beats in speech and music. A non-classical pathway that transfers the signal bottom-up directly via the cerebellum and thalamus to the frontal cortex (red) ensures that sound onsets as well as swift changes in sound quality are detected and ensure that cortical attentional to salient/relevant information can be kept up. Via the thalamus these cortical wakeup calls are also sent to the temporal cortex (red).

The basal ganglia, subcompartmentalized into a ventral and dorsal part, seem to mirror a similar dimensionality in the frontal cortex for temporal sound patterns marked as more or less salient (e.g., Kotz et al., 2013). In particular, the dorsal basal ganglia decode temporally predictable acoustic patterns in speech and music (Grahn & Brett, 2007; Kotz & Schwartze, 2010; Kotz et al., 2009; Salimpoor et al., 2011). These sound patterns are likely marked by saliency/relevance, taking the form of a beat or pulse, that may alternate quasi-periodically in speech or periodically in music. Together with the temporal and frontal cortex the basal ganglia form a network, in which the thalamus takes center stage, and functionally coordinate how we decode and predict saliency/relevance in temporally evolving sound patterns (Frühholz et al., 2016; Kotz et al., 2018). The cerebellum, often undervalued in the literature, is part of the described neural network, as it is sensitive to the temporal onsets of discrete sound events and sudden sound changes (Schwartze & Kotz, 2013). This sensitivity may critically contribute to fast and involuntary detection of saliency/relevance in the sound signal, which prepares the cortical brain structures to focus attention not only on salient/relevant but also new information over time. Consequently, if we want to consider prosody as a dynamically unfolding nonverbal signal that carries salient and relevant information in time, an interface between subcortical and cortical brain structures might be needed to ensure that salient/relevant information is channeled in time to keep up attention to salient markers in complex sound signals such as speech and music.

In summary, we propose an integrative neural perspective on prosody that encompasses processing steps within a neural network in a first attempt to merge prosody in speech and music. Within this network, common and differential coding of complex auditory sound types is possible based on the relative weighting of sound composition and complexity in the respective brain regions comprising this network.

References

Albouy, Philippe, Lucas Benjamin, Benjamin Morillon & Robert J. Zatorre. 2020. Distinct sensitivity to spectrotemporal modulation supports brain asymmetry for speech and melody. *Science* 367(6481). 1043–1047.

Beier, Eleonora J. & Fernanda Ferreira. 2018. The temporal prediction of stress in speech and its relation to musical beat perception. *Frontiers in Psychology* 9. 431.

Boemio, Anthony, Stephen Fromm, Allen Braun & David Poeppel. 2005. Hierarchical and asymmetric temporal sensitivity in human auditory cortices. *Nature Neuroscience* 8(3). 389–395.

Fitch, W. Tecumseh. 2013. Rhythmic cognition in humans and animals: Distinguishing meter and pulse perception. *Frontiers in Systems Neuroscience* 7. 68.

Frühholz, Sascha, Wiebke Trost & Sonja A. Kotz. 2016. The sound of emotions – towards a unifying neural network perspective of affective sound processing. *Neuroscience & Biobehavioral Reviews* 68. 96–110.

Gilbers, Dicky & Teja Rebernik. 2022. A constraint-based approach to structuring language and music. Towards a roadmap for comparing language and music cross-culturally. In: Mathias Scharinger, Richard Wiese, editors. *How language speaks to music: Prosody from a cross-domain perspective*, 71–103. Berlin: De Gruyter.

Grahn, Jessica A. & Matthew Brett. 2007. Rhythm and beat perception in motor areas of the brain. *Journal of Cognitive Neuroscience* 19(5). 893–906.

Koelsch, Stefan. 2018. Investigating the neural encoding of emotion with music. *Neuron* 98 (6). 1075–1079.

Kotz, Sonja A, Anna S. Hasting & Silke Paulmann. 2013. On the orbito-striatal interface in (acoustic) emotional processing. In: Eckart Altenmüller, Sabine Schmidt, Elke Zimmermann, editors. *Evolution of emotional communication: From sounds In nonhuman mammals to speech and music in man*, 229–240. Oxford: Oxford University Press.

Kotz, Sonja A., Andrea Ravignani & W. Tecumseh Fitch. 2018. The evolution of rhythm processing. *Trends in Cognitive Sciences* 22(10). 896–910.

Kotz, Sonja A. & Michael Schwartze. 2010. Cortical speech processing unplugged: A timely subcortico-cortical framework. *Trends in Cognitive Sciences* 14(9). 392–399.

Kotz, Sonja A., Michael Schwartze & Maren Schmidt-Kassow. 2009. Non-motor basal ganglia functions: A review and proposal for a model of sensory predictability in auditory language perception. *Cortex* 45(8). 982–990.

Kumar, Sukhbinder, Katharina von Kriegstein, Karl Friston & Timothy D. Griffiths. 2012. Features versus feelings: Dissociable representations of the acoustic features and valence of aversive sounds. *The Journal of Neuroscience* 32(41). 14184–14192.

Larrouy-Maestri, Pauline, David Poeppel & Peter Q. Pfordresher. 2022. Pitch units in music and speech prosody. In: Mathias Scharinger, Richard Wiese, editors. *How language speaks to music: Prosody from a cross-domain perspective*, 17–41. Berlin: De Gruyter.

McGettigan, Carolyn & Sophie K. Scott. 2012. Cortical asymmetries in speech perception: What's wrong, what's right and what's left? *Trends in Cognitive Sciences* 16(5). 269–276.

Morris, John S., Sophie K. Scott & Raymond J. Dolan. 1999. Saying it with feeling: Neural responses to emotional vocalizations. *Neuropsychologia* 37(10). 1155–1163.

Nolan, Francis & Hae-Sung Jeon. 2014. Speech rhythm: A metaphor? *Philosophical Transactions of the Royal Society B: Biological Sciences* 369(1658). 20130396.

Obleser, Jonas, Frank Eisner & Sonja A. Kotz. 2008. Bilateral speech comprehension reflects differential sensitivity to spectral and temporal features. *The Journal of Neuroscience* 28(32). 8116–8123.

Paulmann, Silke. 2016. The neurocognition of prosody. In: Gregory Hickok, Steve L. Small, editors. *Neurobiology of language*, 1109–1120. London: Elsevier.

Pell, Marc D. & Sonja A. Kotz. 2011. On the time course of vocal emotion recognition. *Plos One* 6(11). e27256.

Pell, Marc D. & Sonja A. Kotz. 2021. Comment: The next frontier: Prosody research gets interpersonal. *Emotion Review* 13(1). 51–56.

Pell, Marc D. & Carol L. Leonard. 2003. Processing emotional tone from speech in Parkinson's Disease: A role for the basal ganglia. *Cognitive, Affective, & Behavioral Neuroscience* 3(4). 275–288.

Pfeifer, Jasmin & Silke Hamann. 2022. Word stress perception by congenital amusics. In: Mathias Scharinger, Richard Wiese, editors. *How language speaks to music: Prosody from a cross-domain perspective*, 105–134. Berlin: De Gruyter.

Poeppel, David. 2003. The analysis of speech in different temporal integration windows: Cerebral lateralization as 'asymmetric sampling in time'. *Speech Communication* 41. 245–255.

Rauschecker, Josef P. & Sophie K. Scott. 2009. Maps and streams in the auditory cortex: Nonhuman primates illuminate human speech processing. *Nature Neuroscience* 12(6). 718–724.

Salimpoor, Valorie N., Mitchel Benovoy, Kevin Larcher, Alain Dagher & Robert J. Zatorre. 2011. Anatomically distinct dopamine release during anticipation and experience of peak emotion to music. *Nature Neuroscience* 14(2). 257–262.

Sammler, Daniela. 2020. Splitting speech and music. *Science* 367(6481). 974–976.

Scharinger, Mathias. 2022. Melody in speech and music. In: Mathias Scharinger, Richard Wiese, editors. *How language speaks to music: Prosody from a cross-domain perspective*, Berlin: De Gruyter.

Scharinger, Mathias & Richard Wiese. 2022. Introduction: How to conceptualize similarities between language and music. In: Mathias Scharinger, Richard Wiese, editors. *How language speaks to music: Prosody from a cross-domain perspective*, 43–69. Berlin: De Gruyter.

Schirmer, Annett & Sonja A. Kotz. 2006. Beyond the right hemisphere: Brain mechanisms mediating vocal emotional processing. *Trends in Cognitive Sciences* 10(1). 24–30.

Schönwiesner, Marc, Rudolf Rübsamen & D. Yves Von Cramon. 2005. Hemispheric asymmetry for spectral and temporal processing in the human antero-lateral auditory belt cortex. *The European Journal of Neuroscience* 22(6). 1521–1528.

Schwartze, Michael & Sonja A. Kotz. 2013. A dual-pathway neural architecture for specific temporal prediction. *Neuroscience & Biobehavioral Reviews* 37(10). 2587–2596.

Selkirk, Elisabeth O. 1995. Sentence prosody: Intonation, stress, and phrasing. In: John A. Goldsmith, editor. *The handbook of phonological theory*, 550–569. Cambridge, MA: Blackwell.

Wildgruber, Dirk, H. Ackermann, B. Kreifelts & T. Ethofer. 2006. Cerebral processing of linguistic and emotional prosody: fMRI studies. *Progress in Brain Research* 156. 249–268.

Zatorre, Robert J., Pascal Belin & Virginia B. Penhune. 2002. Structure and function of auditory cortex: Music and speech. *Trends in Cognitive Sciences* 6(1). 37–46.

Index

aesthetics 9, 29, 30, 43, 46, 50, 52, 58, 61, 62, 85, 142
autocorrelation 9, 55–64

Beethoven, Ludwig van 162, 170
bibliometric analysis 1, 6, 7
brain 4, 17, 24, 61, 62, 77, 106, 107, 110, 142, 145, 147, 149, 150, 259, 260, 262, 263

Chinese 82, 107, 115
chord 62, 71, 72, 75, 77–79, 86–91, 99
congenital amusia 105, 107, 109, 112, 128
constraints 10, 11, 24, 44, 46, 74–77, 81–88, 91, 92, 94–97, 99, 100, 115, 139, 140, 168, 183, 191–193, 196, 207–210, 212–215, 224, 228, 231, 245, 250

duration 2, 7, 10, 11, 23, 34, 45, 46, 50–54, 56, 59, 61, 64, 73, 78, 105, 109–115, 121–123, 126, 127, 136, 138, 161–163, 168–172, 176, 182, 192, 195, 196, 200, 203, 204, 212, 215, 224, 225, 229, 231, 233, 250
Dutch 77, 141, 227, 235

EEG 115, 119, 120, 122, 144–150
electroencephalography. See EEG
emotion 2, 8, 20, 22, 23, 47–49, 74, 80, 106, 107, 259–261
English 11, 12, 73, 81, 83, 84, 87, 95, 107–109, 140, 141, 144, 145, 148–150, 154, 163, 164, 168, 169, 174, 191–193, 195, 196, 223, 225–227, 229–231, 233–238, 242, 244, 245, 247–251
ERP 8, 109, 110, 119, 127, 128, 145, 148–151
evolution 3, 4, 8, 72, 135, 142, 259

F0 18, 22, 24–26, 28, 29, 47–64, 85, 195, 227
Finnish 11, 12, 161, 163–169, 172–174, 182–186
fMRI 148

foot 94–96, 99, 100, 151, 165, 198, 199, 234, 261
French 95, 108, 165, 174, 223–225, 229, 231, 242, 245, 247, 248
functional magnetic resonance imaging. See fMRI
fundamental frequency. See F0

Gamelan music 84
German 29, 46, 55, 59, 73, 105, 108, 110–113, 115, 126, 136, 140, 141, 144–148, 150–155, 164, 168, 174
glissando 49, 51, 52, 63, 98

Hawaiian 82, 86, 87
Haydn, Joseph 11, 191, 192, 196–198, 202, 203, 211, 214, 216–218
Hindi 78, 95
Hip Hop 229

intensity 2, 45, 46, 51, 53, 78, 105, 110–115, 121, 126, 155, 192, 195, 231, 233, 238
intonation 2, 5, 18, 19, 22, 23, 27, 33, 44, 46–48, 51, 52, 71, 74, 81, 91–94, 99, 107, 108, 227, 231, 233, 259
isochrony 97, 154–156
Italian 73, 174

Janácek, Leos 48
Japanese 82, 84, 224, 226, 229, 230, 234, 242, 247, 248

Kreutzer, Conradin 54, 55, 57, 58

length 2, 25, 45, 46, 54–56, 73, 92, 93, 97, 98, 108, 111, 112, 114, 161–164, 166–177, 180–186, 200, 209, 214, 236, 259
lyrics 73, 106, 161, 162, 164–166, 172, 173, 192, 193, 223, 227, 228, 245

Makam music 12, 223, 226, 236–239, 240–247, 250
maximum entropy grammar 191–193, 196, 207, 210, 214, 215

https://doi.org/10.1515/9783110770186-011

melody 1, 8, 9, 17, 18, 21, 25, 28, 30–34, 43–49, 52, 54, 55, 57–62, 64, 71–74, 77, 87, 91–94, 97, 98, 163, 172, 223, 224, 227, 236–238, 248–250

meter 1, 2, 5, 8, 11, 46, 50, 55, 58–60, 64, 72, 107, 117, 118, 136–140, 151, 162, 164, 165, 167, 168, 171, 173, 191–193, 195, 206–208, 211, 214, 223, 224, 226–229, 236–239, 241, 242, 244–246, 248–250, 261

metrical grid 135, 137, 139–141, 151, 166, 168

Metrical Organization 135, 144, 165, 173, 191

mismatch negativity. See MMN

MMN 105, 109–112, 117–120, 122, 124–128

mora 162, 164, 168, 173–177, 179, 182–184, 229

Mozart, Wolfgang Amadeus 137

nPVI 73

Optimality Theory. See OT

OT 10–12, 74–77, 79, 81–84, 86, 89, 92, 95, 96, 99, 100, 193, 209, 210, 214, 245

perception 8, 17–24, 28–31, 35, 45, 50, 51, 61, 62, 72, 78, 82, 85, 87, 105–110, 112–116, 126, 128, 135, 137, 139, 141, 142, 144, 145, 149, 151, 154–156, 230, 235, 247

phoneme 22, 78, 81, 83, 84, 86, 100, 164

pitch 2, 4, 5, 8–10, 12, 17, 18–28, 30, 31, 35, 44–49, 51–53, 62, 63, 72, 73, 78–80, 84, 88, 105–116, 119, 121, 122, 124–128, 161–163, 191–193, 195, 196, 199–201, 204–209, 213–215, 224–227, 229–231, 233, 235, 238–241, 245, 248, 249, 259, 261

poetry 1, 9, 11, 43, 50, 52, 140, 149, 164–168, 197

Polish 231

prediction 61–63, 141–143, 154, 195, 196, 202, 206, 226, 227, 233, 237

predictive coding 11, 61, 62

preferences 9, 21, 34, 55, 96, 139, 165, 182, 197, 208, 211

production 2, 8, 35, 47, 72, 106, 109, 112, 113, 135, 141, 142, 144, 145, 151, 153, 155, 156, 162, 230

prosody 1–6, 8, 11, 12, 17–20, 22, 23, 28, 35, 47, 49, 60, 96, 107, 140, 153, 161, 183, 223–231, 236, 237, 240, 245–251, 259–263

quantity 11, 162–165, 168, 172, 183

Reich, Steve 48

rhyme 50, 56–61, 64, 140, 164, 168, 173, 177, 178, 182, 184

rhythm 4, 5, 10, 11, 45, 46, 51, 52, 64, 72, 73, 80, 95–99, 105, 117, 118, 135–149, 153–155, 162, 163, 166, 173, 193, 237, 238, 259, 260

Russian 155, 168, 174, 235

Schönberg, Arnold 60, 77

Schultz, Johann Abraham Peter 55

scoop 9, 17, 24–34

Scottish 73, 173, 196

singing 2–4, 18, 24, 27, 30, 44, 49, 54, 55, 80, 98, 106, 161, 162, 174, 184, 185

Slovenian 73

sonority 82, 88, 161, 172, 179, 181, 182, 184, 186

Spanish 87, 163, 235

spectral slope 50, 105, 111–115, 126

speech perception 17, 107, 108, 112, 156

stanza 56–59, 61, 63, 140

Strauß, Johann 138

Strauss, Richard 54, 55, 57, 58

Stravinsky, Igor 143, 144

stress clash 95, 96, 99, 140, 145, 146, 148, 149

Swedish 174

syllable 2, 5, 9, 18, 22, 25, 31, 44, 47–59, 61, 63, 64, 71, 75, 77, 78, 80–82, 86, 87, 89, 94, 95, 98–100, 107, 111, 113, 126, 136, 141, 145, 146, 148, 150, 151, 156, 161–166, 168, 169, 172–179, 181–186, 191, 194–201, 203, 207, 208, 223–225, 228, 229, 231–235, 238–247, 249, 259, 261

syntax 2, 5, 72–74, 140, 141, 154

tactus 137, 165–167, 169–171, 173, 182, 196, 199, 200
temporal 2, 4, 5, 19, 25, 50, 53, 72, 98, 106, 112, 139, 141, 142, 145, 154, 155, 162, 224, 260–263
text-setting 11, 12, 63, 161–163, 166–169, 172, 183, 185, 186, 191–193, 195–197, 204, 207, 211, 214, 259
timbre 21, 30, 45, 72, 106
ToBI 47, 51, 52
tone 2, 5, 6, 9, 10, 12, 19–21, 23–31, 34, 43–52, 55, 56, 58, 60, 63, 64, 72, 80–82, 84, 86, 88, 89, 92, 98, 100, 107–111, 114, 115, 127, 192, 193, 195, 196, 199, 200, 204–207, 209, 213–215, 223–225, 227, 229, 230, 233, 234, 249, 259, 261
Turkish 12, 223, 225–227, 230–238, 241–254

universal 1, 2, 9, 10, 12, 71, 72, 75, 76, 78, 80, 82, 84, 87, 95, 97–99, 208, 246

variation 18, 25, 31, 51, 73, 76, 81, 92, 93, 95, 97, 99, 112, 151, 155, 156, 162, 166, 168, 173, 197, 202, 203, 205, 213, 229–232, 235

weight 11, 75–78, 80, 95, 127, 161–165, 167–169, 172, 174, 177, 179, 181–186, 189, 210, 223, 231, 235, 240–242, 245–248
word stress 12, 78, 105, 107, 109–115, 119, 121, 124, 126–128, 141, 148, 150, 151, 164, 183, 192, 194, 223–225, 227, 228, 230, 231–235, 237–239, 242, 244, 246–248, 250

Yawelmani 87, 95

www.ingramcontent.com/pod-product-compliance
Lightning Source LLC
Chambersburg PA
CBHW050519170426
43201CB00013B/2017